CRIME, JEWS AND NEWS

AUSTRIAN AND HABSBURG STUDIES
General Editor: Gary B. Cohen, Center for Austrian Studies,
University of Minnesota

CRIME, JEWS AND NEWS

VIENNA 1895–1914

Daniel M. Vyleta

Berghahn Books
NEW YORK · OXFORD

First published in 2007 by

Berghahn Books

www.berghahnbooks.com

© 2007, 2012 Daniel M. Vyleta
First paperback edition published in 2012

Library of Congress Cataloging-in-Publication Data

Vyleta, Daniel Mark.
  Jews, news and crime : Vienna, 1890-1914 / Daniel Mark Vyleta.
    p. cm. -- (Austrian and Habsburg studies ; v. 8)
  ISBN: 978-1-84545-181-3 (hbk.) -- ISBN: 978-0-85745-593-2 (pbk.)
  1. Jewish criminals--Austria--History--19th century. 2. Jewish criminals--Austria--History-
-20th century. 3. Antisemitism in the press--Austria--History--19th century. 4. Antisemitism
in the press--Austria--History--20th century. I. Title. II. Series.
  GBA679066 bnb
  305.89240436--dc22

2006355560

British Library Cataloguing in Publication Data

A catalogue record for this book is available from the British Library

Printed in the United States on acid-free paper

ISBN 978-0-85745-593-2 (paperback)   ISBN 978-0-85745-594-9 (ebook)

CONTENTS

List of Figures and Tables

Figures

Tables

List of Abbreviations Used in the Endnotes

Archival Sources

ÖS	Österreichisches Staatsarchiv, Allgemeines Verwaltungsarchiv
SaW	Stadtarchiv Wien
PaHS	Privatarchiv Harald Seyrl (Kriminalmuseum, Wien)

Journals

Archiv	*Archiv für Criminalanthropologie und Criminalistik*
Monatsschrift	*Monatsschrift für Kriminalpsychologie und Strafrechtsreform*

Newspapers

AZ	*Arbeiter-Zeitung*
DV	*Deutsches Volksblatt*
Extrablatt	*Illustriertes Wiener Extrablatt*
Krone	*Illustrierte Kronenzeitung*
NFP	*Neue Freie Presse*
NWT	*Neues Wiener Tagblatt*
ÖK	*Österreichische Kriminalzeitung*
ÖW	*Österreichische Wochenschrift*
OR	*Ostdeutsche Rundschau*
RP	*Reichspost*
RW	*Reichswehr*
WIK	*Wiener Illustrierte Kriminalzeitung*
WT	*Wiener Tagblatt*

All references to newspapers are to the main (morning) editions, unless otherwise indicated.

All translations are the author's unless otherwise indicated.

Acknowledgements

This book could not have been written without the generous help of a great number of individuals and institutions. My gratitude goes to the AHRB who funded my doctoral research; to Fitzwilliam College, Cambridge, who provided me with a base, funds and support for renewed research; to my former supervisors Richard J. Evans at Cambridge and Gerhard Botz at Vienna, who generously shared their expertise and continuously inspired me to do better; to Robert Pynsent and Chris Clark who grilled me over my argument's many gaps and catches; to Nicky Hahn Rafter who gave me early encouragement when I really needed it; to Andy Merrilles, Jonathan Kwan and Chantal Wright who revealed as many flaws in my grammar as in my thinking (and many more in my spelling); to my family who quietly cheered me on; and to the many scholars and students who commented on my work at conferences, presentations and on less formal occasions. I also want to thank the *Stadtarchiv* and *Staatsarchiv* of Vienna and the staff at the Österreichische Nationalbibliothek for guiding my researches.

... please excuse my speaking in such a deadfully educated manner, but if one studies at the university, one stumbles upon a great number of foolish books; and without being conscious of it, one begins using idiotic expressions.

Gustav Meyrink, Der Golem (Berlin 1989 [1915]), p. 137

Chapter 1

INTRODUCTION

Murder Most Foul

They found her lying in the woods, half-naked. There wasn't much blood at the scene, nor in her body. On the first of April, 1899, the corpse of Anežka Hrůzová was discovered in the forest of Březina near the Bohemian–Moravian border-town of Polná, with numerous head wounds, and her throat cut from ear to ear. It started as a provincial murder, gruesome but not singularly atrocious; a local affair, historically inconspicuous. Nevertheless, within months, Anežka Hrůzová, a nineteen-year-old assistant seamstress, had become a household name throughout Austria, a name that precipitated waves of veneration and righteous anger. Her own fame, however, was easily overshadowed by that of the supposed villain in this drama, that of Leopold 'Poldi' Hilsner, a Jewish vagabond who was charged with the murder. Before long Hilsner pictures and Hilsner statues were being sold by street-vendors up and down the Danube, as were postcards depicting the outraged villagers standing around the pencilled-in body of the Christian victim-turned-martyr, naked and virgin-white.

The accusation that made such headlines and made heads and newspaper presses spin was that of ritual murder. The Jew had struck again, and conquered Christian maiden-blood. Soon enough Tomáš Masaryk, the future president of the Czechoslovak Republic, was involved in the propagandistic battle surrounding the trial, facing off against Karel Baxa, a future mayor of Prague. After a first conviction and a sensational re-appraisal of the medical report that lead to the retraction of the verdict, the re-trial in Písek attracted even more attention than its predecessor in Kutná Hora. Hilsner was convicted, once again, for assistance in conspiratorial murder. His mysterious accomplices – minutely described by a half-dozen witnesses as two Jews, one hobbling, the other bent, both cigarette smokers – were never found.[1]

If I re-narrate this story in these somewhat racy terms, I do so because I believe it is the only way to get to the root of the issue. The *affaire* Hilsner was not simply a historical fact, a trial, a matter of accused and accuser, of witnesses called and speeches made, justice done or betrayed. The Hilsner murder was a scandal, a paper-devil constructed out of black ink and café gossip, a discursive entity, something whose very existence was tied up with the use of racy language, and bold type.

It is not the aim here to downplay the human tragedies of a young, murdered life and of a conviction based on racial slur and shaky evidence. However, we cannot understand this affair *qua* affair unless we accept it as a radically modern phenomenon – as something deliberately created by investigative journalists, which had an existence separate from the courtrooms in far off Kutná Hora and Písek, in those urban centres of scandal consumption, Vienna and Prague. There were many Hilsners, and only one of them was present at the trials; the others were narrative creations, tightly emplotted as cautionary tales in which moralistic message wrestled with suspense for structural predominance.

It is in this second, discursive existence of the trial – an existence facilitated by the rise of the modern city and of the modern newspaper – that the *affaire* ceases to be explicable simply by reference to village life and local politics, or even to the socio-economic upheavals brought about by a time of rapid change. Its dynamics become governed not by rural patterns of antisemitism and Czech nationalist ambitions, but by the conventions of trial reporting. Hence, if the Hilsner murder is to be understood in terms of a newspaper scandal, it will have to be understood as but one in a series of scandals. As a trial it was merely another chapter in a near continuous sequence of instalments of court-room soap digested by avid consumers of such vicarious drama. Similarly, if contemporaries regarded Hilsner as a criminal, this was done within the parameters of the pre-conceived (if contested) terms of criminality current in his time and place, both those bandied around in the papers and those carefully defined in the budding literature of criminology. More to the point, Hilsner was a Jewish criminal, a category that I will suggest had a separate discursive existence in Vienna and Austria at the time of his trial.

My fascination with the Hilsner trial thus raised any number of questions, all of which beckoned me away from the affair itself and to a wider cultural history of crime and antisemitism. What exactly was the contemporary conception of criminality? Where were popular narratives of crime articulated, and what were the generic rules of this articulation? How far did popular and scholarly conceptions differ? How did antisemitism interact with the language of crime? Within these questions I sensed hidden the chance to write a neglected chapter of the history of modernity.

The Context of Viennese Antisemitism

In order to tell this story, I chose Vienna as my geographic *locus*. The choice was motivated above all by the disturbing levels of antisemitism that so marked the Habsburg city. Not only was Vienna the period's only European capital to have a democratically elected mayor who stood on an explicitly anti-semitic platform, Hitler's propagandistic memoirs retrospectively enshrined the city as the place where he learned to hate the Jew and thus created a legend that turned it into something like the nursery of the 'Final Solution', a legend that has invited the close scrutiny of historians from the 1960s onward.[2]

Despite this rich and vigorous tradition of scholarship on the issue, the nature of Viennese antisemitism around the turn of the last century remains imperfectly understood. The historiography focusing on *political* antisemitism in the last quarter of the nineteenth century traces the emergence of Georg von Schönerer's pan-Germanist movement that embraced an aggressive, racialist antisemitic message. It did so hard on the heels of the 1882 expansion of the franchise, which effectively gave a political voice to the lower middle classes amongst whom such a message could hope to be popular.[3] Von Schönerer's career soon floundered, both because of an imprudent 1888 raid on a liberal, Jewish-owned daily, the *Neues Wiener Tageblatt*, that earned him prison time and the suspension of his political rights, and because of the mete-oric rise of his one-time ally (and one-time fellow liberal), the leader of the Christian Social Party, Karl Lueger.[4] As in the case of von Schönerer, Lueger's antisemitism was fostered by opportunism, whatever his precise personal prej-udices about Jews may have been. He came to embrace an openly antisemitic stance in 1887, and four years later officially founded his party upon an anti-semitic platform.[5] Unlike Schönerer's preoccupations with Aryan and Semitic 'blood', Lueger tapped into older antisemitic tropes that had first been rehearsed in Austria in the throes and the immediate aftermath of the 1848 revolution in which Jews had played a prominent role.[6] He exploited anti-semitism as a convenient, readily available language of anti-modernism and anti-capitalism that appealed to Catholic traditionalists steeped in a long tradi-tion of religious enmity against Jews. This traditional enmity was further encouraged by anxieties concerning 'big capital' amongst petit-bourgeois arti-sans and small traders; these were particularly acute during the years of an eco-nomic downturn that was initiated by the stock market crash of 1873 and lasted into the mid-1890s. Lueger's embracing of an antisemitic message thus allowed him both to tap into the socio-economic discontent of a new stratum of the electorate, and to take over much of the (admittedly small) movement von Schönerer had built, effectively eliminating him as a political force and rival. Some of von Schönerer's most vociferous sympathisers – Ernst Vergani, Ernst Schneider, Robert Pattai and others – joined up with the winning team, and would continue to spout antisemitic invective of a distinctly Schönerian cast throughout the 1890s and beyond. This they did despite the Christian Social Party's gradual re-orientation once Lueger had won the office of major (and the Emperor had given up on his attempts to veto his ascent to office) in April 1897. Not only did they moderate their antisemitic language – Lueger ignored the Jewish Question in his inaugural speech and would on occasion dismiss Jew-baiting as the 'sport of the rabble'[7] – but with the final demise of the political fortunes of the liberal party (they had been on the ropes since 1879 when they lost control of the parliament) and the gradual expansion of the franchise, they began to focus on the Socialists as their main political enemies.[8] Here, too, a certain brand of antisemitic discourse was part and parcel of their political strategy; but if their early incarnation had been one of a social protest movement against big 'Jewish' capital,[9] they now presented themselves as upholders of *bürgerlich* order in the face of an atheist proletariat under cynical Jewish leadership.[10]

The historiographic consensus thus describes the flare-up of overt, often extreme antisemitism in 1880s and early 1890s, in a variety of manifestations ranging from Christian prejudice against Jewish 'usurers' recast as a language of complaint about free-market capitalism to the appropriation of racial ideas that have been traced back to Arthur Joseph de Gobineau's mid-nineteenth-century *An Essay on the Inequality of Races*, Wilhelm Marr's 1879 *The Victory of Judaism over Germandom* and Eugen Dühring's 1881 *The Jewish Question as a Question of Race, Morals and Culture*. Amongst these, the religiously inflected anti-modern antisemitism is seen to have been far more successful than its racial competitor that seemed to attract only a limited number of dedicated adherents, most notoriously university students who provided perhaps the biggest block of von Schönerer's supporters and – disillusioned by Austria's ignoble defeat at the hands of Prussia in 1866 and no doubt fuelled by the usual Oedipal desire to deride their fathers as fools – embraced a vision of a ethnically pure *Großdeutschland* made possible only by the destruction of the dynastic empire whose citizens they were.[11]

Beyond this it has also been a mainstay of historiographic orthodoxy, first put forward by Peter Pulzer's seminal 1964 study *The Rise of Political Antisemitism in Germany and Austria*, and routinely upheld ever since, that while the political antisemitic climate mellowed from the mid-1890s onwards, Jew-baiting and Jew-hatred leapt from the political arena to become culturally ubiquitous and *Salonfähig*, i.e. respectable even amongst the rich and educated.[12] In fact, Steven Beller, in an important study of the importance of Jews for Viennese intellectual and cultural life, has suggested that antisemitism came to serve as social glue for non-Jewish immigrants of diverse nationalities and, by implication, classes.[13] Vienna, then, emerges as a city of omnipresent antisemitism that traverses socio-cultural divides. In Pulzer's words: 'it [antisemitism] succeeded not only among the elite but also among the masses; that is to say, it progressed along both what Mr Hughes calls the 'higher' and 'lower' levels of thought.'[14]

The problem with such an assertion is that it is not easy to provide evidence that would adequately prove the point. Scholars cite the antisemitic invectives circulated by one of the period's rabidly and explicitly antisemitic dailies and point to the undeniable fact that contemporary Jewish voices attest to an increased, often unwanted awareness of their heritage due to their frequent run-ins with antisemitic insults and worse.[15] This in itself does not give a clear picture of the spread, shape and social penetration of antisemitism in Vienna, however: a small minority of radical antisemites, obviously in evidence in the period under consideration, can terrorize a population no less aggravatingly, if qualitatively differently, than universal antipathy and socially sanctioned discrimination. This is not to doubt the fundamental fact that Austrian Jews lived in an antisemitic society; it simply begs the question of the precise nature of this antisemitism, both in terms of its social base and its precise content.

When it comes to giving sociological specificity to the designation of social strata amongst whom antisemitism prospered in the two decades leading up to the Great War, there exists – for all the supposed 'respectability' of Jew-hatred – a long historiographic tradition to point first of all to the uneducated 'masses': it is, after all, what contemporaries did. The liberal parliamentarian Ferdinand Kronawetter's designation of Lueger's and von Schönerer's movements as '*der Sozialismus der dummen Kerle*' (conventionally translated as the 'socialism of fools') has proven influential; we have already noted Lueger's invocation of the 'rabble'. Similarly, modern historians frequently refer to Lueger's politics as those of the 'mob' whose base 'instincts' were mobilised,[16] although one should not forget that his final victory was precipitated by the defection of the poorer end of the *Bildungsbürgertum* – minor officials and teachers, hardly prime mob-material – from the liberal cause.[17] This is not to deny that Lueger inaugurated a more populist form of politics, but the invocation of the 'mob', the 'mass' and the 'crowd' strikes me as problematic, precisely because it so closely echoes contemporary verdicts: there was, at the time, a fashionable fascination with the crowd that connected scholars such as Gustave LeBon, Emile Durkheim and Georg Simmel and, decades later, still provided the impetus for Elias Canetti's Vienna-inspired *Crowds and Power*. Blaming masses for instinctual, irrational behaviour was, in other words, *de rigeur* at the time – the discourse of crowds provided liberals with an antithesis to their cherished self-contained individualism and a vehicle to express their distrust of political democratisation. It might be dangerous then, to recycle their terminology without great care.

The issue is further problematised by the fact that there exists lively debate about the precise position of the Socialist Party – and that of its working-class followers, who in numerical terms would have been well suited to making up a crowd or two – on the issue of antisemitism. Robert Wistrich has argued that the Socialists neither abstained from using antisemitic political rhetoric nor had any real wish to: not only did the protection of Jews, in his view, win no votes, antisemitic anti-capitalist discourse could be used to implicate the Christian Socials (who had a way of courting big Jewish financiers). Wistrich has further argued that their Marxist beliefs led them to accept and endorse the escalation of antisemitism as an inevitable and welcome stage in capitalism's demise.[18] Other scholars – the literary historian Sigurd Paul Scheichl, the German historian Rosemarie Leuschen-Seppel – have maintained, *contra* Wistrich, that the party's forays into antisemitic language needs to be evaluated as qualitatively different from Christian Social invective and warn against stigmatising the Socialists as antisemitic in any straightforward way.[19] As to the working classes themselves, source material giving a clear indication as to their vulnerability to an antisemitic world-view is notoriously hard to come by. Beyond a hard-core petit-bourgeois following of Lueger who might have read one of the papers associated with his movement (not an insubstantial group in a city full of artisans and small industry), it is thus not easy to quantify the number of convinced or 'casual' antisemites. Nor is it clear what sort of language about Jews was most widely disseminated, and what sort of antisemitic narratives were popularly embraced as commonplaces.

The question gains in urgency if we look beyond the literature on political antisemitism in Austria to the often strangely disconnected scholarly literature charting the rise of racist and biological antisemitic narratives. Sander Gilman and Klaus Hödl, for instance, have over the last twenty years or so collated the various antisemitic fantasies regarding Jewish minds and bodies in circulation at the *fin-de-siècle* and beyond,[20] while John Efron has investigated how Jewish scientists themselves negotiated narratives of Jewish racial traits.[21] Their work implies that the tropes of race-language about Jews were much more prevalent than the fate of von Schönerer's political project of racial antisemitism might indicate. At the same time both Gilman and Hödl often rely on juxtaposing individual (sometimes quite marginal) sources across significant spans of time and place and hence fail to give a clear picture of the precise degree and channels of dissemination of the narratives they describe. It is clear, of course, that any number of self-declared intellectuals were smitten with, say, Houston Stewart Chamberlain's racial assertions in his *The Foundations of the Nineteenth Century*, published virtually contemporaneously with Freud's substantially more edifying *Dream Interpretation*: but how much of this had become the topic of every-day bar-room discussion? How much racism made it home to the dinner tables of gentile *Döbling* or those of more earthy *Ottakring*, to name but two city districts in the northwest of Vienna? Outside the fringe circles of self-declared prophets like Guido von List or Lanz von Liebenfels, to what degree did Viennese – above all those Viennese whose political sympathies did not lie with the Christian Social Party – internalise stereotypes about Jews, pass them on to their children and thus prepare the way for the catastrophe of the 1930s and 1940s?[22]

Crime, Antisemitism and the Media

I cannot promise that this book, by itself, will answer all these questions, nor answer them with sufficient precision: it represents one attempt to come to terms with them, within one realm of discourse, that of crime. Talk about crime, I maintain, represents a fortuitous area of inquiry for this investigation for a number of reasons. The first is that the scientific discourse of crime – criminology – was deeply and obviously implicated in creating powerful narrative of biological difference. Ever since Foucault's seminal *Discipline and Punish* it has been regarded, alongside psychology, as a paradigmatic science dedicated to the creation of 'others' – i.e. the demarcation of difference, including physiological and psychological difference – within a segment of the general population, with the implicit aim of this segment's permanent removal from society.[23] This project of 'othering' the criminal has been traced back by some scholars to the very roots of enlightenment discourse about crime;[24] it was certainly central to Cesare Lombroso's *L'uomo delinquente* whose 1876 publication kick-started the discipline of modern criminology.[25] Its emergence has struck historians as no less a centre-piece of modernity than that of racial antisemitism: both involve projects of categorisation that could be turned into exclusionary power. The contemporary emergence of discourses of Jewish and criminal biological difference has often been noted but never been fully explored, nor has there been much analysis of the specifically Austrian contribution to criminal science that dates precisely from the last decade of the nineteenth century.[26]

What is more, criminological knowledge had – to a much larger degree than, say, the theories of clinical psychology or sexology – the potential for mass dissemination, owing to the tremendous popularity of writings about crime, above all of trial reports that furnished a large percentage of what we might nowadays call the entertainment section of daily news. A third quintessential feature of modernity – the rise of mass media, above all the triumph of the newspaper, and the attendant rise (and collapse) of what Habermas has christened the public sphere – thus enters into the parameters of our investigation.[27] If narratives about behavioural abnormalities of minority groups rooted in the biology of their blood were to be transposed from scientific journals and monographs to households up and down the social ladder, newspaper crime-stories would have made the perfect transmitters. Despite this fact, there exists no history of the interaction of the popular knowledge of crime with criminology in this period, nor yet a history of the ways in which crime/trial reporting, perhaps the single most popular genre in the mass press at the turn of the last century, was utilised for antisemitic purposes.[28] This latter omission is particularly unfortunate: the very popularity of crime made it an attractive arena for formulating antisemitic narratives that could be elaborated on a weekly, sometimes daily basis. In order to assess this strategy, it will be necessary to comprehend crime/trial reports as forms of knowledge in their own right that both followed and played upon genre conventions. It was through the manipulation of such conventions that antisemites were capable of developing sustained narratives of Jews and criminality.

At the same time the ubiquity of crime as a news item allows for a direct comparison across the various papers and their respective political allegiances, and thus for an assessment of how far antisemitic narratives, however subtle, had slipped into popular culture and were propagated by publications other than those of a self-consciously antisemitic persuasion. In this context it might be surprising to read that there has been a relative neglect of the Viennese 'gutter' press, certainly if compared to London or Berlin: scholars have either been charmed by the sophistication of the *Neue Freie Presse*, Vienna's most famous and arguably best paper, or sought out the antisemitic dailies like the *Deutsches Volksblatt* with little consideration of how they fit into the city's overall landscape of news production. The *Illustrierte Kronenzeitung*, by far Vienna's most popular, journalistically most innovative, and most determinedly populist paper, has, by contrast, not been systematically utilised. Perhaps Vienna's astonishing wealth of high cultural achievements that can be condensed into a litany of Great Men who all seem to have come to prominence round and about the *Ringstrasse* around the turn of the last century – Klimt, Loos, Hoffmansthal, Freud, Wittgenstein, Kokoschka, Schiele, Mahler, Herzl, Beer-Hoffmann, Schnitzler, Kraus, Krafft-Ebing etc. – has mesmerised historians into paying insufficient attention to more popular genres of cultural expression. It is in these that I hope to unravel the interconnections between those quintessential modern phenomena of antisemitism, criminology and the mass media.

Structure

The main body of the book is divided into six chapters. The first of these, chapter two (entitled 'Scientific Tales of Criminality: Criminology and Criminalistics') features a reassessment of contemporary criminological discourse. It argues that the usual historiographic emphasis on criminology as a science that sought to delineate criminal difference needs to be complemented by an account of criminalistics – the science of detection – that emerged in Austria around the *fin-de-siècle* and articulated a sweeping critique of criminology's most fundamental assumptions. Rather than focusing on the essential deviance of criminals, criminalistics stressed the epistemological challenges of bringing offenders to justice and consequently inquired into the physical procedures and psychological dynamics of the investigative and judicial processes. In this narrative, the criminal did not hold any special status as an anthropological, psychological or sociological 'other', but was understood as a rational participant in these processes.

Chapter three ('Jewish Criminals') uses this survey of contemporary crime science as a springboard to investigate how criminology conceptualised the criminality of Jews. It demonstrates that biological and racial narratives did not dominate the debate about Jewish crime, and that Jewish criminals were most typically marked as modern, rational and predatory upon victims less adjusted to modernity than they themselves. Sociological and historical explanations for Jewish criminal activity thus predominated over tales of heredity and racial attributes, in contrast to, for example, contemporary narratives of Gypsy criminality.

The fourth chapter ('Paper Trials') moves the focus away from the scientific literature to the popular, newspaper discourse about (Jewish) crime. The chapter demonstrates the centrality of trial reporting for the popular imagining of crime and analyses the tropes of trial reporting. These serve to present crime as a contest between observing public and observed criminal, a game that pits observatory sophistication against the criminal's skill at dissimulation. Rather than pathologising criminals, trial reports emphasised their rational cunning, and embedded crime in the social and psychological dynamics of the court room. As such, trial reports shared many of the epistemological assumptions of the criminalistic (as opposed to criminological) construction of criminality.

Chapter five ('Jewish Crimes') is based on the analysis of several hundreds of contemporary trial reports. From this bulk of empirical material the chapter chooses a half-dozen exemplary trial sensations that were all constructed as Jewish crimes by the antisemitic press. It argues that antisemites systematically constructed Jewish criminals as cunning, conspiratorial agents who had mastered the art of evading justice and, in the final analysis, aimed at destroying the very mechanisms of justice. Far from locating Jewish criminality on their bodies or within their minds, these reports stressed their (ab)use of specifically modern knowledges and institutions (science, psychiatry, the press) and aimed to implicate 'Jewry' as a whole in the criminality of individual defendants. By contrast, publications that did not have an overtly antisemitic orientation carefully eschewed marking crimes as Jewish. The chapter thus draws attention to the polarisation of public language about Jews. It closes with a discussion of the coverage of a 1909 'Chinese crime' that provides an illuminating point of comparison in this regard.

Finally, chapter six ('The Hilsner Ritual Murder Trials') re-constructs the popular and criminological responses to the 1899 and 1900 trials of Leopold Hilsner and demonstrates that the logic of the antisemitic portrayal of criminality held sway even in the construction of this Blood Libel accusation. Once again antisemites located the 'Jewishness' of a crime not in the perpetrator's essentialist deviance, but in the alleged Jewish campaign surrounding the trial that aimed to subvert justice. At the same time the Hilsner trials attracted various criminological treatments that similarly concentrated on the effects of the mechanisms of 'suggestion' on both investigation and trial.

A conclusion (chapter seven) summarises the book's findings and places them in the wider context of Austrian history after World War One.

A Brief Note on Method: What Can One Learn from Reading Newspapers?

Crime, Jews and News is a piece of cultural history. It aims to reconstruct some of the ways historical subjects conceptualised (Jewish) criminality by interpreting, above all, contemporary newspaper reports and scientific treatments of crime. This may be deemed problematic. After all, the words disseminated in public and those exchanged in private may not have been entirely of the same order. Clearly it is possible and even probable that newspapers and other popular and indeed scientific outpourings were frequently doubted and resisted by those who consumed them. On the other hand it seems hardly credible that the language of crime hawked by newspaper vendors bore no resemblance to and did not at all impact upon private languages about crime. The most constructive way of looking at these conceptualisations of criminality articulated in press and scientific journals, in novels and true-crime accounts, I suggest, is to regard them as narratives, i.e. stories that order and construct knowledge about criminals and Jews. These narratives can be challenged by counter-narratives, but, they cannot, I believe, be regarded as utterly indifferent to historical actors' 'true beliefs'. As Miri Rubin puts it in her *Gentile Tales*:

> Let us think of narrative as a mode of organising events, unified by a plot ... Whole cultural systems are carried in myths, and myth is carried in rituals and through narratives. People act through narratives and they remember through narrative.[29]

This vision of narrative takes seriously Alasdair MacIntyre's claim that human kind is a story-telling animal, a creature that can only exist and impose meaning upon his or her world through constant narration.[30] Even if the plot and content of such narratives could be challenged – as they were, quite obviously, when rival versions of a trial or rival theories of criminality found circulation – the structure and terminology of these stories allows the historian some sort of access to the contemporary conceptual space. The result is an approximation: an intellectual history not of intellectuals but of various social strata that sketches the shape of their thought rather than its concrete content. That, alas, is the best we can do.

Given my emphasis on textual analysis, it will not surprise the reader that this book contains an unusual number of quotations from the sources. These serve to identify and demonstrate the genre logic of the reports under scrutiny: after all, the point is that the construction of criminality – including Jewish criminality – is deeply tied up with the conventions of reporting and the assumptions inherent therein. Of course one should never forget that such construction did not take place in a vacuum. The genre developed against a reality of crime and that of investigative and judicial practices; it also absorbed and exploited narratives that existed elsewhere, from criminalistic texts through to antisemitic pamphlets, parliamentary speeches, debates about white slavery and so on. However 'literary' the analysis of trial reports and other writings may seem on occasion, therefore, the intention throughout is to make historical rather than purely textual claims. The sources, in other words, yield real social implications for the nature and spread of antisemitism in Vienna 1900, for popular attitudes towards crime and contemporary anxieties about modernity. Close reading is merely a method of unlocking this yield, one that has the additional benefit of allowing the reader to look over the historian's shoulder during the process of interpretation and thus gaining access to the archive in some limited way.

Stylistically I have taken the liberty of using the first person singular when this seemed the clearest and most honest way of phrasing the point. I have taken other small stylistic liberties – all within the boundaries of good academic practice, or so I hope – believing that the historical enterprise has little to gain from the stylistic asceticism practised in the sciences, and indeed that an artificially dry turn of phrase does more to obstruct lucidity than improve it. In all this I hope I have not fallen prey to narcissism. My wish is always simply to communicate.

Notes

1. For a detailed analysis, see: chapter six. For a full reconstruction, see: Jiří Kovtun, *Tajuplná Vražda, Případ Leopoldna Hilsnera* (Prague 1994).
2. Adolf Hitler, *Mein Kampf* (Munich 1943 [1925]), pp. 18–137. In Brigitte Hamann's account, Hitler's rabid antisemitism stems from a later period of his life: Brigitte Hamann, *Hitler's Wien, Lehrjahre eines Diktators* (Munich 1998), p. 502.
3. By 1895 von Schönerer had made the 'removal of Jewish influence from all sections of public life' one of his party's official aims. On von Schönerer and Pan-Germanism, see: Robert S. Wistrich, *The Jews of Vienna in the Age of Franz Joseph* (Oxford 1990), pp. 205–21; A.G. Whiteside, *The Socialism of Fools, Georg Ritter von Schönerer and Austrian Pan-Germanism* (Berkeley 1975).
4. One should note, however, that the pan-Germanists did comparatively well in the 1901 parliamentary election; it was only general suffrage that finally broke their collective backs. Cf. Dirk van Arkel, *Antisemitism in Austria* (Leiden 1964), p. 132.
5. On Lueger, see: John W. Boyer, 'Karl Lueger and the Viennese Jews', in: *Leo Baeck Institute Yearbook* 21 (1981), pp. 125–41; John W. Boyer, *Political Radicalism in Later Imperial Vienna: Origins of the Christian Social Movement 1848–1897* (Chicago 1981); John W. Boyer, *Culture and Political Crisis in Vienna, Christian Socialism in Power 1897–1918* (Chicago 1995); Richard S. Geehr, *Karl Lueger, Mayor of Fin-de-Siècle Vienna* (Detroit 1989); Carl E. Schorske, *Fin-de-Siècle Vienna, Politics and Culture* (London 1981), pp. 133–44.
6. Wistrich, *Jews of Vienna*, pp. 32–5. See also: Reinhard Rürüp, 'The European Revolution of 1848 and Jewish Emancipation' in: Werner E. Mosse, Arnold Paucker, Reinhard Rürüp (eds), *Revolution and Evolution: 1848 in German–Jewish History* (Tübingen 1981), pp. 1–53.
7. Quoted in Bruce F. Pauley, *From Prejudice to Persecution, A History of Austrian Anti-Semitism* (Chapel Hill 1992), p. 46.

8. This is not to claim that the Christian Social Party could not revert to much more open antisemitism on occasion, for example in the aftermath of the 1905 pogroms in Russia that led Lueger to demand the boycotting of Jewish shops and saw him threaten pogroms in Vienna. Cf. Walter R. Weitzmann, 'Die Politik der jüdischen Gemeinde Wiens zwischen 1890 und 1914', in: Gerhard Botz, Ivar Oxaal, Michael Pollak and Nina Scholz (eds), *Eine zerstörte Kultur, Jüdisches Leben und Antisemitismus in Wien seit dem 19. Jahrhundert* (Vienna 2002), pp. 211–12.

9. Van Arkel, *Antisemitism*, p. 193.

10. Cf. Boyer, *Political Radicalism*, p. 402.

11. On Austrian student antisemitism and pan-Germanic *Burschenschaften* (fraternities), see: Robert Hein, Studentischer Antisemitismus in Österreich', in: *Beiträge zur österreichischen Studentengeschichte* 10 (Vienna 1984).

12. See, for instance: Peter Pulzer, *The Rise of Political Antisemitism in Germany and Austria* (New York 1964), p. 189; Peter Pulzer, 'Spezifische Momente und Spielarten des Österreichischen und des Wiener Antisemitismus', in: Botz et al., '*Zerstörte Kultur*, pp. 129–44, esp. pp. 134–39; Wistrich, *Jews of Vienna*, p. 236; Boyer, *Political Radicalism*, p. 113; Pauley, *From Prejudice*, pp. 34, 46.

13. Cf. Steven Beller, *Vienna and the Jews 1867–1938, A Cultural History* (Cambridge 1989), p. 193.

14. Pulzer, *Political Antisemitism*, p. 30.

15. In Arthur Schnitzler's phrase: 'It was not possible, especially not for a Jew in public life, to ignore the fact that he was a Jew.' Arthur Schnitzler, *My Youth in Vienna*, translated by Catherine Hutter (New York 1979), p. 6.

16. Wistrich, *Jews of Vienna*, pp. 220, 236; Pauly, *From Prejudice*, pp. 27, 37, 53.

17. Cf. Boyer, *Political Radicalism*, p. 228 and passim.

18. Robert S. Wistrich, 'Sozialdemokratie, Antisemitismus und die Wiener Juden', in: Botz et al., *Zerstörte Kultur*, pp. 187-95; Robert S. Wistrich, *Socialism and the Jews, The Dilemmas of Assimilation in German and Austro-Hungary* (London 1982).

19. Sigurd Paul Scheichl, 'Nuancen in der Sprache der Judenfeinde', in: Botz et al., *Zerstörte Kultur*, pp. 165–85; Rosemarie Leuschen-Seppel, *Sozialdemokratie und Antisemitismus im Kaiserreich, Die Auseinandersetzung der Partei mit den konservativen und völkischen Strömungen des Antisemitismus 1871–1914* (Bonn 1978).

20. Sander Gilman, *The Jew's Body* (New York 1991); Sander Gilman, *Jewish Self-Hatred: Anti-Semitism and the Hidden Language of the Jews* (Baltimore 1986); Sander Gilman, *The Case of Sigmund Freud, Medicine and Identity at the Fin-de-Siècle* (Baltimore 1993); Klaus Hödl, *Die Pathologisierung des jüdischen Körpers* (Vienna 1997).

21. John M. Efron, *Defenders of the Race, Jewish Doctors and Race Science in Fin-de-Siècle Europe* (New Haven 1994).

22. For a survey of fringe race theoreticians in Vienna c. 1900, see: Hamann, *Hitlers Wien*, pp. 285–336.

23. Michel Foucault, *Discipline and Punish*, translated by A. Sheridan (New York 1977); Peter Strasser, *Verbrechermenschen, Zum kriminalwissenschaftlichen Erzeugen des Bösen* (Frankfurt am Main 1984).

24. Piers Beirne, 'Inventing Criminology: The "Science of Man" in Cesare Beccaria's Dei Delitti e Della Pene', in: Piers Beirne (ed.), *The Origins and Growth of Criminology, Essays on Intellectual History 1760–1945* (Dartmouth: Aldershot 1994), pp. 777–820; Maren Lorenz, *Kriminelle Körper – Gestörte Geister, Die Normierung des Individuums in Gerichtsmedizin und Psychiatrie der Aufklärung* (Hamburg 1999); Peter Becker, *Verderbnis und Entartung, Eine Geschichte der Kriminologie des 19. Jahrhunderts als Diskurs und Praxis* (Göttingen 2002).

25. David G. Horn, *The Criminal Body, Lombroso and the Anatomy of Deviance* (London 2003).

26. On the importance of the Austrian criminalist Hans Gross, see: Roland Grassberger, 'Österreich und die Entwicklung der Kriminologie zur selbstständigen Wissenschaft', *Wissenschaft und Weltbild* 18, 4 (1965), pp. 277–89; Peter Becker, 'Die Rezeption der Physiologie in Kriminalistik und Kriminologie: Variationen über Norm und Ausgrenzung', in: Philipp Sarasin and Jakob Tanner (eds), *Physiologie und industrielle Gesellschaft. Studien zur Verwissenschaftlichung des Körpers im 19. und 20. Jahrhundert* (Frankfurt am Main 1998), pp. 453–90; Peter Becker, 'The Criminologists' Gaze at the Underworld, Towards an Archaeology of Criminological Writing', in: Peter Becker and Richard Wetzell (eds), *Criminals and Their Scientists: The History of Criminology in International Perspective* (Cambridge 2006), pp. 105–36. Gross's contribution is discussed in detail in chapter two of this book. For the intellectual context of Austrian criminology and the relationship of scientific innovation to other forces of 'modernity', see: Allan Janik and Stephen Toulmin, *Wittgenstein's Vienna* (New York 1973); William M. Johnston, *The Austrian Mind, An Intellectual and Social History 1848–1938* (Berkeley, Cal., 1972); Erna Lesky, *Die Wiener Medizinische Schule* (Graz 1978 [1965]); Edward Timms, *Karl Kraus, Apocalyptic Saint, Culture and Catastrophe in Habsburg Vienna* (New Haven 1986); Jaques LeRider, *Modernity and Crises of Identity, Culture and Society in Fin-de-Siècle Vienna*, translated by Rosemary Morris (Cambridge 1993); László Péter and Robert B. Pynsent (eds), *Intellectuals and the Future in the Habsburg Monarchy 1890–1914* (London 1988).

27. Jürgen Habermas, *Strukturwandel der Öffentlichkeit, Untersuchungen zu einer Kategorie der bürgerlichen Gesellschaft* (Frankfurt am Main 1996 [1961]). For a useful primer, see: Craig Calhoun, 'Introduction: Habermas and the Public Sphere', in: C. Calhoun (ed.), *Habermas and the Public Sphere* (Cambridge, Mass. 1992), pp. 1–48.

28. For various attempts to reconstruct popular attitudes towards criminality from literary sources and/or newspapers, see: Birgit Kreutzahler, *Das Bild des Verbrechers in Romanen der Weimarer Republik, Eine Untersuchung vor dem Hintergrund anderer gesellschaftlicher Verbrecherbilder und gesellschaftlicher Grundzüge der Weimarer Republik* (Frankfurt am Main 1987); Isabella Claßen, *Darstellung von Kriminalität in der deutschen Literatur, Presse und Wissenschaft 1900 bis 1930* (Frankfurt am Main 1988). See also: Konstantin Imm and Joachim Linder, 'Verdächtige und Täter. Zuschreibung von Kriminalität in Texten der "schönen Literatur" am Beispiel des Feuilletons der "Berliner Gerichtzeitung", der Romanreihe "Eisenbahnunterhaltungen" und Wilhelm Raabes "Horaker" und "Stopfkuchen",' in: W. Frühwald (ed.), *Zur Sozialgeschichte der deutschen Literatur von der Aufklärung bis zur Jahrhundertwende* Vol. 1 (Tübingen 1985), pp. 21–96.

29. Miri Rubin, *Gentile Tales, The Narrative Assault on Late Medieval Jews* (New Haven 1999), p. 2.

30. Alasdair MacIntyre, *After Virtue, A Study in Moral Theory* (London 1981), p. 197.

Chapter 2

SCIENTIFIC TALES OF CRIMINALITY: CRIMINOLOGY AND CRIMINALISTICS

Historiography and Criminology

Two spectres haunt the historiography of criminology into which we wish to inscribe the Jewish criminal: the spectre of Cesare Lombroso and that of Michel Foucault.[1] Lombroso and his famed creation, l'uomo delinquente, have long been accepted as a convenient cipher for the momentous shift within nineteenth-century thought about crime, away from a forensic and moral understanding centred upon the criminal act, to a medical understanding centred upon the agent.[2] Similarly, there is wide agreement amongst historians of criminology that while Lombroso's theory of atavism, in which criminality was reduced to biological difference that could be physically located upon the body of a criminal, was rejected within twenty or thirty years by most scholars throughout Europe, his idea that any science of crime worth its salt had to concern itself with what sets the criminal deviant apart from the great mass of men and women found wide resonance. French criminologists for instance, argued that deviance could be acquired through destructive degenerative habits such as alcoholism and sexual promiscuity, but also that degeneration could be inherited.[3] German criminology, too, sought to strike a balance between acquired and inherited criminal deviance,[4] and even Lombroso himself was happy to juxtapose, if not exactly reconcile, rival models of criminality – each new edition of L'uomo delinquente seemed to add a new factor (including degeneracy, moral insanity and epilepsy) to the causes of born criminality.[5] What we witness here, then, is the process of a 'soft' adaptation of Lombroso's vision, stripping his thesis of all its particulars but leaving in place the focus on the criminal and leading to a more and more sophisticated study of criminal bodies and minds, i.e. the gradual 'medicalisation' of the criminological endeavour.[6]

Hand in hand with this narrative of the rise of determinist models of crime runs a narrative of exclusion that owes much to Michel Foucault's 1975 work on the French penal system, and his subsequent theoretical work on the connection between knowledge and power.[7] Crudely put, Foucault suggests that the emerging new scientific discourse on crime, criminals and their punishment constituted a distinct system of knowledge that aimed at securing exclusionary power over those it identified as deviants. The identification of criminals as distinct from the general population, in other words, allowed for their surgical removal from society; the medicalisation of criminology went hand in hand with its potential and ambition for social engineering.[8] Criminological knowledge is thus connected to eugenic measures such as forced sterilisation in the early and mid-twentieth century.[9] Indeed, some historians such as Peter Becker argue that this exclusionary potential can be traced all the way back to the beginnings of the nineteenth century, when crime theorists marked criminals as 'other' by pointing to their habitual moral dissipation, allowing them to trace their criminality in their biographies independently of any given criminal offence.[10]

The twin focus upon medicalisation and exclusion has led to a relative neglect of other aspects of the contemporary criminological discourse, which I believe are crucial if we are to develop an accurate picture of how narratives of Jewish crime were integrated into it. The most important of these, I will argue, was the emergence of a criminalistic discourse of crime, which combined interest in policing and identification technology with a trenchant critique of the mainstream criminological endeavour. In order to contextualise its emergence, it is helpful to first highlight some of the failures and incoherences inherent to criminal anthropology/psychology around 1900.

For one thing, the initial promise central to Lombrosian criminology – the hope that criminals could be accurately identified independently from their acts – was largely frustrated. It required a finite set of agreed upon signs, ideally of a physical nature, that could be read upon the body of criminals. Lombroso, of course, provided numerous lists of such stigmata, which were continuously augmented by his followers by ever new and – it must be said – rather outlandish indices of crime. Thus, in the year 1901 alone, the publications by self-conscious Lombrosians included analyses of (criminal) hip-bones, thumb-lines, levels of blood-pressure, the quantity of mucus in the corners of the mouth, the length of the second toe, the sebum-gland located in criminal cheeks, the size of the Adam's apple, and the existence and shape of fingernail lines, none of which had featured much in earlier lists of criminal stigmata.[11] Elsewhere in Europe the focus upon degenerative signs also caused problems, both because the morphology of such signs was thought to be extensive and because scholars were well aware that degeneracy and criminality could not be simply conflated. Indeed more and more voices suggested that no criminal typology existed, and that degenerative signs among prison populations were shared with the population at large. Johannes Jaeger's study of prisoners' writings, for instance, stressed that the 'criminal in no way represents a typical variety of the *genus humanum*, [and] that the same morphological and psychological variations hold sway among criminals [as among non-criminals]'.[12] Abraham-Adolph Baer similarly maintained that criminals did not constitute a unitary type, and that the signs of degeneration found by Lombroso were also found among the general population.[13] Hand in hand with these arguments for the lack of distinctiveness of criminals went something of a pathologisation of the general public. The Swiss psychiatrist August Forel, for instance, stressed the limited rationality of 'normal' human beings.[14] Paul Näcke, a German psychiatrist based in a Saxon mental institution in Hubertusburg (from 1889 to 1912), went even further: his book on female criminality and insanity argued that 'the latent disposition [for deviance] is so widely spread, that no-one is safe from turning criminal or insane due to strong outside influences.'[15] His views were echoed by advocates of degeneration theory outside the field of criminology: cultural critics such as Max Nordau and Paul Möbius linked modern civilisation's state of cultural decay to an endemic biological decline.[16] Here, too, it was not merely a minority class of deviants that was afflicted, but large portions of society.

Statistical approaches towards crime, first conceived in the mid-nineteenth century, and popular throughout the late nineteenth and early twentieth centuries, implied that crime was better studied as an aggregate rather than mapping onto the individual offender, and often implicitly challenged medical thought about crime by suggesting that sociological factors such as religion or vocation shaped criminality.[17] Lombroso himself began to explore statistical correlations of crime with a variety of cultural and 'racial' factors (climate, nationality, hair colour, complexion etc.), in effect inscribing the individual deviant into a sociological space and thus blurring the line between criminal 'others' and the general population.[18] It is also important to keep in mind that neither Lombroso nor any of his Italian, French or German colleagues suggested that all criminal activity could be explained by reference to determinist models of crime. Estimates of how many criminals could indeed be classed as congenitally criminal, '*minderwertig*' ['psychologically inferior'] or 'abnormal' fluctuated widely, even within individual authors, at times estimating a proportion of as little as twenty percent.[19] Indeed, scholars like Gustav Aschaffenburg cautioned, the criminal population also included those rational enough to consciously avoid having themselves tattooed or using criminal cant because they had become aware that these had been designated as markers of criminality.[20] The 'pathologisation' of the general population thus went hand in hand with doubts about the width of applicability of determinist models of crime.

The practical and theoretical challenges posed by reliably locating criminal distinctiveness also articulated themselves in the failure of criminology to impact decisively upon prophylactic measures against crime. Increasingly, congenital criminality was proven by reference to recidivism, i.e. the recurrance of criminal acts whose history could be followed thanks to the rise of reliable identification technology, i.e. Bertillon's anthropometric system, and – gradually – dactyloscopy (fingerprinting). Only in retrospect could psychological, anthropological and social narratives of deviance be imposed upon these recidivists, a version of writing *ex post facto* criminal biographies that had a long tradition throughout the nineteenth century. Despite attempts to make policing 'scientific' by introducing criminological thought into the education of crime practicioners such as policemen and investigative judges – evident in Salvatore Ottolenghi's School for Scientific Policing in Rome and in various German police manuals of the early twentieth century – the practical ability of criminology to pinpoint those it wished to exclude was far from obvious.[21] It is against this background of a divided, contested, and in many ways ineffectual discipline that one should analyse the emergence of the science of criminalistics, as spearheaded by the Austrian investigative judge turned academic Hans Gross.

Criminalistics and Crime

Hans Gross (1847–1915) was born a Catholic, raised and educated in Graz. He worked as an investigative judge for close to thirty years, before turning academic, serving as a professor of penal law first at Czernowitz, then Prague, then Graz, where he founded the Institute of Criminalistics and a Criminal Museum.[22]

Gross made three sizeable contributions to the science of criminality. The first was the *Handbuch für Untersuchungsrichter* ('Handbook for Investigative Judges'), first published in 1893 and soon followed by six editions and countless translations;[23] the second its companion volume *Criminalpsychologie* ('Criminal Psychology') that proved similarly successful;[24] the third a journal entitled *Archiv für Criminalanthropologie und Criminalistik* ('Archive for Criminal Anthropology and Criminalistics'), launched in 1898. Significantly, all of these publications were written as explicit critiques of the criminological (i.e. criminal–anthropological and criminal–psychological) agenda described above. His introductory essay in the first issue of the *Archiv* maintained that the key problem of criminal anthropology was that, from the outset, it had falsely understood itself as

> the science of the physical and mental *distinctiveness* of the criminal. One had already included the assumption, that such a distinctiveness exists, into the definition [of the criminal] ... We know today what constitutes a *crime*. What, however, one is to understand under the heading '*criminal*' nobody has as of yet explained.[25]

Gross's own work, he vowed, would not rest on such a priori assumptions. Furthermore Gross believed that his critique of criminology added up to a coherent system that allowed alternative access to the problem of criminality.

This was made explicit by adding the specification 'as a system of criminalistics' to the third and all subsequent editions of the *Handbuch*, and self-enshrining himself in its preface (by way of quoting a New York newspaper) as the founder of a new school of criminology: the 'psychological (realistic–psychological) school'.[26] The claim soon found acceptance among his colleagues.[27]

This Grossian 'school' of criminology was based on a number of principles: the insistence on non-reductive data collection and its 'phenomenological' interpretation; the widening of the sphere of inquiry to include not only the criminal but also the crime-scene and all those people partaking in the investigation of a crime; and the problematisation of the acts of perception and memory themselves, with the attendant drive to distinguish those who produced reliable knowledge from those who did not.[28] Criminals retreated into the background of the inquiry and were implicitly held to be mostly rational actors who were not anthropologically and psychologically distinct from the main population.

In order to unpack this Grossian programme, let us have a more detailed look at his *oeuvre*. One of the first things to strike the reader is the encyclopaedic ambition evident in all of his work: the *Handbuch* and *Criminalpsychologie* were not merely long books, they were explicit attempts to collect all available knowledge on their respective subject matters.[29] The *Archiv*, likewise, was named precisely for its ambition to bring together all further bits and pieces of knowledge.[30] None of Gross's publications aimed at providing a sweeping, overarching thesis of the criminal. Indeed, the criminal as an internally stable category was virtually absent in Gross's writing, most conspicuously so in his two books. Rather the *Handbuch*'s main aim was to provide a thorough initiation of the investigator into the craft of hunting down criminals, touching on topics such as interpreting footprints, ciphers or gun-shot wounds, to hands-on advice on how best to sketch a crime scene with pencil and paper. It equipped the hunter of criminals with all the technical knowledge required to interpret the material evidence surrounding crime. *Criminalpsychologie* provided a similarly comprehensive, practical guide for interpreting non-material evidence.[31] Far from delving into criminals' psychopathology, it offered a wealth of guidance on how to question witnesses and suspects alike, along with detailed observations about the psychology of the court-room, including the psychology of judges, jurors and participating audience.[32] The book argued that the mental act of perceiving crime in its widest sense in itself demands detailed and careful analysis:

> Crime, of course, exists objectively, and Cain would have murdered his brother Abel, even if Adam and Eve had already been dead at that point [i.e. if they had not been around to witness the crime], but for us each crime nevertheless exists only as we perceive it – as it comes to our awareness through all the means allowed by the laws of criminal procedure. All these means are based on sense-perception, on the perception of the judge and his assistants, that of witnesses, accused and expert witnesses. All these perceptions must be mentally digested, and to learn about the rules

that determine such digestion, one is in need of a special branch of general psychology, *i.e. of a pragmatic applied psychology that inquires into all the states of mind that will come into question in the determination and evaluation of criminal actions*.[33]

Gross explicitly attacked contemporary criminal psychology for limiting itself to the 'lore of criminal motives, or (after Liszt) the research into the criminal's psyche, explained physiologically'.[34] In both *Handbuch* and *Criminalpsychologie* the crime scientist's sphere of inquiry was thus systematically widened. Gross maintained that the 'truth' about a crime and a criminal was intimately tied up with a technically flawless recovery of his or her fingerprint or the accurate assessment of a witness statement.

Together the *Handbuch* and *Criminalpsychologie* thus provided a systematic collection of truth-tools that aimed at getting to the bottom of all criminal activity.[35] Their ambition to function as reference works, detailing every single possible permutation of observed crime, is as striking as their focus beyond the criminal: on the things that could be observed at a scene of crime, and on the minds of those who did the observing.[36]

Gross's preoccupations cannot be explained until one realises that his conception of what was to be read upon bodies and within minds rejected the reductivism that underlay mainstream criminology, and that he was profoundly mistrustful of the average person's ability to arrive at good knowledge of his or her own accord. Where Lombroso and those working in a criminological mould, narrowly defined, investigated criminal bodies and minds within a closed semantic system of signifiers leading back to the simple 'fact' of the criminal's deviance, Gross advocated a total reading of all available signs surrounding the crime and their individual interpretation. *Criminalpsychologie*, for instance, devoted long sections to reading people's physiognomies, clothes, walks, hands and voices,[37] in an observatory act Gross called 'phenomenological ... [i.e.] the systematic collection of those external symptoms, which are caused by inner processes'.[38] This act of clue-reading was unaffected by whether or not the observed subject was criminal or not; it was a 'normal-psychological semiotics'.[39] In his discussion of footprints, for example, Gross in no way differentiated between criminal and non-criminal footprints, discussing the prints made by pregnant women side-by-side with those made by sailors or drunks.[40] Nor did Gross assume that an observed surface sign was tied to a stable signifier: an emotion, for instance, did not register the same way on the skin of every person at each instant.[41] Gross did not provide a reductive system, but rather removed the hope for a semiotic dictionary of phenomenological observation into the utopian distance.[42] The only guide Gross could offer was a list of his own experiences and observed correlations, and guidelines on how one was to school one's eye, for instance by observing people speaking on the telephone and reading their body language without hearing what was being said.[43] In Gross's view, experience alone would provide expertise and make the world legible.[44]

This call for observatory experience in turn was tied to Gross's deep mistrust of the powers of untrained perception and memory, and the belief that dissimulation was at the very heart of criminal activity.[45] More than three hundred of *Criminalpsychologie*'s five hundred pages were dedicated to the problem of perception/memory, commenting in detail on all available senses, and the dangers of false memory, hallucinations, and misperceptions.[46] The *Archiv*, similarly, printed numerous articles on these issues.[47] The mistrust of perception and memory was particularly focused on the witness.[48] This made sense in light of Gross's above-quoted assertion that 'crime ... exists only as we perceive it'.[49] The witness, Gross maintained, frequently misperceived, or was unable to distinguish true memory of a perceived event from made-up memory based on an external stimulant.[50] Consequently the crime-specialist had to be trained to question witnesses in such a way as to distinguish true perception from false perception. He also had to be trained in reading material facts directly, and thus leave behind his dependency on other people's sense perceptions.[51] This crime expert advocated by Gross was not the post-Lombrosian criminologist who made spurious assertions about the link between psychological or physiological markers and criminal deviance, but an expert able to correctly perceive and judge a crime. The experienced, scientifically trained expert alone became the guarantor for good knowledge. Everyone else was in danger of becoming a 'plaything of the senses'.[52]

Gross's books and journal provided training manuals of how to become such an expert, as well as collecting each and every discrete fact about crime that had been gathered by a reliable method and individual. Leafing through the *Archiv* one is quite simply astonished by the ambition of Gross's project: 'I ask each reader not to assume that any observation he has made is insignificant,'[53] he wrote in the *Handbuch*, and consequently any possible observation that could at all have bearing on the subject matter of crime was welcomed in the *Archiv*'s pages, with article titles ranging from 'Effects of a Water Shot,' 'Poisonings via Rectum and Vagina,' 'Criminal Ciphers of Freistadt,' 'A Criminalistic–Chemical Investigation of Glue', 'Ant-Baths as Therapy,' and 'Further Details about Electrocutions,' to 'Homosexual Kisses.'[54] Gross's epistemological model was purely cumulative and descriptive, a safeguard against the weak observatory powers of the public on the one hand, and the overconfident pronouncements of Lombrosian and other criminologists on the other. His collection mania was rounded off by the creation of a criminal museum in Graz that served as an archive for physical objects relating to crime.[55]

At the same time Gross's emphasis on criminal tricks, frauds and tools suggested that the criminals themselves were largely a rational and professional class, best studied in terms of their technique and social organisation.[56] In an article on modern forms of criminality, he stressed the ingenuity of many a criminal, without any suggestion that this criminal intelligence should be read as a sign for a determinist disposition towards crime as it sometimes was by other authors who saw in 'genius' a sign of deviance.[57] This is not to argue that

Gross denied that hereditary abnormalities could explain a specific criminal's actions and that their investigation should be neglected. Indeed, in 1913 he became one of Austria's earliest advocates for the sterilisation of degenerates.[58] However, Gross did not allow the existence of biological deviants amongst criminals shape his vision of criminology's agenda as a scientific discipline. At no point did he attempt to provide a typology of criminals to rival those circulated by several contemporary criminologists. He thus went a long way towards replacing the dichotomy of normal citizen and criminal enshrined by criminal anthropology and psychology, with a dichotomy between rational expert (a minority class) and muddle-headed layman.

It is here that Gross's inquiry connected with the theories of the degeneration of the wider public voiced by Paul Näcke, who was one of the *Archiv's* core contributors. In Gross the public – as represented by the witness – was not directly described as degenerate, but was characterised as weak-willed, easily confused and unreliable. Gross's own comments on the danger of degenerates destroying society through a kind of inverse selection (voiced in an article dealing with vagrants, gamblers and drunks that made no reference to more serious criminal activity) drive home his closeness to Näcke's position.[59] Criminology's vision of degenerate criminals preying on normal citizens was effectively inverted into a vision of normal criminals preying on proto-degenerate citizens.

It might be objected at this point that Gross was essentially a policeman and not a man of science and should thus not be considered in the same light as a Liszt, a Ferri or an Aschaffenburg, or else that Gross was simply a conservative, more tied to a view of the criminal surviving from the previous century and pursuing a scientific trajectory that led directly back to mid-nineteenth century figures such as Avé-Lallemant and Ludwig von Jagemann.[60] Yet, it is evident from the journals that Gross, far from being a marginal figure, was considered a colleague by Liszt, Näcke, and Aschaffenburg alike. They were familiar with Gross's work,[61] just as Gross was with theirs: he routinely reviewed criminological texts in his journal and himself published articles in Aschaffenburg's *Monatsschrift*.[62]

Indeed it would be a mistake to separate criminalistics and criminology too stringently, despite the above noted epistemological incompability of the two.[63] Across Europe it was criminologists who hailed identification technologies – i.e. criminalistic detective technology – as an important innovation; in Italy, the above mentioned Salvatore Ottolenghi struggled to reconcile the knowledges produced by criminalistics and criminology even while Gross made a point of separating them as distinct disciplines.[64] As late as 1912, at the seventh international congress for criminal anthropology in Cologne, criminalistic exhibits and lectures featured alongside those of a criminal anthropological/psychological nature,[65] and at least one of the 'criminological' contributions echoed Gross by focusing on the need for a psychology of the police, the investigator, and (curiously enough) of the victims of crime.[66] One should add that

Aschaffenburg's *Monatsschrift* covered many issues dear to Gross's heart, most prominently the question of witness reliability.[67] Similarly, the *Archiv für Criminalanthropologie und Criminalistik* catered for several conceptualisations of crime, carrying its dual name with no apparent discomfort. It did give voice to Lombrosian approaches to criminality (including Gross's own occasional ventures into more deterministic criminology), even if its general tendency was to argue against such conceptualisation.[68] One should also note that Gross's school of criminalistics as an academic discipline dominated the Austrian criminological enterprise into the late 1960s and beyond.[69] There seems to be few grounds, then, to dismiss Gross as a non-scientist whose views were marginal and not taken seriously by the criminological establishment.

Nor do Grossian criminalistics represent the simple re-issue of nineteenth-century writings about criminality, despite similarities in theme and encyclopaedic ambition: Gross's project not only included psychological preoccupations entirely absent in Avé-Lallement *et al.*; it also called for an entirely new level of technical expertise on the side of the criminalist, devoting attention to specialist topics such as forensic photography, the importance of dentistry for identification or the various minituae of evidence collection.[70] Finally, the very fact that Gross wrote after Lombroso – that all of his texts were deeply informed by the contemporary debate in which he himself partook – would be enough to place his writing into a different order: whatever conservatism one might perceive in it, it was formulated as a direct response to contemporary development and as a way of re-writing the rules and aims of criminological research.

Gross's 'criminalistic' project inspired a series of detective manuals, both in the German speaking world – most notably Niceforo's and Lindenau's *Die Kriminalpolizei*, and Gustav Roscher's *Großstadtpolizei* – and elswhere in Europe.[71] It stands within an alternative tradition of thought about crime whose focus was not on criminal distinctiveness. This is not to claim that criminalistics replaced other criminological inquiry. Rather, Gross and his followers represented a rival model to more biologically or psychologically based constructions of criminality favoured by such Austrians as Moriz Benedikt, a Viennese medical doctor who engaged with Lombroso's ideas, or the sexological pioneer Richard von Krafft-Ebing whose *Psychopathia Sexualis* devoted a section to criminal sexual deviance. Even if Grossian criminalistics did not become the predominant parameter of scientific thought about crime, however, the questions he raised about the status of observation and description (as opposed to analytical reduction) and about the weakness of perception and memory found among witnesses, were central to a variety of criminological debates raging at the turn of the last century. They had a wide currency among crime scientists in Vienna and elsewhere in Europe, and also form part of the context into which scholars and newspapers narrated tales of Jewish crime.

Malleable Selves, Unstable Truths

Criminology, it was often noted by its critics, threatened to undermine notions of moral autonomy. By depicting criminals as being subject to biological and social forces outside their control, criminologists challenged notions of culpability upon which modern law codes had been constructed. It is true, of course, that Enlightenment thought had already tempered its notion of the the freedom of the will with the constraints of 'habit' and the demands of the 'passions', an equation that underlay Cesare Becaria's celebrated plea for more rational and less barbaric law codes, *Of Crime and Punishment* (1764). Nevertheless one is right to observe an erosion of the idea of personal autonomy towards the end of the nineteenth century. From Marxism to Durkheimian sociology to the emerging science of psychoanalysis, the self began to be conceptualised not as the unitary, rational and autonomous entity evoked by Cartesian thought but rather as deeply penetrated by forces beyond its control. This idea of a malleable self found a multitude of a articulations within criminological and criminalistic discourse: Hans Gross, for instance (himself afraid of the dilution of the notion of moral culpability brought on by the new criminology),[72] argued that gestures, performed by witnesses or defendants in order to convince the jury of the authenticity of a certain emotion, could themselves generate the enacted emotions.[73] Liars would thus come to believe their own lies, and were themselves unable to differentiate their true selves from their enacted selves.[74] Crucially, the debates centering on the theme of the malleable self did not typically focus upon the criminal. In other words, a discourse existed within professional criminological journals, which routinely invoked non-criminals as non-autonomous actors. This discourse, by no means limited to Gross and his admirers, served to further the corrosion of clear lines of delineation between pathological perpetrators driven by deterministic forces and autonomous and rational victims and bystanders.

This erosion found its clearest expression in the vast literature on suggestion that emerged in the last decade of the nineteenth century.[75] It had its roots in the fascination with hypnotism characteristic of the 1870s and 1880s, which itself owed much to a long-standing fascination with mesmerism.[76] Towards the end of this period, the advocates of the so-called Nancy school of hypnotism were winning the argument against the view that a hypnotic state could only be induced in subjects displaying degenerate/hysterical symptoms. From a theory that viewed hypnotic suggestability as a function of deviance, it was beginning to turn into a theory that described a psychological process to which the general population was subject.[77] Gradually, the interest shifted away from the formal process of luring a person into a trance-like state for therapeutic reasons, and focused instead on the various ways by which fully awake and conscious individuals could be induced to commit acts they had not themselves willed, or remember things they had not themselves experienced. For some scholars like Hypolite Bernheim, hypnotism and suggestion became near synonymous, with the former phenomenon being dissolved in the latter.[78]

According to the literature, suggestion could be triggered by other people's influence, by images or words encountered in a newspaper, even by words that were overheard in the street. Reported manifestations of suggestion ranged from numerous accounts of false witness statements – a witness's claim to have observed detailed facts about some criminal activity that was precipitated by false memories implanted by newspaper or police reports – to actual criminal activities, such as rape or blackmail.[79] One pioneering study of suggestion, written by the Munich psychologist Albert v. Schrenck-Notzing, for instance recounts the case of a maid who managed to

> continually suggest the feeling of guilt [for acts of destruction against the parent's most valuable pieces of property perpetrated by the maid herself] in the child that had been placed in her care, so that for nine months she [the girl] willingly endured all punishments and made detailed confessions acquired via suggestion, without once betraying her tyrant.[80]

The domestic dimension of such an example serves as a potent symbol for the immediacy of the threat encapsulated by the theory of suggestion: not only was one not safe in one's own house from quasi-criminal activity, but one's own self could be compromised by friends and strangers alike. Schrenk-Notzing explicitly noted that suggestibility was not merely a symptom among psychologically abnormal people, but could in principal affect all human beings.[81] It is no wonder, then, that journal articles and monographs entitled 'Suicide Through Suggestion,'[82] *Suggestion and Hypnotism in Ethnic Psychology*,[83] *Suggestion and its Social Importance*,[84] 'Suggestion and falsification of memory,'[85] *Hypnotism and Suggestion in Life and Education*,[86] 'An Olfactory Illusion Caused by Suggestion,'[87] and 'Mass-Suggestion'[88] began to litter the professional journals and shelves. There also existed an attendant discourse on the proclivity of *Schundliteratur* – bad literature, in particular cheap crime thrillers – to produce criminal imitators.[89]

The debate about suggestion within criminological circles centred primarily on the damage it did to the authorities' attempt to find and bring to justice the perpetrators of crime. Suggestion caused false perceptions both at the crime scene and in the court room. Paul Näcke, for instance, recounts the case of a mother, a wife and a sister who unanimously and falsely identified the corpse of a drowned man as their son, husband or brother, all under the influence of suggestion.[90] In another article Näcke bemoans the suggestibility of judges who were unconsciously swayed by the defendants' wealth and status, leading to biased judgements.[91] It is for this reason that suggestive forces could effectively be criminalised. Newspapers in particular were targeted for spreading suggestion.[92] The only antidote to suggestion, one should equally note, was the expert who could spot it when it occurred, and assess the truth situation of a crime independent of reports coming from suggestible witnesses. Schrenck-Notzing acted in the Berchthold case as precisely this kind of expert, not only correctly identifying instances of suggestion acting on the witnesses, but also successfully telling them apart from conscious attempts at perjury.[93] Gross's emphasis on physical evidence over witness statements was another solution to the problem of suggestion.[94]

Another contemporary debate within criminology/criminalistics centred on the question of whether or not one could make investigative use of the presumed inability of the will to control the unconscious. 'Psychological Fact-Diagnostics' ['*Psychologische Tatbestandsdiagnostik*'] was a detective technique developed by two of Hans Gross's former Prague students, Max Wertheimer and Julius Klein. It proposed that it should be possible 'to search a man's soul for the psychological effects of a factual occurrence, without relying on his claims'.[95] Suspects or witnesses could, of course, not be stopped from lying, but their dissimulation, so Wertheimer and Klein postulated, would have psychological repercussions that could be measured. Unsurprisingly, their method drew the attention of the budding science of psychoanalysis. Carl Gustav Jung contributed one of the key essays of the debate, and Sigmund Freud published an interesting comparison between this new criminological method and that of psychoanalysis in the *Archiv* itself.[96]

In effect Wertheimer and Klein sought to establish a forerunner of the lie-detector test, albeit one based on psychological symptoms of deception rather than physiological ones.[97] Typically a list of one hundred words was read out to the suspect, twenty of which were deemed 'stimuli words' which might have psychological–physiological effects (words like 'murder'). The suspect was to reply with quick, one-word associations. Both the kind of answer given and the time required were measured and later analysed by the expert. This act of interpretation did not follow hard-and-fast rules, but rather depended on the precise circumstances of each particular case, analogous to the Grossian concept of clue-reading. 'Psychological Fact-Diagnostics' received much attention in a variety of journals, and was hotly debated.[98] Its utility was contested, the difficulties of interpretation and limitations noted.[99] At the same time, the underlying assumption that minute observation of discrete details could reveal hidden secrets was universally accepted, as was the assumption that the method principally worked on all subjects equally, implicitly denying any essentialist psychological difference between criminal and non-criminal.

The criminological debate about simulated insanity also combined a stress on expert readings of clues with the assumption of a treacherous, non-unitary self. A variety of authors within criminological and psychological circles articulated their belief that offenders, in order to escape execution or to secure better food, frequently attempted to imitate a variety of clinical symptoms mimicking insanity.[100] One contribution to this debate vividly described how the evaluating psychological expert could see through the simulation by paying attention to minute details:

He knows how to read it already in his [the criminal simulator's] eye. Never does it glow in the phosphorous light of the maniac, never does it speak of the drab dispassionateness of the melancholic man, never does it display the lively distrust of the paranoid or the frightened insecurity of the epileptic patient. The eye of the simulator that always scrutinises its surroundings, to decipher the impression that one forms about his behaviour, remains the eye of the criminal – a mobile, attentive, cold and dark eye.[101]

Interestingly – and ironically – both investigator and investigatee were here described as clue-readers in the Grossian sense: the criminal's eye was 'shifty' not because it was criminal, but because it displays the criminal's attentiveness to the details of the investigator's reactions. It was precisely this rational inquisitiveness that gave the simulator away and differentiated him or her from the mentally ill who could be classified by reference to stable signifiers such as the tell-tale 'phospherous glow' of mania. The same article, however, also warned psychologists that on occasion the simulation enacted by the patient was itself a symptom of an underlying mental malady – an opinion shared by Johannes Bresler and Gustav Aschaffenburg.[102] The author, C. C. Falkenhorst, presented the example of a clinically paranoid inmate who simulated epilepsy. The expert – and Falkenhorst established an explicit dichotomy between rational, trained experts ('*Sachverständige*') who were capable of coming to an accurate appraisal of what constituted reality, and laymen (he used the word 'unitiated' – *Uneingeweihte*) who were not – thus could not rely on the patient's confession of his or her simulation.[103]

Concurrent with these debates was the development of the rival identification technologies of the Bertillon System (the anthropometric measurement of eleven body parts and a shorthand physical description of convicts) and dactyloscopy.[104] Both techniques nicely illustrate some of the tensions running through criminology at the turn of the last century. As identification technologies they do not themselves in any way differentiate between criminal and non criminal: anyone can be processed and reliably identified through them. Indeed they implicitly denied that knowledge observed in particulars (the lines inscribed in a thumb, the length of the skull) could establish anything beyond these particulars – in direct opposition to Lombrosian criminology in which such particulars lead back to the knowledge of criminal type. Drawing on the terminology of the medieval ontological debate, Alan Sekula has characterised these rival systems as 'realist' and 'nominalist', respectively.[105] Gross's focus on the individual clue and the individual criminal, who is not simply a representative of a type was clearly 'nominalist' in this sense: it eschewed reductivism, avoided typologies, and relied solely on the collection of a maximum number of particulars. The triumph of the new identification systems similarly owed much to its nominalist persuasion: a set of measurements or prints pointed to nothing beyond the identity of the processed person. At the same time, however, significant research efforts were made, particularly in the case of dactyloscopy, to prove the existence of typologies hidden within the data: race and heredity were to be traced directly in the print.[106] The research did not go unchallenged and was largely ignored by crime practicioners. Once again we uncover a discipline suspended between the dream of reductive typologisation of criminals and evidence that pointed against clear lines of delineation between criminals and the general population.

The point of this section, and indeed the chapter, is to redress the balance within a literature that all too often stresses criminology's tendency to narrate criminals as a distinct group by foregrounding debates in which the lines between rationality and irrationality, criminal and non-criminal were blurred in a variety of (often contradictory) ways. Gross's encyclopaedic–phenomenological project should be located within these debates: seen in this context his preoccupations cease to be marginal worries of an ex-practitioner with no real connection to mainstream criminology. Indeed they can be located at the centre of pressing questions about the self underlying much of the discipline. The next section will demonstate that this criminological preoccupation with the malleable self was disseminated in more popular forms and indeed was a commonplace in contemporary Austrian cultural output.

Popular Criminology

Criminological and criminalistic ideas about criminality found some degree of popular dissemination in Vienna through the launch, in April 1907, of the *Österreichische Kriminalzeitung*, a specialist publication that wished to act as a 'central organ for policing and criminal science' and promised to 'enlighten readers about the practices of the criminal world, offer them access to their secret dwelling places ...'.[107] Its circulation numbers were limited until it began to combine its treatment of criminological topics with the peddling of trial scandals much in the manner of other Viennese dailies: then circulation quickly shot up to some 30,000.[108] Its pages were filled with an eclectic collection of information about criminal practices, criminological theories and case studies. One could find articles about the reliability of child witnesses and female witnesses,[109] sexual perversions,[110] the role of the police in prostitution,[111] the favoured strategies of pederasts looking for company,[112] letters written by homosexuals,[113] the criminality of 'American Negroes',[114] or the fictionalised report about the life and times of 'Silk-Jeanette,' a woman of the *demi-monde*.[115] In many ways the paper thus made similar reading to Hans Gross's *Archiv*: it collected information, if of a somewhat racier nature, and with a more obvious emphasis on the socio-economic causes of crime that 'often, even in the majority of cases of crime' were to be held responsible for creating criminals.[116] Despite this professed conviction that unjust social circumstances precipitated crime, the paper – just like the *Archiv* – would time and again highlight issues concerning malleable selves, the powers of suggestion, the unreliability of senses and memory. An article entitled 'Forensic Medicine and Psychiatry:

Face-Changes of Criminals', for instance, inquired whether new methods in plastic surgery would enable future criminals to change their appearance fully, thus avoiding discovery.[117] Along with the obvious danger raised by this possibility, the article considered whether a new, more handsome face would bring forth in a criminal a new sense of pride 'which will create a new person in [his or her] personality, that works against [his or her] low instincts.'[118] Right next to the article we find a commercial advertisement for a beauty *crème* that promises a 'generous, well-formed bosom', i.e. offers the kind of physical change the article considers.[119] Gross's notion that acted-out emotions could lead to real emotions was here put into the context of permanent physical change. While the possible effects were depicted in a positive light, the underlying anxiety that the self was malleable by outside influences shines through. Other examples include the charge of a mis-trial that claimed the jury had fallen sway to suggestion,[120] the phenomenon of copy-cat crimes due to the human 'instinct for immitation'[121] the above-mentioned articles on witness reliability, and an indictment of female suggestibility that had disastrous effects on a 'feminised' justice system.[122]

The Malleable Self in Popular Culture

If the *Österreichische Kriminalzeitung*'s impact on Austria's popular imagination must ultimately be judged marginal, there exists plenty of evidence that concerns about the suggestibility and epistemic unreliability of 'modern man' highlighted within criminological/criminalistic discourse had an independent life in wider, popular culture. Reference to bad memory and false perception was common in contemporary Austrian fiction. Gustav Meyrink's *Golem* presents a hero who cannot remember his own childhood trauma, and repeatedly is unable to distinguish dream from reality, false memory from real memory.[123] Arthur Schnitzler's *Der Weg ins Freie* recounts an episode where a failed actress's fantasy of being a famous stage-name becomes so real for herself that others around her re-configure their perceptions and memories until they too are dazzled by her talent.[124] Alfred Kubin's *Die andere Seite* dreams up a mysterious city at the other side of the world whose inhabitants' very sensations and perceptions are controlled by the suggestive powers of the city's mysterious king-god.[125] Even the lowest strata of literature, such as the cheap novel *Suggestion, Roman aus der Berliner Gesellschaft*, or throwaway newspaper *feuilletons*, would centre their stories around the concept of suggestion without any fear of not being understood by their readers.[126] Indeed hypnotism had been turned into a household concept through the *Ringtheater* performances of the Dane Carl Hansen as early as 1880: afterwards children could be seen playing at hypnotic suggestion in school-yards.[127] Newspapers also reported on the problem of suggestible witnesses,[128] and on the dangers of bad literature precipitating crimes (even though newspapers also clearly disseminated such literature).[129]

Meanwhile, Karl Kraus's *Fackel* fought a concentrated campaign against the bad use of language, particularly in the press, that did not allow its consumers to gain knowledge of 'the facts' but rather forced upon them opinions and judgements without their knowledge.[130] The emerging science of psychoanalysis –much discussed by Gross[131] – was also rooted in a mistrust of memory, and did much to deconstruct a firm barrier between the normal and the insane. It also, like Gross, suggested an open-ended reading of clues as the best way of getting to the bottom of his patients' mysteries.[132] At the same time the cultural critic Georg Simmel disseminated his own take on mass psychology and mass criminality through a series of articles in the Viennese weekly *Die Zeit*.[133] Simmel argued for a vision of the masses in which a dominant personality's gestures and facial expressions could directly induce others to copy such motions and thus invoke the acted-out emotions within his imitators.[134] Gross's concerns can thus be described as being very much in tune with his culture.

Why would such concerns with the reliability of perception and memory find such sustained expression in *fin-de-siècle* Austria, specifically Vienna? Gross's own distrust of the witness might best be explained by his professional experience. As an investigative judge he was in charge of witness and suspect interviews which may easily have generated a deep mistrust in people's mental abilities and independence. The typical interview was conducted in a series of sessions over a period that would stretch for several weeks, sometimes as much as a quarter of a year.[135] The witness's or suspect's answers were written down in a single coherent text, interrupted only by the signatures of those in attendance at the end of any given session of interviews. The resulting report could approach a hundred pages full of contradictory information, conflations and no indication in how far the interviewer had 'led' his witness.[136] Each such report was then reiterated in a cacophony of witness statements within the courtroom itself, stretching over hours and days. Add to this the anxieties about the jury system, which introduced yet another human link in this chain of memory and perception that Gross distrusted.

In themselves, however, the frustrations inherent in the practice of criminal investigations are insufficient to explain why memory and perception should also be problematised by criminologists with no comparable investigative experience, as well as by the psychoanalysts, novelists, philosophers and cultural critics enumerated above. Why would they share Gross's preoccupations? Without wishing to reduce scientific inquiry and cultural discourse solely to a function of socio-economic and political developments, I want to suggest that at least part of the answer is provided by the rise of mass culture that fell into precisely the same time period. Lueger's (and Hitler's) Vienna was a city of mass politics, of mass papers, of common people serving as witnesses and jurors. It was precisely in this period that newspaper circulation numbers suddenly mushroomed as a result of a change in the law. The Christian Social Party had risen on a political platform that was nothing if not determinedly populist,[137] and in 1907, after years of debate, universal, free, male suffrage was introduced. Ten years previously, in 1897, Vienna's electric tram system had been inaugurated, granting wide sections of the populations rapid mobility within the city, hence also a visibility unknown in previous days.[138] In a time when the 'little man' was rising, it is not surprising that bourgeois criminologists worried about the prospect that these masses could succumb to suggestion and be controlled by forces other than autonomous reason – an observation, incidentally, that also awed young Hitler, if one is to believe his account of watching the Socialist 'dragon' of 250,000 protesting workers take over Vienna's streets in September 1911.[139] Simmel's analysis of 'mass psychology' gave direct articulation to this bourgeois fear of the masses – of demonstrations, riots, democracy and the socialist movement.[140] He claimed that the vast majority of people were unable to cope with the economic and mental independence demanded by modern life. The debate on suggestion is thus comparable to the debates about neurasthenia and degeneration: in all three, anxieties about modernity found formulation.[141] These anxieties were focused above all on the modern city with its density of population, the constant interaction between strangers, and the sheer pace of city life. The influences that could play upon this modern city dweller were utterly unpredictable: any dominant force, willing or unwilling, could precipitate false seeing, hearing, remembering. Crime could flourish in this environment. As such, suggestible masses were a threat to civilisation *per se* and suggested crime narratives in which the social environment of crime rather than the individual criminal's deviance was at the heart of the investigation. It was these anxieties that antisemites exploited in their construction of Jewish criminality.

Notes

1. A version of parts of this chapter (with a longer consideration of the historiography of criminalistics) appears in: Daniel M. Vyleta, 'Was Early Twentieth Century Criminology a Science of the 'Other'? A re-evaluation of Austro-German criminological debates', *Cultural and Social History*, 3, 4 (2006).

2. Some scholars trace biological and determinist narratives of crime back to the eighteenth century. Cf. Lorenz, *Kriminelle Körper*; Beirne, 'Inventing Criminology', pp. 777–820. For recent studies on Lombroso's criminological thought, see: Horn, *The Criminal Body*; Mary Gibson, *Born to Crime, Cesare Lombroso and the Origins of Biological Criminality* (Westport, Conn. 2002).

3. Robert A. Nye, *Crime, Madness and Politics in Modern France, The Medical Concept of National Decline* (Princeton 1984), pp. 98 ff.

4. Richard F Wetzell, *Inventing the Criminal, A History of German Criminology, 1880–1945* (London 2000), pp. 39–71.

5. Gibson, *Born*, pp. 23 ff.

6. I am here using Richard Wetzell's influential phrase. Cf. Richard F. Wetzell, 'The Medicalization of Criminal Law Reform in Imperial Germany', in: Norbert Finzsch and Robert Jütte (eds), *Institutions of Confinement, Hospitals, Asylums, and Prisons in Western Europe and North America 1500–1950* (Cambridge 1996), pp. 275–83.

7. Foucault, *Discipline and Punish*. On the enormous influence of Foucault on the history of criminology, see: David Garland, 'Criminological Knowledge and its Relation to power, Foucault's Genealogy and Criminology today', in: *The British Journal of Criminology* 32, 4 (Autumn 1992), pp. 403–22.

8. For a strong version of this exclusion thesis, see: Gustav Strasser, *Verbrechermenschen, Zum kriminalwissenschaftlichen Erzeugen des Bösen* (Frankfurt am Main 1984).

9. Wetzell, *Inventing*, p. 237 ff.

10. Becker, *Verderbnis*; Peter Becker, 'Kriminelle Identitäten im 19. Jahrhundert, Neue Entwicklungen in der historischen Kriminalforschung', in: *Historische Anthropologie* 1 (1994), p. 149.

11. Cf. Paul Näcke's review of 1901 Italian criminological literature in: 'Die Hauptergebnisse der kriminalanthropologischen Forschung im Jahre 1901', in: *Archiv* 9 (1902), pp. 141–52. The reviewed works are: Coscia, 'Caratteri feminili e atavici nei bacini dei criminali', in: *Archivio di psich. Forensico* (1901) [hip-bones]; Fere, 'Note sur une anomalie du pli d'opposition du pouce', in: *Comptes rendus de la Société de Biologie* (1901) [thumblines]; Andenio and Ugo Lombroso, 'Contributo allo studio dell' asimmetria di pressione negli epilettici, nei delinquenti e nelle prostitute', in: *Archivio di psich. Forensico* (1901) [blood-pressure]; Fasaro, Cesare Lombroso, Treves and Olivetti, 'Le pieghe laterali dei solchi vestibolari della bocca', *Archivio di psich. Forensico* (1901) [mucus]; Frasetto, 'Cenni preliminari sul nuovo carattere ereditario (prevalenza del secondo dito sull' alluce) nel piede dei criminali', in: *Archivio di psich. Forensico* (1901) [toe-length]; Cesare Lombroso, 'Sulla cortezza dell' alluce negli epilettici, nei criminali e negli idioti', in: *Archivio di psich. Forensico* (1901) [also: toe-length]; Krakow, *Die Talgdrüsen der Wangenschleimhaut* (Königberg 1901) [sebum gland]; Salvi, 'Di alcune anomalie della laringe in individui delinqenti', in: *Archivio di psich. Forensico* (1901) [Adam's apple]; Treves, 'Intorno alla frequenza ed al significato della striatura ungueale traversa nei normali, nei criminali e negli alienati', in: *Archivio di psich. Forensico* (1901) [fingernail lines].

12. Johannes Jaeger (ed.), *Hinter Kerkermauern, Autobiographien und Selbstbekenntnisse, Aufsätze und Gedichte von Verbrechern, Ein Beitrag zur Kriminalpsychologie, Mit einem Vor- und Nachwort von Univ.-Prof Dr Hans Gross* (Berlin 1906), p. 6.

13. Abraham-Adolph Baer, *Der Verbrecher in anthropologischer Beziehung* (Leipzig 1893).

14. August Forel, *Ueber die Zurechnungsfähigkeit des normalen Menschen* (Munich 1907).

15. Paul Näcke, *Verbrechen und Wahnsinn beim Weibe mit Ausblicken auf die Kriminalanthropologie überhaupt, Klinisch-Statistische, Anthropologisch-Biologische und Craniologische Untersuchungen* (Vienna 1894), p. 174. See also: Wetzell, *Inventing*, p. 52.

16. Max Nordau, *Entartung* (Berlin 1886); Max Nordau, *Die conventionellen Lügen der Kulturmenschheit* (Leipzig 1889 [1883]); Paul Julius August Möbius, *Ueber Entartung* (Wiesbaden 1900); Paul Julius August Möbius, *Geschlecht und Entartung* (Halle 1903). On Nordau, see: Robert B. Pynsent, 'Conclusory Essay: Decadence, Decay and Innovation', in: Robert B. Pynsent (ed.), *Decadence and Innovation, Austro Hungarian Art at the Turn of the Century* (London 1989), pp. 128–40; P. M. Baldwin, 'Liberalism, Nationalism and Degeneration: The Case of Max Nordau', *Central European History* 13 (1980), pp. 99–120. For the history of degeneration-theory more generally, see: Daniel Pick, *Faces of Degeneration, A European Disorder c. 1848–1918* (Cambridge 1989); Patrick Brantlinger, *Bread and Circuses, Theories of Mass Culture as Public Decay* (Cornell 1983); Arthur Hermann, *The Idea of Decline in Western History* (New York 1996); Sander L. Gilman and J. Edward Chamberlin (eds), *Degeneration: The Dark Side of Progress* (New York 1985); Joachim Radkau, *Das Zeitalter der Nervosität, Deutschland zwischen Bismark und Hitler* (Munich 1998); Marianne Schuller, '"Entartung," Zur Geschichte eines Begriffs, der Geschichte gemacht hat', in: Heidrun Kaupen-Haas and Christian Saller (ed.), *Wissenschaftlicher Rassismus, Analysen einer Kontinuität in den Human- und Naturwissenschaften* (Frankfurt 1999), pp. 122–36.

17. This is not to claim that statistical methods were, *a priori*, incompatible with biological explanations of crime. See: Piers Beirne, 'Adolphe Quetelet and the Origins of positivist criminology', *American Journal of Sociology* 92, 5 (March 1987), pp. 1140–69. However, much of the turn of the century debate on criminal statistics eschewed any clear reference to stable criminal typologies.

18. One should note that Lombroso never reconciled this statistical work with his theory of atavism. Cf. Cesare Lombroso, *Crime, Its Causes and Remedies*, translated by Henry P. Horton (London 1911 [1896/7]). The Italian edition was published in three volumes, as the fifth edition of *L'uomo*: Cesare Lombroso, *L'uome delinquente* Vols. I-III, ed. F. Bocca (Turin 1896-7). The German edition was published in 1902 as: Cesare Lombroso, *Die Ursachen und Bekämpfung des Verbrechens*, translated by H. Kurella and E. Jentsch (Berlin 1902).

19. The figure refers to an examination of 405 prisoners discussed in Gustav Aschaffenburg's influential *Das Verbrechen und seine Bekämpfung: Kriminalpsychologie für Mediziner, Juristen und Soziologen, ein Beitrag zur Reform der Strafgesetzgebung* (Heidelberg 1903), p. 168. Aschaffenburg's numbers fluctuated depending on his specific empirical basis. Lombroso's later work tended to estimate that around 35 percent of criminals were 'born criminals' (cf. Lombroso, *Crime*, pp. 376).

20. Aschaffenburg, *Verbrechen*, p. 161.

21. Gibson, *Born*, pp. 127 ff; Peter Becker, 'Vom "Haltlosen" zur "Bestie". Das polizeiliche Bild des Verbrechers im 19. Jahrhundert', in: Alf Lüdtke (ed.), *"Sicherheit" und "Wohlfahrt". Polizei, Gesellschaft und Herrschaft im 19. und 20. Jahrhundert* (Frankfurt am Main 1992), p. 113.

22. Cf. Johnston, *Austrian Mind*, pp. 94–5; Emanuel Hurwitz, *Otto Gross, Paradies Sucher zwischen Jung und Freud, Leben und Werk* (Zurich 1979), pp. 36 ff.; Jacques Le Rider, 'Hans Gross, criminologue, et son fils Otto Gross, "délinquant sexuel" et psychoanalyste', in: Britta Rupp-Eisenreich und Justin Stegl (eds), *Kulturwissenschaft im Vielvölkerstaat, Zur Geschichte der Ethnologie und verwandter Gebiete in Österreich ca. 1780–1918 / L'Anthropologie et L'Etat Pluri-Culturel, Le cas de l'Autriche, de 1780 à 1918 environ* (Vienna 1995), pp. 229–40; LeRider, *Modernity*, pp. 127 ff.; Martin Green, *Mountain of Faith, The Counterculture Begins, Ascona 1900-1920* (London 1986), pp. 18 ff.

23. Hans Gross, *Handbuch für Untersuchungsrichter als System der Kriminalistik (Dritte Vermehrte Auflage)* (Graz 1899). In the following analysis I will consistently be referring to this, the third edition, of the text.

24. Hans Gross, *Criminalpsychologie* (Graz 1898).

25. Hans Gross, 'Aufgabe und Ziele', in: *Archiv* 1 (1898), pp. 1–2. Gross's emphasis. See also: Hans Gross, 'Wesen und Aufgabe der Kriminalanthropologie', in: Hans Gross, *Gesammelte Kriminalistische Aufsätze* Vol. 2 (Leipzig 1908), pp. 309–17.

26. Gross, *Handbuch*, II.

27. Alfred Kloß, 'Buchbesprechung: Hans Gross, Handbuch für den Untersuchungsrichter als System der Kriminalistik, 4. Auflage' in: *Monatschrift* 1 (1904/5), p. 601.

28. For a discussion of the epistemology of this detective "method", see: Carlo Ginzburg, 'Morelli, Freud and Sherlock Holmes: Clues and Scientific Method," translated by Anna Davin, *History Workshop* 9 (1980), pp. 5–36.

29. Cf. Gross, *Handbuch*, I-V; Gross, *Criminalpsychologie*, VI.

30. Cf. Gross, 'Aufgabe und Ziele', pp. 1–3.

31. Hans Gross, *Criminalpsychologie*, p. vi.

32. Cf. Ibid., pp. 1–3. See also: Hans Gross, *Handbuch*, p. ii.

33. Ibid., p. 3. Gross's emphasis.

34. Ibid.

35. Cf. Roland Graßberger, 'Österreich und die Entwicklung der Kriminologie zur selbstständigen Wissenschaft', *Wissenschaft und Weltbild* 18, 4 (1965), pp. 285 ff; Karl-Heinz

Hering, *Der Weg der Kriminologie Der Weg der Kriminologie zur selbständigen Wissenschaft* (Mainz 1966), pp. 189 ff.

36. Gross also published a dictionary of criminalistic terms that made this ambition explicit. Hans Gross, *Encyclopädie der Kriminalistik* (Leipzig 1901).
37. Gross, *Criminalpsychologie*, pp. 51–124. See also: Gross, *Handbuch*, pp. 102 ff.
38. Gross, *Criminalpsychologie*, p. 51.
39. Ibid.
40. Gross, *Handbuch*, p. 467. Peter Becker, 'Die Rezeption der Physiologie in Kriminalistik und Kriminologie: Variationen über Norm und Ausgrenzung', in: Philipp Sarasin, Jakob Tanner (eds), *Physiologie und industrielle Gesellschaft. Studien zur Verwissenschaftlichung des Körpers im 19. und 20. Jahrhundert* (Frankfurt am Main 1998), pp. 453–90; Peter Becker, 'The Criminologists' Gaze at the Underworld, Towards an Archaeology of Criminological Writing', in: Peter Becker and Richard Wetzell (eds), *Criminals and Their Scientists: The History of Criminology in International Perspective* (Cambridge 2006), pp. 105–36.
41. See, for example, Gross's discussion of scorn and spite in his *Handbuch*, p. 117.
42. Ibid., p. 51. See also: Gross, 'Aufgabe und Ziele', pp. 1–3.
43. Gross, *Criminalpsychologie*, p. 54.
44. Gross, *Handbuch*, p. 102.
45. Hans Gross, 'Wesen und Aufgabe', p. 316.
46. See also the sections on perception in the *Handbuch*: Gross, *Handbuch*, p. 52–97.
47. For example: A. Oskar Klaussmann, 'Zeugen-Prüfung', in: *Archiv* 1 (1898); Hans Gross, 'Augenzeugen', in: *Archiv* 1 (1899), pp. 340–1; Hans Gross, 'Buchbesprechung: L. William Stern, *Zur Psychologie der Aussage, Experimentelle Untersuchungen über Erinnerungstreue* (Berlin 1903)', in: *Archiv* 11 (1903), pp. 292–3; Hans Schneickert, 'Zur Psychologie der Zeugenaussage', in: *Archiv* 13 (1903), pp. 193–211; Hans Gross, 'Buchbesprechungen: L. William Stern (hrsg.) *Beiträge zur Psychologie der Zeugenaussage, Mit besonderer Berücksichtigung von Problemen der Rechtspflege, Pädagogik, Psychiatrie und Geschichtsforschung* (1904), und: William Stern, *Die Aussage als geistige Leistung und als Verhörsprodukt, Experimentelle Schüleruntersuchungen* (Leipzig 1904)', in: *Archiv* 16 (1904), pp. 371–6. Albert Hellwig, 'Zur Psychologie der Zeugenaussage' in: *Archiv* 17, pp. 202–3; E. v. Karman, 'Ein Schema zur Psychologie der Zeugenaussage', in: *Archiv* 61 (1914), pp. 167–74. The literature on witnesses overlaps with that on suggestion discussed below.
48. Gross, *Criminalpsychologie*, pp. 11, 20–1; Gross, *Handbuch*, pp. v, 56–108.
49. Gross, *Criminalpsychologie*, p. 3.
50. On the contemporary discourse of the problem of good seeing, cf.: Daniel Pick, 'Stories of the Eye', in: Roy Porter (ed.), *Rewriting the Self*, pp. 186–99; Jonathan Crary, *Techniques of the Observer, On Vision and Modernity in the Nineteenth Century* (Cambridge, Mass. 1990); Martin Jay, *Downcast Eyes, The Denigration of Vision in Twentieth Century French Thought* (Berkeley 1993), pp. 113–16, 149 ff. See also: Hans Gross, 'Zur Wahrnehmungsfrage', in: *Gesammelte Kriminalistische Aufsätze* 2, pp. 117–22; Hans Gross, 'Zur Frage des Wahrnehmungsproblems', in: ibid., pp. 123–8; Hans Gross, 'Die Macht der Einbildung', in: ibid., pp. 167–8; Hans Gross, 'Die Aussage von Zeugen in Todesgefahr', in: ibid., pp. 172–4; Hans Gross, 'Das Verstehen der Zeugen und die Einbildung', in: ibid., pp. 175–6.
51. Gross, *Handbuch*, p. v. Gross's emphasis. One should note that the witness debate had several sub-genres. One of these dealt with the degree to which children and menstruating women could be useful witnesses. See for example: Hans Gross, 'Buchbesprechung: Richard von Krafft-Ebing, *Psychosis Menstrualis, Eine klinisch-forensische Studie* (Stuttgart 1902)', in: *Archiv* 9 (1902), pp. 242–3: R. Wollenberg, 'Wie haben wir uns gegenüber der Menstruierenden als Zeugin zu verhalten?', in: *Monatsschrift* 2

(1905/6), pp. 698–705; 'Die Zeugenaussage der Frau', in: *ÖK*, 11 July 1907, p. 5. Franziska Lamott, 'Liebe, Tod und Strafrecht, Strategien der Angstabwehr in der Kriminologie der Jahrhundertwende', p. 91, misrepresents the debate as being much more unitary than it was.

52. Gross, *Criminalpsychologie*, p. 4.

53. Gross, *Handbuch*, p. 2.

54. O. Hauer, 'Wirkung eines Wasserschusses', in: *Archiv* 1 (1898); Georg Sticker, 'Vergiftungen vom Mastdarm und von der Scheide aus', in: *Archiv* 1 (1898); Hans Gross, 'Die Gaunerzinken der Freistädter Handschrift', in: *Archiv* 2 (1899) – 1739 pictures of secret signs employed by criminals here testify to what length Gross would go in his quest for full encyclopaedic documentation; Hans Schöfer, 'Eine kriminalistisch-forensische Untersuchung von Klebstoff', in: *Archiv* 34 (1909), pp. 251–60; Albert Hellwig, 'Das Ameisenbad als Heilmittel', in: *Archiv* 28 (1907); Paul Näcke, 'Weiteres zur elektrischen Hinrichtung', in: *Archiv* 16 (1904); Paul Näcke, 'Der Kuß Homosexueller', in: *Archiv* 17 (1904), p. 177.

55. Susanne Regener, 'Metaphysik des Bösen: Zur Anschauungspraxis von Kriminalmuseen', in: Heidrun Kaupen-Haas and Christian Saller (ed.), *Wissenschaftlicher Rassismus*, pp. 304–26. Regener claims that Gross tried to establish criminal typologies with his exhibitions of criminal and criminalistic paraphernalia, but the evidence suggests otherwise.

56. Hans Gross, *Handbuch*, sections XV ('Ciphers'), XVII ('Theft'), XVIII ('Fraud').

57. Hans Gross, 'Moderne Verbrecher', in: Gross, *Gesammelte Aufsätze* 2, pp. 342–52.

58. Hans Gross, 'Zur Frage der Kastration und Sterilisation', in: *Archiv* 51 (1913), pp. 316–25. See also my comments on Gross's theory of pathological superstition amongst certain criminals in chapter six.

59. Hans Gross, 'Die Degeneration und das Strafrecht', in: ibid., pp. 1–12. Hans Gross, 'Degeneration und Deportation', in: ibid., pp. 70–76. For an argument that the article represents the essence of Gross's theory of criminality (and an implicit attack against his psychoanalyst, anarchist son, Otto), see: Franziska Lamott, 'Professor Dr Hans Gross gegen seinen Sohn', in: Jean Clair, Cathrin Pichler und Wolfgang Pircher (Hrsg.), *Wunderblock, Eine Geschichte der modernen Seele, Ausstellungskatalog* (Vienna 1989), pp. 611–19; Lamott, 'Liebe', pp. 82–94. In my view the article is an attempt to distinguish between a petty, degenerate criminality and criminality 'proper' that was enacted by rational actors.

60. Friedrich Christian Benedikt Avé-Lallement, *Das Deutsche Gaunertum in seiner socialpolitischen, literarischen und linguistischen Ausbildung zu seinem heutigen Bestande*, 4 Vols. (Leipzig 1858–62); Ludwig von Jagemann, *Handbuch der gerichtlichen Untersuchungskunde* (Heidelberg 1838). One might also mention: Rudolph Alois Fröhlich, *Die gefährlichen Klassen Wiens, Darstellung ihres Entstehens, ihrer Verbindungen, ihrer Taktik, ihrer Sitten und Gewohnheiten und ihrer Sprache. Mit belehrenden Winken über Gaunerkniffe und einem Wörterbuch der Gaunersprache* (Vienna 1851).

61. See for instance: Alfred Kloß, 'Buchbesprechung: Hans Gross, Handbuch für den Untersuchungsrichter als System der Kriminalistik, 4. Auflage' in: *Monatsschrift* 1 (1904/5), pp. 601–3; Robert Gaupp 'Zeitschriftenschau: Archiv für Kriminal-Anthropologie und Kriminalistik Bd. 20, 22', in: *Monatsschrift* 3 (1906/7), pp. 435, 569. As mentioned above, Paul Näcke was one of the *Archiv*'s key contributors.

62. For example Hans Gross, 'Buchbesprechung: Adolf Baer, *Der Verbrecher in anthropologischer Beziehung* (Leipzig 1893)', in: *Archiv* 1 (1899), pp. 135-6; Hans Gross, 'Buchbesprechung: Cesare Lombroso, *Ursachen und Bekämpfung des Verbrechens* (Berlin 1902)', in: *Archiv* 9 (1902), p. 245; Hans Gross, 'Hausarrest als Strafmittel', in: *Monatsschrift* 2 (1905/6), pp. 209–19.

63. Contra: Wetzell, *Inventing*, pp. 61-2, 104-5.

64. Cf. Gibson, *Born*, pp. 135–9; S. Ottolenghi, 'Wissenschaftliche Polizei und Criminalanthropologie' in: Gustav Aschaffenburg and Dr. Partenheimer (eds), *Bericht über den VII. Internationalen Kongreß für Kriminalanthropologie* (Heidelberg 1912), pp. 478–82. On the German debate on this issue, see also: Prof. Hübner, 'Über die Ausgestaltung des Universitätsunterrichts in der Kriminalpsychologie und Kriminalistik', in: ibid., pp. 288–96.

65. Cf. ibid., pp. 506 ff.

66. Robert Sommer, 'Der Gegenwärtige Stand der Kriminalpsychologie', in: ibid., pp. 265–76.

67. F. Siemens, 'Zur Psychologie der Aussage, insbesondere von Kindern', in: *Monatsschrift* 2 (1905/6), pp. 36–54; R. Sommer, 'Zur Psychologie der Zeugenaussagen', in: *Monatsschrift* 4 (1907/8), pp. 181–2; F. Schmidt, 'Zur Psychologie der Zeugenaussagen', in: *Monatsschrift* 5 (1908/9), pp. 321–34; O. Lippmann, 'Die Technik der Vernehmung von psychologischem Standpunkte', in: *Monatsschrift* 7 (1909/10), pp. 331–9.

68. Lombroso himself published in Gross's *Archiv*: Cesare Lombroso and A. Bonelli, 'Ein Fall schwerster Beschuldigung eines Unschuldigen, Erläutert durch die Kriminalanthropologie', in: *Archiv* 11 (1903), pp. 322–7.

69. Graßberger, 'Österreich und die Entwicklung', p. 286.

70. See: Gross, *Handbuch*, pp. 170 ff on collecting hairs at the crime scene; Hans Schneickert, 'Photographieren von Leichen', in: *Archiv* 18 (1905), p. 268; Hans Gross, 'Zahnheilkunde und Kriminalistik', in: Gross, *Gesammelte Aufsätze* 1, pp. 250–4.

71. A. Niceforo und Heinrich Lindenau, *Die Krimalpolizei und ihre Hilfswissenschaften* (Groß-Lichterfelde-Ost 1910); Gustav Roscher, *Großstadtpolizei, Ein praktisches Handbuch der deutschen Polizei* (Hamburg 1912). Niceforo openly acknowledges his debt to Gross and describes criminalistics as a 'branch of criminology' (p. xlvi). He also dedicates a chapter to the interrelation of criminological and criminalistic knowledge (pp. 436–44). On Roscher see: Becker, 'Vom "Haltlosen" zur "Bestie", p. 103 and *passim*.

72. Gross, *Handbuch*, p. 104.

73. Gross, *Criminalpsychologie*, p. 59.

74. Ibid., p. 60.

75. Key examples include: Albert von Schrenck-Notzing, *Über Suggestion und Erinnerungsfälschung im Berchthold Prozeß* (Leipzig 1897); Albert von Schrenck-Notzing, *Kriminalpsychologische und Psychopathologische Studien, Gesammelte Aufsätze aus den Gebieten der Psychopathia Sexualis, der gerichtlichen Psychiatrie und der Suggestionslehre* (Leipzig 1902); Hyppolite Bernheim, *Die Suggestion und ihre Heilwirkung*, translated by Sigmund Freud, ed. M. Kahane (2nd Edition) (Leipzig 1896); August Forel, *Der Hypnotismus: seine psychophysiologische, medizinische, strafrechtliche Bedeutung und seine Handhabung* (Stuttgart 1891); Arthur Nussbaum, *Der Polnaer Ritualmordprozess* (Berlin 1906). Lombroso himself contributed to the literature surrounding the concept, focusing, among other things, on the suggestive powers of born criminals over occasional criminals and the suggestibility of women. See, for instance: Cesare Lombroso and Guglielmo Ferrero, *Criminal Woman, the Prostitute, and the Normal Woman*, translated by and with a new introduction by Nicole Hahn Rafter and Mary Gibson (Durham, NC 2004), pp. 78, 192 ff.

76. On the history of the therapeutic uses of hypnotism and the shift to suggestion in a waking state, see: Alan Gould, *A History of Hypnotism* (Cambridge 1992), pp. 427, 559–60; Sander Gilman, 'Psychotherapy', in: W. F. Bynum and Roy Porter (eds), *Companion Encyclopaedia of the History of Medicine* Vol. 2 (London 1993), pp. 1029–49; Paul Lerner, *Hysterical Men, War Psychiatry and the Politics of Trauma in Germany, 1890–1930* (Ithaca 2003), pp. 86 ff. On the link between mesmerism and hypnotism, see: Vincent Buranelli, *The Wizard from Vienna* (London 1976), pp. 205–17.

77. Cf. Jean-Roch Laurence and Campbell Perry, *Hypnosis, Will and Memory, A Psycho-Legal History* (New York 1991), pp. 194 ff. On the debates over hypnotism amongst

Viennese medical circles, and the victory of the Nancy School's theory of hypnoid states, see: Frank J. Sulloway, *Freud, Biologist of the Mind, Beyond the Psychoanalytic Legend* (New York 1979), pp. 42–9.

78. Cf. Gould, *History*, pp. 547–8.

79. Alexander Margulies, 'Suggestibilität im postepileptischen Zustande', in: *Archiv* 28 (1907), pp. 73–90; C. Lombroso, A. Bonelli, 'Kriminelle Suggestionierung an einem schwachsinnigen Alkoholiker', in: *Archiv* 11 (1903), pp. 327–37; August Drähms, *The Criminal, His Personnel and Environment* (New York 1900), p. 324. Cf. Laurence and Perry, *Hypnosis*, pp. 234, 241ff. On the related discourse about crimes committed on and by hypnotised subjects, see: Gould, *History*, 498 ff. and Ruth Harris, *Murder and Madness, Medicine, Law and Society in the Fin-de-Siècle* (Oxford 1989), pp. 155–207.

80. Von Schrenck-Notzing, *Kriminalpsychologische Studien*, p. 119.

81. Ibid.

82. Paul Näcke, 'Selbstmord durch Suggestion', in: *Archiv* 10 (1902), p. 169.

83. Otto Stoll, *Suggestion und Hypnotismus in der Völkerpsychologie* (Leipzig 1904).

84. W. von Bechterew, *Suggestion und ihre soziale Bedeutung*, translated by R. Weinberg (Leipzig 1899).

85. Dr. Placzek, 'Suggestion und Erinnerungsfälschung', in: *Archiv* 2 (1899), pp. 132–9.

86. Theodor Altschul, *Hypnotismus und Suggestion im Leben und in der Erziehung* (Vienna 1900).

87. Albert Hellwig, 'Eine suggestiv bewirkte Geruchsillusion', in: *Archiv* 50 (1912), pp. 165–6.

88. Hans Schneickert 'Massensuggestion', in: *Archiv* 18 (1905), p. 265; Friedrich Sturm, 'Massensuggestion', in: *Archiv* 42 (1911).

89. For example: Wilhelm Börner, *Die Schundliteratur und ihre Bekämpfung* (Vienna 1908); Ernst Schulze, *Die Schundliteratur, Ihr Wesen, Ihre Folgen, Ihre Bekämpfung* (Halle 1911); Albert Hellwig, 'Die Beziehung zwischen Schundliteratur, Schundfilms und Verbrechen, Das Ergebnis einer Umfrage', in: *Archiv* 51 (1913), pp. 1–32; Brunner, *Unser Volk in Gefahr, Ein Kampfruf gegen die Schundliteratur* (Düsseldorf 1909); H. Heldt, *Die Schundliteratur* (Leipzig 1908); Karl F Kočmata, *Jugend und Schundliteratur, Eine energisches Wort gegen systematische Volksvergiftung* (Vienna n. d. (1908?)). See also: Rudolf Schenda, *Volk ohne Buch, Studien zur Sozialgeschichte der populären Lesestoffe 1770–1910* (Munich 1977), pp. 241–7, 449.

90. Paul Näcke, 'Macht der Suggestion', in: *Archiv* 7 (1901), pp. 339–40. See also Paul Näcke, 'Noch einmal: Macht der Suggestion', in: *Archiv* 8 (1901/2), pp. 210–11 on a similar case.

91. Paul Näcke, 'Stand und Reichtum als Suggestionsfaktoren', in: *Archiv* 49 (1912), pp. 187–8.

92. For a weak form of this accusation, see: Adolf Ledening, 'Wirkung von Gerichtssaalsberichten', in: *Archiv* 20 (1905), pp. 55–8. Others were less coy about pointing the finger: von Schrenck-Notzing, *Kriminalpsychologische Studien*, pp. 115 ff; Nussbaum, *Der Polnaer Ritualmordprozess*, pp. 6 ff.

93. Von Schrenck-Notzing, *Über Suggestion*, *passim*; von Schrenck-Notzing, *Kriminalpsychologische Studien*, pp. 114–16.

94. Gross, *Handbuch*, p. v.

95. Max Wertheimer and Julius Klein, 'Psychologische Tatbestandsdiagnostik', in: *Archiv* 15 (1904), p. 72. See also: Max Wertheimer, *Experimentelle Untersuchungen zur Tatbestandsdiagnostik* (Leipzig 1905).

96. Carl Gustav Jung, 'Die psychologische Diagnose des Tatbestandes', in: *Juristisch-psychiatrische Grenzfragen, Zwanglose Abhandlungen*, ed. A. Finger, A. Hoche and J. Bresler, Bd. 4, Heft 3 (Halle 1906), pp. 1–47. Sigmund Freud, 'Tatbestandsdiagnostik und Psychoanalyse', in: *Archiv* 26 (1907), pp. 1–10.

97. Physiological responses to external stimuli were the subject of a separate inquiry. See, for example: Cesare Lombroso and A. Bonelli, 'Ein Fall schwerster Beschuldigung eines Unschuldigen, Erläutert durch die Kriminalanthropologie', in: *Archiv* 11 (1903), pp. 322-7. On the evolution of the lie detector, see: Eugene Block, *Lie Detectors: Their History and Use* (New York 1977); David G. Horn, 'Blood Will Tell: The Vascular System and Criminal Dangerousness', in: Christopher Forth and Ivan Crozier (eds), *Body Parts: Critical Explorations in Corporeality* (Lanham, Md. 2005).

98. On the debate, see: Paul Näcke, 'Die Feinde der Assoziations-Psychologie', in: *Archiv* 28 (1907), pp. 199-201; Hans Gross, 'Zur psychologischen Tatbestandsdiagnostik', in: *Gesammelte Kriminalistische Aufsätze* Vol. 2, pp. 317-27; Alfred Groß, 'Zur psychologischen Tatbestandsdiagnostik', in: *Monatsschrift* 2 (1905/6), pp. 182-4; Otto Kraus, 'Psychologische Tatbestandsdiagnostik', in: *Monatsschrift* 2 (1905/6), pp. 58-61; W. Weygandt, 'Zur psychologischen Tatbestandsdiagnostik', in: *Monatsschrift* 2 (1905/6), pp. 435-44; Carl Gustav Jung, 'Zur psychologischen Tatbestandsdiagnostik', in: *Monatsschrift* 3 (1906/7), pp. 365-72; M. Lederer, 'Die Verwendung der psychologischen Tatbestandsdiagnostik', in: *Monatsschrift* 3 (1906/7), pp. 163-72; A Löffler, 'Zur psychologischen Tatbestandsdiagnostik', in: *Monatsschrift* 3 (1906/7), pp. 173-84; Hoegel, 'Die "Tatbestandsdiagnostik" im Strafverfahren', in: *Monatsschrift* 4 (1907/8), pp. 26-40; Fr. Mohr, 'Kriminalpsychologische Tatbestandsforschung', in: *Monatsschrift* 4 (1907/8), pp. 442-4; Ch. de Montet, 'Assoziationsexperimente an einem kriminellen Fall', in: *Monatsschrift* 6 (1909/10), pp. 37-46; Alfred Gross, 'Die Associationsmethode im Strafprozess', in: *Zeitschrift für die gesamte Strafrechtswissenschaft* 26 (1906), pp. 19-40; Alfred Gross, 'Kriminalpsychologische Tatbestabdsforschung', in: *Juristisch-Psychiatrische Grenzfragen* 5,7 (1907), pp. 1-56; William Stern, *Psychologische Tatbestandsdiagnostik, Beiträge zur Psychologie der Aussage* 2 Vols. (Leipzig 1903-6).

99. Cf. Carl Gustav Jung, 'Die psychologische Diagnose des Tatbestandes', pp. 370-2.

100. C. Falkenhorst, 'Zur Psychologie des Verbrechens', in: *ÖK*, 30 Sept. 1907, 3-4; *ÖK*, 7 Oct 1907, pp. 3-4; Bolte, 'Ueber einige Fälle von Simulation', *Allgemeine Zeitschrift für Psychiatrie und psychiatrisch-gerichtliche Medizin* Bd. 60 (1903), p. 47; Johannes Bresler, *Die Simulation von Geistesstörungen und Epilepsie* (Halle 1904); Paul Näcke, 'Echte und falsche Epilepsie', in: *Archiv* 34 (1909), p. 344. Gross himself addresses the issue in his *Handbuch*, pp. 252-9.

101. Falkenhorst, , 'Zur Psychologie', p. 4.

102. Johannes Bresler, *Die Simulation von Geistesstörungen und Epilepsie* (Halle 1904), pp. 201-3; Aschaffenburg, *Verbrechen*, pp. 169-70.

103. Falkenhorst, 'Zur Psychologie', p. 4.

104. On a history of these, see: Simon A. Cole, *Suspect Identities, A History of Fingerprinting and Criminal Identification* (Cambridge, Mass. 2001); Chandak Sengoopta, *Imprint of the Raj, How Fingerprinting Was Born in Colonial India* (London 2003).

105. Allan Sekula, 'The Body and the Archive', pp. 353-4. Some of Sekula's arguments are taken up in: Celia Lury, *Prosthetic Culture, Photography, Memory and Identity* (New York 1998), pp. 51-7.

106. Cole, *Suspect Identities*, pp. 94 ff.

107. *ÖK*, 1 April 1907, p. 1 ('Programmartikel').

108. *ÖK*, 23 Sept 1907, p. 1: 'guaranteed circulation of 30,000.' On the newspaper's re-orientation towards scandals, see also: *ÖK*, 2 Sept 1907, p. 2 ('In eigener Sache').

109. *ÖK*, 16 May 1907, pp. 3-4; *ÖK*, 11 July 1907, p. 5.

110. *ÖK*, 16 May 1907, p. 7 (concerning a man's fantasy to have his wife drink his urine).

111. *ÖK*, 18 July 1907, p. 2.

112. *ÖK*, 12 Aug 1907, p. 5.

113. *ÖK*, 19 Aug 1907, p. 6.

114. *ÖK*, 11 Nov 1907, p. 6.

115. '*Die Seiden-Jeanette, Der Wahrheit nacherzählt von Otto Hartinger*', in: *ÖK*, 18 July 1907, p. 2.
116. *ÖK*, 1 April 1907, p. 1. At times the paper would also run quite technical, scholarly articles, like the piece on simulating insanity discussed above, that could equally have appeared in a specialist journal; famous criminologists/psychologists like August Forel were also known to contribute (for example *ÖK*, 16 Sept 1907, p. 2).
117. 'Gerichtliche Medizin und forensische Psychiatrie: Gesichtsveränderungen für Verbrecher', in: *ÖK*, 4 July 1907, p. 7. On the issue of plastic surgery (this one concerning noses), see also: A. Abels, 'Häßliche Nasen und ihre Verbesserung', in: *Archiv* 39 (1910), pp. 359–60.
118. 'Gerichtliche Medizin und forensische Psychiatrie: Gesichtsveränderungen für Verbrecher', in: *ÖK*, 4 July 1907, p. 7.
119. Advertisement: *ÖK*, 4 July 1907, p. 7
120. *ÖK*, 25 July 1907, p. 2.
121. *ÖK*, 2 Sept 1907, p. 4.
122. *ÖK*, 12 Aug 1907, p. 2.
123. Gustav Meyrink, *Der Golem* (Berlin 1998 [1915]), pp. 57, 83, 97.
124. Arthur Schnitzler, *Der Weg ins Freie* (Frankfurt am Main 1990 [1908]), pp. 165–6.
125. Alfred Kubin, *Die andere Seite* (Reinbek bei Hamburg 1995 [1909]), pp. 60, 62–3, 69, 136, 157.
126. R. Austerlitz, *Suggestion, Roman aus der Berliner Gesellschaft*, Hölzer's Romanbibliothek Vol. 42 (Vienna n. d.); *DV*, 3 Jan 1895, p. 1.
127. Mikkel Borch-Jacobson, *Remembering Anna O., A Century of Mystification*, translated by Kirby Olson (New York 1996), pp. 64–6.
128. See, for example, the reports on a twelve-year-old child witness: *Extrablatt*, 16 Dec 1906, pp. 4–5; *Krone*, 15 Dec 1906, p. 4.
129. See reports of (attempted) murders and invectives against *Schundliteratur* in: *DV*, 8 June 1907, pp. 5–6; *DV*, 8 Aug 1909, 9; *RP*, 13 Aug 1904, p. 7. The August 1909 coverage of 'Another Victim of Detective Novels' in the *Deutsches Volksblatt* ran concurrently with a serialised novel entitled: *Chased – Detective Novel* by Edmund Mitchell.
130. Cf. Janik and Toulmin, *Wittgensteins Wien*, pp. 91 ff, 143. See also: Jörg Henning, 'Gerichtsbestattung in deutschen Tageszeitungen 1850–1890', in: Jörg Schönert (ed.), *Erzählte Kriminalität*, p. 349.
131. Hans Gross, 'Buchbesprechung: Sigmund Freed [sic!], *Die Traumdeutung*', in: *Archiv* 7 (1901), p. 168; Hans Gross, 'Buchbesprechung: Sigmund Freud, *Ueber den Traum*', in: *Archiv* 10 (1903), pp. 340–1; Hans Gross, 'Buchbesprechung: Sigmund Freud, *Zur Psychopathologie des Alltagslebens*', in: *Archiv* 18 (1905), pp. 271–2. The positive reception of Freud in the *Archiv* points to the fact that Freud was not quite the spurned genius he styled himself as. Cf.: Marina Tichy and Sylvia Zwettler-Otte, *Freud in der Presse, Rezeption Sigmund Freuds Psychoanalyse in Österreich 1895–1938* (Vienna 1999).
132. Cf. Peter Gay, Freud, *A Life for Our Time* (London 1988), pp. 80, 92–5.
133. Georg Simmel, 'Massenpsychologie', in: *Die Zeit*, 23 November 1895, pp. 119–20; Georg Simmel, 'Ueber Massenverbrechen', in: *Die Zeit*, 2 October 1897, pp. 4–6. Both reprinted in: David Frisby (ed.), *Simmel in Wien, Texte und Kontexte aus dem Wien der Jahrhundertwende* (Vienna 2000), pp. 43–9, 91–9. See also: Gustave Le Bon, *Psychologie des foules* (Paris 1896), which Simmel discusses in 'Massenpsychologie'.
134. Georg Simmel, 'Ueber Massenverbrechen', p. 96.
135. In the 1895 Gustav Eichinger murder investigation, the chief suspect was questioned over a period of more than seven weeks (SaW, Gerichtsakt, Box unnumbered, Fasz. 92, No. 1185 (Eichinger 1895), Doc. No. N/A (?c. 10)); in the fraud case of 'Kubowsky und Konsorten' the main defendant was questioned for more than fourteen weeks

(SaW, Gerichtsakte, Box A11, Fasz. 177–8, No. 2780 (Kubowsky 1905), Doc. No. 27ff.) Other case files corroborate these as typical time brackets.

136. Gross, for one, was keenly aware of the danger of suggestion when questioning witnesses: Gross, *Criminalpsychologie*, p. 11.
137. Hamann, *Hitler's Wien*, pp. 396–8; John W. Boyer, *Political Radicalism*.
138. Maren Seliger and Karl Ucakar, *Wien, Politische Geschichte 1740–1930, Entwicklung und Bestimmungskräfte Grossstädtischer Politik, Teil 2: 1896–1934* (Vienna 1985), pp. 901–7.
139. Adolf Hitler, *Mein Kampf* (Munich 1943 [1925]), pp. 42-4. Cf.: Hamann, *Hitler's Wien*, pp. 255–6; Ian Kershaw, *Hitler, 1889–1936: Hubris* (London 1998), p. 36.
140. Simmel, 'Massenpsychologie', p. 119.
141. Cf. Radkau, *Zeitalter*, pp. 173-7.

Chapter 3

Jewish Criminals

In Search of Racial Criminality

On the surface of things there is plenty of reason to anticipate a criminological construction of Jewish criminals as biologico-racial others.[1] Was not crime science's shift of attention towards physiological abnormalities upon criminal bodies mirrored by an ever more racialist discourse surrounding Jews that similarly stressed physical markers? Indeed, one only needs to scratch the surface to uncover suggestive similarities between 'the born criminal's' physiological and behavioural stigmata as established by 'positivist' criminology and the antisemitic stereotypes of Jewish physiological and behavioural difference. Criminals had dark complexions and big noses, as did Jews; criminals spoke in a secret language that enabled them to evade the supervision of the authorities, as did Jews; criminals were driven by abnormally strong sexual appetites, as were Jews; criminals had a distinct, asymmetrical gait, as did the weak-footed Jews; criminals were prone to certain kinds of mental diseases; the Jews, too, were known to be disproportionally prone to insanity.[2] The list, culled from the work of Sander Gilman, could be further augmented if one reads contemporary anthopological data on the Jewish 'race' and compares it to further Lombrosian criminal stigmata: criminals and Jews shared a proclivity for 'brachycephalic' skulls for instance; they were both disinclined to physical labour, they both had bad skin, and so on.[3] One could also add that *fin-de-siècle* attempts to essentialise groups by means of photographic super-exposition – a process in which various negatives of faces belonging to a distinct human category were faintly exposed on top of each other in order to arrive at a (fuzzy) positive that was understood as representing an 'ideal type' of this category – included Jews, criminals, and consumptives, implying that Jewishness was regarded as a type of anomaly comparable to criminality or disease.[4] For Sander Gilman, the chief chronicler of these parallels between the narratives about Jew and criminal, they feed into clear narratives of Jewish criminality. He especially highlights Jewish sexual criminality as a wide-spread *topos* of the time, going so far as to claim that the 'face of the Jew and that of the sexual criminal had merged in the course of the *fin-de-siècle* in the figure of 'Jack the Ripper' as an eastern European Jew.'[5]

The main problem with this thesis, I will argue, is the absence of any example where criminological literature would directly and immediately collapse 'the criminal' and 'the Jew' into a single figure. The parallels between criminal and Jewish stigmata function solely on the level of analogy. Nor was this analogy much taken up in the wider antisemitic discourse, which followed a quite different logic in its construction of Jewish crime. The thesis overestimates the dominance of Lombroso's vision criminality in both popular and scholarly discourse.[6] In fact, one of the striking aspects of the period's criminological output is the relative dearth of material that would make specific claims about Jewish criminality in a manner that could be usefully integrated into the history of criminology as an exclusionary science. The material that does exist is strewn over several decades, and various bodies of words. It is this material to which I shall now turn in order to analyse it both in the light of my reading of *fin-de-siècle* crime-science, and of Gilman's thesis.

Mid-Nineteenth Century Conceptions of Jewish Crime

The idea of Jewish criminality was not new at the end of the nineteenth century. As a theme it can be traced back to the eighteenth and seventeenth centuries.[7] This narrative found one of its most coherent expressions in A.F. Thiele's 1842 publication of the first of two volumes on *Jewish Crooks in Germany*.[8] Thiele served as a 'Royal Prussian Criminal Executive' and his book grew out of his personal acquaintance with an 1831 Berlin court case against a Jewish criminal organisation. The book offered analyses of the nature of Jewish criminality, and presented several case-studies of Jewish criminals and their 'gangs', along with a list of the most popular Jewish criminal strategies and a dictionary of Jewish criminal terms. His starting point was to differentiate between ordinary offenders who committed crimes due to 'poverty or misery or passion', and 'crooks' ['*Gauner*'] who committed them '*con amore*', and lived as part of a criminal society, that 'constitutes a separate society within the state that is hostile to all bourgeois interests,' governed by its own language and laws.[9] The crook, then, was envisioned as the inhabitant of a criminal underworld that was both mirror and antithesis of middle-class existence. This underworld was defined by rules, language, networks of association and, above all, its inhabitants' profession.[10] Since these professional criminals were far more dangerous than the dilettante driven by need, it was upon them that Thiele's study focused.

Thiele went on to explain that he would concentrate on Jewish crooks in particular, both because the Christian crook had already been covered by the literature, and because the Jewish crook was the 'most dangerous'.[11] This danger Thiele located largely in Jewish criminal competence: Jewish crooks were cunning, skilled at planning crimes and skilled at their execution;[12] their agility during break-ins was 'enhanced to a phenomenal degree';[13] they left no evidence behind, and, in the event of getting caught, made excellent liars.[14] Significantly, this homage to Jewish skill at criminal activity was consistently communicated in a comparative dimension: Jews were depicted not simply as skilled criminals, but as *better* criminals than their Christian counterparts. In fact Thiele located Jewish criminal distinctiveness largely in this heightened level of their criminal skill, rather than in any specific type of criminal activity or its style of execution.

The key aspects of this Jewish criminal competence were then further related to specific sociological features of the Jewish underworld. Thus part of the criminal superiority of Jews vis-à-vis Christians was explained by their stronger bonds of solidarity within these underworld networks, fostered by their marriage patterns: Jewish crooks only married other Jewish crooks, and brought up their children as crooks.[15] As a result whenever two Jewish criminals met they immediately recognised each other as members of a 'separate society' and 'become 'chawern' (comrades) and steal together'.[16] Thiele also maintained that Jewish crooks typically masked themselves as itinerant traders, a particularly cunning disguise since traders had no fixed abode, hence were hard to trace.[17] Indeed, according to Thiele, Jewish criminals identified trade with theft to such a degree that in their language the two terms had become synonymous.[18]

Thiele's list of Jewish criminality's sociological features was clearly rooted in the observation of the realities of Jewish life in Germany: their cohesion and separateness from mainstream society, their practice of not marrying outside the faith, the simple fact that a disproportionate number of Jews were engaged in trade and hence were frequently on the move. By collapsing this lifestyle with the largely fictional narrative of a cohesive underworld, Thiele created an image of the Jewish crook, who embodied mid-nineteenth century bourgeois fears about a professional, organised and skilled 'counter-class' of criminals, and whose identifying mark lay precisely in the purity of this embodiment.

When it came to defining who should and should not be included in the category under discussion, Thiele argued for an inclusive definition, effectively attributing a contagious quality to Jewish forms of crime:

> The term Jewish crook denotes not only Jews, but also those professional, Christian villains, who are connected to the former, commit their crimes in conjunction with them and thus, as far as their personalities, their language, their habits and manners when stealing are concerned, acquire, in a manner of speaking, somewhat of a Jewish air.[19]

Significantly this dynamic of contagion could only run one way: 'No Jew coming in contact with Christian thieves will live according to their habits or change his convictions according to these; the other way around the opposite happens every time.'[20] Thiele proved this 'Judification' of Christian crooks by recounting how some Christian criminals started going to synagogue along with their partners in crime, and even partook in their rites: for Thiele these Christians had entered the Jewish underworld, hence become Jews as far as their criminal typology was concerned.[21]

In his account, then, Jews were defined as a religious and sociological category. They were depicted as forming a separate, cohesive underworld within Germany, one that could expand by imposing its ways upon inhabitants of rival, less dangerous, underworlds. Thiele painted this picture in a language devoid of a racial or even ethnic understanding of Jews. Nor did he dip into any of the medical or psychological terminology so prevalent in the *fin-de-siècle*: the imitation of Jewish criminals by Christians was not, for instance, narrated in terms of suggestion. Nevertheless we encounter the germ of a narrative that put Jews into a powerful and dangerous position both as cunning executioners of crime, and as a wider corruptive force. We shall see how this germ developed as the cultural understanding of crime, subjectivity and society evolved.

Thiele's contribution is remarkable, but also extraordinary, in that it has no real equivalent in the literature about crime for the next eighty or so years: no other German scholar of crime devoted an entire monograph specifically to the study of Jewish criminality. At the same time it proved influential, and his name and book appeared in most criminological bibliographies for the next two generations. Its wisdom was oft echoed (if adjusted to the relevant milieu), as in Karl Wilhelm Zimmermann's 'practical guide' to the *Thieves of Berlin* that warns us that Jewish crooks are more cunning than their Christian equivalents, because of their mastery of the art of hiding among respectable people, a disguise that is facilitated by their treatment of crime as a professional trade much like any other.[22] Thiele's account also found its critics, however. Avé-Lallement's monumental *Das Deutsche Gaunerthum* devoted considerable space to the discussion of the role of Jews in German criminality, and shared Thiele's assessment that Christian crooks took on Jewish habits, including religious rites, after prolonged exposure.[23] However, Avé-Lallement explicitly rejected Thiele's idea that there was a specifically Jewish criminality that was distinct from its Christian equivalent.[24] Indeed, he argued that Jews (and Gypsies) were merely the most visible members of the criminal caste, and hence were believed to be much more prevalent then they were – in a footnote he went as far as remarking that it was Christian 'intolerance' that produced a skewed view of Jewish involvement in crime.[25] Later in the century Avé-Lallement was at pains to stress that European Jews 'have become Aryan' (on the basis of their skull shapes), i.e. to explicitly refute any claims to an essentialist difference between Jews and non-Jews.[26] The status of Jewish criminality was therefore contested, and the question of racial difference (or lack thereof) began to be explicitly raised only towards the century's end.

Lombroso and Jewish Crime

The closest *fin-de-siècle* echo to Thiele's project was provided by a number of chapters devoted to Jewish criminality in various key texts, most significantly perhaps Lombroso's own discussion in the fifth and last edition of *L'uomo delinquente*.[27] The chapter was located in a section devoted to crime's 'social causes'. 'Race' was treated as one such social cause, best evaluated by that modern tool of social science, statistics. One should take note though that 'race' here is used to denote and compare different ethnic groups within nation states for example the Gallic as opposed to the Ligurian race in France. Lombroso set about his task methodically, first discussing Austrian, Italian, and French criminal patterns, moving on to the links between skull shapes, hair colour and crime within a given race.[28] His results concerning the significance of race for criminal patterns varied significantly from case to case. His discussion of Austrian criminality, for instance, stressed that no clear conclusions could be drawn about the comparative susceptibility of the various Austrian 'races', as education, 'civilisation' and work habits had a significant impact here that overshadowed racial difference.[29] Only after he had dealt with the races within various European countries, and deliberately set apart from these, did Lombroso turn to the criminality of Jews and Gypsies, a pairing that already had a certain tradition within the scholarly discourse on crime (for example in Avé-Lallement).[30] Gilman's vision of the potential of criminology as a new kind of antisemitic discourse seemed to find validation in Lombroso's very first sentence: 'The influence of race upon criminality becomes plainly evident when we consider Jews and Gypsies ...'. However, he immediately added a key qualifier:

> ... although [this influence] manifests itself very differently in the two races. The statistics of some countries shows a lower rate of criminality for the Jews than for their Gentile fellow citizens, which is all the more remarkable since, because of their usual occupations, they have to be compared not with the population in general, but with the merchants and petty tradespeople, who have, as we shall see, higher rates of criminality.[31]

The implications were not only that if race did have an influence on Jewish crime rates, this influence was one that caused their criminality to be potentially lower than that of other races, but also (and paradoxically) that race might not be such an important factor for determining criminality after all, since profession seemed to also play a very significant role.[32]

Lombroso went on to describe Jews as prone to certain kinds of crime: they were 'master-rogues' with 'exceptional cunning', practised usury, forgery and smuggling.[33] This list of criminal professions was, however, itself broken down for the various nations, which Jews inhabited, strongly suggesting that these crime-traditions were contingent, passed down along family lines and not a function of biology.[34] Having reinforced criminal stereotypes redolent of Thiele's thesis, Lombroso was at pains to demonstrate that the time of the great

Jewish criminal dynasties and gangs was a thing of the past, and that the 'causes [that] formerly impelled the Jews to these crimes' were 'greed for gold, discouragement and desperation, exclusion from office and from all public assistance, the resistance against the stronger races from which they had no other means of defence ...'.[35] Lombroso thus listed largely exogenous causes that could be reduced to a rational reaction against social pressures, rather than racial predisposition. Indeed Lombroso added that 'it is fair to note that from the time when the Jews have been permitted to enter political life their tendency to special crime [sic!] has diminished.'[36] The Jews, then, were let off lightly by Lombroso, certainly if compared to the Irish, the Sicilians or the Gypsies whose criminal patterns were described (and condemned) in far less ambiguous terms.[37] According to Lombroso, Jews were not particularly prone to criminality, nor did their race conclusively explain the kind of criminality they did indulge in.

It is also remarkable that the entire section on race, indeed the entire part of the book devoted to 'social causes' of crime (climate, level of civilisation, density of population) did not make any reference to the thesis of atavistic criminality which propelled Lombroso's name to household fame. Not with a single word did Lombroso try to map Jewish 'racial' physical features onto the kind of physical stigmata he employed to identify the 'born criminal'. The analysis of race drifted above this original thesis, seemingly unconnected. Even when he concluded that a disproportional number of Jews suffered from mental disorders,[38] this was not put into the context of the rest of his theory that at this stage of its development nearly equated certain kinds of mental disorder (most notably epilepsy) with a criminal disposition.[39] Rather, Lombroso somewhat cryptically explained this tendency with reference to the 'intellectual work' favoured by Jews, and thus effectively neutralised its significance for the context of crime.[40]

Lombroso's final formulation of his original thesis thus played out the contested and irreconcilable nature of various contemporary criminologies, rather than presenting a coherent synthesis. His initial reductive system stood eroded by the quasi-sociological treatment of crime that was juxtaposed with but not reconciled to his vision of the born criminal. Nevertheless it is significant that the prime advocate of criminological reductionism avoided any clear identification of the nature or causes of Jewish criminality: it emerged rather out of a complex web of national allegiance, tradition, history, as well as potentially 'racial' inclination. From an antisemitic point of view none of this provided much grist for the mill, particularly once it was coupled with Lombroso's thesis of the transracial validity of racial stigmata espoused elsewhere.[41]

There is a certain temptation to find an answer to Lombroso's unwillingness to treat Jewish criminality as racial criminality, and his reluctance to relate race to criminal anthropology more generally, in his own Jewish identity. In this manner one could explain the avoidance of his own theory's supposed latent implications on the grounds of personal bias. While there was, of course, no necessary connection between the faith and ethnic identity into which a contemporary was born, and his or her stance towards the 'Jewish question' – the Jewish writer Otto Weininger's antisemitism being a case in point[42] – it is clear from Lombroso's other writings, most notably his 1894 text *L'antisemitismo e le scienze moderne* that he was indeed an active opponent of antisemitism as well as a staunch assimilationist.[43] *L'antisemitismo* argued both that Jews were not a 'true' Semitic race – i.e. that racial antisemitism had no scientific, ethnic grounds – and that antisemitism was an irrational prejudice that was passed on from generation to generation, and should itself be regarded as a symptom of psychological atavism.[44] At the same time the text did develop certain themes about Jewish behavioural patterns, though it is less than clear what these patterns were based upon. Lombroso stressed, for instance, that Jews were 'representative of modernity,'[45] and highlighted their cleverness, their skill at lying, their chameleon-like aptitute at wearing masks.[46] Elsewhere he described Jews as forming the 'nucleus of bourgeois capitalism' (*Genio et degenerazione*), and drew attention to the alleged custom of prostituting daughters among pre-Mosaic Jews (*La donna delinquente*).[47] While, as I will argue, many of these themes were absolutely central to contemporary antisemitic constructions of the criminal Jew, one notes that Lombroso located Jews at the opposite end from atavistic, pre-modern criminals. His assimilationist politics did not allow for a description of Jews in terms of anthropometric difference. At times he implies that Orthodox Jews were culturally backward, but he never rooted this in biology, race or even physique.[48]

Lombroso's avoidance of a biologisation of Jews becomes even more significant once one realises that biological/anthropometric language describing Jewish difference was in circulation around the turn of the century, and that this language was by no means by definition antisemitic, but was used by those Jewish thinkers who wished to prove their racial singularity and hence their claim to nationhood.[49] The Zionist *Die Welt*, for instance, published a long article that cheerfully described (and statistically 'proved') Jews to be small-bodied, short-limbed, and thick-lipped, with dark hair and eyes, brachycephalic skulls, lots of facial and bodily hair, broad foreheads, big noses and small chests.[50] The article went on to depict Jews as a race of poor physical workers who were intelligent but not creative. Galton's composite pictures of Jews were similarly commissioned for philosemitic reasons, to depict the true beauty and nobility of an essentialist Jewish 'type', even if Galton's own reading of the pictures was less than admiring (beauty being in the eye of the beholder).[51] At times Jewish weakness and lack of vigour could even be directly employed for philosemitic (often specifically Zionist) ends, as in the utilisation of Jewish 'neurasthasia' to argue for a need for Jewish 'regeneration' in a new Israel.[52] The point is that the language of anthropological difference was not in any way owned by antisemites. A determinedly philosemitic follower of Lombroso could have used its vocabulary to 'prove' the incompatibility of the Jewish 'racial type' with the criminal type, just as an antisemitic student of Lombroso's could have equated the two. What is striking, therefore, is that no criminologist ever did: to my knowledge no clear example of the construction of a specifically Jewish 'born criminal' exists in the contemporary criminological literature in any language.[53] Cultural degeneration as a function of modernity was, or course, routinely connected to Jews, but this did not typically translate into a claim that Jews as a race were physiologically degenerate. Here and elsewhere they were framed more as poisoners than as the poisoned.

Jewish Crime in German Criminological Journals

As noted above, dedicated inquiry into Jewish forms of criminality was a rare event in the contemporary criminological discourse. Going through a decade and a half's worth of articles in the two journals that arguably dominated Austria's criminological horizon in the first decade of the twentieth century – Hans Gross's *Archiv* and Gustav Aschaffenburg's *Monatsschrift für Kriminalpsychologie und Straftechtsreform* – one finds perhaps twenty that touch on the topic of 'Jews and Crime' in some form or other. The vast majority of these articles did not conceptualise crime as a function of 'race' and tended to focus on specific crimes: close to a dozen contemporary books and articles, for instance, dealt with ritual murder accusations.[54] They offered case studies of various accusations (or else reviews of books dealing with the phenomenon of blood libel), along with an analysis that typically if not universally amounted to a dismissal of the charge. Those, like Hans Gross, who were willing to entertain the idea of ritual murder, usually pointed out that it was not impossible that some Jewish sect was subject to some sort of blood superstition that could be found in many of the world's religions.[55] Occasionally other 'typically Jewish' criminal activities are highlighted: for instance the question of whether or not Jews were more likely to commit perjury.[56] Here the accusation was clearly tied to causes located within Jewish culture, namely the belief that even the most minute damage perpetrated upon the Talmud (for example pricking it with a needle) invalidated any oath sworn upon it. Once again no claim was made for some sort of essentialist – let alone pathological – difference that would set Jews, as a group, apart from the rest of the population; nor did the charge of 'Jewish perjury superstition' find universal support.[57]

There were a few exceptions to this reluctance to treat Jewish criminality as a function of race. The first of these, entitled simply 'Race and Crime' was penned by Paul Näcke and sought to affirm the existence of a stable (hence biologically based) 'Jewish character' composed of traits such as greed.[58] Näcke did not however name any specific physical or psychological signifyers that would denote Jewish criminals. Nor did he attempt to establish any clear tie between the actual criminal behaviour observed in Jews and these supposed Jewish traits, apart from a fleeting reference to prostitution.[59] Elsewhere Näcke stressed the 'alien' morality of Jews, and blamed their 'unpleasant characteristics' on their incestuous marriage patterns.[60] Again it remained unclear what sort of criminality would emerge from these characteristics. Näcke's other writings show him as an outspoken opponent of Italian criminological positivism and as someone upholding the ubiquity of degenerative hereditary traits within the wider population. His antisemitism thus ill fitted his criminological persuasions and he never managed to frame a coherent thesis of the criminal Jew. The issue of what might constitute a typical Jewish crime was, in any case, largely approached from a different angle.

Jews as Modern Criminals

In fact it was the statistical approach exemplified by Lombroso's comparison between various nations' crime statistics, rather than competing typologies of Jewish racial essence, that soon provided the main arena for discussing Jewish criminal difference. The debate raged in the pages of Aschaffenburg's *Monatsschrift*, a number of key monographs, and a more specialised (and Zionist) publication entitled *Zeitschrift für Demographie und Statistik der Juden* [Journal for Demography and Statistics of the Jews].[61] By and large the numbers produced in this statistical exchange tended to affirm Lombroso's verdict that Jewish criminality typically was somewhat lower than that of the overall population in general, and markedly lower as far as violent crimes were concerned: a detailed 1896 Berlin study put Jewish criminality in Austria at eighty-four percent of that of the Christian population.[62] It also, however, tended to maintain that Jews – independent of their 'host' country – displayed a predisposition towards certain kinds of crimes, namely economic crimes such as fraud, embezzlement, forgery etc., and that here they far outstripped the criminality of the Christian population. The debate thus focused on various explanatory models to explain this abnormality.

Several scholars argued that the statistical abnormality was best explained by reference to Jewish patterns of occupation, arguing that a disproportional number of Jews were engaged in trade and that their crime figures, if compared to Christian merchants only, displayed no anomaly.[63] If anything, scholars like Rudolf Wassermann argued, Jewish crime patterns reflected the overall crime patterns of the future (capitalist) world, crime patterns that already existed in advanced capitalist cultures like the United States, or among the commercially orientated Greeks.[64] Indeed, he noted that in places where Greeks and Jews lived side by side, Jews were displaced into professions involving physical labour while Greeks controlled trade, i.e. that, for all the capitalist orientation of the Jews, this was by no means a necessary feature of their constitutions, and by extension that their proclivity towards commercial crime was contingent rather than in any sense 'natural'.[65]

This conclusion, however, was contested by an authority no less weighty than the eminent German criminologist Franz von Liszt, who in a 1907 discussion of the issue declared:

The assumption we have held up to now that Jewish criminality can be fully explained by reference to the criminality of professions, is wrong. In other words: the Jewish merchant is not equal to the Christian merchant in terms of his criminality; in some areas he comes off better, in some on the other hand worse.[66]

Lizst admitted that he did not know how to explain what caused this difference between Christian and Jewish merchant, but others were less coy about giving a clear answer. Thus the Dutch head of the 'Bureau for Legal Statistics', Jan de Roos, maintained that it was Jewish racial traits that not only shaped their criminal patterns, but also their occupational choices: both were functions of the 'natural predisposition of the central nervous system' and hence Jewish life revolved around commercial ambitions 'both in the social as in the antisocial activities'.[67] These racial traits included a preference for mental over physical work, an attendant lack of physical strength and courage, and greed, as illustrated by their participation in sexual crimes only in the secondary function as hawkers of pornography.[68] Consequently Jews did not commit many violent crimes (they were too puny and afraid), did not resist state authorities (again they lacked the courage) but excelled in all that called for 'cunning, calculation and thought'.[69]

It is striking to see how in de Roos's hands statistical figures that by and large showed Jews to be upstanding citizens could be turned into instruments of racial condemnation, how even the 'abnormally' low figures in crimes such as murder or resistance were re-interpreted as signs of Jewish racial weakness and lack of manly vigour. Like Näcke's article discussed above, Roos's physiological view of Jewish criminality in which the nervous system rooted a people in certain characteristic patterns 'that one already finds in the Bible', was the exception rather than the rule, a point that is driven home by the fact that Roos cites and quotes Näcke as his sole support for his assertions.[70] One should also note that even in these rare cases when a biological narrative of Jewish crime was attempted, this had little to do with the initial parameters of the debate surrounding criminal atavism/degeneracy. After all, it was precisely not the crude criminal activities of the atavistic man-beast that were the focus of investigation here, but rather crimes acted out within civilisation, by some of its own, civilised members, however compelled these might be by their racial nature.

What does become clear from the statistical debate, however, is that it made sense to contemporary commentators to break down criminal patterns according to racial allegiance, and specifically in terms of Jews versus non-Jews. Even Wassermann, who claimed that his investigation into Jewish criminality was motivated largely by the desire to practice his grasp of the new science of statistics, and who argued against Jewish criminal difference, could ultimately not avoid affirming an analytical model in which the stratification of criminal data according to race (however defined) made sense. Yet this search for Jewish difference via the medium of quantification had little to do with anthropological or psychological modes of investigating the individual criminal. The Jew here became an abstract figure, stretched out on the rack of averages, not a tangible villain who could be hunted down and removed from society.

Many of the ideas voiced by de Roos, and indeed Wassermann, can be found in a systematised form in Hugo Herz's *Verbrechen und Verbrechertum in Öster-reich*, which in terms of offering a systematic narrative of Jewish criminality is the closest *fin-de-siècle* equivalent to Thiele's project on Jewish crooks. His book included a lengthy section on the 'Criminality of Gypsies and Jews', offering a socio-historical account of Jewish criminal genealogy – once again one should note the pairing with Gypsies, to which I will turn presently.[71] Here, with unashamedly teleological gusto, Herz emplotted 'the Jew' as one of the key motors of nineteenth-century economic history, narrating the 'capital-ist productive organisation,' as 'the mission of Judaism'. This love affair between 'the Jew' and the 'Manchester system', had according to Herz a decisive influence on criminality:

> In the antisocial world of criminality, Jewish capitalism and acquisition ethics resulted in the growth of new kinds of crime that replaced the physical force of pre-vious days with criminal cunning: crimes of exploitation of the inexperienced and of those ignorant of business matters ...[72]

In this narrative, Jews created modern economic crime by pushing the bound-aries of legal capitalist business practice beyond what should be regarded as eth-ical. The law was slow to catch up in the early days of capitalism, too enamoured with the dogma of non-intervention. Once invented, these new economic crimes quickly spread to non-Jews:

> One need only to think of stock market, insurance, lottery and mortgage frauds, white slavery etc., in which Jews not only provide a large number of criminal ele-ments, but in which native delinquents in their actions, their habits and language copy the Jewish criminals.[73]

Thus Jews successfully 'judaised' crime, even as they 'capitalised' the economy; they effectively brought into being a whole new criminal scene. The parallels to Thiele's 'contagion' paradigm are obvious. Moreover, Herz's conclusion that modern crime centred not on atavistic acts of violence, committed by over-sexed, pathological freaks (tattoos and all), but on the cunning exploita-tion of criminal spaces opened up by the civilisatory process, binds in neatly with the image of the modern, wily Jew found in Lombroso. According to Herz, modern crime split society not into the antagonistic pairing of born criminals versus 'normal' citizens, but into a class-based pair of manipulator and manipulatee. Criminals themselves could be subdivided into those who were pushed into crime because of economic hardship, but were badly equipped for it intellectually, and those who prospered in this modern world of criminality that so resembled the capitalist mode of production at large:

On the one hand criminals of genius, who in terms of their productivity, their inventive powers of imagination, and technological tools stand head and shoulders above anything that has come before, on the other the proletarian masses who are forced upon the path of immorality but lack any criminal skill or identity.[74]

Herz's book provided as close to a systematic criminalisation of the Jew as could be found in any contemporary piece of criminological writing. The Jew emerged as an economic manipulator, a creative, intelligent, armchair criminal, whose scams were so successful that they seduced others – non-Jews – into imitation. Moreover, Jews were clearly identified with the forces of modernisation, urbanisation and capitalism, a view popular among conservative, petit-bourgois populations, both in a wider historical perspective, and especially after the stock market crash in 1873 and the consequent political collapse of liberalism in Vienna.[75]

Herz's conflation of Judaism and capitalism, incidentally, found various echoes amongst contemporary sociologists, above all in Werner Sombart's 1911 publication of *Die Juden und das Wirtschaftsleben* (The Jews and Economic Life).[76] The Berlin professor argued for a distinct and genetically based Jewish psychological disposition that predisposed them to economic success within a capitalist system.[77] The rationality of the Jewish religion, the history of diaspora and oppression further shaped them into capitalism's primary protagonists. Unlike Herz, Sombart did not consider Jewish criminal activity, although he did note that economic behaviour that had been regarded unethical and quasi-criminal in the seventeenth and eighteenth centuries had become 'self-evidently proper' under capitalism.[78] Sombart's views were echoed by a variety of scholars but also drew heavy criticism, particularly for its argument about the genetic/racial underpinnings of Jewish behaviour, which went against the beliefs of much of the German sociological establishment.[79]

While Herz's quasi-socialist indictment of capitalism itself as a source of crime was unique within Austrian criminology, it is hard not to notice the compatibility of the picture he offers with the concerns voiced by Hans Gross and other contemporary criminologists. Gross's concern with the sensory perception of crime, and the attendant discourse about a degenerate, weak-willed society, could easily accommodate an antisemitic argument that constructed Jews as intelligent arch-criminals who took advantage of other people's mental limitations. It was compatible, too, with the statistical debate, which – in its antisemitic overtones – stressed the cunning of Jews, their adroitness at maneuvering the innovations of the modern world, their aptitude to exploit existing structures against ignorant victims.

The Jew conjured up in these narratives was one who would commit cunning crimes, or else act to widen criminal spaces, for example by selling pornography, which was understood not only as an offence in itself, but also – given the 'suggestible' power of its subject matter – as a cause of crime (prostitution, indecency, sexual assault) further down the line.[80] Dissimulation was often a key ingredient of Jewish criminality, including, as Ann Golding has argued on evidence from earlier in the century, the simulation of insanity for illicit purposes.[81] All these narratives conceptualised a wilful and rational criminal, even if this criminal's motives were shaped by his or her racial constitution, and they all stressed the symbiosis of Jewish criminality with the forces of modernity, i.e. the capitalist economy and the atomised society of the modern city wherein they dwelled.[82] It became possible to portray Jews not only as rational, city-bound criminals preying on the weak, but, in the last consequence, as destructive of 'good' knowledge itself, with the aim of facilitating crime. We shall see this narrative emerge when we consider the constructions of Jewish crime in the antisemitic press.

Jews and Gypsies

The Jew, in the contemporary criminological literature, was not then conceptualised as a physiological other, but as a hyper-rational actor, whose criminal activities exemplified civilisatory progress rather than opposed it. Gilman's thesis that to some degree Lombrosite criminal stigmata and contemporary antisemitic discourse approached each other in the period under discussion is not brought out by the evidence. It works much better if one considers the scholarly treatment of Gypsies rather than Jews.[83] We have already noted that Jews and Gypsies were frequently juxtaposed in the discussion of racial influence on crime (although Gross is a notable exception here, as he does not offer a discussion of Jewish crime at all). Neither group fitted neatly into the otherwise nation-based mode of categorisation that dominated such studies – neither Jews nor Gypsies had a *Heimat*, and yet they both were seen to have an inner cohesion that forbade their subsumation into the category of their host-countries, although attempts at this were made by those who argued a strong case for assimilation (Rudolf Wassermann, or the Jewish scientist Alfred Ploetz being key examples).[84] Another reason why they could easily be paired up was that far from being perceived as very similar they provided scholars like Herz and Lombroso with a perfect study in contrast: for these scholars they represented antithetical models of criminality.

Consider, for instance, Lombroso's introduction to Gypsy criminality: 'With the Gypsies the case is quite different [from the Jews]. They are the living example of a whole race of criminals...'.[85] They are characterised as 'cowardly' and 'vicious', sensual, noisy and, when cornered, 'have been known to throw their own children at the head of their opponent ...'; they have been suspected of 'cannibalism', and they have an 'atavistic genius' for music.[86] Lombroso systematically removed Gypsies from common humanity and described them as atavisms incarnate, a race from before civilised time, although even here he stopped short of explicitly relating this indictment to his (transracial) theory of criminal atavism. Herz similarly attached atavistic-primordial characteristics to Gypsies: they 'represent ... a dangerous and peculiar type of criminality' that was a function of their 'biological peculiarity'.[87] Despite the enormous socio-economic changes that gave rise to modern Jewish crime, Gypsies continued to reproduce the crime-patterns of the seventeenth and eighteenth centuries, based around gangs of interrelated robbers. Herz described this criminality as 'primitive' and hence as ultimately less dangerous than modern, Jewish crime: his description of the Gypsies bore clear echoes of Thiele's description of a Jewish underworld some half-a-century before.[88] Unlike that of Thiele's Jewish criminals, however, the Gypsies' skill at criminal activities was described not in terms of intelligence or training, but rather in terms of instinct. For instance, Herz maintained that Gypsies, while unable to use the sophisticated tools of modern burglars and thieves, could open chests of drawers etc. 'with an uncanny skill using only a knife, a bent nail or doing it in some other primitive way'.[89]

Indeed it is striking how much the metaphor of animal behaviour and animal skill – a key point in Lombroso's thesis of atavism – crept into the descriptions of Gypsies, both in Herz and, more surprisingly perhaps, in Gross's *Handbuch*, that Herz quoted at length. Gypsies were compared to 'wild beasts' because like certain animals they 'wander in the winter months'.[90] They were said to have the 'agility and suppleness of weasels,' the 'eyes of owls and the ears of foxes'[91] and were animated by an 'animal sensuality'.[92] A Gypsy would slink around potential crime sites 'like a fox', and would only be given away by his or her pungent animal smell that was like 'fat and mouse smells combined' and that clung to the walls long after he or she was gone.[93] On this metaphorical level, too, we are thus consistently reminded that 'the gypsy differs completely from every civilised human being, even the coarsest and most degraded kind,' i.e. that he represented a racially cohesive other, that moved and lived in a herd, and hence was hardly human at all.[94]

Gross's own chapter on Gypsies represents an oddity in his own published opus: it indulged in crude prejudice and communicated a dogmatism about the essence of this type of criminal that was conspicuously absent in the vast majority of his output. This is not to say that his tone of writing was ever less than confident, or indeed bigoted, but this confidence (and bigotry) were usually poured into the description of discrete facts and methods, justified by his direct and prolonged experience of these 'particulars' (for example whether or not liars necessarily blush). The Gypsies are the only example where Gross attributed traits to an entire group of people, rather than to an individual, and thus symbolised a marked break with his general methodology: he even went so far as to include a chapter on the Gypsies' 'physical traits' that included such gems as their pathological dislike of wind, and their propensity to heal wounds faster than normal human beings, a 'trait that may be oriental in origin'.[95]

Why is it then that Lombroso, Herz and Gross, for all their conceptual differences, unanimously condemned Gypsies as criminality incarnate, but treated Jews either as the next evolutionary step in the development of crime

(Herz), as an analytical unit whose criminality was best understood within historical and sociological parameters (Herz and Lombroso), or else simply remained silent about them as Gross did, who, except for a brisk passage that described a type of mail fraud popular among Russian Jews and a throw-away line about Jewish behaviour in the court-room had nothing at all to say about the criminality of Jews as a group?[96]

The most convincing answer, I believe, was that Jews were integrated in society to such a degree – visible, familiar, accepted (grudgingly or not) – that to disseminate crude typologies within a discourse of science had no resonance, simply because of the lack of empirical evidence. The Gypsies on the other hand were sufficiently foreign, distinct, and separate that virtually any old prejudice could safely resurface within the scholarly literature, and be accepted as true. Gross's own lapse from his usual doubts that knowledge about the criminal was simply not possible yet in any essentialist sense ('what ... one is to understand under the heading '*criminal*' nobody has as of yet explained'[97]) illustrates the point: how far outside the civilised pale must he have regarded the Gypsies as residing, to throw his usual caution about the problems of fact-establishment (not to mention his avid dislike of Lombroso) to the wind, and write a twenty-one-page chapter that effectively enshrined them as an animal race of *uomi deliquenti*?[98]

The Jews might have once been regarded a similarly peripheral category prior to their legal emancipation – and there are elements of this in Thiele's treatment of the Jews as a cohesive other, forming its own underworld – but by the turn of the nineteenth century they certainly could no longer be regarded as anything else than in a key sense integrated, into crime no less so than society. Consider in this context the discourse about criminal language. Language was absolutely central to mid-nineteenth century accounts of criminality: written in the wake of the literature of (romantic) nationalism that highlighted the role of language in constituting identity, arguments for a criminal language were crucial for the formulation of a vision of a criminal underworld as an anti-society and anti-nation.[99] In Gilman's interpretation the proximity of the Jewish-German dialect to criminal cant is a significant point of antisemitic anxiety.[100] Indeed, mid-nineteenth century texts about the criminal recognised this proximity. Thiele's 1842 account, for instance, systematically collected Jewish 'criminal' words in a dictionary spanning some 134 pages and 2718 words.[101] Avé-Lallement's *Das Deutsche Gaunertum*, too, devoted the majority of the third of its four volumes to the 'Jewish-German language', providing its first coherent 'grammar'.[102] He, however, stressed that the language of crooks was in no way identical with the Jewish–German tongue, but rather had simply borrowed terminology to save itself the effort of inventing a terminology all its own.[103] Where Thiele regarded Jewish criminal cant as a separate and important repository of criminality, Avé-Lallement, writing half a generation later, relegated the Jewish input into criminal language to a co-incidental and historical role.[104]

Later on in the century, Hans Kurella – Lombroso's translator and chief exponent of Lombrosian criminological ideas in the German speaking world - found 'signs of atavism' in the criminal use of language, and, like Avé-Lallement, commented on the Jewish and Gypsy origin of many a term in the professional argot of criminals.[105] He also maintained, however, that German criminal language – specifically in Berlin – was moving away from the use of Jewish terms, and embracing local slang.[106] He went on to list a number of criminal terms, marking a small number as 'Hebrew' in origin.[107] Lombroso himself also mentioned the use of Hebrew/Jewish German terms in Dutch and German criminal cant, but made it clear that the association was purely historical and regional.[108] Gross's *Handbook* chose not to differentiate Jewish and non-Jewish words in its own dictionary of criminal terms, and indeed words of recognisably Jewish origin were rare in this collection ('*Goi*,' '*Schickse*,' '*schächten*' and '*schäkern*' are the only ones that are immediately recognisable), despite a reference to the historical importance of Jewish terminology.[109] The various contributors to the *Archiv* who wanted to add to this particular enterprise of data collection tended to break it down in terms of nationality, but here the logic was governed by a recognition that criminals in different countries had their own professional terminology, not by a desire to implicate a single language as inherently influential in criminal circles.[110] Amongst the many articles on this topic published in the *Archiv*, there was no separate contribution on Jewish criminal language, and indeed Gross, reviewing a book on criminal cant, at one point complained that certain words listed are 'no criminal words but rather provincial terms of Jewish words ...,' i.e. that the one has been falsely identified as the other.[111] Thus Thiele's attempt to separate and single out 'Jewish language' as a privileged repository of criminality was by the early years of the twentieth century replaced by a more general project of collecting words based solely on geography and milieu. Within this latter project Jewish words had no separate conceptual existence.[112] On a small scale the discussion of criminal language mirrored the wider developments within a criminology that was disinclined to deal with entire population groups as homogenous criminal types – unless, that is, they were regarded as utterly foreign to society, as Gypsies were, or within the realm of statistical analysis that as a methodology depended on precisely such pre-conceived units.

Race in the Early Twentieth Century

By the end of the period here considered, this tension between the statistical approach that treated Jewish criminality as a distinct analytical unit to be investigated *en* aggregate, and those who like Gross approached Jewish criminal activity only by means of case-studies that made no *a priori* (nor indeed *a posteriori*) claim for their distinctiveness, was being decided in favour of the former.[113] Race was slowly being turned into a key, if contested, unit of criminological analysis and began to take on the more strictly biological meaning it would hold a generation later. In 1906 the term 'race' was still ambiguous enough even within scientific circles for authors to feel a need to define it at the beginning of their articles, for example as a 'purely anthropological, not politico-historical terminus'.[114] In legal contexts the term would remain contested for decades, as is shown by the 1921 court rulings concerning Article 80 of the Treaty of St. Germain that established who within the erstwhile empire had rights to Austrian citizenship: an administrative court first ruled that the treaty's use of 'race' should be interpreted in a biological sense, then repealed its decision and chose to understand the term as synonymous with 'nationality'.[115] Moreover, even those criminologists who embraced a biological meaning of 'race' continued to find it difficult to fill the word with meaning, and to tie it to clear signifiers. As I have argued above, there is no single scholarly contribution in this period that would clearly list Jewish racial traits as broken down by physiological and psychological differences.[116] What did exist were occasional affirmations of Jewish susceptibility to insanity, but this did not become a widely disseminated medical idiom until the 1920s.[117] In the *fin-de-siècle* discourse surrounding crime, the analytical unit 'race' existed primarily in the abstract, as a statistical category largely devoid of any definitive set of attributes. It was left to popular antisemitic narratives to provide these attributes.

One should add that the statistical debate about race transcended Jews. In 1906 the 'Anthropological Society of Vienna' collected data comparing various races' tendencies towards different mental illnesses, including 'moral insanity', i.e. that mental disorder that prevented a person from differentiating right from wrong (a category first developed by James Prichard at the beginning of the nineteenth century and one that most *fin-de-siècle* criminologists, including Gross, no longer invoked with any regularity).[118] The racial categories under discussion includes 'Jews,' 'Slavs,' 'Germans,' 'Italians' and 'Hungarians,' i.e. featured no clear differentiation between a political or historical understanding of race and an anthropologised one. The results of this investigation were varied: Germans were shown to have a tendency towards depression and combined forms of paranoia, while Slavs were more likely to fall prey to 'phantastic-hallucinatory paranoia'; Jews were prone to hereditary degeneration, and hypochondria; Hungarians, along with Jews, had a slightly heightened propensity towards 'the megalomaniac variety of paralysis' and so on.[119] None of these results offered much in terms of conclusive evidence about the link between race and insanity, let alone race and criminality. Indeed the report draws our attention to the fact of how easily a supposed 'racial' correlation could be downplayed rather than accepted when this was desirable: the report indicated that Germans in Vienna were more likely sufferers of 'moral insanity' than any of the other races under discussion, but this was quickly explained away through 'purely local factors (the milieu of a big city, the local Viennese German population)'.[120] The abstract statistical category 'race' could thus provide highly flexible evidence. Its correlations depended largely on the analytical choices made prior to the actual act of counting (what after all was to be correlated with what?) and the results could either be accepted as sufficiently explained by reference to 'race', or else rejected by recourse to an exogenous category (typically milieu) not present in the statistical analysis. For the antisemite, in other words, this was a goldmine for prejudice, functioning quite independently from the actual numbers it produced.

White Slavery

Finally, there did exist a strong cultural identification of Jews with one sort of crime that generated a scholarly discourse all its own: the Jew as *Mädchenhändler* (literally 'trader-in-girls' or 'white slaver' in the somewhat more salacious contemporary English phrase), i.e. as a supplier of white, unwilling prostitutes to brothels throughout the world. The debate surrounding *Mädchenhandel* emerged in the 1880s and became a conventional topic in newspapers and journals, amongst women's groups and antisemitic agitators across Europe by the early 1890s. The trade was highly international in nature: many of the young women were bound for destinations in the New World where gender imbalances were common due to predominantly male migration patterns, and prostitution flourished. Steamboats and the telegraph facilitated a worldwide market that saw women shuttled from Poland to Germany to Constantinople, the Far East or the emerging cities of Latin America.[121] Starting in England from around 1885, charitable societies full of reformist zeal began to focus on the issue, raising public awareness and also giving birth to a series of commercial publications and, later, films that cashed in on the peculiar combination of moral disgust and sexual titillation offered by the material.[122] It would be misleading to read the outlandish claims and yelps of outrage of both reformist and commercial publications simply as the expressions of a moral panic that had taken hold of Europe. Rather, the White Slavery debate is best placed into a wider contemporary discourse about sex, in which invocations of disgust and sanitary scruples could coexist with voyeuristic pleasure. Alongside pamphlets about the horrors of the trade in women, Europe's population was busy consuming lascivious material like Zola's *Nana* (1880), 'Walter's' sexual memoirs (*My Secret Life*, published anonymously in eleven volumes under a pseudonym in Amsterdam between 1880 and 1894)) and 'Josephine Mutzenbacher's' autobiographical musings on her road from incest to the whorehouse (*Die Geschichte einer wienerischen Dirne, von ihr selbst erzählt*, published in Vienna 1906 and most likely written by Felix Salten, the inventor of Bambi) in record numbers.[123] Prostitution itself was a highly controversial issue that provoked a wide variety of contemporary responses: prostitutes could be celebrated as the truest incarnations of female sexuality by literary figures such as Kraus and Wedekind or stigmatised as anthropological deviants by Lombroso and his followers; they could be regarded as a necessary evil that needed to be

regulated but ultimately contributed to the functioning of society, or condemned as a health hazard in an age when the bane of syphilis held a central
space in bourgeois consciousness.[124] The *Mädchenhandel* discourse held additional fascination because it conjured up a world in which female innocence
and ignorance was exploited, and women were forced into a promiscuous life
of vice through no fault of their own. In reality, many of the prostitutes bound
for overseas brothels at least claimed that their profession was an active choice
rather than a function of victimisation, which goes a long way towards explaining why the many organisations formed throughout the 1890s recorded such
limited success in saving 'unfortunates'.[125]

In Austria the *Mädchenhandel* discourse focused above all on Galicia and
Bukovina, two impoverished regions in the east of the empire with large Jewish populations, where many of the prostitutes in question originated: Buenos
Aires in particularly was said to be awash with Jewish prostitutes from Galicia.[126] The fight against enforced prostitution and the international trade in
women was centralised in 1902 in the hands of the interdenominational (and
hence Christian dominated) *Österreichische Liga zur Bekämpfung des Mädchenhandels* [Austrian league against the trade-in-girls]; Jewish 'vigilance commit-
tees' that had formed in response to the Galician situation were soon forced to
merge with this central organisation.[127] Given that so many Jews were involved
in the trade, and given that these were *Ostjuden*, suspect even to the assimilated
Jewish elites of German-speaking Austria and Germany, it is no wonder that
the issue attracted antisemitic attention. The theme of 'white slavery' began to
become a mainstay of antisemitic rhetoric in the 1890s in such publications as
Alexander Berg's *Judenbordelle* (Berlin 1892) and Joseph Seidl's *Der Jude des
Neunzehnten Jahrhunderts* (first published in Graz in 1899). In 1892, twenty-
seven traffickers – all Jewish – were tried in a Lemberg court for the charge of
transporting twenty-nine females (twenty of these themselves Jewish) to various destinations abroad. Ten days of hearings resulted in twenty-two convictions, and gave antisemitic publications plenty of time to rehearse the theme –
for example by surveying the 'full extent' of the international trade in vice.[128]

The narrative logic of the antisemitic invective against Jewish white slavery
can be well observed in Joseph Schrank's comparatively subtle 1904 survey of
the theme, under the title of *Der Mädchenhandel und seine Bekämpfung*. Schrank
was an expert on the topic and had published extensively on aspects of prostitution and trade in women since the mid-1880s.[129] Consequently he was elected
president of the afore-mentioned *Österreichische Liga zur Bekämpfung des
Mädchenhandels* despite his clear antisemitic leanings. These are evident in his
practice of citing antisemitic newspapers – including the rabid *Deutsches Volksblatt* – and antisemitic tracts like Berg's radical, in its final lines exterminatory,
Judenbordelle as sources of factual evidence, as well as in his lengthy and
approving quotation from a highly controversial antisemitic interpellation by
the Christian Social parliamentarian Schlesinger that, in the context of the
Lemberg trial, asked 'His Excellency, the Minister President' what measures he

was going to take 'against the harmful offences against all perpetrated by the Jewish people in Austria'.[130] Despite these antisemitic leanings, Schrank denied that his book was 'tendentious in any political, religious or national direction'.[131] Consequently, the antisemitic logic was woven into the fabric of his work, rather than being worn on its sleeve.

In this logic, Jewish traders in women emerged as calculating, highly professionalized and, of course, immoral. Their immorality was motivated by boundless greed: it lay in their ability to trade in human beings as though they were any other type of commodity.[132] Principally these attributes were shared by all traders in women, but Jews seemed to have a specific propensity for the job, and as a result held something close to a monopoly on the trade: '[the traders] are generally in almost all states only Jews'.[133] In this Vienna was no exception, where wine-cellars were said to be packed with Jewish traders on the look-out for victims.[134] While Schrank admitted that the poverty of eastern European Jews may have played a role in this, he immediately went on to assert that economic hardship could hardly be the only cause.[135] His numerous examples of individual Jewish traders stressed their 'devilish cunning': they lured their victims with their gentle manners and with streams of ingratiating presents, or else drugged them with opiates; they communicated with one another utilising clever codes; wore false beards and wigs, and used false names, enabling them to avoid the authorities by switching identities time and again; their unscrupulous rabbis faked marriage certificates and allowed traders to marry their victims *en masse*; and they organised their trade in such a manner that even when arrested only a fraction of their offences could be proven against them.[136] In short, once again Jews were depicted as master criminals who were marked, above all, by their callous criminal competence.

This narrative of the Jewish criminal becomes even clearer when it is compared to other national narratives implicit to Schrank's study. The contrast is particularly stark in the case of the English, whose levels of vice were much decried by the author. However, his entire discussion here shifted its point of view from supply to demand. Schrank dwelled on the English propensity towards sexual perversion – 'In England four sexual phenomena commonly exist, namely: bought marriages, the mania for deflowering, child abuse and flagellation mania' – and lost not a word about the characteristics or habits of English pimps.[137] In other words, the discourse shifted away from hyper-rational Jewish traders to perverse consumers, and, in passing, to the drunk and disorderly parents of the unfortunate victims.[138]

When the victims themselves came to be discussed, one can similarly witness a subtle differentiation by nationality and religion. German victims, for instance, were identified as having been tricked outright, or else as being driven by need and deprivation.[139] Hungarian girls were marked as *leichtsinnig* ['careless' or 'negligent'], implying that they were not without responsibility for their fates.[140] French women were even less obviously victims, and indeed prostitution by force was seen not to be an issue in Paris, because 'there are so many women prone to vice in Paris that there is no need [to trick or force them into brothels].'[141] When it came to Jews, Schrank knew better than not to admit that the vast majority of the Jewish controlled trade involved Jewish women, although he made an exception for Constantinople where, he claimed, Jews primarily sold Christian girls to Turkish customers.[142] And while he accepted that it was poverty that drove Jewish women into the traders' arms,[143] he elsewhere maintained that it was poverty spiked with greed: 'among these [Jewesses in Buenos Aires brothels] there are many who willingly passed themselves over to the traders, to make so much money through prostitution abroad that they could return home and marry or set up a business'.[144] Logically, of course, this claim threatened to undermine much of Schrank's own invective about the traders' great cunning and greedy amorality – how difficult could it be to convince willing 'wares'? – but in this manner Schrank was able to implicate Jews at both ends of the trade, and differentiate between worthy victims and Jewish ones, whose sense of profit, just like the traders', overrode any moral objections.

Schrank's logic in narrating Jewish participation in 'white slavery' is confirmed by far more explicit German antisemitic publications, even by those that employed overtly racist definitions of Jews and blamed their antisocial behaviour on racial characteristics buried in their blood. Alexander Berg's above-mentioned *Judenbordelle* [Jew-brothels], for instance, introduces a pseudo-Darwinian framework in the introduction to this pamphlet that was sold, despite some attempt by the authorities to stop its distribution, up and down Berlin's Friedrichstraße in 1892.[145] Here Jews (and 'Semites' in general') were said to display atavistic, bestial characteristics: humanity's cultural advances had served simply to increase their 'criminal consciousness' by increasing their cunning.[146] Indeed they resembled that 'cleverest and most malicious' of animals, the 'ant-lion' that traps hapless ants without remorse or mercy.[147] Despite this biological claim about the Jewish racial propensity towards crime (a claim that separates Berg's populist hate-rag from most scholarly publications of the period), Berg's actual indictment of the Jewish girl-trader highlighted the same characteristics found in Schrank, namely their cunning exploitation of their victims' need and innocence, their ability to treat the trade in humans matter-of-factly, just like any other sort of trade, and their insidious competence.[148] The main difference was that Berg, unlike Schrank, has no compunctions in making the demonstrably false claim that German (i.e. Christian) maidens were the Jews' principal victims – he maintained that fifty percent of all prostitutes worldwide were Germans – and to boldly insist that *all* brothel-keepers and *Mädchenhändler* were Jews.[149] Otherwise the narrative of Jewish criminals as rational exploiters of modern socio-economic conditions [*Lebensnot*] was unaffected by Berg's biological frame.[150]

Of course, antisemitic narratives of white slavery did tap into sexual anxieties surrounding the defilement of Christian virgins; in fact Berg dwelled on this fear time and again, conjuring up a virtual race-war that was conducted through the defilement of 'the female portion of Aryan peoples'.[151] It is important to note, however, that Jews were narrated primarily as the profit-orientated facilitators of this defilement, not as sexual predators overcome by bestial needs. Schrank, for one, consistently narrated the seduction of females by traders as acts of clever dissimulation that were motivated purely by rational profit-thinking. At no point was there an implication that the traders 'tested' their wares themselves (the closest it came to that was the story of a Jewish trader making her victims take a bath to assess their physical attributes);[152] nor is there any implication that Jewish women signed up to prostitution due to their 'natural lewdness'. Indeed, sexual desire – and sexual perversity – were only mentioned in connection with the English, the Turks and the Chinese.[153] Berg's fringe publication mentioned 'Jewish lewdness' precisely twice, both times in connection not with brothels or white slavery, but by way of explaining how even in societies where licensed brothels were illegal (i.e. in Germany) Jews forced women into prostitution – he claimed that Jewish factory owners seduced female staff, who then had little choice but to become prostitutes.[154] Despite this accusation, which he made in passing (it was clearly motivated by having something bad to say about Jewish behaviour in Germany itself), Berg, too, narrated white slavery as a rational, economic crime, with no sexual basis. Tellingly, when it came to articulating the full horror of the situation, he provided a racial list of 'consumers' that explicitly omitted Jews: thanks to Jewish 'soul-sellers',

> the whole world, indeed the lowest races and the dregs of humanity – the negroes, the Chinese, slaves and mulattoes, the Hottentots, the Turks and Samojeds [Siberian tribesmen who were held to be particularly filthy and savage] – all are able to slake their animal thirst on the betrayed and sold daughters of precisely the German Nation.[155]

The rape of German womanhood was thus narrated as orchestrated but not enacted by Jewish criminal activity.[156]

As such the construction of Jewish *Mädchenhandel* conforms to the construction of Jewish criminals found in Herzl and the statistical debate analysed above. White slavery was precisely the kind of cowardly, non-physical crime de Roos described as Jewish, and that fitted Herz's definition of modern crime as an extension of capitalist commercial activity. What the white slavery discourse highlighted, over the other criminalisations of Jews already discussed, was the international dimension of Jewish criminal activity. It raised the spectre of a Jewish solidarity in crime that transcended the key category of the age – nation – and played into the hands of an antisemitic discourse about a worldwide conspiracy, led by the mysterious *Alliance Israelite*.[157] Reason, modernity, organisation and cunning thus consistently remained at the heart of the different permutations of the narrative of Jewish criminality.

Finally, one should add that antisemitic constructions of the trade in women contrasted starkly with treatments by non-antisemites, and should not be mistaken for a neutral, or mainstream treatment. Other authors were likely to note in passing that Galician Jews were involved in the crime, and otherwise dwelled on social problems that allowed this monstrosity to prosper amongst their midst, for example the dangerous influence of modern fashion. Some went so far as to recommend a change to Swiss-style military service (i.e. periodic short spells of service) to end the unhealthy effects of long-term barracks life, the reduction of factory work-hours so that working-class women could raise their daughters properly, and relentless opposition to the 'fast-living lifestyle' [*flottes Leben*] of contemporary youths.[158] Here, Jewish criminality played no role whatsoever.

Conclusion

Within criminological discourse Jewish criminality, then, was framed above all as a modern and rational criminality. It was on occasion related to their 'racial nature', but this equation rarely strayed into a dedicated determinism, nor did it maintain that an anthropology of Jewish criminality could be written. I have related this strategy of narrating Jewish criminality to currents within contemporary criminology that did not recognise a firm distinction between criminals and non-criminals and that spent significant energies on mapping the implications of an unreliable, suggestible public upon the process of fighting crime. The existence of these anxieties opened up the possibility of popular narratives of crime in which interest in the culprit's inborn/acquired propensity towards crime was by far eclipsed by a focus upon the interaction between manipulative criminal and a public susceptible to such manipulation.

This is not to claim that the only criminal envisioned by determinist criminologies was violent and irrational and hence that such criminologies were necessary incompatible with a narrative of criminal as rational manipulator. Lombroso's, Liszt's or Aschaffenburg's respective theories could all accommodate a perpetrator who on the surface of things was in possession of impressive mental faculties. However, their projects typically focused upon demonstrating deviance behind the guise of wilful rationality. In the lurid newspaper narratives of crime that follow, this presumed essentialist deviance of the criminal was of little interest. Rather, they converted crime into a contest between the public-as-audience and the criminal-as-performer. As such they stressed the Grossian virtues of expert observation and 'phenomenological' description, while eschewing determinist concepts of crime almost entirely.

Notes

1. Parts of this chapter have appeared in: 'Jewish Crimes and Misdemeanours: In Search of Jewish Criminality', *European History Quarterly* 35, 2 (2005), pp. 299–325.

2. Sander L. Gilman, *The Case of Sigmund Freud, Medicine and Identity at the Fin de Siècle* (Baltimore 1993), pp. 169 ff; Sander L. Gilman, *The Jew's Body* (New York 1991), pp. 12, 50. See also: Sander Gilman, *Jewish Self-Hatred: Anti-Semitism and the Hidden Language of the Jews* (Baltimore 1986); Klaus Hödl, *Die Pathologisierung des jüdischen Körpers* (Vienna 1997).

3. See, for instance: M. Kreuzer, 'Ueber anthropologische, physiologische und pathologische Eigenheiten der Juden', in: *Die Welt* 27–9 (5, 12 and 19 July, 1901). One should note that this anthropological study was philosemitic in intent and published in a Zionist weekly.

4. On the most significant exponent of this method, see: Francis Galton's *Inquiries into Human Faculty and Its Development* (New York 1883, reprinted Bristol, England 1998); Francis Galton, 'Photographic Composites', in: *The Photographic News* 29 (April 17/24 1885), pp. 234–45. See also: Nicholas Wright Gillham, *A Life of Sir Francis Galton, From African Exploration to the Birth of Eugenics* (Oxford 2001), pp. 215–19; K. Pearson, *The Life of Francis Galton* (Cambridge 1914–30), Vol. II, p. 293; Sekula, 'The Body', pp. 364–73.

5. Gilman, *Case of Sigmund Freud*, p. 174. Gilman refers to the newspaper coverage of the Jack the Ripper murders in this context. For a close textual analysis of the antisemitic aspects of this coverage, see: L. Perry Curtis, *Jack the Ripper and the London Press* (New Haven 2002), pp. 123–30.

6. For a complementary critique of Gilman's claim that Jewishness and insanity are neatly collapsed throughout the nineteenth century, see: Ann Golding, *Sex, Religion, and the Making of Modern Madness, The Eberbach Asylum and German Society 1815–1849* (Oxford 1999), p. 163.

7. On eighteenth and nineteenth-century narratives of Jewish criminality, see: Uwe Danker, *Räuberbanden im Alten Reich um 1700, Ein Beitrag zur Geschichte von Herrschaft und Kriminalität in der Frühen Neuzeit* (Frankfurt am Main 1988), pp. 318–31; Otto Ulbricht, 'Criminality and Punishment of the Jews in the Early Modern Perood', in: R. Po-Chia Hsia and Hartmann Lehmann (eds), *In and Out of the Ghetto, Jewish- Gentile Relationships in Late Medieval and Early Modern Germany* (Cambridge 1995), pp. 49–70; Mordechai Breuer and Michael Graetz, *German-Jewish History in Modern Times Vol. 1: Tradition and Enlightenment 1600–1780*, (ed.) Michael A. Mayer and Michael Brenner, translated by William Templer (New York 1996), pp. 247–51.

8. A.F. Thiele, *Die jüdischen Gauner in Deutschland, ihre Taktik, ihre Eigenthümlichkeiten und ihre Sprache nebst ausführlichen Nachrichten der in Deutschland und an dessen Grenzen sich aufhaltenden berüchtigten jüdischen Gauner, Nach Kriminalakten und sonstigen zuverlässigen Quellen bearbeitet und zunächst praktischen Criminal- und Polizeibeamten gewidmet, 1. Band, 2. Auflage* (Berlin 1842 [1842]), p. vi. Much of Thiele's argument was anticipated in: K. Schwenken, *Notizen über die berüchtigsten jüdischen Gauner und Spitzbuben welche sich gegenwartig in Deutschland und an dessen Grenzen herumtreiben nebst genauer Beschreibung ihrer Person, nach Criminalakten und sonstigen zuverlässigen Quellen bearbeitet und in alphabetischer Ordnung zusammengestellt* (Marburg 1820).

9. Thiele, *Die jüdischen Gauner*, III, p. 2.

10. Cf. Richard J. Evans, *Tales from the German Underworld* (New Haven 1998), 151; Peter Becker, 'Kriminelle Identitäten', pp. 142–57.

11. Thiele, *Die jüdischen Gauner* 1, V, p. 3.

12. Ibid., p. 10.

13. Ibid., p. 21.

14. Ibid., p. 18.

15. Ibid., pp. 16–18.

16. Ibid., p. 16.

17. Ibid.

18. Ibid.
19. Ibid., p. 10.
20. Ibid.
21. Ibid.
22. Karl Wilhelm Zimmermann, *Der Dieb in Berlin oder Darstellung ihres Entstehens, ihrer Organisation, ihrer Verbindungen, ihrer Taktik, ihrer Gewohnheit und ihrer Sprache. Zur Belehrung für Polizeibeamte und zur Warnung für das Publikum. Nach praktischer Erfahrung* (Berlin 1847), pp. 31–2.
23. Avé-Lallement, *Das Deutsche Gaunerthum* Vol. I, p. 16; Vol. II, p. 32.
24. Ibid., Vol. III, p. 197; Vol. IV, pp. 256–8.
25. Ibid., Vol. I, pp. 15, 17.
26. Friedrich Christian Benedict Avé-Lallement, *Physiologie der deutschen Polizei* (Leipzig 1882), p. 43. See also his list of Jewish contributions to European culture. Ibid., p. 42.
27. Cesare Lombroso, *L'uomo delinquente*. I will be quoting here from the English edition of the text, *Crime, Its Causes and Remedies*.
28. Lombroso, *Crime*, pp. 26–35.
29. Ibid., p. 26.
30. Ibid., pp. 36–42.
31. Ibid., pp. 36–7.
32. For Austria, however, Lombroso's statistics suggest that Jewish crime rates were marginally higher than those of the Gentile population. Ibid., p. 38.
33. Ibid.
34. Ibid., pp. 38–9.
35. Ibid., p. 39.
36. Ibid.
37. Ibid., pp. 23 (Irish criminality), 30–1 (Sicilian criminality), 39–42 (Gypsies).
38. Ibid., p. 39.
39. Ibid., pp. 365–84.
40. Ibid., p. 39
41. Ibid., pp. 365 ff; cf. Strasser, *Verbrechermenschen*, pp. 57–62.
42. Otto Weininger, *Geschlecht und Charakter* (Vienna 1904 [1903]), pp. 409–52; on the debate surrounding Weininger's 'Jewish self-hatred' see: Allan Janik, 'Viennese Culture and the Jewish Self-Hatred Hypothesis: A Critique', in: Oxaal, Pollak and Botz (eds), *Jews*, pp. 75–87; Chandak Sengoopta, *Otto Weininger, Sex, Science and Self in Imperial Vienna* (Chicago 2000), pp. 42–3.
43. Cesare Lombroso, *L'antisemitismo e le science moderne* (Turin 1894); translated into the German as: Cesare Lombroso, *Der Antisemitismus und die Juden im Lichte der modernen Wissenschaft*, translated by H. Kurella (Leipzig 1984), pp. 10–28. Cf. Nancy A. Harrowitz, *Antisemitism, Misogyny and the Logic of Cultural Difference, Cesare Lombroso and Matilde Serao* (London 1994), pp. 41–61.
44. Ibid. See also: Cesare Lombroso, *Der Verbrecher (Homo Delinquens) in anthropologischer, ärztlicher und juristischer Beziehung*, translated by M.O. Fraenkel (Hamburg 1890–96), Vol. 1, p. 535. Mariacarla Gadebusch Bondio, *Die Rezeption der Kriminalanthropologischen Ideen von Cesare Lombroso in Deutschland* (Husum 1995), pp. 111–14.
45. Lombroso, *L'antisemitismo*, 100; cf. Harrowitz, *Antisemitism*, p. 47.
46. Harrowitz, *Antisemitism*, pp. 43–7.
47. Ibid., pp. 52, 57. Lombroso and Ferrero, *Criminal Woman*, p. 102.
48. Harrowitz does claim that Lombroso ascribes atavism to Jews, but like Gilman she can make this argument only by analogy. See: Harrowitz, *Antisemitism*, pp. 48, 52.
49. On the Jewish/Zionist use of race science, see: John E Efron, *Defenders of the Race, Jewish Doctors and Race Science in Fin-de-Siècle Europe* (New Haven 1994), pp. 9–12, 76–8, 123–6, 174.

50. M. Kreuzer, 'Ueber anthropologische, physiologische und pathologische Eigenheiten der Juden', in: *Die Welt* 27–9 (5, 12 and 19 July, 1901).

51. Francis Galton, 'Photographic Composites,' in: *The Photographic News* 29 (April 17, 1885); Joseph Jacobs, 'The Jewish Type, and Galton's Composite Photographs,' in: *The Photographic News* 29 (April 24, 1885), pp. 234–45. See also: *Jewish Encyclopaedia*, 12 Vols. (New York 1901–1906), Vol. 12, p. 294; Efron, *Defenders*, pp. 62–88.

52. Cf. Radkau, *Zeitalter*, p. 333. One should remember that terms like 'nervousness' were themselves part of a complex and contested vocabulary. Emile Durkheim for instance argued that neurasthenics were by nature innovative and hence the true motors of progress in modern society. Ibid., p. 267.

53. For a good summary of the question about the distinctiveness of a Jewish race, see: Ritchie Robertson, *The Jewish Question in German Literature, 1749–1939, Emancipation and its Discontents* (Oxford 1999), pp. 164 ff.

54. For example: Anonymous, *Der Konitzer Mord, Ein Beitrag zur Klärung* (Breslau 1900); Albert Hellwig, *Ritualmord und Aberglaube* (Minden i.W. n.d.). Many such books were reviewed by Hans Gross in his *Archiv*: Hans Gross, 'Buchbesprechung: Anonymous, *Der Konitzer Mord, Ein Beitrag zur Klärung* (Breslau 1900)', in: *Archiv* 4 (1900), pp. 363–5; Hans Gross, 'Buchbesprechung: D. Chwolson, *Die Blutanklage und sonstige mittelalterliche Beschuldigungen der Juden, Eine historische Untersuchung nach den Quellen* (Frankfurt am Main 1901 [1880])', in: *Archiv* 9 (1902), pp. 240–1; Hans Gross, 'Buchbesprechung: Carl Mommert, *Menschenopfer bei den alten Hebräern* (Leipzig 1905)', in: *Archiv* 24 (1906), p. 176; Hans Gross, 'Buchbesprechung: Carl Mommert, *Der Ritualmord bei den Talmudjuden* (Leipzig 1905)', in: *Archiv* 24 (1906), p. 176; Hans Gross, 'Buchbesprechung: Maximilian Paul-Schiff, *Der Prozeß Hilsner, Aktenauszug* (Vienna 1908)', in: *Archiv* 29 (1908), p. 314; Hans Gross, 'Buchbesprechung: Albert Hellwig, *Ritualmord und Aberglaube* (Minden i.W. n.d.)', in: *Archiv* 59 (1914), p. 377. See also my discussion in chapter six.

55. The argument, of course, allowed antisemites to continue with their defamations of 'Jewish butchers' - Gross's antisemitism is evident here as it is elsewhere in his work.

56. Albert Hellwig, 'Jüdischer Meineidsaberglaube', in: *Archiv* 41 (1911), pp. 126–41.

57. For example M. Eschelbacher's 'Jüdischer Meineidsaberglaube?', in: *Archiv* 54 (1913), pp. 130–9 attacks Hellwig's assertion as to the existence of such a belief.

58. Paul Näcke, 'Rasse und Verbrechen', in: *Archiv* 25 (1906), pp. 64–73.

59. Ibid., p. 66.

60. Näcke, *Verbrechen*, p. 176.

61. For an alternative discussion of some of this material, see: Gilman, *Case of Sigmund Freud*, pp. 179 ff. Gilman focuses on sexual crimes, specifically incest, even though the debate he discusses touches on such crimes only very marginally, and then largely to de-sexualise Jews.

62. Das Comite zur Abwehr antisemitischer Angriffe in Berlin (ed.), *Die Kriminalität der Juden in Deutschland* (Berlin 1896), p. 56. The figures are based on convictions.

63. Rudolf Wassermann, *Beruf, Konfession und Verbrechen. Eine Studie über die Kriminalität der Juden in Vergangenheit und Gegenwart* (Munich 1907); Rudolf Wassermann, 'Die Kriminalität der Juden in Deutschland in den letzten 25 Jahren (1882–1906)', in: *Monatsschrift* 6 (1909/10), pp. 609–18. Cf. also: *Die Kriminalität der Juden in Deutschland*; A. Ruppin 'Der Rassenstolz der Juden', *Zeitschrift für Demographie und Statistik der Juden* 6 (1910), pp. 88–92; Ludwig Fuld, *Das jüdische Verbrecherthum, Eine Studie über den Zusammenhang zwischen Religion und Kriminalität* (Leipzig 1885).

64. Wassermann, 'Die Kriminalität', pp. 612–13.

65. Ibid.

66. Franz v. Liszt, 'Das Problem der Kriminalität der Juden', in: *Festschrift für die juristische Fakultät in Giessen zum Universitäts-Jubiläum*, hrsg. Reinhard Frank (Giessen 1907),

p. 377. Gilman misrepresents Liszt's contribution to the debate as being basically identical with Wassermann's. Cf. Sander Gilman, *Case of Sigmund Freud*, p. 182.

67. J.R.B. de Roos, 'Über die Kriminalität der Juden', in: *Monatsschrift* 6 (1909/10), pp. 196, 204.

68. Ibid., p. 196.

69. Ibid.

70. Ibid. The quotation is taken from Näcke's article 'Rasse und Verbrechen'.

71. Hugo Herz, *Verbrechen und Verbrechertum in Österreich, Kritische Untersuchungen über Zusammenhänge von Wirtschaft und Verbrechen* (Tübingen 1908), pp. 167–92.

72. Ibid., p. 173.

73. Ibid.

74. Ibid., p. 318.

75. Cf. van Arkel, *Antisemitism*, pp. 7, 169.

76. Werner Sombart, *Die Juden und das Wirtschaftsleben* (Leipzig 1911). For similar views, see: Lazar Felix Pinkus, *Die Moderne Judenfragen, Von den Grundlagen der jüdischen Wirtschaftsgeschichte und des Zionismus* (Breslau 1903); Georg Simmel, 'Die Philosophie des Geldes', in: *Georg Simmel Gesamtausgabe* Vol. 2 (Frankfurt am Main 1989 [1892]), p. 305.

77. Sombart, *Die Juden*, pp. 328–34, 384–402. See also: Friedrich Lenger, *Werner Sombart 1863–1941, Eine Biographie* (Munich 1994), pp. 187–201; Derek Penslar, *Shylock's Children: Economics and Jewish Identity in Modern Europe* (Berkeley 2001), pp. 165–73.

78. Sombart, *Die Juden*, p. 179.

79. Lenger, *Werner Sombart*, pp. 201–7. Sombart himself attacked a crude conception of race, and endorsed a more dynamic vision of Jewish identity, which he termed 'genetic'. See: Sombart, *Die Juden*, pp. 384–400.

80. Cf. Kočmata, *Jugend*, pp. 9 ff.

81. Golding, *Sex*, pp. 162–82.

82. On the notion of rational Jews as the negative image of enlightenment ideals of rationality, see: Robertson, *Jewish Question*, pp. 181, 194.

83. On nineteenth-century thought on and treatment of Gypsies, see: Rainer Hehemann, *Die 'Bekämpfung des Zigeunerwesens' im Wilhelminischen Deutschland und in der Weimarer Republik, 1871–1933* (Frankfurt am Main 1987), pp. 87–90, 403–14; Joachim S. Hohmann, *Geschichte der Zigeunerverfolgung in Deutschland* (Frankfurt am Main 1981), pp. 66–71.

84. Alfred Ploetz, *Die Tüchtigkeit unserer Rasse und der Schutz der Schwachen* (Berlin 1895), pp. 130–42.

85. Lombroso, *Crime*, p. 39.

86. Ibid., p. 40.

87. Herz, *Verbrechen*, pp. 157–8.

88. Ibid., p. 160.

89. Ibid., p. 164.

90. Ibid., p. 165. Cf. Gross, *Handbuch*, pp. 337, 352.

91. Gross, *Handbuch*, p. 340. Quoted in: Herz, *Verbrechen*, p. 163.

92. Ibid., p. 167.

93. Gross, *Handbuch*, p. 339.

94. Ibid., pp. 333–4.

95. Ibid., p. 352.

96. Ibid., pp. 348, 556.

97. Gross, 'Aufgaben und Ziele', p. 2. Gross's emphasis.

98. Arno Pilgram makes a similar argument about present-day police narratives of eastern European criminality. These, too, tend to become the more outlandish the more 'exotic' the criminals under scrutiny. Cf. Arno Pilgram, 'Wirklichkeitskonstruktionen

im Vergleich: Polizei und Unternehmer im Ost-West-geschäft über "Organisierte Kriminalität"', in: Martina Althoff *et al.* (ed.), *Integration und Ausschließung, Kriminalität und Kriminalpolitik in Zeiten gesellschaftlicher Transformation* (Baden-Baden 2001); Hermann Kuschej and Arno Pilgram, 'Fremdenfeindlichkeit im Diskurs um "Organisierte Kriminalität"', in: Karin Liebhart *et al.* (ed.), *Fremdbilder-Feindbilder-Zerrbilder* (Klagenfurt 2002).

99. Cf. Benedict Anderson, *Imagined Communities, Reflections on the Origins and Spread of Nationalism* (London 1983), pp. 66–79.

100. Gilman, *Jewish Self-Hatred*, pp. 209 ff.; Gilman, *Jew's Body*, pp. 11 ff.

101. Thiele, *Die jüdischen Gauner* Vol 1, pp. 193 ff.

102. Avé-Lallement, *Das Deutsche Gaunerthum*, Vol. III, pp. 186 ff.

103. Ibid., Part IV, pp. 254–61.

104. Avé-Lallement's findings were anticipated by Casper Dietrich Christensen, a Kiel policeman. See: Dankert, *Räuberbanden*, p. 327.

105. Hans Kurella, *Naturgeschichte des Verbrechers, Grundzüge der criminellen Anthropologie und Criminalpsychologie* (Stuttgart 1893), p. 220.

106. Ibid., p. 222.

107. Ibid., pp. 224–7.

108. Lombroso, *Verbrecher*, Vol. 1, p. 388.

109. Gross, *Handbuch*, pp. 286, 292–333.

110. Sommer, 'Ueber die Mexikanische Gaunersprache', in: *Archiv* 28, 3.+4. Doppelheft (1907), pp. 209–14; Ernst Lohsing, 'Tschechoslawisches in der Gaunersprache', in: *Archiv* 13 (1903), pp. 279–85; Vladimir Čačič 'Kroatische Wörter im Vocabulare der Gaunersprache des Großschen Handbuchs für Untersuchungsrichter', in: *Archiv* 9 (1902), pp. 298–310; Max Pollack, 'Wiener Gaunersprache', in: *Archiv* 15 (1904), pp. 171–205. The last named does include Yiddish words, but does not identify them as Jewish. In his list of criminal sources for the listed words the vast majority of criminals are identified as 'Catholic'.

111. Hans Gross, 'Buchbesprechung: August Schacht, *Rottwälsch oder Kaloschensprache, Ein Blick in die Geheimnisse des Gaunerthums* (Berlin n.d.)', in: *Archiv* 4 (1900), p. 352.

112. For a technical, linguistic analysis of the actual links between criminal language and Jewish German, see: Paul Wexler, 'Languages in Contact: The Case of Rotwelsch and the Two Yiddishes', in: Po-Chia Hsia and Lehmann (eds), *Ghetto*, pp. 109–24.

113. On the rise of statistical analyses of racial criminality in the 1920s, see: Arno Pilgram, *Kriminalität in Österreich, Studien zur Soziologie der Kriminalitätsentwicklung* (Vienna 1980), pp. 113 ff.

114. Näcke, 'Rasse und Verbrechen', pp. 64–73.

115. Cf. Pauley, *From Prejudice*, pp. 86–8.

116. Of course anthropological studies of Jewish or 'Semitic' anthropometric data existed, but these were not exploited by criminologists.

117. Radkau, *Zeitalter*, pp. 331 ff.

118. A. Pilcz, 'Vergleichende rassenpsychiatrische Studien', Anthropologische Gesellschaft in Wien, Sitzung vom 16. Januar 1906 as printed in: *Monatsschrift* 2 (1905/6), p. 754.

119. Ibid.

120. Ibid.

121. Edward J. Bristow, *Prostitution and Prejudice, The Jewish Fight against White Slavery 1870–1939* (New York 1983), pp. 34, 111ff.

122. Ibid., pp. 41, 236ff. See also: Mark Thomas Connelly, *The Response to Prostitution in the Progressive Era* (Chapel Hill 1990).

123. Bristow jumps to this conclusion on what I believe to be rather slender evidence: while many tracts about the issue were published, it is doubtful that their popularity proves that a popular 'panic' took place. Bristow, *Prostitution*, pp. 37–8, 41–2.

124. Peter Gay, *Schnitzler's Century, The Making of Middle-Class Culture 1815–1914* (New York 2002), pp. 130–2; Anna Hauer, 'Sexualität und Sexualmoral in Östereich um 1900, Theoretische und Literarische Texte von Frauen', in: Wiener Historikerinnen (ed.), *Die ungeschriebene Geschichte, Historische Frauenforschung, Dokumentation 5. Historikerinnentreffen* (Vienna 1985); Nike Wagner, *Geist und Geschlecht, Karl Kraus und die Erotik der Wiener Moderne* (Frankfurt am Main 1982), p. 159 and *passim*. See also the short discussion of a 1909 brothel novel: Karin Jušek, 'Ein Wiener Bordellroman, Else Jerusalems "Heiliger Skarabäus,"' in: Heide Dienst and Edith Saurer (eds), *Das Weib existiert nicht für sich* (Vienna 1990), pp. 123–42; Marion A. Kaplan, *The Jewish Feminism Movement in Germany, The Campaigns of the Jüdischer Frauenbund, 1904–1938* (London 1979), pp. 139–47.

125. Bristow, *Prostitution*, pp. 106, 240–1.

126. Some surveys put the proportion of Jewish prostitutes in Buenos Aires brothels at as high as ninety percent. Cf. Deutsches Nationalkomitee zu internationaler Bekämpfung des Mädchenhandels (ed.), *Der Mädchenhandel und seine Bekämpfung* (Berlin 1903), p. 8. On Austrian *Mädchenhandel*, see also: Lothar Höbling, 'Der Österreichisch-Ungarische Mädchenhandel in den Akten des Bundesdirektionsarchivs Wien', (MA Diss. Univ. Wien 1996); Anna Staudacher, 'Die Aktion "Girondo". Zur Geschichte des internationalen Mädchenhandels in Österreich-Ungarn um 1885', in: Dienst and Saurer (eds), *Weib*, pp. 97–138; Kaplan, *Jewish Feminism*, pp. 103–45. On the Galician conditions that fostered Jewish prostitution, see: Klaus Hödl, *Als Bettler in der Leopoldstadt, Galizische Juden auf dem Weg nach Wien* (Vienna 1994), pp. 67–74.

127. Bristow, *Prostitution*, p. 263.

128. Ibid., pp. 73–80, 250–1. For antisemitic coverage in the Viennese dailies, see especially *DV*, 22 October–1 November 1892. For an antisemitic 'summary' of the affair, see: Alexander Berg, *Judenhyänen vor dem Strafgericht zu Lemberg, ein bestätigender Nachtrag zu seiner Schrift 'Judenbordelle'* (Berlin 1893).

129. Josef Schrank, *Die Prostitution in Wien in historischer, administrativer und hygienischer Beziehung*, 2 Vols. (Vienna 1886); Josef Schrank, *Die Regelung der Prostitution in Kairo* (Vienna 1890); Josef Schrank, *Die amtlichen Vorschriften, betreffend die Prostitution in Wien in ihrer administrativen, sanitären und strafgerechtlichen Anwendungen* (Vienna 1899); Josef Schrank, 'Prostitution in Madrid', in: *Deutsche Vierteljahrsschrift für öffentliche Gesundheitspflege* Vol. 31, 3 (1889).

130. Josef Schrank, *Der Mädchenhandel und seine Bekämpfung* (Vienna 1904), pp. 30, 41, 91, 250; quotation from p. 92. The full text of Schlesinger's interpellation can be found in: *Stenografisches Protokoll über die Sitzungen des Hauses der Abgeordneten des österreichischen Reichsrats in den Jahren 1892 und 1893*, 9. Session, Vol. 7 (Vienna 1893), 11 Nov. 1892, pp. 7638ff.

131. Schrank, *Mädchenhandel*, p. iii.

132. See for example Schrank's story of an unscrupulous female trader who is simply and repeatedly identified as 'the Jewess'. Ibid., p. 14.

133. Ibid., 41. Schrank is here quoting a report from the antisemitic *Reichspost* from 30 July 1899. For further statements on the predominance of Jews in this criminal profession, see: ibid., pp. 29, 96.

134. Ibid., p. 38.

135. Ibid., p. 41.

136. Ibid., pp. 14, 15, 26–9, 59, 91.

137. Ibid., pp. 49–50. Schrank's vision of English perversity is much influenced by the framework given to prostitution by the 1885 articles in W.T. Stead's *The Maiden Tribute of Modern Babylon*, which focused on the sale of young virgins. For an analysis of this, see: Judith Walkowitz, *City of Dreadful Delight, Narratives of Sexual Danger in Late-Victorian London* (London 1992), pp. 85 ff.

138. Schrank, *Mädchenhandel*, p. 51.
139. Ibid., pp. 38, 53.
140. Ibid., p. 42.
141. Ibid., p. 52.
142. Ibid., p. 58.
143. Ibid., p. 40.
144. Ibid., p. 42.
145. Bristow, *Prejudice*, p. 251.
146. Alexander Berg, *Judenbordelle, Enthüllungen aus dunklen Häusern* (Berlin 1892), pp. 5–6.
147. Ibid., p. 7.
148. Ibid., pp. 21–8. The same narrative appears in Joseph Seidl, *Der Jude des 19. Jahrhunderts, oder warum sind wir Antisemiten?* (print run 11–14,000, Munich 1900), pp. 87–9.
149. Berg, *Judenbordelle*, pp. 10, 36.
150. The theme of unfavourable modern conditions, and their links to 'Jewish' capitalism, was periodically reiterated by Berg. Cf. ibid., pp. 9, 21, 34.
151. Ibid., p. 10.
152. Schrank, *Mädchenhandel*, p. 91.
153. Ibid., pp. 59, 64.
154. Berg, *Judenbordelle*, pp. 28, 33. Berg is here re-rehearsing an older antisemitic narrative that blamed Jews for society's moral decay. This narrative did not usually make reference to criminality. See, for example, Thomas Frey (a.k.a. Theodor Fritsch) *Antisemiten-Katechismus, Eine Zusammenstellung des wichtigsten Materials zum Verständnis der Judenfrage* (6th ed., Leipzig 1888), pp. 18–19. Elsewhere Frey marks Jews as sexually 'passionless' and characterised by extreme 'self-control' (ibid., pp. 12–13). He provides no analysis of white slavery, and treats Jewish crime as a function of unscrupulous business strategies (ibid., p. 16).
155. Ibid., p. 36.
156. Bristow repeatedly suggests that white slavery accusations represent the 'sexualisation' of ritual murder accusations, on slender evidence. If the phrase is taken to mean that the sexual implications of Jews doing away with young Christian maidens latent in ritual murder affairs were literalised in the antisemitic treatment of white slavery, this ignores the fact that Jews were not primarily constructed as sexual predators in antisemitic treatments of the issue. Bristow, *Prejudice*, pp. 4, 46, 82.
157. For the origins of the narrative of a Jewish world conspiracy, and its fin-de-siècle incarnation, see: Norman Cohn, *Warrant for Genocide, The myth of the Jewish World Conspiracy and the Protocols of the Elders of Zion*, Brown Judaic Studies 23 (Chica, Calif. 1981 [1969]), pp. 25–31, 54–9.
158. S. Mexin, *Der Mädchenhandel* (Basel 1904), pp. 78–9.

Chapter 4

PAPER TRIALS

> No sooner was I awake than I sat down to answer Henri van Blarenberghe. But before doing so, I wanted just to glance at *Le Figaro*, to proceed to that abominable and voluptuous act known as *reading the paper*, thanks to which all the miseries and catastrophes of the world during the past twenty-four hours – battles that have cost the lives of fifty-thousand men, crimes, strikes, bankruptcies, fires, poisonings, suicides, divorces, the shattering emotions of statesmen and actors alike – are transmuted for our own particular use, though we are not ourselves involved, into a daily feast that seems to make a peculiarly exciting and stimulating accompaniment to the swallowing of a few mouthfuls of coffee brought in response to our summons.
>
> Marcel Proust, 'Final Sentiments of a Parricide.'[1]

Following the enormous proliferation of printed matter that accompanied the various 1848 revolutions – fuelled by the need to spread the revolutionary message, and helped along by the temporary relaxation of censorship laws – the newspaper established itself across Europe as a central institution of bourgeois life.[2] By the start of the twentieth century (and in some European countries much earlier) it had consolidated on this success through the birth of mass journalism. Urbanisation and growing literacy rates facilitated the gradual penetration of a much broader strata of society, in particular those who lived in the *fin-de-siècle* urban centres of London, Berlin, Paris, or Vienna.[3] Contemporaries were well aware of the cultural importance of the newspaper within their lives, and of the papers' symbiotic relationship with the city, to which it provided a guide as well as a commentary.[4] One need not take Proust's word for this, who, not unusually for a bourgeois commentator, if with greater literary flourish, highlighted the frivolity of newspaper consumption as well as its hypnotic power. Contemporary cultural critics and sociologists like Albert Schäffle, Max Weber or Ferdinand Tönnies,[5] ever growing circulation numbers, the centrality of newspapers in late nineteenth century fiction – particularly detective fiction, from Poe to Collins, Conan Doyle and beyond – as well as the self-congratulatory celebrations of their commercial and cultural success found within the papers' columns themselves all attested to the importance of that daily (and often twice daily) fix of news to which contemporaries had grown accustomed.[6] Historians tend to agree with this contemporary verdict, and mark out newspapers as a key agent of social change, specifically the rise of individualism, the growing division between private and public spheres, and the spread of secularisation: by the late nineteenth century, for a significant part of the population, 'communion with the Sunday paper had replaced churchgoing.'[7]

In Austria the rise of the mass paper was a somewhat deferred process, held back by the triple obstructions of high taxation on newspaper advertisements (the *Inseratsteuer*), strict limits on the degree to which sensitive political material – including parliamentary debates – could be reported (*Kolportageverbot*) and the existence of the *Zeitungsstempel*, a newspaper tax that had made the publication of a cheap, small-format paper well-nigh impossible.[8] Government intervention in journalistic output was traditionally very high: prior to 1848, Vienna was home to no more than three daily papers, all of which were either government controlled, or else heavily censored.[9] These various obstructions gradually disappeared, and the lifting on the *Zeitungsstempel* on the second of January 1900 finally opened the doors for the rise of a genuine mass-paper, the *Illustrierte Kronenzeitung*, which reigned supreme as the most successful national paper until the rise of a new and even more determinedly popular press after the First World War eventually began to challenge its position.[10]

In spite of this delayed rise of a newspaper mass culture, Vienna's contemporary journalistic landscape was both varied and expansive, with a total circulation of Austrian German-language dailies in 1905 running well over 500,000 copies, the majority of which were bought and consumed by the capital city's population of around 1.8 million.[11] Given that newspapers were often shared within a household and among colleagues, or else read in one of Vienna's many cafés, the dissemination of news among the urban population must have been considerable.[12] Virtually all these papers contained daily reports on crimes and trials within Vienna and beyond.

Before jumping head-first into an analysis of crime reporting in contemporary newspapers, one should perhaps consider what such an analysis can possibly uncover. How much does the construction of criminality found in newspapers tell us about how contempories talked and thought about criminality? Historically, this question is notoriously hard to answer, and any evidence presented would almost invariably be anecdotal. Contemporary commentators, like the above mentioned sociologist Albert Schäffle, or indeed those criminologists worried about the 'suggestive' power of printed matter, were inclined to stress the power of papers to create, change or destroy public opinion.[13] Habermas's influential thesis about the exclusion of the public from political debate from the second half of the nineteenth century onwards, likewise stresses the influence of sensationalist papers over the public: their role was both to manipulate opinion and to dazzle their readers by presenting politics purely in terms of a spectacle in order to ensure their passivity.[14] Empirically based studies on reading behaviour, however, urge us to question this assumed passivity and lack of critical faculty. Arno Pilgram, for instance, argues against the glib assumption that present-day media consumers are not aware of the process of deliberate selection and sensationalist magnification with which crime-stories are put together.[15] Indeed, he points out that very often the readers of the so-called 'boulevard' or 'gutter' press are the ones most critical of their own reading habits, chiding their papers' reporting standards as shoddy, their emphasis on scandal as 'trashy' and 'immoral', and their general tone as deliberately hyperbolic. Recent work on the Weimar political press, similarly stresses the lack of correlation between the public's voting behaviour and their paper consumption.[16] While neither example should be imposed upon the Viennese readership, they warn us against a simple model that assumes that the contemporary reader was an uncritical vessel into which papers could pour their partial truths without any resistance.[17] Indeed, as I shall argue, there existed a self-reflective discourse *within* contemporary papers on the machinations of the press and their truth-distorting habits. In this manner they actively added to the circulation of a language that might very well generate a culture of distrust towards newspaper coverage of crime.

This tale of potential consumer scepticism towards the accuracy of the vision of the world constructed by newspapers does not, however, render newspapers useless as historical sources that provide insight into the public's understanding of criminality. The question that demands investigation is whether potential consumer scepticism towards their papers was more significant than the fact of consumption itself. What was being consumed here was clearly language. What was being resisted, to a small or large degree, was, however, not so much the language but rather the veracity of the newspapers' coverage about crimes. In other words, even if newspapers were frequently and commonly disbelieved – and perhaps disbelieved in precisely those terms coined by newspapers in their numerous articles that criticise other paper's attempts at dissimulation – the words in which these dubious stories were communicated were still consumed en masse. This language represented what could publicly and decently be said, and must have had a crucial impact on the conceptual vocabulary available to the public. Embedded within this conceptual vocabulary was a specific knowledge about criminality. While rival, private conceptualisations of crime may also have existed, there is no real justification in treating those as more important or 'authentic' than those disseminated day-in-day-out by the press: it is, after all, in public articulation and not in private thought that culture and society 'take place'.

In this context one may also wonder, how much the knowledge created by the papers was shaped by government censorship (regulated by Article 302 of the contemporary Austrian legal code), even after the lifting of the *Kolportage-verbot* at the turn of the century. Indeed, the confiscation of papers on the grounds that their contents constituted 'agitation' was a regular if not frequent event.[18] The 'agitation' in question, incidentally, could be of antisemitic, anti-Protestant, anti-Catholic or anti-capitalist nature, and virtually all papers here discussed, including the illustrious *Neue Freie Presse*, were at times subject to this charge.[19] While this indicates that the government set limits to what could be said in *fin-de-siècle* Vienna, a look at trial documents also indicates that for the most part, officials were loath to gag the media. This becomes clear when one studies the correspondence surrounding a 1905 'secret' trial concerning a sexual crime, to which public access was denied. The authorities here decried their 'powerlessness' in curbing paper coverage and the dissemination of the trial 'almost down to the word'.[20] One can only conclude that public discourse in *fin-de-siècle* Vienna was rule-bound, but that there was ample room to manoeuvre within these rules and that the trial report in particular represented a journalistic space that could not easily be censored. This was one of the reasons why it proved such fertile ground for antisemitic agitation.

The Viennese Papers

Tables 4.1 and 4.2 provide an overview of the papers whose trial and crime reporting are analysed in this book.[21] These include the *Deutsches Volksblatt* (antisemitic, racialist) and *Kikeriki* (antisemitic and satirical), the *Reichspost* (Catholic-antisemitic), *Vaterland* (Catholic with antisemitic leanings), the *Illustriertes Wiener Extrablatt* and the *Illustrierte Kronenzeitung* (populist/liberal and populist, respectively), the *Arbeiter-Zeitung* (socialist) and the *Neue Freie Presse* (highbrow liberal). Occasional reference will be made to the *Ostdeutsche Rundschau* (antisemitic), *Die Welt* and the *Österreichische Wochenschrift* (Zionist and self-consciously Jewish, respectively), Karl Kraus's *Die Fackel* (uncategoriseable) and the *Neues Wiener Tagblatt* (liberal).[22] I have excluded non-German language papers circulated in Vienna on the grounds of their typically very small circulation numbers. Zionist and other self-consciously Jewish publications rarely had regular crime coverage and therefore do not receive detailed analysis in this thesis, with the exception of the *Österreichische Wochenschrift*'s coverage of the Hilsner trial, a journal that was edited by the Rabbi Joseph Samuel Bloch.

All the papers named here covered crime on a daily basis. Overwhelmingly this coverage took the shape of trial reports, overshadowing reports on crimes in a ratio that was routinely upwards from three-to-one.[23] Viennese dailies all carried a regular trial column, and, as we shall see, individual issues of the more popular papers could on occasion cover little else but a single trial sensation. These reports enjoyed tremendous popularity and could be central to a paper's commercial success.[24] There can be little doubt that they were avidly consumed and much discussed by contemporaries.[25] These reports need to be understood as a distinct literary genre whose rules can be described and analysed. Buried within these reports lay coherent strategies of how to think about criminality,

Table 4.1 Publication and circulation data of key Viennese newspapers

Table 4.1 provides publication and circulation data for the Viennese newspapers under scrutiny. It also indicates the relative importance trial reporting had for individual papers, and classifies the papers according to political orientation.

Paper	Frequency of circulation	Date of first publication	Circulation c. 1900/1910	Illustrations	Political orientation	Length of trial columns
Deutsches Volksblatt	twice daily	1888	c. 50,000 (1904)/25,000	N	antisemitic	***
Reichspost	daily	1895	6,5000/2,3000	N	Catholic-antisemitic	**
Vaterland	twice daily	1860	c. 7,000/5,000	N	Catholic	*
Kikeriki	twice weekly	1860	data not available	Y	antisemitic (satirical)	N/A
Illustrierte Kronenzeitung	daily	1900	100,000 (1906)/200,000 (1912)	Y	populist	****
Illustriertes Wiener Extrablatt	twice daily	1872	c. 30,000 (1904)	Y	populist (liberal)	****
Arbeiter-Zeitung	daily	1889	24,000/54,000 (1914)	N	socialist	***
Neue Freie Presse	twice daily	1864	55,000/50,000 (1914)	N	liberal	***

The 'Length of trial' column denotes the average space devoted to trials. **** indicates that trials were covered daily, at an average of more than three columns, and would, on occasion, constitute more than half of the paper's total daily news. Both papers marked with **** were illustrated dailies, and dedicated a substantial part of their illustrations to the topic of crime. *** indicates that coverage was regular and substantial. Occasional issues carried no coverage, but on other days coverage could fill as many as twelve or more columns. ** indicates that coverage was regular but often short. Major trials could still fill up to nine columns, but otherwise coverage could be as short as a quarter column. * indicates irregular coverage. Even major trials were unlikely to be reported in more than two columns.

Table 4.2 Newspaper characteristics (overview)

Table 4.2 provides a discursive overview of the main characteristics of the Viennese newspapers under scrutiny.

Deutsches Volksblatt Radically and dedicatedly antisemitic paper edited by Ernst Vergani, covering everything from local and international politics, business news (including investment advice), sports, trials and other sensations. German-nationalist and racialist. Significant advertising, frequent and lengthy serialised novels. Length could vary from 12 to 22 pages.*

Reichspost The main propagandistic voice of the Christian Social Party. Catholic, conservative, antisemitic. Political, foreign and local news, the latter focused entirely upon Vienna. Length typically 12 pages.

Vaterland The monarchy's leading Catholic paper. Mostly political and foreign news. Much of its cultural news explicitly addressed religious/church-political issues. Opposed extreme nationalism. Competed with the *Reichspost* for readers, though less populist in nature. Length usually 8, occasionally 12 pages.

Kikeriki Antisemitic satirical magazine, that provided a mixture of humorous poems and songs, cartoons, jokes, fake letters and articles, and commentary. Xenophobic and irreverent, routinely satirising the monarchy and the government. An anthropomorphised rooster was its symbol. Length alternated between 4 and 10 pages.

Illustrierte Kronenzeitung Austria's biggest and most populist paper post-1903. Small format. Made its name with the coverage of the Hungarian Draga Maschin murder, to which it sent its own correspondents and illustrator. Mostly trial and local news, small advertisements. Question and answer columns. Frequent and lengthy serialised novels. Its founder, Gustav Davis, published the conservative, monarchist *Reichswehr*. Length typically 16 pages.

Illustriertes Wiener Extrablatt A populist paper with liberal leanings. The first major German-language illustrated paper in Austria, and one of the first illustrated papers in Europe. Favoured sensationalist and local news over political news. Stressed its devotion to king and emperor. Often moralistic in tone. Frequent and lengthy serialised novels. Length typically 16 pages.

Arbeiter-Zeitung The 'central organ of Austrian Social Democracy' (sub-title), with frequent contributions by key party leaders (such as Viktor Adler). Mostly local political and party political news, but also covered wider cultural issues. Some advertisements and serialised novels. Length typically 10–12 pages.

Neue Freie Presse Vienna's premier bourgeois/liberal paper with a high standard of journalism, a well-known *feuilleton*, detailed political and economic news, and an air of objectivity and rationality that irked Karl Kraus and other critics who saw it as a destructive social force. Famed art and music critiques. Its main competitor was the *Neues Wiener Tagblatt*, that had a similar flavour. Lengthy advertisement section. Length 22–32 pages.

---

* All references to length refer to morning editions on a weekday (not Monday).

that ran across the various papers – strategies that answered the readers' basic need to understand their lives and the events taking place in their city and their country in terms of narrative patterns.[26] Our initial task then, is to systematically describe how these papers constructed criminals, what methods they used to identify them, and to relate these strategies to the contemporary debates within criminology and criminalistics already discussed. The next section will provide the close analysis of a paradigmatic murder sensation, that of Franziska Klein and Johann Heinrich Klein. Only then can we turn to the problem of how antisemitic publications could exploit the genre of crime and trial reports by spinning tales of Jewish crime.

The Klein Murder Scandal

The murder trial of Franziska and Johann Heinrich Klein was one of the period's most remarked upon sensation trials, outdone only by the outrage that surrounded the Dreyfus Affair (1894 to 1899), the Hilsner ritual murder trials (1899 and 1900) and the killing of the Serbian royal couple (1903). The case makes fascinating reading. On the eleventh of October 1904 the corpse of Johann Sikora, aged seventy-one, was discovered in a sack, hidden under the Kleins' living-room sofa in their flat in Magdalenenstraße 78 in Vienna's sixth district. Both of the corpse's legs had been cut off at the knee in order to make it fit. The Kleins – who had only married on the fourth of September, and were therefore frequently referred to as a 'honeymoon couple' – had run off to Paris, but were arrested in due course and extradited by the French authorities. They faced trial in Vienna from the twenty-sixth to the twenty-ninth of April, 1904. In the course of the trial it was revealed that Franziska Klein, a former nun, had turned to prostitution within a week after her marriage, which had itself been the result of a personal advertisement in the papers. Sikora was one of her customers, and had courted her some six years previously, a relationship that ended – according to Franziska Klein – with her being raped by both Sikora and an unnamed friend. Klein also maintained that either Sikora, or else his friend, was the father of a daughter whose whereabouts she described as unknown. Despite this earlier association, Sikora seems not to have recognised Franziska Klein ('By God, with his many affairs he had no way of remembering').[27] According to the prosecutor she had lured Sikora into her flat on the third of October and together with her husband murdered him, and, with the help of a hatchet, dismembered his corpse. Then they had taken Sikora's keys and robbed his apartment. Initially the couple considered smuggling the corpse out with the help of two wooden crates, but gave up on the idea and announced their departure for Budapest on the sixth of October, escaping to Paris instead. Awaiting the trial, Franziska Klein published her life-story in a series of letters in the *Neues Wiener Tagblatt*.[28] She first confessed to the murder, effectively acquitting her husband of any guilt, then retracted and attempted to demonstrate his sole responsibility for Sikora's death. On the twenty-ninth of April, Franziska Klein was convicted of robbery and murder, and sentenced to death, a sentence that was subsequently commuted to lifelong imprisonment by imperial pardon. Johann Heinrich Klein received an eight-years prison sentence for being an accessory to her crimes.[29]

Reporting Murder

Looking over the reports of the trial in the contemporary press, one is struck first of all by the sheer quantity of ink devoted to the sensation. For the duration of the trial the more populist papers literally wrote about little else, the *Illustrierte Kronenzeitung* leading the pack with a coverage of forty-three (small format) pages, including six title pages with full-page pictures over the course of seven days.[30] On the twenty-seventh of April alone – the morning edition after the first full day of trial – more than ten of the paper's sixteen pages were devoted to the Kleins, including no fewer than six pictures.[31] The other major illustrated paper, *Das Illustrierte Extrablatt*, did not lag far behind, with more than twenty-five large format pages, and four title pictures, in the morning editions alone.[32] The evening editions added another eleven pages to this count, including numerous pictures and a four page 'separate edition' of the paper focusing solely on the trial.[33] Nor did the 'quality' press regard the sensation as beneath their contempt: the illustrious *Neue Freie Presse* devoted between five and seven columns (at three columns a page) to the trial in each of its morning editions, with somewhat lighter coverage in the evening;[34] the earnestly socialist *Arbeiter-Zeitung* only slightly less, in proportion to its shorter length.[35] The antisemitic *Deutsches Volksblatt*'s coverage peaked at a dozen columns; it averaged six to eight in most morning editions, and three to four in the slim evening supplement.[36] Given the astonishing wealth of the coverage that was put into public circulation, one must assume a more than passing familiarity with the case by all but Vienna's most reclusive inhabitants.

In terms of the presentation of the trial on the newspaper page, we encounter a desire within virtually all the daily papers to allow the reader to experience the drama of the courtroom at first hand by providing lengthy word-for-word excerpts of witness statements and the questions asked by judge, prosecutor and attorney – the closest approximation of a 'live' report a printed medium could provide (and a method also employed for reporting parliamentary debates). Occasionally these exchanges were paraphrased or rendered in reported speech; parts of the trial that were judged boring, insignificant or undesirable in their political implications were either dropped or summarised in brief. Editorial influence was exerted by the choice of which material was printed, by highlighting certain words or phrases, and by organising the material into coherent sections that received a separate sub-headline. These sub-headlines aimed not so much at communicating the gist of the next paragraph's content, as at drawing the reader's attention to a specific detail or statement and in this manner constructed significance and sequence for the reader. Real editorial commentary was limited to an opening paragraph, typically inserted into the report on the penultimate day of the trial, and could at times be turned into a separate article that explored the 'broader issues' at hand. It was in the form of such an editorial (or, in illustrated papers, as a graphic representation) that a major trial could make the front page of even the most respectable newspaper.[37]

Picturing Criminals

Another stable element of the trial report was some sort of description of the courtroom itself, of the defendant or defendants, and of the public in attendance and their behaviour. These descriptive paragraphs could be found at the beginning or the end of most reports, particularly on the first and last days of the trial. In the illustrated press this descriptive aspect was in the first instance visual. It is indeed hard to explain the *Kronenzeitung*'s significant commercial success without reference to its daily circulation of high-quality images drawn by Ladislaus Tuszynski, even though one should note that the '*Krone*' was not the first Austrian paper to sport illustrations, and that of all its predecessors only the *Illustriertes Wiener Extrablatt* could claim respectable circulation numbers.[38] The front cover was a particular selling point, and it typically offered the reader various kinds of visual information. The *Kronenzeitung*'s cover on the twenty-eighth of April 1905, for instance, showed a collage of images taken from three separate points of view (Figure 4.1). At the top we see a scene in which one of the expert witnesses is being asked to demonstrate the use of the axe for the mutilation of Sikora's body, rendered from the point of view of a front-row seat within the audience. The reader was provided with a snapshot of the reality of the courtroom: the liveliness of the scene vouchsafed for its authenticity, its draughtsmanlike precision for its accuracy. The paper thus offered the reader a simulacrum of 'having been there' through something like the visual equivalent of its 'live' reporting style. Through the paper's pen he or she became an omnipresent if invisible witness, observing the event accurately and impartially: in Ranke's phrase, *wie es eigentlich gewesen*.

The bottom half of the picture was split into two images. On the right there was a view of the auditorium, that was characterised mainly by female spectators in lavish hats, some of them clutching opera glasses. Here the point of view was essentially that of the judge: the spectator's gaze was inverted and the audience itself became the spectacle. This was a privileged gaze, in the sense that it came from beyond the barrier separating actors and audience. Implicitly the paper's readers were told that they no longer partook in the (ill-behaved, sensationalist) crowd and were invited to study it, too, as part of the spectacle. This sense of privilege was highlighted by the third image of the collage, a close-up of the

Figure 4.1 Klein Trial. Collage of images.
Source. Title page: *Illustrierte Kronenzeitung*, 29 April 1905.

Präsident (i.e. the judge within the contemporary Austrian legal system) as he was demonstrating a piece of evidence, encircled by a thin black line suggesting a detective's magnifying glass. The paper, in other words, was offering the reader a chance to meet one of the court room's main protagonists face-to-face and study them in detail. Together the three images not only established a sense of dramatic space – the court room was mapped in its outlines – but through its blending of different images and perspectives facilitated a number of different knowledges and attendent roles: participation in the drama as invisible witness, access to insider details barely visible for the normal observer (approximating a detective's gaze), and the sociologist's perspective of stuying the crowd as a crowd. One is reminded of the way in which current news-reel images are a careful amalgam of close-ups and sweeping, 'bird's eye', 'establishing shots'.

Looking through the various title pages of the Klein case, it is evident that these visual strategies were typical, if not always employed in unison. The *Illustriertes Wiener Extrablatt*, for instance, frequently favoured a single image on its title page, most typically drawn from the spectators' point of view, thus emphasising participation over privileged access (cf. Figure 4.2), or else tried to

Figure 4.2 Franziska Klein towering over the judge, hearing aid in place. The point of view is that of an audience member in an excellent, front-row seat: the reader is invited to join in and partake in this dramatic moment.
Source. Title page: *Illustriertes Wiener Extrablatt*, 27 April 1905.

establish the court room as a dramatic space (cf. Figure 4.3). Apart from the use of the 'split image' technique for their title pages, the illustrated papers were also fond of quasi-forensic pictures providing images of the crime scene, i.e. imitating the gaze of police and investigative judge (Figures 4.4 to 4.8).

Figure 4.3 The picture establishes the court room as a dramatic space, while at the same time playing up the majesty of the court. The point of view is that of an audience member who leans back and lets his eyes wander over the scene.
Source. Title page: *Illustriertes Wiener Extrablatt*, 30 April 1905.

Die Ottomane, unter der sich der Sack mit der Leiche Sykora's befindet.

Figure 4.4 Crime scene illustration. Ottoman under which murder victim was hidden.
Source. *Illustriertes Wiener Extrablatt*, 26 April 1905, Abend-Separatausgabe, p. 3.

Die Leiche Sykora's im Sacke.
(Nach der polizeilichen Thatbestandsaufnahme.)

Figure 4.5 Crime scene illustration. Close-up of dismembered body.
Source. *Illustriertes Wiener Extrablatt*, 26 April 1905, Abend-Separatausgabe, p. 4.

Figure 4.6 Analysis of suicide. One should note that while the *Krone* did not offer images exemplifying the kind of forensic gaze found in the *Extrablatt* during the Klein trial, it provided such drawings in other cases. The image above demonstrates another variety of this gaze. A mixture of photographic snap-shot and diagram, the image traces the arc of a man's fall from a cliff (the victim, postman Josef Neumann, had first shot himself at the top of the cliff). In its desire to reconstruct the forensic facts of the incident (i.e. the angle of the fall) it mirrored similar diagrams in contemporary criminalistic texts, but mixed this technical aspect with a sensational flair that allowed the viewer to visually partake in the suicide.
Source. *Illustrierte Kronenzeitung*, 16 June 1909, p. 9.

Figure 4.7 Newspaper floor-plan of crime scene. The floor-plan in the bottom right corner closely resembles contemporary police sketches of crime scenes and constitutes an obvious imitation of these.
Source. Title page: *Illustriertes Wiener Extrablatt*, 14 June 1909.

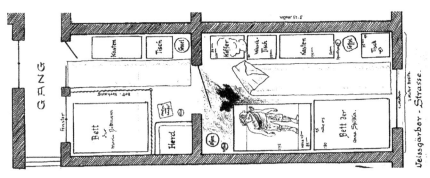

Figure 4.8 Police floor-plan of crime scene.
Source. SaW, Gerichtsakte, Box A 11, Fasz. 108 (Sosztarich 1899), illustration 3/1.

Reading Criminals

One should perhaps not be surprised at the presence of descriptive imagery in an era before the television screen transported the image of each and every public figure into the news consumer's living room. What is interesting to observe, however, is that the descriptive strategies were not confined to visual representations, and that the paper that used images in the most sophisticated fashion – the *Illustrierte Kronenzeitung* – was also the paper that devoted most attention to linguistic strategies of description, which occurred in a quantity that is deeply alien to the present day reader.[39] One should bear in mind that a paper like the populist *Krone* in a very real sense was existentially dependent on its trial reports: it had no political affiliation, no Page One editorial commentary – the so-called *Leitartikel* that was a standard feature of most dailies – no *feuilleton*, and no permanent correspondents outside Austria, i.e. very little foreign news, and the little it had was only second-hand and with a day's delay. It was legendarily cheap, selling at no more than the price of a bread roll, and scrupulously popular, sticking to its editor-in-chief's maxim 'if we are wise, we'll remain stupid [*San ma g'scheid, bleib' ma blöd*]'.[40] What it did provide was entertainment: serialised fiction, riddles, lengthy advice columns answering readers' questions (from how to counter hair-loss to solving mathematical problems), and – above all – sensations.[41] Trials made the most memorable sensations, both because of their internal complexity – there was much to write about – and because of the frequently scandalous nature of the subject matter. The *Krone* was thus the first Austrian paper to be explicitly structured around sensation-reporting, and it perfected many of the journalistic strategies that had been germinating in the papers over the quarter-century prior to its launch. Discursive description was central to these strategies.

Consider for instance the description of Franziska Klein offered on the first day of the trial:

> She: a woman dressed in black, still youthful, displaying a cool calm. A pale, well-formed, almost beautiful face, with childlike, soft features. A fur boa, coquettishly thrown around her shoulders, augments the pallor. Not even the eyelashes, that throw deep shadows over the eyes, move ... If it weren't for the play of the excited small hands, hidden away in fingerless gloves, the deep breaths with which she suppresses her anxiety – she would resemble a dressed-up doll.[42]

The description provided here was more than a simple enumeration of the physical facts of Klein's appearance. Rather these facts were integrated into a discursive act that aimed at establishing knowledge about the defendant. Thus Klein's fur boa was described as a manifestation of her coquetry. This coquetry was located not in the accessory itself, but in the way Klein had 'thrown [it] around her shoulders.' It implied the deliberate use of her sexuality to influence the judgement of the court. At the same time it was precisely this cunning strategy that gave her away as a less than savoury character and gave her an air of *femme fatale.* A similar dynamic existed between Klein's show of calmness and impassiveness, and the observer's shrewd gaze that both noted the artificiality of her calm (via the comparison with the dressed-up doll) and the subtle signs (her deep breaths, the play of her hands) that gave this calm away as a mask. The resulting characterisation was that of a woman who was in control of herself, a calculating creature. At the same time the description established the journalist – and through the journalist the reader who re-enacted the journalist's gaze in his or her act of reading – as a careful observer who was capable of reading not only the semiotics of the enacted personality, but also the semiotics of dissimulation, both of which resided on the observed surface of the defendant's body. The interpretation of the defendant's character was thus intrinsic to the act of description itself.

Similar descriptive strategies were employed for Franziska Klein's husband, although here the journalist's interpretative service for the reader was made much more explicit:

> Mr Klein, who follows her closely, is completely different. Also calm. But his calm is the resigned calm of a gambler, who has accepted his losses.
>
> He attempts to create the impression of being carefree. His glance flies coolly over the auditorium. Now he recognises an acquaintance, with a half-ashamed, half-friendly smile. Then he calmly looks over the jurors. But the gaze that is meant to seem so clear is unsteady and in spite of his self-control an evil flash sometimes runs through it, especially when he furtively glances at his wife. That gaze makes his face appear ugly ...
>
> And it's a handsome face. Good complexion, framed by a pointed beard, the points of the moustache are rolled up, the black hair is slicked back. He could be called good-natured, were it not for that fatal gaze.[43]

Mr Klein, it was established, could not be trusted. He looked respectable and calm, but the careful observer could easily penetrate both fronts and unmask him both as nervous and potentially dangerous.

Indeed the mask, and the theatrical display, were central metaphors, and were repeatedly pitted against the public's observatory power. The *Krone* was quite explicit in warning its readers of the dangers of being misled by careless observation: 'Franziska Klein,' it wrote,

> will attempt to blind us with her undeniable mental superiority. She will – but how can one predict ahead of time what a person like Franziska Klein, who with every moment changes her details, her mood, who cries, deeply depressed, one moment, and smiles victoriously the next, will do? Perhaps today she will strike the pose of a sinner broken in her soul, drowning in desperate tears, perhaps she will face her judges with boldly flashing eyes, declaiming her innocence. Whichever way she decides her role is to be interpreted.[44]

The *Krone*'s warning about Franziska's powers for distorting the truth went hand in hand with an implicit promise: read us and you will see through the dissimulation, even of this cunning criminal mastermind, who is attempting to 'blind' us. One notes the visual imagery of the passage, and by extension how tied-up this act of truth establishment was with the reading of visual clues. It is also obvious that establishing the defendant's criminality (or lack thereof) did not need to make any reference at all to his or her criminal act: it resided in the body, not as a stable signifier – Lombroso's large ears and bushy eyebrows – but rather in minute details that hinted at the distance between the enacted self and a true self. It was this discrepancy, i.e. the act of dissimulation itself, that served as a primary marker of criminality.

Readers of nineteenth-century fiction and its commentators may be reminded at this point of certain features of Balzac's realism. Here, too, one finds incredibly rich descriptive passages that anticipate those uncovered in Viennese trial reports. Here, too, seemingly innocent details are magnified and take on tremendous meaning.[45] The difference lies that in Balzac's mid-century epistemology the individual could still be unproblematically apprehended as partaking of a stable type.[46] In the court reports the only common denominator between unmasked defendants was merely their shared act of deception. In fact, 'significant description' as found in the above examples more closely imitated the criminalist's gaze than Balzac's attempt at sociology through fiction. The papers attempted to read the 'phenomenological' clues residing in the defendants' appearance and mannerisms in much the same manner as Gross recommended in his *Criminalpsychologie*: both were interested simply in catching the suspect at 'it'. Indeed Gross clearly approved of the papers' detective gaze. When it came to printing the transcript of a 1907 Viennese trial sensation in the *Archiv*, he included information missing from the original transcript, namely the 'significant description' provided by one of the papers.[47]

While the *Krone* was perhaps the most innovative practitioner of this descriptive technique, virtually all the other contemporary papers also provided detailed descriptions of the Kleins that served as 'readings' of the defendants' personalities. Thus the *Neue Freie Presse*, Vienna's most highbrow daily, similarly integrated a description of Franziska Klein's costume and appearance into a clear narrative of dissimulation:

Franziska Klein is the most interesting defendant to appear in a trial that has stirred the public in a long time. This woman, who even before the night of horrors of the third of October had fallen into the pit of big-city vice, presents herself [*präsentiert sich*] with the self-confidence and delicacy of an educated lady, used to the best societal form. Despite the horror and repulsion one experiences when one considers the terrible crimes with which she has been charged, one can nevertheless not deny that she knows how to impress with her pleasing appearance, her refined manners, her skilled way with words, and her very posture... With the exquisite talents, which the defendant today displayed, she reminds one of those wild beasts with splendid furs, with grace in their movements and beauty even as they leap at the victim, which humanity has to regard as dangerous enemies. The quick-wittedness which the defendant displayed today, the speed and confidence of her arguments during the rhetorical duels, frequently caused a stir among the spectators, that, while not to be interpreted as assent to her words, have to be regarded as the involuntary respect for her dialectics.[48]

One should note here how Klein's eloquence itself, along with her pleasant appearance, were read as part of a mastery of a 'criminal toolbox' that marked her out as especially dangerous. Indeed, as a look at the *Illustrierte Extrablatt* shows us, her criminality could be read in the most trifling of her actions:

> And how she moves, how she throws back her skirt, how she passes her boa on to the clerk, when it gets too heavy for her, and thanks him with a quiet nod, when he arranges the arm-chair for her. All this she does with breeding, like the actresses who play sophisticated ladies [*Damen von Welt*] on the stage.[49]

Once again the journalist proved himself an expert observer who was able to differentiate between good manners and enacted good manners, and – through his description – allowed the reader access to this subtle reading of the criminal body as a sign system of dissimulation. Klein's weakness, her elegance, her breeding, and even her supposed deafness (Klein employed a hearing aid throughout the trial) were scrutinised and judged as part of a master-plan to hide the truth of her guilt: 'What she wants to hear she hears. One has to repeat to her every statement. Thus she wins time to think through her answer.'[50] Her husband, the *Extrablatt* noted, was unable to match this deviousness through a similar arsenal of his own.[51] A clear hierarchy of villainy was thus established within a few hours of the trial's beginning.

Lest it be thought that the Klein case was unique in its descriptive gusto, or that murderers alone could evoke this kind of sustained attention, a look at the 1905 Kubowski fraud trial – analysed in greater detail in chapter five – reassures us that this strategy was routinely employed. Once again, the visual representation of the courtroom comes as a carefully constructed amalgam of points of view, combining the audience's view of the defendants with the close-up – again drawn within a magnifying-glass circle – of Anna Kubowski herself (cf. Figure 4.9). Once again one also notes the role of description, in juxtaposition with the defendants' biography, as an exercise of clue-reading that effectively transformed the courtroom into something analoguous to a crime scene – a space that needed to be carefully observed and analysed:

> She is an interesting person, no doubt. She knows how to play at being the 'lady' in spite of her relative lack of education. The court she greets with a curtsey [*Hofknix*]. When she dries her eyes with her handkerchief, she does so with grace. And the break she uses to act out the role of loving daughter. She walks over to her old father who sits feebly in his wheelchair, and touches his forehead. As she does so her right hand flashes her – rosary, that encircles her wrist. A golden cross dangles from it and clangs when it brushes against the metal of his chair. Her full figure is clothed in an elegant, tailored black dress – Anna Kubowski comes dressed in mourning.[52]

Figure 4.9 Kubowski Trial. Study of defendants.
Source. Title page: *Illustrierte Kronenzeitung*, 26 September 1905.

As in the Klein case this description of the defendant's actual behaviour in court – her minute gestures, her bearing – are understood as clues to her true self. Of central interest is the discrepancy between what Anna Kubowski aims to communicate about herself, and the journalist's analysis: the signifiers she employs carry a meaning intent on fooling the public, but it is precisely this attempt at dissimulation that gives her away. Thus Kubowski's physical appearance and actions might strike the casual observer as respectable, positive, even wholesome: she wears sombre black, she carries religious icons, she displays both loving affection for her ageing father and admirable manners in her behaviour towards the court. However, on close observation, all these trappings of decency prove to be false: her black dress is 'elegant' and 'tailored' and hence mock-modest, her religiosity and daughterly affection overly ostentatious, her curtsey is a fake curtsey, the grace with which she wields the handkerchief suspect. The journalist, here in his role of expert observer, once again engages in a feat of unmasking, and passes this observatory sophistication on to his readers who are now able to watch with the detective/journalist's trained gaze. They are not fooled by the act, and indeed it is Kubowski's attempt to fool them that most clearly identifies her as criminal, quite independently of the crime she has committed or the evidence presented in court.

Indeed, contemporaries showed an acute awareness that the papers' strategy of meaningful description served the purpose of marking out heroes and villains, irrespective whether they were employed to characterise defendants or witnesses, lawyers and jurors. For instance, on the twenty-ninth of September, the antisemitic *Volksblatt* printed a speech about the Dreyfus scandal made by the Christian Social parliamentarian Pattai in Vienna's Musikverein.[53] This speech, in its printed version, contained a lengthy section sub-headed 'The Jew Press':

> The trial [i.e. the trial coverage] was introduced with dramatic narrations, as though it were a theatre play, and the descriptions were even worse. Each witness was characterised and certain types were established. A witness for Dreyfus's defence was usually described with flowing hair and strong eyebrows; honesty would stare out of his eyes, and he would start speaking with a simple voice, but under the power of his propositions soon everybody was convinced. (Laughter). Other witnesses, who spoke against Dreyfus, were called ridiculous, stubborn, close to imbecility, insane, people who embarrass themselves when they open their mouths, even if they were the army's best generals...or famed scholars like *Bertillon* ...[54]

Despite such invective the *Deutsches Volksblatt* also employed meaningful description to mark out villains, if perhaps not with such evocative perfection as the *Kronenzeitung*. Here, however, it chose to highlight the power of papers to themselves dissimulate, i.e. to wrongly depict the events of the courtroom with an aim of fooling the public. In other words, the *Volksblatt* attacked the papers for an act of manipulation that implicitly identified them with the criminals under scrutiny. We will return to this strategy of criminalising all forms of supposed dissimulation time and again as we study antisemitic strategies in narrating Jewish crime.

The papers' exercises in clue reading were not limited to the defendants' bodies: they also imitated Gross's approach towards crime in the reading of other available clues about the suspect. Thus Franziska Klein's letters received attention not only as documents that offered information about who Klein wanted the public to believe her to be (and thus, through critical reading, insight into who she truly was), but were also considered in terms of form and style. The *Extrablatt* printed a sample of her handwriting, by which its readers were free to judge for themselves, while the *Krone* offered the following, graphological characterisation:

> The letters are written in a firm, confident hand; the text is broken up only by rare, irrelevant corrections. The sentences that Franziska Klein judged as being of special importance, she has underlined repeatedly. Both the flowing handwriting and the style of the letters point to her good education.[55]

The letters, too, were thus seen to attest to her education, her forthrightness, and ultimately to the danger of her criminality. One also notes with some mirth how much this description of Klein's letters serves as a fair summary of the *Krone*'s own style. Its sensationalism, its brazen clarity, its need to highlight for the reader the juiciest bits were here found in a murderer's letter that was written for publication by another paper. Suspected murderer and paper here spoke the same language, pointing to a strange sort of symbiosis: the murderer existed as a public figure only within the pages of the dailies, and the dailies sold issues precisely through their construction of such criminals. The clue reading became a circular exercise in which the murderer provided legible clues directly to the papers in a format that already conformed to the papers' stylistic demands.

Naturally, observation rendered as significant description was only one of the tools employed to mark out criminality and guilt. It was, for instance, routinely coupled with a biographical tale of the defendants' downward spiral, i.e. put into the context of a longer trajectory of transgression, deception and crime. Hence virtually all the papers narrated Franziska Klein's youth in the convent, her flight, her prostitution ('Franziska Klein has an eventful past. She has been a nun, ran away from the convent, changed religions, worked for a while as a teacher, got into conflict with the law, and eventually became a lady of the *demi-monde*'),[56] as well as her husband's bad business sense, his debts, his schemes to pay these back, his cheating.[57] As a strategy to establish criminality this comes as no surprise, and closely resembles early to mid-nineteenth century criminological texts that made such biographical investigation of a criminal's unsavoury past a central aspect in their localisation of criminality.

It is important, however, to note that this biographical dimension was secondary and supplementary for establishing the Kleins' guilt. There is an important sense that sufficient evidence for the personalities and actions of the defendants should, and could, be gathered within the court room itself and by extension that the crime itself could be solved only by the pieces of puzzle generated and reviewed within its walls. This evidence was in part provided by the witnesses, but also by the appearance and behaviour of the suspects and their interaction with witnesses, audience, jury and each other. It is a version of what Richard Sennet, in his discussion of the Dreyfus case, has called a 'trial by character,' which need not make any reference to the crime to establish guilt.[58]

Within the boundaries of the trial report 'character' was established via observation and the descriptive rendering of this observation, rather than through simple reference to behaviour *outside* the courtroom.[59] The centrality of descriptive detail to the understanding of trial reports is further corroborated by Karl Kraus's mockery of these: Kraus, in his own coverage of the Klein case, and the concurrent Navratil murder case, sought to ridicule the papers' obsession with minute facts, oblivious, it seems, to the privileged place these self-same facts held in contemporary criminalistic science.[60]

If the papers' gaze – and through the papers, the public's gaze – was criminalistic in nature, this holds true not only for its desire to read clues, but also in its judgement of the nature of such clues. Nowhere, throughout the various papers' coverage of the trial, was there any attempt to essentialise the defendants, to stamp them as incarnations of some stable criminal type. At the same time there was some sort of recognition that criminal stereotypes did exist. The *Neue Freie Presse*, for instance, explicitly noted that Klein, if anything, looked like a *Giftmischerin* – a 'female poisoner' – but contrasted this appearance with the actual violence of the crime for which she was prosecuted.[61] Similarly Mr Klein was attested not to 'display a murderer's physiognomy, indeed, not even the physiognomy of any criminal.'[62] The notion of stable criminal signifiers was invoked only to be dismissed. The message enshrined in such references to criminal stereotypes was that real-life criminals did *not* in fact conform to such generic categories, familiar, perhaps, from the world of penny-dreadfuls.

Finally, one should also note in passing that the authenticity demanded of the innocent was a trope not entirely new to the *fin-de-siècle*. In fact the question of dissimulation had dominated the agenda in French Revolutionary discourse, to name but one example: one of the demands of the terror had been the virtue of transparency, a Republican virtue that would allow immediate access to a man's loyal heart.[63] However, one should note that dissimulation traditionally was above all a politician's crime, who stood accused of deceiving the public. In the *Krone*'s coverage of the Klein affair – and in dozens of other court scandals in this period – the charge was transferred to the ordinary criminal. The deception now took place right there in court where it either fooled or was uncovered by the observing public.

Gender and the Court Room

While the journalist's expert gaze could of course be consumed, and through consumption assimilated, by readers of either gender, one should note that this gaze was overtly constructed as masculine. In this it mirrored the *flâneur*'s gaze that literally hunted the city for impressions and whose abilities to observe metropolitan life have similarly evoked comparisons to the detective's.[64] The *flâneur*'s feuilletonistic strategy of describing these impressions, however, was marked by a 'feminine' passivity. It allowed the city to inscribe itself upon his consciousness rather than imposing itself upon the scrutinised object.[65] The court reporter's writing style was more overt in converting the passivity of spectatorship into the masculine enterprise of judging: his observation and description was goal-driven in the same manner that criminalistic observation was.[66]

Within this context, there can be little surprise that – as indicated by my choice of the Klein and Kubowski trials – female defendants were particularly closely studied by their papers. The point was not that only women could display inauthenticity and hence criminality. There were, after all, plenty of male defendants, many of whom were described in considerable detail. Rather, the implicit suggestion was that criminality per se was feminine because it involved donning a mask. The intricate nature of female toilette highlighted this association. The male, truth-seeking gaze could, of course, penetrate beyond such masquerading. Since the feminisation of Jews was also a common contemporary theme – most overtly in the writings of Otto Weininger[67] – the association of Jewish crime with skilful dissimulation within the antisemitic press (discussed in detail in the next chapter) also followed the gendered logic of the court journalist's gaze.

This dynamic between male spectator and female spectacle, male righteousness and female deception, was augmented by the general consensus in the papers that women who attempted to 'read' defendants or witnesses frequently failed in this endeavour. In their coverage of the Klein case, for instance, the *Arbeiter-Zeitung* – hardly the most mysogynist of Viennese papers – played up the the slippage between two kinds of expert gaze: that of the criminalist watching a supposed murderess, and that of the (female) fashion commentator, evaluating a lady's toilette.

> Nobody has sat in the dock as elegantly as her for quite some time. Above all the clothes. A new, black silk blouse covers the solid body of the woman, who is of below average height. The beautiful, black woollen skirt sits tightly around the slim waistline under her belt. And she also wears a long fur collar, also black, shining, and, of course, elegant. One has only noticed a single mistake in her get up. The sleeves of the blouse are too long and nearly reach down to her fingers ... The fact that only the waist-line of the small lady is slim, and thus does not correspond to mass-produced sizes, certainly explains the deficiency of the blouse. But her figure is nevertheless not bad. Nor is her face ...
>
> And how elegantly she holds herself [*sie sich gibt*], the most expert ladies admired! She displays the smallness of her feet, and the nobility with which she moves her hand, and that she knows how to turn her head in a dignified manner.[68]

The gaze of the 'expert ladies' in the audience was here juxtaposed with that of the journalist who drew the readers' attention to the 'dignified manner' in which Klein 'knows how to turn her head', i.e. to the theatrical falsity of her gestures. The paragraph thus served to characterise not only Klein, but also the female audience in attendance whose very way of looking at the defendant was analysed. Unlike the reporter this audience misread what was on display; it mistook the court room for a fashion room.

Indeed, the frequent criticisms voiced by the papers about the audience's inappropriate behaviour in court (manifested by noise, overt display of excitement, the use of opera glasses to see better) invariably stressed the misbehaviour of women.[69] While part and parcel of the general feminisation of mass culture characteristic of the period,[70] this sort of criticism also aimed to highlight the difference between journalist and (implicitly male) reader who studied the scene in silence and the sensationalist, feminised mass in attendence who were as exposed to view – and to analysis – as the other participants of the trial. We will return to this theme of the wedge driven between the private news consumer and the public that was under observation, when we have a closer look at the theatrical metaphor so typical of contemporary court reports.

Truth and the Courtroom

A further characteristic of the trial reporting on the Klein case that was central to contemporary trial reports in general was the problematic relationship of factual reporting and fiction, and the subtleties of the truth claim made by the papers. As we have already noted in the defendants' descriptions, the language in which the trial was rendered borrowed heavily from that of fiction and drama. References to the 'floorboards ... [of] the stage of life',[71] the 'first act of the great drama,'[72] the 'tragic book of life,'[73] the 'gala performance'[74] and the *Schauspiel*[75] ('play', 'performance' or 'spectacle'; literally: the 'game of looking') were ubiquitous throughout the reports. Franziska Klein's defence council blurred the line further by quoting Shakespeare in his final plea.[76] The slippage between the real world and the world of fiction that was present on this lexical level was readily acknowledged by the *Extrablatt*: 'The great trials – of course – represent a piece of theatre ... From the stage on which blood is shed, from the theatre of an illusionary reality, it's only a small step to the reality of life.'[77]

While some of the papers rejected such linguistic equalisation of fact and fiction as 'greedy sensationalism'[78] and used it to implicate their rival papers' deplorable tendency to obscure truth and turn the court room into a 'place of brutalisation and perversity',[79] the *Extrablatt* argued that this theatricality and drama was an inherent aspect of trials themselves: 'But it is not the papers that create sensations. Life creates them. The newspaper is a mirror to that which life holds up to it.'[80] In other words, the papers, the *Extrablatt* claimed, did not fictionalise fact, but the facts of the courtroom were themselves like fiction. Hence theatrical language was realistic language. Given the papers' claim that the criminals were actors, wilfully employing a barrage of semantic signs to play innocent, this interpretation was consistent with the manner in which trials were perceived: a contest between fiction and fact, truth and lie, dissimulated selves and penetrating gazes.[81]

But there was a further ambivalence to the nature of the sort of truth established in the court room which was once again readily acknowledged – even given central attention – in these narratives of the trial. Consider, for instance, this remarkable series of quotes taken from successive editions of the *Arbeiter-Zeitung*:

> Many details have been revealed to the jury over the past three days, but still the crime can be interpreted in a wide variety of ways. Many combinations are possible, as concerns the time of the murder, the point in time when the deed was first conceptualised, the motivations involved, and the participation of husband and wife in the complex of actions, which, if not legally, then in actual fact, make up the crime ...[82]
>
> It is a great number of pieces of circumstantial evidence [*Indizien*] that the witnesses had to report, pieces of evidence, naturally, of which many, taken by themselves, prove nothing ...[83]
>
> Who is the murderer? Who killed the old man who arrived in the night from the third to the fourth of October in the expectation of a tender hour of love? ... Whether husband or wife committed the murder is virtually a matter of chance ... Whether guilt and punishment have been justly measured out will not remain without acute doubts.[84]

Two aspects of the open-endedness of the kind of truth established by the court were here accentuated: on the one hand there was a recognition that over the course of several days of trial a myriad discrete truth problems were raised that were never conclusively resolved within the court procedure: no master account of *what really happened* on the night of the murder was given, into which all the conflicting claims made by various witnesses were neatly integrated. The trial remained at the level of juxtaposed truth-versions. On the other hand, the *Arbeiter-Zeitung* more generally acknowledged that the jury's verdict was just that: an opinion from which others would differ. This verdict then was a human version of the truth, based on human perception and judgement.[85]

The other papers similarly acknowledged that the truth of the crime and of the defendants' guilt had no absolute validity outside the courtroom, that it was heavily caught up with its procedures and therefore ultimately elusive.[86] Theirs was an understanding of crime that could not and would not isolate the truth of the act from the mechanisms of perceiving and arriving at this truth, and as such is closely related to the understanding of crime we have found in Hans Gross's analysis. It is interesting to observe that the papers' reaction to this realisation was also similar to Gross's: they, too, acknowledged the importance of expert witnesses and they, too, widened their sphere of interest from focusing on the supposed criminal alone to a consideration of all the agents participating in the act of truth establishment.

In an epistemological regime in which the criminal particular could not be classified by simple reference to some criminal type, and in which conflicting

truth claims made by various witnesses were never resolved, it comes as no surprise that expert witnesses received detailed attention by the papers. Indeed, the third day of reporting was largely devoted to their statements, their demonstrations of *Realia* (physical pieces of evidence) – the rope, the hatchet, an anatomical model of an Adam's apple – and their technical verdicts on the defendants' physical ability to commit the murder. Two of the *Kronenzeitung*'s precious front covers were devoted not to either of the defendants, but largely to these experts' activities, depicting them in the very act of providing (and proving) their expertise (see Figures 4.1 and 4.10).[87] As for Gross, the potency of their statements was seen to stem from both the depth and the narrowness of their expertise, and no attempt was made on the side of the papers to raise doubts about their findings. In a spectacle of uncertain truths the expert witnesses were accepted to wield something of a monopoly over solid fact.

The psychologist who testified to Franziska Klein's sanity (she claimed having been confused, 'crazily in love' with her husband – themes familiar from the criminological literature) was part of this group of experts, but, as we shall see in other trials, represented a far more contested type of expertise. After all, the psychiatrist did not deal with the tangible, forensic clues of the crime scene, but with the mental disposition of the defendants – the very thing with which the papers' dual strategies of description and biographical analysis attempted to come to terms. The papers' analyses – in so far as they build up the Kleins as dangerous criminals – depended crucially on the basic assumption of the defendants' sanity and their conscious dissimulation of innocence. In the Klein case, the psychologist's verdict that 'Franziska Klein is neither generally insane, but at most shows, in a certain sense, a characteristic form of intelligence'[88] confirmed this assumption and hence was welcomed without comment.

But the attention paid to the expert witnesses needs also to be understood in the context of the papers' interest in *all* participants of the trial. From the sensationalist *Krone* to the erudite *Neue Freie Presse*, the papers unanimously refused to reduce the trial to the contemplation and analysis of the defendants. Judge, jury, witnesses, lawyers, audience 'are all characters in [the] drama',[89] and as such were all subject to the papers' scrutiny, although rarely described at the length devoted to the defendants. In the illustrated press all these characters were depicted in a variety of pictures (see Figures 4.11 and 4.12); the *Extrablatt* even included a photograph of the jurors.[90] In some trials one finds a detailed appraisal of lawyers' performances in terms reminiscent of theatre criticism: their rhetorical skills, emotional involvement and integrity were scrutinised and evaluated.[91] This interest in all the trial's participants need not be dismissed as mere gossip, a way of stretching the story. Rather, as for Gross, one can read it as a function of the papers' understanding of legal truth as precisely the product of the complex interactions taking place at court. The court room was thus transformed into a social space worthy of exploration, its disparate elements fused together by the mystery of the crime that lay at its centre.

Figure 4.10 Klein Trial. Expert Witnesses.
Source. Title page: *Illustrierte Kronenzeitung*, 28 April 1905.

Theatre and Public, Public Theatre

The public in attendance was central to this contemplation of the court room as a social sphere of interaction. References to the public – and the German word *Publikum* denoted both the spectators of a specific event as well as the public at large, semantically conflating those in attendance with society *per se* – were ubiquitous in trial reports.[92] Particular attention was paid to the behaviour of the audience within the courtroom – their clothes and accessories, their sympathies,

Den Geschwornen wird der blutige Sack gezeigt.

Figure 4.11   Kubowski Trial. Witnesses examine bloody bag.
Source. *Illustriertes Wiener Extrablatt*, 28 April 1905, p. 12.

MARIE ZOUHAR   TISCHLERMEISTER BARDA   MARIE STIPPEL.   JOSEFINE SIMADA

Zeugen im Prozesse Klein.

Figure 4.12   Kubowski Trial. Study of witnesses.
Source. *Illustriertes Wiener Extrablatt*, 29 April 1905, 11.

their reactions to what they were experiencing – as well as to the general interest and attention paid to the trial, the street scenes and reactions, and (another well-worn trope) the regular fights to gain entrance.[93] What is one to make of the interest in the public, over and beyond saying that the conventions of crime reporting routinely conflated any knowledge of a criminal act with knowledge about the social event that served to examine and judge it? The answer, I believe, lies in taking seriously the idea that a court room was a theatre.

In the contemporary papers, I have argued, there was a sense that it was in the court room where the crime really *happened*, or, at the very least, where it was re-enacted, in the sense that the trial was not merely the locus of where the formal truth about the criminal action was established and officially sanctioned, but also the central event where criminal and public met, where the defendants' characters were evaluated, and where the public re-experienced the crime. This interactive dimension has prompted historians like Larry Wolff to highlight the similarities of court room and theatre stage, a simile we have already described as ubiquitous within the papers' own reports.[94]

In order to fully appreciate this simile, however, it needs to be put into the context of the contemporary experience of theatre. This is not an entirely straightforward task because, like so much of society, theatrical conventions at the turn of the last century were caught in a process of transformation.[95] On the one hand the important changes of the beginning of the century still shaped the experience of watching a play, opera or operetta. These can best be understood as a process of disassociation between street and stage. In the eighteenth century street and stage clothing bore a resemblance to each other – one being a hyperbolic version of the other. Moreover (much to the chagrin of Jean-Jacques Rousseau), a sense of *performance* was common to actors on the street as well as on the stage, making a dynamic interaction between players and spectators possible.[96] The nineteenth century, by contrast, erected a wall between the two worlds. Costumes became just that, clothing obviously and purposefully differentiated from street dress.[97] Lights began to be dimmed during performances, physically separating actors and audience. It became bad form – particularly in bourgeois theatre – to speak during a performance; applause came to be deferred to the end of the performance.[98] On the street, too, things were changing; Richard Sennett describes a law of silent spectatorship descending upon the streets of the European metropolis.[99] One observed quietly and privately. Finally, just as identity became a secret entity, jealously guarded and only accessible to seasoned observers who could read an intricate fabric of external clues, the theatre actor came to be tied to the conventions of melodrama, in which identity was reduced to clearly delineated roles – villain, rescuer, virginal victim – that, in contrast to real people, could be apprehended even by the most dim-witted of theatre goers.[100] As the century carried on there was an increasing drive towards 'realistic' painted scenery that falsely implied that the stage represented the world accurately.[101] In a word: the stage became a place where actors played out the fantasy of a world in which everyone could be readily read by an inscrutable audience that sat passively and in the protection of a self-policed and silent darkness. Despite the legibility of the stage actor, the period also witnessed the rise of the theatre critic, usually in the form of journalists; at the same time theatre programmes began to explain the performance even before it had been witnessed.[102] The habitual transferral of one's critical judgement, and the reliance on guidance for how to watch and understand a performance, thus became part of the silent spectatorship of the theatre going public.

In the second half of the nineteenth century, however, and particularly in its last quarter, the absolute dominance of conventionalised melodrama came to be challenged by a series of movements, the most significant of which, in our context, was the rise of 'naturalism'. The shift was gradual and haphazard. Three dimensional box-sets with real furniture and props began to be used. Actors were trained to deliver lines 'naturally'. Ibsen, Strindberg, Chekhov wrote plays in which the dialogue concealed rather than revealed the emotions of their speakers. Stanislavski suggested that actors should gather deep biographical and psychological understanding of their characters, rather than merely displaying them by utilising a pictorial code shared with the audience in order to represent the character's identity.[103] In Vienna naturalism began to be fostered at the *Burgtheater* under Max Burckhardt's direction (1889 to 1912), although more conventional theatre continued to thrive in Austria and elsewhere in Europe at least until the start of the First World War.[104] Naturalism, of course, was itself quickly superseded by any number of movements: theatre had entered the flux of modernity that tore it from experiment to experiment.[105]

Despite these winds of change, the theatre of melodrama provides perhaps the most important point of comparison to the court trials under discussion.[106] The language of the reports often harkened back to melodramatic convention: they invoked fixed roles in the court room, including villain, upright witness, devious lawyer, and the innocent victim. However, one also notes immediately that the court room was nothing like the 'modern' theatre stage: the audience did interact loudly and rambunctiously with the 'drama' (clapping and booing in reaction to the events, a feature of contemporary vaudeville and popular theatre), the lights were not dimmed, and, as shown above, the principal actors on stage needed to be read with considerable subtlety to be unmasked in their lack of authenticity.

Indeed it was crucial to the reports that the scenes witnessed were *real*, and that their reality lay precisely in the fact that the people under scrutiny were not professional performers, but 'normal' members of the public, who had been plucked off the street and pushed out into the limelight. In this, then, the court room was ritualised street scene, rather than theatre – i.e. it provided precisely the sort of 'realism' cherished by the new naturalist theatre. Nevertheless, melodramatic patterns of good and evil were imposed upon the proceedings; this was possible because the journalistic/detective gaze provided access to the performers' true selves with a reliability that was unattainable by the common, street observer. In doing so the court journalist imitated the theatre critic's role in shaping the audience's reaction. Viewed through the expert gaze that analysed minute details in its test of authenticity, reality could be dissolved into the fantasy of melodrama: in other words, if one viewed the real world closely and expertly enough, it revealed itself as adhering to the reassuring moral clarity of theatrical convention after all.

It is also important to note that newspapers did not treat the court proceedings as a stage, but rather the entire court room. That is to say that, within the logic of the court report, the audience in attendance, too, were actors. Indeed one notes that one of the features of late nineteenth-century drama, particularly in Germany and Austria, was its fondness for large crowd scenes.[107] In the courtroom the crowd was, of course, not scripted: they behaved as they wished, often to the chagrin of the judge. However, in the papers' coverage of the trials, the audience was watched much like all other participants in the trial. This act of watching was recorded, often in elaborately descriptive ways: 'on all cheeks the excitement conjured up red blossoms ... and, in the midst of all this, the jewels in the female spectators' rosy earlobes shone and sparkled, like dew in the sun.'[108] The papers, in turn, passed on this act of watching to their own audience, the readers, as we have already noted when contemplating one of the *Krone*'s cover pictures.[109] Effectively this enabled the papers' readers to observe the *Publikum* – both audience in attendance and the public *per se* – as 'other', i.e. without identifying themselves with, and having their individuality dissolved in, this public. This placed the consumer of trial reports in a role that stood in diametric opposition to the goals of a functioning public sphere, which (according to Habermas) include self-identification of newspaper readers with the public they read about, and their attendant, critical self-observation.[110] The court report invited instead a stance of alienation bred from observatory superiority.

The readers were thus turned into the true – i.e. passive, silent, critically guided – spectators of the trial, whilst the audience in attendance – the *Publikum* – were dissolved into the spectacle and became part of it. The awareness that what was being witnessed was indeed a spectacle was thus highlighted rather than obscured. By transforming public space into a stage-performance that could be fully illuminated, the newspapers could celebrate public transparency without challenging the privacy of the individual newspaper reader. In the same article that defended the papers' so-called sensationalism, the *Extrablatt* also made explicit this new role of the paper that provided knowledge about the public:

> Who bemoans the fact that the control over life becomes ever more public and more perfect, that every word that is spoken in a public space is directed at the whole world? The public certainly doesn't ... Humanity is becoming purer, the air sharper in front of this merciless mirror that hides or veils nothing that is human.[111]

The reader alone escaped the papers' scrutiny by embracing the role of an anonymous, invisible voyeur. *In extremis* the courtroom as *theatrum mundi* was thus elevated to provide knowledge not only of a specific criminal mystery but of society itself; at the same time the reader/detectives were disassociated with this society that was being made known. Their voyeurism was a private pleasure.

Finally, one may note a tension between the theatrical and overtly moralising agenda of unmasking villains on the evidence of their lack of authenticity, and the implicit transformation of court trial into a detective riddle that journalist and reader solved through private acts of observation.[112] Melodrama and the modern detective yarn are not, after all, obviously compatible genres. Indeed there was a sense that the moralistic language featured by many papers – although the *Krone* was relatively restrained in this, less ashamed in its celebration of sensation *qua* sensation – was conventional rather than sincere. One is tempted to argue that there was in fact little investment in the moral truths uncovered: the journalist vocalised outrage, but it was not required that the reader actually be outraged.[113] The reader, after all, remained passive in his or her encounter with the sensation. Those people who actually did become outraged enough to go to the courtroom (never more than a tiny minority of those fascinated by the events) were, as we just saw, quickly turned into part of the spectacle that was being observed. The journalist's report, then, was formally outraged at the moral depravity of the crime on behalf of his readers, giving the reader free rein to indulge in the pleasure of following his detective gaze and watching the twists and turns of the case unfold.

Playing Detective: The Hunchback's Treasure

One should perhaps put these comments about the role of the public in trial coverage, its relationship to the reader and indeed the above-described conflation of fact and fiction into the context of one of the *Krone*'s most successful projects, a serialised novel running under the snappy title of *The Hunchback's Treasures*.[114] In the novel's rather convoluted plot the hunchbacked villain blackmails an aged, respectable nobleman over a certain indiscretion committed by the nobleman's son. The hunchback's goal is not simply to obtain money, but to drive the old man insane by forcing him into a cruel (and rather absurd) game of detection: the blackmailer will hide silver capsules containing money around the city and provide the nobleman with clues as to where he can find them. If he does not find the capsule, his name will be publicly besmirched. The first set of clues describes how the villain prowls the streets of Vienna at night, walking up Alserstraße in the ninth Viennese district towards Hernals in the seventeenth. He walks up to a street lamp, then chooses an erratic path through some minor streets until he comes upon the 'cold, iron bars' of a 'portcullis' behind which there are graves. He walks along the outside wall and puts a silver capsule down in some hiding place before running off into the storm and the night. 'Now they shall search,' he mumbles as he marches off, 'now they shall search.'[115]

This then was the framework: a spurious story-line, clumsily written, setting up an unlikely game of wits between the nobleman and the criminal. The twist, of course, was that the *Krone*'s readers themselves would participate in this detective game: they were to impersonate the nobleman's private detectives and were asked to follow the trail of clues in real life. The concept was new enough to puzzle the readers, many of whom kept looking for the silver capsules within the newspaper pages themselves, bombarding the Krone's editorial rooms with their cut-out pictures and demanding their money.[116] By the time the story's first capsule had been hidden, however, the instructions on how to participate in the detective game had been re-printed a sufficient number of times to lure a large number of treasure seekers out towards Hernals early on the twenty-second of October, 1903. The *Krone's* title page on that day proudly announced: '*The first silver capsule can be found today!*'[117] The next day the paper celebrated its first successful detective, a civil servant by the name of Josef Lorenz, who gave a detailed account of how he came to find the 'treasure':

This morning ... I entered the newsagents at Neubaugasse 40 next to Siebensterngasse and I noticed the announcement on the front-page ... I bought the paper, which I usually only read later in the day, and carefully read through the newest part of the novel. I came to the conviction that the treasure could only be located in the enclosure around the Schmelz-cemetery.
– Do you know that area so very well?
As well as any Viennese. But the *clues* were quite *explicit*: 'From Hernals, through streets and alleyways, past a wide plain with no houses, the portcullis ...'. All this should have told any reader that only there could the treasure lie hidden.
– What did you do then, when you had become convinced that you had guessed at the right area to look for the capsule?
I immediately took a tram to the area. I must have arrived around seven in the morning. Many hundred people had already gathered around the cemetery: men, women and children had come out just like me to look for the treasure. But nobody had found it at the time of my arrival.
– How do you explain that these many people were unable to find a treasure that was not hidden away all that well really?
That's simple. These people just didn't understand *how* to go about the search. Some looked for it on top [of the gravestones], others were digging in the ground with sticks, with no plan and no thought put into the search.
– Well, now we're getting to the most interesting part: how did you find the treasure?
I calmly strolled along the outside of the cemetery, my eyes always on the ground. Since the novel specifically stated that the hunchback bent down, the capsule had to be on the ground. Suddenly I noticed a few steps ahead a stone very close to the cemetery wall. This stone looked like a good hiding place and I immediately thought: 'This is where the treasure will be hidden.' There was still some distance between me and the stone and many people passed it without heed. When I reached it the stone still lay there untouched. I *lifted it* and – *the silver capsule lay gleaming at me*. I quickly picked it up, put it in a pocket and moved away. This happened so quickly that no more than a few people even noticed my finding the treasure, despite the fact that a large number of people surrounded me.[118]

One should note how closely Lorenz's account (or rather his account as narrated by the paper) followed the conventions both of the detective literature of the time and those of the trial report, and indeed scientific accounts of detective work: it was literally an exercise in clue-reading, in which the minute details could be followed by the clear-headed detective where his many hundred competitors failed, coupled with the exercise of shrewd observation that identified the rock as the only plausible hiding-place. Lorenz had become, in Peter Fritzsche's phrase, a 'citizen detective'.[119] At the same time it was precisely his expertise (and the reader's vicarious participation in this expertise) that set him apart from the public as such: the article stressed the ignorance of the other treasure hunters who paid not a second glance to this rock and consequently passed not a foot from the capsule, unawares. In other words, the *Krone* here reiterated the criminological narrative of the masses whose observatory powers were minimal, and under whose very noses decisive actions could take place wholly undetected. As before, we note how much reporting on crime – real or fictional – depended on a dichotomy of observatory expertise vs. widespread ignorance that criminals could exploit.

In the visual coverage that accompanied *The Hunchback's Treasures* the paper reiterated its role as an observer of the public: the cover page of the fourteenth of October, for instance, depicting various Krone readers in the act of reading the paper and setting off on their search for the treasure. Rather than denying that it was actively involved in the process of news/sensation-creation, the *Krone* celebrated this role openly. Crime, as a theme of newspaper coverage, thus needs to be continuously read from the perspective of a press that was conceived of as an active agent within the public sphere and whose role it was to literally guide its readers' eyes towards significance. Moreover, reporting on crime was always also a means of reporting on the state of society. Herein lies the key to antisemitic strategies to narrate Jewish crimes.

Antisemitism in the Klein Case

In order to introduce the logic of antisemitic narratives of Jewish crime, let me for one last time turn to back to the Klein case in order to explore its antisemitic dimension. It might come as something of a surprise that there should be such a dimension. Neither of the Kleins was, after all, Jewish. Franziska Klein, it is true, had converted from Catholicism to Protestantism when marrying her husband, and reconverted to Catholicism during the investigative process, but it is hard to see how this confessional interlude should provide antisemitic mileage for even the most dedicated Jew-baiter. Indeed, looking at the *Reichspost*, the newspaper most closely associated with the Christian Social Party, we can discern some early confusion as to how a 'Jewish' dimension could be introduced into the discussion of the case: 'Heinrich Klein,' it wrote in its initial description of the two defendants, 'sports a beard ... and hence looks remarkably like a Jew.'[120] The *Deutsches Volksblatt* – an even more rampantly antisemitic publication edited by Ernst Vergani who had supported von Schoenerer's racialist pan-Germanic movement before aligning himself with the Christian Socials – echoed this, when it introduced Heinrich Klein as wearing 'a jet-black beard' and as being 'of a remarkably Jewish type.'[121] What is remarkable here is not only that the Volksblatt should try to convert the Protestant Klein into a crypto-Jew – a signification tied simply to the style of his beard – but the feebleness of this assoication. For where, indeed, could one go with this alleged resemblance?

The answer is nowhere, for both the *Reichspost* and the *Volksblatt* soon abandoned this initial attempt to 'judify' Heinrich Klein via his appearance. Rather they identified a more convincing 'Jewish' angle. Already in its coverage of the day preceding the trial, the *Reichspost* had drawn attention to the Jewishness not of the defendants but of their lawyers: 'the defence councils are *Dr Morgenstern* (!) for the wife and *Dr F. Elbogen* (!) for the husband.'[122] The *Volksblatt* not only identified the Kleins' lawyers as Jewish and immoral,[123] but also that part of the (female) audience whose rambunctious behaviour and inappropriate dress ('sensational hats and sensational make-up') were implicated as sabotaging the court's dignity and judicial duties.[124] It also made much of the fact that the Kleins' *Kupplereianzeigen* ('procuring advertisements') had been printed in what it identified as a 'Jew paper', and repeatedly used this fact to indict the Jewish immorality that underlay the whole murder affair.[125]

What may appear as a relatively incoherent strategy here was given full expression in the antisemitic satirical magazine *Kikeriki* that printed its main contribution to the Klein scandal under the heading of 'Singer, Klein und Morgenstern,'[126] Singer being the editor-in-chief at the 'Jewish' *Neues Wiener Tagblatt*. The half-page article explained that Singer's paper not only printed Klein's prostitution advertisements, but also her letters with the aim of 'nothing less than to *influence the Viennese jurors*'.[127] In other words, this 'Jewish procurer-paper [*Kuppel-Blatt*]',[128] so vastly immoral that *Kikeriki* described it as being 'pregnant with the atmosphere of the rutting season,'[129] was here depicted as wilfully attempting to mislead justice and help Franziska Klein avoid her just deserts. The *Neues Wiener Tagblatt* was, however, only able to do so with (the Jew) Morgenstern's help, who arranged the printing of Klein's letters. *Kikeriki* went on to explain that while this may seem very inconsiderate of the Jew Morgenstern vis-à-vis his Jewish colleague Elbogen, who was labouring to get Franziska's husband off the hook, Elbogen himself had employed the very same strategy in an earlier criminal trial.[130] The goal of this sort of strategy, *Kikeriki* indicted, was to generate 'cheap propaganda for the accused' that would result in the 'captivation of naïve juror-minds'.[131] Morgenstern and Elbogen were unmasked as being masters in the use of precisely such '*Judenkniffe* (Jewish tricks)'; with the help of a Jewish newspaper they worked to destroy the administration of justice.[132]

Figure 4.13 'The robbers of past and present.'
Source. *Kikeriki*, 30 April 1905, p. 7.

The same edition of *Kikeriki* featured a two-panel cartoon under the heading of 'The robbers past and present' (cf. Figure 4.13).[133] The left panel depicted a seedy tavern; at the table a bunch of shady characters, drinking, gambling and spilling beer. The door stood ajar, a Jew, denoted by his grotesquely large nose and thick lips, had just entered the establishment. The bottom caption read: 'Spiegelberger: "Let us go into the Bohemian woods and start a robber gang."' The right panel also showed a room with a table, where three Jews were sitting and three more were standing, all with their heads bowed in conspiracy. All had big noses, Jewish beards and felt hats. Here the caption read: 'Jews: 'Let's move to Vienna and found a non-political paper.'[134] While it is important to notice the stress on the danger of immigration of eastern Jews, as is the identification of Jews with a long tradition of crime, the crucial point here is the criminalisation of the whole sphere of news production that purported to be apolitical, but in fact distorted truth – much as the *Neues Wiener Tagblatt* stood accused of having done a few pages earlier.[135] The difference between the cartoon and the article lay in the clear visual identification of Jews in the former: in an antisemitic fantasy Jews were all clearly differentiable by their very appearance. In reality they could be traced only by reference to their Jewish names (Singer, Morgenstern, Elbogen) and through the identification of their 'Jewish tricks'.

This then was the logic with which a trial could be re-interpreted in an antisemitic key. Precisely because crime was seen to be so tied up with the process of truth recovery, and because this process was seen to depend on the wider interaction of defendant, jury, public and papers, virtually any trial was open to the accusation of a miscarriage of justice. Jewish forces could easily be identified as the primary instigators of such miscarriages, particularly when Jews were involved in this wider network of the trial: not necessarily as defendants (although we shall encounter this variety as well), but as lawyers or journalists, psychologists, expert witnesses, or simply as the public. This, of course, conforms to our argument that criminological science was in these years beginning to focus on issues other than the identification of criminal difference and was considering problems of truth establishment and the dangers of dissimulation and suggestion. One need not argue here that the antisemitic publications consciously tapped into criminological discourse about the fragility of knowledge, but simply that the Jewish perversion of knowledge became a theme within antisemitic coverage of crime concurrently with this discourse. After all, trial reporting was merely a mode of writing about society. Hence the social threat posed by Jews could be systematically exposed by antisemitic writing on crime. The truest Jewish crime, we shall see, was nothing other than the total destruction of objective access to truth itself.

Notes

1. Marcel Proust, 'Final Sentiments of a Parricide', in: Friedrich R. Karl and Leo Hamalian (eds), *The Existential Imagination, From de Sade to Sartre* (London 1973), p. 112.
2. In Britain the triumph of the press occurred as early as the 1810s and 1820s. Cf. Paul Johnson, *The Birth of the Modern* (London 1991), 948–50; Ivon Asquith, 'The Structure, Ownership and Control of the Press 1780–1855', in: George Boyce, James Curran and Pauline Wingate (eds), *Newspaper History, from the seventeenth century to the present day* (London 1978), pp. 98–118. On the rise of journalism as a profession, see: Jean K. Chalaby, *The Invention of Journalism* (London 1998).
3. For a brief introduction to German language mass papers, see: Ernst Bollinger, *1840–1930: Die Goldenen Jahre der Massenpresse* (Freiburg, Schweiz 1996). On the rise of German press power, and its connection to the reporting of scandals, see: Andreas Schulz, 'Der Aufstieg der vierten Gewalt, Medien, Politik und Öffentlichkeit im Zeitalter der Massenkommunikation', in: *Historische Zeitschrift* 270 (2000), pp. 65–97.
4. Cf. Peter Fritzsche, *Reading Berlin 1900* (Cambridge, Mass. 1996), pp. 8, 60.
5. Cf. Albert Eberhard Friedrich Schäffle, *Bau und Leben des sozialen Körpers* (Tübingen 1881); Max Weber, 'Rede auf dem ersten deutschen Soziologentage in Frankfurt 1910', in: *Gesammelte Aufsätze zur Soziologie und Sozialpolitik* (Tübingen 1924), 434–41; Ferdinand Tönnies, *Kritik der öffentlichen Meinung* (Berlin 1922). All these texts and their authors are discussed in: Hanns Hardt, *Social Theories of the Press, Early German and American Perspectives* (London 1979).
6. In Germany the rise of the newspaper and its reading public is well documented. See: Rolf Engelsing, *Massenpublikum und Journalistentum im 19. Jahrhundert in Nordwestdeutschland*, Schriften zur Wirtschafts- und Sozialgeschichte Vol. 1 (Berlin 1966); Rolf Engelsing, *Analphabetentum und Lektüre, Zur Sozialgeschichte des Lesens in Deutschland zwischen feudaler und industrieller Gesellschaft* (Stuttgart 1973); Kurt Koszyk, *Deutsche Presse im 19. Jahrhundert* (Berlin 1966); H. Diez, *Das Zeitungswesen* (Leipzig 1919). For Vienna specifically, see: Stephan Schreder, *Der Zeitungsleser, Eine soziologische Studie mit besonderer Berücksichtigung der Zeitungsleserschaft Wiens* (Vienna 1934).
7. Elisabeth L. Eisenstein, 'Some Conjectures about the Impact of Printing on Western Society and Thought: A Preliminary Report', in: *Journal of Modern History* 40, 1 (1968), p. 41. Cf.: Anderson, *Imagined Communities*, p. 39.

8. Kurt Paupié, *Handbuch der österreichischen Pressegeschichte Band 1: Wien* (Vienna 1960), p. 12; Hugo Falkmayer, *Die Presse in der österreichischen Gesetzgebung* phil. Diss. (Vienna 1951). For contemporary accounts, see: Fritz Austerlitz, *Pressefreiheit und Presserecht, Eine Studie über den Preßgesetzentwurf* (Vienna 1902); Max Burckhard, *Der Entwurf eines neuen Pressegesetzes* (Vienna 1902); Max Garr, *Die Inseratsteuer* (Vienna 1909).

9. Cf. Richard Grunberger, 'Jews in Austrian Journalism', in: Josef Fraenkel (ed.), *The Jews in Austria, Essays on Their Life, History and Destruction* (London 1970 [1967]), p. 83.

10. Paupié, *Handbuch*, pp. 12–19, 173ff. Hans Dichand, *Illustrierte Kronenzeitung, Die Geschichte eines Erfolges* (Vienna 1977), pp. 1–100. See also: Bollinger, *1840–1930*, pp. 110–15.

11. 500,000 is an extremely conservative estimate based on the aggregate of circulation numbers listed in Paupié, *Handbuch*, pp. 82–178. This estimate excludes local (for example district-based) papers. The total number of different publications is staggering: in 1907 alone, for instance, 164 new German-language 'periodicals' were founded. Cf. 'Verzeichnis der im Jahre 1907 neu erschienenen und erloschenen periodischen Druckschriften', in: ÖS, Druckschriften IV Allg., Pressedelikte 3038A, No. 164.

12. Rudolf Schenda estimates 2.6 readers per circulated newspaper in Bremen in 1902. The numbers are likely to be at least as high in Vienna. Rudolf Schenda, *Volk ohne Buch, Studien zur Sozialgeschichte der populären Lesestoffe 1770–1910* (Munich 1977), pp. 451–2.

13. Hardt, *Social Theories*, 65–6. For a Viennese voice asserting the influence of the contemporary press over its readers, see: Severus Verax, *Die öffentliche Meinung von Wien. Wiener Pressegeschichten* (Zurich 1899).

14. Habermas, *Strukturwandel*, 258–63; James Curran, 'Mass Media and Democracy', in: James Curran and Michael Gurevitch (eds), *Mass Media and Society* (New York 1991), pp. 82–117.

15. Arno Pilgram, 'Zur Auswirkung der Kriminalitätsdarstellung in den Massenmedien, Annahmen und ihre Folgen', in: *Österreichische Zeitschrift für Soziologie* 4 (1979), p. 112.

16. Bernhard Fulda, 'Press and Politics in Berlin, 1924–30', unpublished Ph.D. thesis (University of Cambridge 2003), chapter one.

17. Rudolf Schenda argues that readers at the turn of the last century were less critical and more willing to believe their newspapers than modern-day readers, as does Rolf Engelsing. Schenda, *Volk*, pp. 493–4; Engelsing, *Massenpublikum*, pp. 130–1.

18. ÖS, Druckschriften IV Allg. 1900, Pressedelikte, 3039.

19. Ibid.

20. ÖS, Jutizakten VI – l – Schweiz Beer, No. 24141/5. The trial in question is the Beer trial, discussed in greater detail in chapter five.

21. For further information about the respective papers and Austrian news culture in general, see: Paupié, *Handbuch*, pp. 88–176; Dichand, *Kronenzeitung, passim*; '50 Jahre', in: *Extrablatt*, 25 March 1922 (Festnummer), pp. 1–2; *AZ*, 1 Jan 1925 (Festnummer), *passim*; 'Sechzig Jahre Arbeiter-Zeitung', in: *AZ*, 1 Jan 1949, pp. iv–v; Holiczki, 'Die Entwicklung der Gerichtsberichterstattung', pp. 224–42; Otto Petting, *Wiens antisemitische Presse* (Vienna 1896); Jakob Margarethe, 'Das Deutsche Volksblatt und seine politische Geschichte in den Jahren 1889–99' (Ph.D. Diss., Univ. Wien 1937); Joseph Draxler, 'Vergleich der Zeitungen Reichspost und Vaterland in Bezug auf die Probleme der Zeit von 1894–1911' (Ph.D. Diss. Univ. Wien 1948); Ingrid Walter, 'Moriz Benedikt und die Neue Freie Presse' (Ph.D. Diss., Univ. Wien 1950); Adam Wandruszka, 'Geschichte einer Zeitung. Das Schicksal der 'Presse' und 'Neuen Freien Presse' von 1848 bis zur zweiten Republik', (Ph.D. Diss., Univ. Wien 1958); Walter Haney, 'Die Illustrierte Kronenzeitung, ein Beitrag zur Geschichte der Wiener Presse' (Ph.D. Diss. Univ. Wien 1950); Ruprecht Kunz, 'Die Geschichte der Arbeiterzeitung

von ihrer Gründung zur Jahrhundertwende' (Ph.D. Diss. Univ. Wien 1949); Mario Molin-Pradel, 'Friedrich Austerlitz, Chefredakteur der Arbeiter-Zeitung' (Ph.D. Diss., Univ Wien 1963); Olga Auer, 'Beginn der Parteipresse in Österreich mit besonderer Berücksichtigung der Parteientwicklung' (Ph.D. Diss. Univ. Wien 1951); Franz Stamprech, 'Die kleinen Blätter Wiens' (Ph.D. Diss. Univ. Wien 1954), pp. 32–43; Rainer Mayerhofer, 'Die Entwicklung der Lokalberichterstattung in der Wiener Tagespresse von 1848 bis 1900' (Ph.D. Diss. Univ. Wien 1972).

22. On the Jewish press in Vienna, see: Jacob Toury, *Die jüdische Presse im Österreichischen Kaiserreich, Ein Beitrag zur Problematik der Akkulturation 1802–1918* (Tübingen 1983).

23. The ratio refers to the total length of coverage rather than number of incidents.

24. The *Illustrierte Kronenzeitung*'s circulation history being a case in point here. Cf. Dichand, *Kronenzeitung*, pp. 25–7. Similarly, the *Neues Wiener Tagblatt* was helped along by its report on a Munich murder. Cf. Heinrich Pollak, *Dreißig Jahre aus dem Leben eines Journalisten* (Vienna 1894).

25. One need only look at the lively discussions precipitated by crime and trials amongst Hamburg workers. Cf. Richard J. Evans, *Kneipengespräche im Kaiserreich. Stimmungsberichte der Hamburger Politischen Polizei 1892–1914* (Reinbek bei Hamburg 1989), p. 182.

26. It is, in other words, not my goal to uncover the political agenda buried in the respective crime reports, largely because most contemporary papers wore this agenda on their sleeves. In this my study differs from other historical treatments of crime reports in newspapers. See, for instance: Eric A. Johnson, *Urbanisation and Crime, Germany 1871–1914* (Cambridge 1995), pp. 53–95; Alexandra Ledl, 'Die Gerichtssaalsberichterstattung in der ersten österreichischen Republik in den Parteiorganen der Christlich-Sozialen und Sozialdemokraten von 1918 bis 1939' (Ph.D. Diss., Univ. Wien 1990).

27. *AZ*, 27 April 1905, p. 7.

28. *NWT*, 23 April 1905, pp. 11–12.

29. This account of the trial is largely reconstructed from the various accounts in the papers, and the few remaining records of the case filed under ÖS VI l Frankreich K 11. For sensationalist re-narrations of the case see: Max Edelbacher and Harald Seyrl, *Wiener Kriminalchronik* (Vienna 1993), p. 104, and Diechand, *Kronenzeitung*, pp. 41–2.

30. *Krone*, 26 April 1905, pp. 1, 9–11; *Krone*, 27 April 1905, pp. 1–11; *Krone*, 28 April 1905, pp. 1–11; *Krone*, 29 April 1905, pp. 1–8; *Krone*, 30 April 1905, pp. 1–7; *Krone*, 2 May 1905, pp. 1, 9–10.

31. *Krone*, 27 April 1905, pp. 1–11.

32. *Extrablatt*, 27 April 1905, pp. 1, 7–13; *Extrablatt*, 28 April 1905, pp. 1, 7–13; *Extrablatt*, 29 April 1905, pp. 1, 8–12; *Extrablatt*, 30 April 1905, pp. 1–2, 8–12.

33. *Extrablatt*, 26 April 1905, Evening Edition, pp. 1–2; *Extrablatt*, 26 April 1905, Evening Edition 'Separatausgabe', pp. 1–4; *Extrablatt*, 27 April 1905, Evening Edition, pp. 1–3; *Extrablatt*, 28 April 1905, Evening Edition, pp. 1–4.

34. *NFP*, 26 April 1905, pp. 9–10; *NFP*, 26 April 1905, Evening Edition, pp. 3–5; *NFP*, 27 April 1905, pp. 9–11; *NFP*, 27 April 1905, Evening Edition, pp. 4–5; *NFP*, 28 April 1905, pp. 8–10; *NFP*, 28 April 1905, Evening Edition, pp. 4–5; *NFP*, 29 April 1905, pp. 9–10; *NFP*, 29 April 1905, Evening Edition, pp. 3–4; *NFP*, 30 April 1905, pp. 12–14.

35. *AZ*, 26 April 1905, p. 8; *AZ*, 27 April 1905, pp. 6–8; *AZ*, 28 April 1905, pp. 6–7; *AZ*, 29 April 1905, pp. 6–8; *AZ*, 30 April 1905, pp. 9–10.

36. *DV*, 26 April 1905, p. 8; *DV*, 26 April 1905, Evening Edition, pp. 1–3; *DV*, 27 April 1905, pp. 7–11; *DV*, 27 April 1905, Evening Edition, pp. 1–2; *DV*, 28 April 1905, pp. 7–10; *DV*, 28 April 1905, Evening Edition, pp. 1–3; *DV*, 29 April 1905, pp. 7–9; *DV*, 27 April 1905, Evening Edition, p. 2; *DV*, 30 April 1905, pp. 1–3, 9–10.

37. The straightforward stenographic report was a hallmark of a more traditional reporting strategy dating from the mid-century; at the turn of the century it was integrated

into more and more overt editorial intervention, of the kind described here. Cf. Holiczki, 'Die Entwicklung', pp. 91–108, 112–16; Klaus Marxen, 'Zum Verhältnis von Strafrecht und Gerichtserstattung in der zweiten Hälfte des 19. Jahrhunderts', in: Schönert (ed.), *Erzählte Kriminalität*, p. 372.

38. Cf. Holiczki, 'Die Entwicklung', pp. 145–8, 249. Holiczki's circulation numbers seem inflated compared to other sources.

39. For theoretical reflections on the relationship between verbal and pictorial description, see: Nelson Goodman, *Languages of Art* (Indianapolis 1976), p. 222; W.J.T. Mitchell, *Iconology, Image, Text, Ideology* (Chicago 1986), pp. 66–7.

40. Hans Dichand, *Illustrierte Kronenzeitung*, p. 18.

41. For the question and answer columns, see in particular the *Krone*'s Monday editions.

42. *Krone*, 27 April 1905, p. 2.

43. *Krone*, 27 April 1905, pp. 2–3.

44. *Krone*, 26 April 1905, p. 9.

45. Richard Sennett, *The Fall of Public Man* (London 1986), pp. 154ff.

46. Erich Auerbach, *Mimesis: The Representation of Reality in Western Literature*, translated by Willard R. Trask (Princeton 1968), 469ff.

47. Transcript, 'Der Prozess Riehl und Konsorten in Wien', in: *Archiv* 27 (1907), pp. 1–111. The paper in question is *Die Zeit*. Gross corrected the paper's coverage by comparing it to official court sources but left in place long descriptive passages on all the defendants.

48. *NFP*, 27 April 1905, p. 9.

49. *Extrablatt*, 27 April 1905, p. 7.

50. *Extrablatt*, 28 April 1905, p. 8.

51. Ibid.

52. Ibid., p. 4.

53. *DV*, 29 Sept 1899, pp. 2–4.

54. Ibid., p. 3.

55. *Krone*, 26 April 1905, p. 10.

56. Ibid. See also: *AZ*, 26 April 1905, p. 5, etc.

57. Ibid.; *Extrablatt*, 27 April 1905, p. 7, etc.

58. Sennet, *Fall*, p. 248. Sennet's discussion focuses on Emile Zola's *J'accuse*.

59. In this the strategy of the reports differs from Zola's *J'accuse*, and also from the 'trials of character' described by Harry Cocks in his discussion of nineteenth century sodomy trials: H.G. Cocks, 'Trials of character: the use of character evidence in Victorian sodomy trials', in: R.A. Melikan (ed.), *Domestic and international trials, 1700–2000, The Trial in History Vol. II* (Manchester 2003), pp. 36–53.

60. Kraus mockingly lists the sub-headlines of the coverage in the *Illustriertes Extrablatt* (for example 'The hands of Mr Klein'; 'The Calm of the Sphinx'; 'The treacherous underwear') and concludes: 'In this rich display, one has not even forgotten to describe the buttons on Miss Navratil's jacket.' Karl Kraus, 'Zum Prozeß Klein', in: *Die Fackel*, May 1905, reprinted in: Karl Kraus, *Sittlichkeit und Kriminalität* (Frankfurt am Main 1987 [1908]), pp. 163–4.

61. *NFP*, 26 April 1905, Evening Edition, p. 3.

62. Ibid.

63. Hannah Arendt, *On Revolution* (London 1973), pp. 98–108; Lynn Hunt, *Politics, Culture and Class in the French Revolution* (London 1992), pp. 19–20.

64. Dana Brand, 'From the Flâneur to the Detective, Interpreting the City of Poe', in: Tony Bennett (ed.), *Popular Fiction, Technology, Ideology, Production, Reading* (London 1990), pp. 224–5. See also: Walter Benjamin, *Charles Baudelaire, A Lyric Poet in the Era of High Capitalism* (London 1983), pp. 40–3. For an excellent summary of the issues, see: John Jervis, *Exploring the Modern* (Oxford 1998), pp. 76ff.

65. Elizabeth Wilson, 'The Invisible Flâneur', in: Sophie Watson and Katherine Gibson (eds), *Postmodern Cities and Spaces* (Oxford 1995), pp. 59–79.

66. On the masculine gaze of the criminologist and criminalist, see: Nicky Hahn Rafter, 'Space, Gender, and Representation in Lombroso's "La donna delinquente"', unpublished conference paper, IFK Vienna, 14 December 2001.

67. Sengoopta, *Weininger*, pp. 61–4.

68. *AZ*, 27 April 1905, p. 6.

69. Cf. Richard Evans's comments on 'female crowds' in the 1913 Sternickel trial in Frankfurt an der Oder. Evans, *Rituals*, p. 472.

70. Lyn Pykett, *Engendering Fictions, the English Novel in the Early Twentieth Century* (London 1995), pp. 33ff.

71. *NFP*, 28 April 1905, p. 8.

72. *Extrablatt*, 27 April 1905, p. 7.

73. *Extrablatt*, 30. April 1905, p. 2.

74. *AZ*, 27 April 1905, p. 6.

75. *Krone*, 26. April 1905, p. 9.

76. Cf. for instance *AZ*, 30 April 1905, p. 10.

77. *Extrablatt*, 30 April 1905, p. 2.

78. *RP*, 3 May 1905, p. 5.

79. Ibid.

80. *Extrablatt*, 30 April 1905, p. 2.

81. Cf. Richard Evans's discussion of the Kürten trial in 1931, in which the defendant is similarly identified as an 'actor'. Evans, *Rituals*, p. 599.

82. *AZ*, 29 April 1905, p. 6.

83. *AZ*, 28 April 1905, p. 6.

84. *AZ*, 30 April 1905, p. 9.

85. See also Ludger Hoffmann's discussion of the truth process in trials. Ludger Hoffmann, 'Vom Ereignis zum Fall, Sprachliche Muster zur Darstellung und Überprüfung von Sachverhalten vor Gericht', in: Schönert (ed.), *Erzählte Kriminalität*, pp. 87–114.

86. Cf. *RP*, 27 April 1905, p. 9; *Krone*, 28 April 1905, p. 2; *Extrablatt*, 28 April 1905, p. 7; *NFP*, 27 April 1905, p. 9.

87. *Krone*, 28 April 1905, title page; *Krone*, 29 April 1905, title page. See Figures 4.1 and 4.12.

88. Here quoted from: *Krone*, 28 April 1905, p. 3.

89. *Extrablatt*, 30 April 1905, p. 2.

90. *Extrablatt*, 28 April 1905, p. 5.

91. For example *NFP*, 29 Oct 1904, Evening Edition, p. 3.

92. *NFP*, 28 April 1905, Evening Edition, p. 4; *NFP*, 29 April 1905, Evening Edition, p. 3; *NFP*, 30 April 1905, p. 14; *RP*, 28 April 1905, p. 6; *RP*, 27 April 1905, p. 6; *Extrablatt*, 30 April 1905, p. 9; *Krone*, 27 April 1905, p. 2; *Krone*, 30 April 1905, p. 2; *AZ*, 26 April 1905, p. 8. *AZ*, 27 April 1905, p. 6, etc.

93. Ibid. For fights at the entrance, see in particular: *NFP*, 30 April 1905, p. 14.

94. Larry Wolf, *Postcards from the End of the World, An Investigation into the Mind of Fin-de-Siècle Vienna* (London 1989), pp. 80 ff.

95. For an excellent introduction to nineteenth-century theatre, see: Michael R. Booth, 'Nineteenth-Century Theatre', in: John Russell Brown (ed.), *The Oxford Illustrated History of Theatre* (Oxford 1995), pp. 299–340.

96. On Rousseau's condemnation of theatricality, see: Lionel Trilling, *Sincerity and Authenticity* (Oxford 1971); E. J. Hundert, 'The European Enlightenment and the History of the Self', in: Porter (ed.), *Rewriting*, pp. 72–83.

97. Iris Brooke, *Western European Costume, 17th to Mid-19th Centuries, and Its Relation to the Theatre* (London 1940); James Laver, *Drama, Its Costume and Décor* (London 1951).

98. Sennett, *Fall*, p. 206.
99. Ibid., p. 210.
100. Ibid., p. 174. Michael R. Booth, 'Nineteenth-Century Theatre', p. 329.
101. Ibid., p. 300; Richard Southern, *The Seven Ages of the Theatre* (London 1962), pp. 253–67.
102. Marvin Carlson, *The German Stage in the Nineteenth Century* (Metuchen, NJ 1972), p. 91; Sennett, *Fall*, p. 209.
103. Martin Esslin, 'Modern Theatre 1890–1920', in: Brown (ed.), *History of Theatre*, p. 356.
104. Carlson, *The German Stage*, p. 195.
105. On the rise and fall of naturalism on German language stages, see: Michael Patterson, *The Revolution in German Theatre 1900–1933* (Boston 1981), pp. 32 ff.
106. On the continuing importance of melodrama throughout and beyond the nineteenth century, see: Michael R. Booth, 'Nineteenth-Century Theatre', p. 339; Nina Auerbach, *Private Theatricals, The Lives of the Victorians* (Cambridge, Mass. 1990), p. 15.
107. On the 'flexible', 'individualised' crowds of Georg II of Saxe-Meininger's theatre, and those of his imitators, see Booth, 'Nineteenth-Century Theatre', p. 336.
108. *Krone*, 27 April 1905, p. 2.
109. Cf. Figure 4.1 and analysis above.
110. Cf. Michael Warner, 'The Mass Public and the Mass Subject', in: Calhoun (ed.), *Habermas*, p. 381.
111. *Extrablatt*, 30 April 1905, p. 3.
112. Martin Wiener describes this decline of a moral view of crime and its replacement by an analytical enjoyment of crime puzzles in his discussion of late nineteenth-century crime literature. See: Martin J. Wiener, *Reconstructing the Criminal, Culture, Law and Policy in England, 1830–1913* (Cambridge 1990), p. 224.
113. This reading implies a careful division between public, 'objective' existence and private enjoyment (objectively outrage has been voiced, therefore it need not be experienced subjectively). It is congruent with the sentiments voiced in the quotation by Proust that opens this chapter. For a discussion of the conventions and techniques of melodrama in the nineteenth-century novel, see: Peter Brooks, *The Melodramatic Imagination, Balzac, Henry James, Melodrama and the Mode of Excess* (New Haven 1995).
114. 'Die Schätze des Buckligen', *Krone*, 14 Oct. 1903, pp. 1, 8, 12–13.
115. *Krone*, 22 Oct. 1903, pp. 11–12.
116. *Krone*, 20 Oct 1903, p. 8.
117. *Krone*, 22 Oct. 1903, p. 1.
118. *Krone*, 23 October 1903, p. 5.
119. Fritzsche, *Reading Berlin*, pp. 83–5; Peter Fritzsche, '"Eyes Peeled!" Anonymity, Anxiety and Surveillance in the Metropolis', unpublished paper presented at the IFK Vienna, 14 December 2001. Fritzsche discusses the example of a simulated man-hunt organised by a popular Berlin daily in 1919.
120. *RP*, 27 April 1905, p. 6.
121. *DV*, 26 April 1905, evening edition, p. 2.
122. RP, 26 April 1905, p. 10. Here and throughout, the emphasis is the original's.
123. *DV*, 30 April 1905, p. 1.
124. Ibid., p. 2.
125. Ibid., pp. 1–2, 9.
126. *Kikeriki*, 30 April 1905, p. 2.
127. Ibid.
128. Ibid.
129. Ibid.
130. One should note that Friedrich Elbogen was a member of the Austrian Israelite Union and could thus be targeted as Jewish with particular ease.

131. Ibid.
132. Ibid.
133. *Kikeriki*, 30 April 1905, p. 7.
134. Ibid. The German both adjusts the orthography to indicate Jewish 'Mauschel', and puns on the word 'Zeit'ung' in order to allude to the liberal (i.e., in an antisemite's dictionary, Jewish) weekly *Die Zeit*.
135. On the antisemitic narrative of the Jewish power over the press, see also: 'Junius' (pseudonym), *Das Judenthum und die Tagespresse: Ein Mahnwort in ernster Stunde* (Leipzig 1879). Cf. Robertson, *Jewish Question*, p. 181.

Chapter 5

Jewish Crimes

Antisemitic periodicals such as the *Deutsches Volksblatt* connected Jews to the theme of criminality with astonishing regularity. A 'busy' month like March 1900 could witness more than thirty instances in which a headline or opening paragraph established a connection between the two – and that refers to the morning editions alone. Even an uneventful month (say, September 1910), and the most conservative of counts, reveals around a dozen instances of such connection. In other words, an avid reader of this newspaper stood to encounter the theme of Jewish crime at least twice a week, and more likely four or five times. To give another sort of quantitative measure: a given month provided about 450 column centimetres about Jewish crimes (though months in which the figure was closer to 1,200 column centimetres also occurred); anything between fifteen to forty percent of the ink spilled on trials in a given month's coverage contributed to the grand project of identifying Jews and crime. Whilst financial transgressions were the most common crimes to be associated with Jews, virtually any sort of criminal activity received attention, from thefts to sexual scandals to violent crimes and murder.

One can easily imagine that prolonged exposure to such a constant reiteration deeply ingrained the connection between Jews and crime into the antisemitic mind-set. No other ethnic or political group was equally systematically slandered. Even the socialists were only occasionally singled out for abuse in the context of crime, and here only in specific types of criminal setting (largely cases of political *Ehrenbeleidigung*, i.e. insults of personal honour). Indeed, when the socialists were singled out for an attack this was frequently combined with unmasking them as Jews into the bargain.[1] There can be little doubt that crime, and specifically trial reporting, were central to the antisemitic narratives spun by the *Volksblatt* and like-minded papers.

Despite the centrality of Jewish criminality within antisemitic papers – the *Volksblatt*'s coverage found a clear echo in other antisemitic publications, most prominently so in the Christian Social paper *Die Reichspost* – the precise characteristics of this motif are not immediately obvious. Most of these reports, after all – whether they covered an actual crime, or concerned a trial – did little more than mention the Judaism of one of the involved. Frequently, they were content with doing little more than identifying a given criminal as Jewish, as in the trial of two Jews who stole coffee from their employer in September 1905,[2] or the trial of a Jewish pub-owner in Berlin who physically attacked an official sent to impound some of his property in March of the same year.[3]

Moreover, a significant proportion of reports managed to connect Jews to criminal acts despite the absence of a Jewish suspect or defendant. In something like a third of the trials (and closer to a half of the crime reports) that were billed in some way or other as 'Jewish', the involvement of any Jewish party involved was rather peripheral. One example for such a report is provided by the Klein case discussed in the previous chapter, in which Jewish lawyers and newspapers were criminalised. Another would be the case of a Jewish landlady suing one of her tenants – the *Volksblatt*'s coverage narrated her as an example of a Jew abusing the justice system for her personal, financial gain.[4] This sort of association of Jews with crime despite the lack of any actual illegal activity on the side of the Jews in question, was taken *ad absurdum* in a 1905 murder trial in which the victim was Jewish: the trial was consistently billed under the heading of 'The murdered Jewess.'[5] In such reports we encounter the sustained and seemingly desperate attempt to associate Jews with criminality, no matter how. One may well ask how this strategy could possibly be thought to be successful.

In order to decode the antisemitic vision of Jewish crime that gave narrative meaning to these hundreds upon hundreds of incidental reports about some Jewish indiscretion or other, and at the same time elucidate why it was possible to frame crimes as Jewish in which no Jewish perpetrator could be located, one needs to turn to antisemitic reports on sensation trials. These trials invited long and detailed coverage in which a story about Jews and crime could be gradually developed over a series of days, and could be buttressed by front page editorials that would spell out the significance of the events 'witnessed'. The previous chapter has analysed the genre tropes associated with these reports, including their use of theatrical metaphors, their passion for locating criminality in the court room itself, their understanding of, and interest in, the public, and their tendency to understand trials as social laboratories in which far more could be observed than the mere guilt of an individual. The present chapter concentrates on a series of sensations that were explicitly built up as Jewish crimes by antisemitic papers. These trials all centred on Jewish defendants. Given that they were major sensations, they were all covered by the whole range of Viennese newspapers of the period under consideration. This allows us to assess how widespread the use of antisemitic tropes about crime was in Vienna around the turn of the last century. Given that business crimes were most widely associated with Jews – and that statistically these were indeed the type of crimes Jewish Austrians were most commonly convicted for – let us first turn to a series of scandals concerning financial fraud.

Business Crimes – Introduction

More than forty percent of crimes and trials involving Jewish perpetrators/ defendants concerned some variety of financial crime, including anything from '*Krida*', i.e. the fraudulent obfuscation of bankruptcy, to schemes of money forgery, con-artistry, or embezzlement.[6] Indeed, the lines between such offences and immoral, but technically legal, business activities were deliberately blurred by antisemitic commentators. Drawing on an exaggerated but factual link between liberal-capitalism and Jews, Jewish businessmen were systematically depicted as the very incarnation of capitalist abuse of the laws, and it was often the 'immoral' utilisation of free market forces that were decried by antisemites as typically Jewish, quasi-criminal activities.

Examples of such charges include the *Volksblatt*'s commentary on the aggressive (hence unfair) advertising campaign by the Jewish bread factory Mendl, which published details about its rivals' lack of sanitation in the production process.[7] Similarly, one finds the *Volksblatt* attacking the 'Jewish' business practice of offering unfair mortgage rates to an innocent and unsuspecting rural population,[8] or else claiming that Jewish businessmen financed their enterprises by going into debt way over their heads and thus precipitated bankruptcies.[9] Yet another example of this dynamic is provided by the paper's exposure of a Jewish spirit factory's use of slightly small barrels in order to increase its profits.[10] The antisemitic press was quick to seize upon such cases in whatever form possible, articulating a vision of Jewish crime as capitalist crime that closely correlates to Hugo Herz's. The problem, the antisemites maintained, was that Jews partook in 'deals' [*Geschäfte*], rather than professions [*Berufe*] and that the former, even where legal, were essentially a form of 'day-to-day theft'.[11]

This routine criminalisation of Jewish/capitalist business methods found expression in the antisemitic press's frequent association of Jewish defendants with Jewish spectators or indeed Jewish victims of crime. This strategy was helped along by the reporting conventions of contemporary trial reports. These, as we have seen, routinely investigated the public in attendance, the jury, the defence lawyer and the other papers' coverage with the same beady-eyed detective's gaze that served to unmask the defendants. Thus, in the trial of two artificial flower manufacturers – consistently designated as 'the Jew Springer' and the 'Jew Goldenberg' in the antisemitic press – who (along with other charges) stood accused of having forged bills of exchange and obfuscated their business's bankruptcy, the pair was associated with the audience who 'recruit themselves from Jews, as seems to be always the case in these kinds of trials' through descriptive observation: one of the defendants was described as 'stud[ying] the spectators with great audacity, occasionally nodding to an acquaintance'.[12] Implicitly, such familiarity suggested minimal difference between defendant and auditorium; the only difference between the Jewish businessmen on either side of the railing that separated the two, we are told, was that some Jewish crooks got caught, while the others did not. Springer and Goldberg were merely examples of ubiquitous Jewish abuse, a point that the *Volksblatt* made explicit by giving them the tag of *Musterjuden* ('exemplary Jews').[13] Indeed, both the *Deutsches Volksblatt* and the *Reichspost* explicitly covered the trial under headings that implicated all Jews – the former with the headline of 'Jews as Businessmen',[14] the latter with 'Jewish Business Ethics'.[15] A third strategy that is evident from this minor, if prolonged, trial, was the attempt to identify Jews with cunning crime. In the present case – hobbled by the trial's triviality – this was done negatively, via a complaint about the defendants' uncharacteristic lack of originality:

> The business manipulation of the two accused Jews Springer and Goldberg is neither original nor Jewish-cunning, but rather took place every-day ordinary [*sic*]. One is, by virtue of numerous preceding cases in which Jews play the lead role, used to their pulling off some uncommon crime of commerce, being familiar with all the tricks of illegal business behaviour.[16]

'True' Jewish crime was usually revealed precisely through its level of criminal competence.

If a minor scandal like the trial of these unfortunate flower manufacturers raised these themes only obliquely, it found full expression in the scandal surrounding an organised gang of Galician defrauders under the leadership of one Nuchem Schapira.

Business Crimes – Nuchem Schapira's False Fifties

On the second of December 1893, on board a train running from Cracow to Trzbinia, the Viennese businessman Arnold Gastfreund made the acquaintance of one Roman Herz, who shared his compartment. The two began talking, first in German, then in English, and after establishing some sort of preliminary interest, Herz made Gastfreund an exceptionally lucrative, if illegal business proposition: he offered to sell him high quality forgeries of Austro-Hungarian money bills, at twenty percent of the nominal price, plus a commission of five percent for every additional buyer Gastfreund could find. Herz got off in Trzbinia, leaving behind a London address. Gastfreund, upon his return to Vienna, reported the incident to the police. Their research soon unearthed a large-scale fraud based in London and Galicia. Businessmen in Galicia – virtually all of them Jewish – were systematically approached and offered the above described 'proposition'. If they declared themselves willing to buy the forgeries they were invited to London (or, occasionally, to Rotterdam, Berlin and

Breslau) to go through with the exchange. After handing over the money, the buyer was cheated out of his part of the bargain: the forgeries did not actually exist. The buyer was either simply lost in the maze of an unfamiliar city, or a fake arrest was staged, in which his supposed business partner was led away before he had a chance to hand over the forgeries.[17]

The fraud was organised and executed by a group of partners, all Jewish, six of whom stood trial for nine cases of fraud and twelve cases of attempted fraud in February 1895: Nuchem Schapira, his wife, Sarah Schapira, Jossel Herz (also known as Roman Herz), Moses Baumgarten, Ello Aaron Frischling and Schlome Berger. Nuchem Schapira was identified as the head of the consortium. Since both the injured parties and the defendants were Austro-Hungarian citizens, the trial took place in Vienna's criminal court.

One of the first things one notices in all the newspaper coverage of the trial – antisemitic and other – is the total absence of any sort of pathologisation of any of the criminals involved. Despite a systematic build-up of Schapira and one or two others, most notably Herz, as arch-criminals, no suggestion was made that their choice of career could be explained by determinist mechanisms. In fact, the cold rationality of the main criminal actors was repeatedly stressed: their intelligence and professionalism acted as markers for their criminal danger.[18] Nuchem Schapira's biography, for instance – the tale of his criminal career – was presented in the language of deliberate choice and professionalisation.[19] When he spoke in court, his words were reported as deliberately chosen, coherent, intelligent.[20] Here, as elsewhere, defendants were not to be explained by rules that did not equally apply to other human beings.

As in the Klein case, 'significant description' was employed as a narrative device for conveying criminal danger, by stressing some of the defendants' apparent respectability, while at the same providing some minute clues that pointed to their criminal nature. Thus Roman Herz, who was built up as a key criminal by both the *Neue Freie Presse* and the *Arbeiter-Zeitung*, was described in the following terms:

> Roman Herz distinguishes himself from the other defendants by his nobler appearance, more careful clothes and more intelligent physiognomy. His face, whose pallor has been caused by fourteen months in jail, has energetic features. His head, with its grey hair, is respectably bald. He wears whiskers and gazes fixedly through his glasses, the way short-sighted people tend to do.[21]

Only a careful reading of his pallor and perhaps of his fixed gaze brought about by his (metaphorical?) short-sightedness may give the careful observer some indication of the criminal that lurked beneath this pleasant exterior.[22] If this description is somewhat less sophisticated than the examples we have encountered before – although its identification of apparent respectability with particularly dangerous criminality is clear as Herz is exposed in the course of the report as a dangerous liar who almost managed to fool the police's identification system and pass himself off as someone else[23] – one should remember that this trial took place nearly five years before the *Krone*'s conception: the genre of the trial report had not yet found its master practitioner.

The witnesses, most of them victims of the money-fraud, were by contrast presented as both stupid and morally defunct. They spoke with the heavy accent of their region, and were frequently the involuntary instigators of the spectators' laughter.[24] Even the police investigator characterised these victims of the fraud as 'easily fooled Galician Israelites', highlighting their susceptibility towards crime.[25] In all newspapers referred to here the basic dynamic of this particular crime narration was one of superior criminals taking advantage of their victims' stupidity. One should note that even the antisemitic dailies, which presumably bore no love for the poor Jewish populations of the east (and did their best to criminalise them along with the defendants – see below) tapped into this language of exploitation. Echoing a phrase used by the prosecutor, the *Reichspost* at one point described Galicia as having been 'almost looted' by the activities of Schapira and companions.[26] '[H]undreds of people were pushed onto the path of crime,' the paper continued, attributing a weakness of will to the victims that contrasted starkly with the intelligence and forcefulness of the perpetrators.[27]

Hand in hand with this emphasis on the criminals' rationality went the interest in the criminalistic aspects of the crime. All the papers devoted extended paragraphs to the fraud's actual criminal procedure, in a manner reminiscent of the *Archiv*'s collection of criminal techniques.[28] We learn, for instance, that the potential buyers were, after much bargaining, sent samples of the forged money. These 'forgeries' were in fact real bills that had been 'split' down the middle, i.e. that were printed only on one side of the bill, hence appearing like incomplete versions of highly sophisticated forgeries. The papers, and through the papers the public, delighted in a mastery of such technical facts of the case. Through such mastery, one could play at partaking in the investigative aspects of the case.

It was when it came to dealing with the Judaism of the accused, that the papers' strategies in covering the case diverged radically. The *Neue Freie Presse*, along with all other liberal papers, reported on the trial with no acknowledgement of the defendants' religion, and often with a deliberate policy of suppressing any information that would remind the reader of their Judaism. Thus the *Neue Freie Presse* paraphrased the heavily accented German of the defendant Frischling, making but a single quick reference to his interpreter,[29] and rendered the caftan he wore in court – something of a symbol for eastern Jewry – as a 'long, grey coat.'[30] When it reported on a statement made by one of the defence lawyers, condemning a vitriolic attack made by a Viennese paper against their 'personal honour', it never mentioned that this attack was of a rampantly antisemitic nature, nor indeed revealed the name of the antisemitic paper in question, the *Ostdeutsche Rundschau*.[31] When the personal data of the accused were listed, their religious affiliation was not conveyed.[32] The more populist *Illustrierte Wiener Extrablatt* and the socialist *Arbeiter-Zeitung* likewise made no mention of the defendants' Judaism, but were unwilling to lose all the involuntary humour arising through the defendants' and witnesses' Galician/Jewish use of words. These were integrated into the 'live' reports, and received no further commentary. The *Arbeiter-Zeitung* also did not shy away from a description of the clothes that identified the defendants' origin, and at one point used 'Polish–Jewish–German' when characterising their dialect.[33] Even the *Vaterland* – Catholic and on occasion antisemitic[34] – simply identified Schapira and his associates as 'international crooks'.[35] Reading papers whose editorial policy was not explicitly and brazenly antisemitic, the defendants' Judaism thus turned into an incidental, nigh on invisible background fact.

In the dedicatedly antisemitic dailies, by contrast, this was a Jewish case through and through. The short opening paragraph and headline of the *Deutsches Volksblatt*'s coverage of the case used the words 'Jew' and 'Jewish' no less than five times.[36] Similarly the *Reichspost* repeatedly reminded us of the defendants' religion/ethnicity, and highlighted the defendant Frischling's *Mauschel* (technically the western Yiddish of Bohemia and Moravia that was imitated by antisemites to designate Jewish speech and dialect more generally) by placing his interview at the very beginning of its fifth day of reporting.[37] In its description of the criminal procedure employed by the defrauders, the *Volksblatt* inserted a sub-headline: '*Criminal Language* [*Gaunersprache*],' explaining that Schapira's letters to his customers were written '*in the Hebrew alphabet*' and had cunningly disguised the true nature of the transactions from any prying eyes by referring to the 'forged' money solely as 'goods' or 'linen'.[38] Non-antisemitic papers also frequently marked this criminal technique, but they did not place this fact into a context of a Jewish narrative. It was through the simple assertion of the case's Jewishness that such technologies were turned into a symptom of *Jewish* criminal cunning.

One can find precisely the same dynamic at work when it came to quoting prosecutor Kleeborn's final statement that marked Schapira as a dangerous dissimulator, indeed as a perfect criminal in a Grossian scheme:

> The highest, purest possession of humankind is truth ... Nuchem Schapira is *the most diametrical opposition, the personified negation of the concept of truth* and I may be allowed to say that whatever he said, was a lie, whatever he thought, was a lie. He is so immersed in his lie, that I believe he would even lie when this brings him no advantage, from sheer habit. Schapira is the epitome of the perfect, serene criminal.[39]

Naturally this statement made its way into virtually all the papers, and one can easily see how this characterisation would have had ample resonance against a background of criminological thought that problematised questions of dissimulation. In the *Deutsches Volksblatt* and likeminded publications, however, it took on a different dimension: here such a statement could be easily read as the characterisation of a specifically *Jewish* criminal, simply by virtue of the fact that the whole crime had already been framed as distinctly Jewish.

However, the endless repetition of the defendants' Jewishness was but one ingredient in the creation of this framework. The witnesses and defence lawyers were equally identified as Jewish, and systematically criminalised alongside Schapira and his accomplices, as was, *in extremis*, the entirety of Jewish Galicia. The *Deutsches Volksblatt*, for instance, highlighted the fraud victims' greed,[40] and noted that the 'examination of the witnesses ... was deliciously humorous, in particular those parts of the statements when the witnesses were not quite sure how they could get out of a tight spot so that they wouldn't end up in the dock themselves.'[41] The *Reichspost* likewise made sure to establish the Jewishness of the witnesses, either by simple designation ('as the first witness the *Jewish* brandy-seller Josef Schiffmann is sworn in')[42] or, in the case of another witness, via his description as a 'full-blooded Jew, with ringlets and caftan'.[43] It then went on to unmask these witnesses as proto-criminal themselves:

A friend of our paper informs us of the following: 'You might be interested to hear, that Mr Gutsfreund [sic!], who has been merited with so much in the discovery of the Jewish money-fraud ring, has his permanent residence in the Café Donauhof where he, together with his brother, brokers clever little stock deals ...'[44]

The *Reichspost*'s point here was that the Gastfreund/Gutsfreund should not be seen as somebody who furthers the cause of truth, but rather as a crook at heart, whose performance in the courtroom was, above all, phoney.[45]

On the final day the *Reichspost* went yet a step further in this strategy of implicating Jews other than the defendants. Its attention now turned to the defendants' Jewish lawyers,

who with all their subtleties and hair-splitting tried to get even THESE crooks off the hook. Requests for extradition were demanded, nationalities challenged, police work was criticised – not to find the *truth* as a Jewish lawyer admitted with a cold smile – but to find the right to look for that little door through which the criminals could disappear once again to the criminal quarter in London. One of the Jewish lawyers ... was so bold to remind the jury not to be influenced by the present [atmosphere of] anti-Judaism.[46]

In this manner the lawyers were themselves effectively criminalised, for they stood accused of protecting Jewish crime with illicit manoeuvres that perverted the very ideals of justice. As in the Klein case, we find a narrative of Jewish crime linked to an accusation of truth distortion. One also notices the tendency, already observed in the Springer/Goldenberg case, to widen the antisemitic attack in these trials to encompass more than just the actual criminals.

The satirical *Kikeriki* stretched this campaign of defamation even further until it included virtually all Jews. Its issue on the twenty-fourth of September features the following 'song' on its cover page, presumably sung from a 'Jewish perspective':

Oh Muse, sing with the lyr-a
The song of Nuchem Schapira
Wherever his face he shows
The heart of our people he knows
For gain without sweat
Night and day do we fret
What is it, the highest good we call?
It's full pockets with no work at all[47]

The song was followed, for several weeks, by a sheer endless stream of Schapira jokes that played up the fact that Schapira was unable to differentiate illegal from normal business,[48] or else intimated that if every person involved in the scandal were arrested 'half of Israel will end up behind bars.'[49]

The single most aggressive piece of antisemitic journalism – precipitating the defence lawyer's comments which were remarked upon above – was printed in the *Ostdeutsche Rundschau*, yet another antisemitic daily and something of a fringe publication, with a circulation of around 2,500 in 1895.[50] Describing the courtroom for the very first time, it chose the following terminology:

> The dock is filled with true figures from half-Asia. Their ranks are almost unpleasantly disrupted by judicial soldiers [*Justizsoldaten*] ... Behind the half-Asians from Polakia [sic!] their modernised and civilised tribesmen have taken their seats, differentiated only by those exterior features that can be changed through human influence. They are here to defend the former.[51]

The racialist reference to the 'Asiatic' nature of the defendants was a knowing nod to Karl-Emil Franzos' tales and sketches, originally published in the 1870s in the *Neue Freie Presse*, that critiqued the cultural backwardness of *Ostjuden* under the title 'Out of half-Asia'.[52] Antisemitic racialism here attempted to align itself with liberal prejudices concerning eastern Jewry's alleged barbarism, then tied it – unusually enough for a trial report in this period – to the invocation of immutable Jewish physical features. Above all, however, the report sought out an association of the lawyers with the criminals they defended, i.e. reiterated the key trope found in the other antisemitic publications.

Looking over the defence strategies of these lawyers, one notes that their own narrative of the crime did not rest on entirely different assumptions from those presented in the press at large, nor, curiously, from those present in the antisemitic press. The very last piece of evidence that defence counsel Friedmann wanted recorded by the court, for instance, was his defendants' low level of education. He wanted to highlight that none of the accused had any formal education apart from going to Jewish school.[53] Mrs Schapira, in fact, had not been to school at all. The point he was trying to make was clear: how could these people be such cunning master criminals, if they lacked even rudimentary education?

Then, in his final defence speech, he changed tactics somewhat. He openly accepted that his defendants acted immorally, but disputed that what they had done added up to a criminal offence according to the statutes of the law. By way of explaining this misunderstanding, he told an antisemitic joke aimed at characterising the victims who represented the core of witnesses in the trial:

> *The imagination of Schapira's co-nationalists makes every little thing appear to them like fraud.* It's just like in the well-known anecdote, in which a Polish Jew comes to the judge and declaims most excitedly that just now two people have been killed. 'Who are the two?' asks the judge. 'Well, the first is myself and the other is on his way, Mr Lawyersir.'[54]

In Friedmann's joke it was the Jewish witness who totally perverted the meaning of truth, presumably for his own gain. Antisemites should not be assumed to have had a monopoly on the language of antisemitism, especially where eastern Jews were concerned.

Nuchem Schapira was back in the headlines some ten years later, once again as the master-mind behind a new money/forgery scandal. In the coverage of the investigation, much of what characterised the 1895 trial was re-rehearsed: again he was described as a 'perfect criminal'[55] and liar, an 'excellent teacher in the school of criminality,' who sat in London 'like a spider in the middle of his web.'[56] Again the forgers' 'cunning criminal tricks'[57] were fully reported on, as were the details of the criminal investigation.[58] Once again all newspapers that were not explicitly antisemitic avoided mentioning the criminals' religious identity,[59] while those with antisemitic persuasions milked the occasion for all that it was worth, as indicated by the *Reichspost* caption: '*Fake Fifties – Real Jews*'.[60]

Interestingly, all the papers assumed the readers still to be familiar with the name of Schapira – a fact that points both to the cultural importance with which trials were regarded, and simply to the fact that a perfect crook like Schapira did not show up in the dock every day. This was all the more true from an antisemitic perspective: Jewish master criminals were thin on the ground, as the criminal statistics rightly indicated. More typically Jews were involved in criminal cases – economic and otherwise – in much more peripheral roles. Let us turn, then, to yet another fraud consortium, that of Anna Kubowsky, and her dastardly lawyer Leopold Amster.

Anna Kubowski's Jewish Lawyer

The Kubowski fraud was tried in the Viennese *Schwurgericht* from 25 to 30 August 1905, and revolved around the fraudulent practice of employing several individuals for the same position. The position in question was that of administration official, i.e. a person hired to supervise several houses of flats. In order to ensure their honesty it was customary for such administration officials to hand over a considerable cash deposit to the house owner at the beginning of their employment. By employing several such officials, a significant sum of deposits could be amassed. The defendants of the Kubowski case – Anna

Kubowski, a 38-year-old widow, her father Chrysanth Lenzhofer, her lover Josef Kadletz, her lawyer Leopold Amster, in whose office the employment contracts had been signed, one of Amster's solicitors, Josef Boreczyk-Glatzer, and the real estate agent Leopold Zacharias – were charged with plotting to cheat the unwitting officials out of their cash deposits. Various further charges of fraud rounded off the accusation.[61]

In theory neither the relative blandness of the offence (no murder or sexual scandal, the sums of money involved were substantial but hardly a fortune), the complex legal situation surrounding this case of multiple fraud, nor the lack of a society figure among the ranks of the defendants, seems to offer much in the way of raw material to move the public imagination; it is hardly the stuff criminal legends are made of. Yet, for a solid week, the *Kronenzeitung* made it the main focus of its journalism, devoting some twenty-six pages to the case. The other dailies similarly gave the scandal substantial space throughout the lengthy five-day trial, above all the *Deutsches Volksblatt* which covered it as a Jewish crime.

As in the Schapira case – and indeed the Klein trial – all the papers treated the perpetrators as rational criminals whose criminality could be assessed by the close study of their performance in court. The medical language of pathology entered the courtroom at one point, but only to characterise a witness and his 'pathological tendency towards lying'.[62] While the witness's statement was incidental to the case itself, it is interesting to observe that the papers were familiar with – and did not hesitate to disseminate – medical jargon, but consistently refused to utilise it in order to explain the defendants' behaviour. The characterisation of criminals as deliberate and rational actors, therefore, was not a function of the papers' ignorance about the availability of medical/determinist narratives of behaviour. Rather, medical/determinist models of criminal actors simply ran against the papers' mode of writing about crime.

In most of the papers Anna Kubowski received the lion's share of attention: her life of depravity that included a lover killed at her husband's hands, as well as her appearance and actions, were closely analysed. The only other defendant who received anything approaching this level of scrutiny was Leopold Amster, the fraudulent lawyer. The *Krone*, for instance, described his entry into the courtroom in the following manner, once again transforming the courtroom into a surrogate crime scene by subjecting Amster to an exercise of clue-reading:

> Only after all the other defendants have taken their seats does he appear at the entrance to the courtroom. He hesitates for a moment, as though it takes a great act of will for him to enter, then he pushes himself trough the door and sits down on an empty chair next to the defendant Lenzhofer. He is wearing a black salon suit, gloves and top hat, the latter only, one suspects, to show that he has not been arrested. He has brought his advocate's satchel, too. He attempts to appear calm, but a quiver in his face betrays his nervousness. He positions his chair in such a manner that he turns his back on the audience/the public [*Publikum*].[63]

The paper thus demarked Amster as criminal by noting the discrepancy between what he wished to communicate (the report explicitly refers to this as '*sich darstellen*' – to display oneself, highlighting the performative aspect of the defendant's role) and what the seasoned observer could discern from this very attempt – a strategy we have already marked as characteristic. Dress and accessories (top hat and satchel) were clearly understood as being part of a semantic code that Amster consciously employed. Every little facet was significant – the way he entered, which chair he chose. He almost got away with looking respectable, it is implied, but the minute details of the scene – the hesitation at the door, the pained attempt to set himself apart from the other defendants, the quiver in his face – gave him away to the journalist. If the description is somewhat briefer than Kubowski's (see Chapter 4), then this carries its own significance: the *Krone* ranked his villainy as inferior to hers.

Turning to the 'Jewish dimension' of the case, and reading the coverage of the *Krone* against that of the *Deutsche Volksblatt*, one is struck immediately by the differences in the respective frames provided for the trial. The Krone ran its story under the heading of '*The Fraud Trial Kubowski*'; the *Volksblatt* as '*The Jew Dr Amster as Defendant (A major fraud trial)*'.[64] Here Amster was moved into the very centre of attention, billed as 'yet another Jewish lawyer' to be found in the dock.[65] He was repeatedly identified as 'the Jew Amster'; his religious affiliation was highlighted in the text when his personal details were listed ('born 26 January 1871 in Lemberg, registered in Vienna, *Jewish* ...');[66] he had his own sub-headline and the attendant paragraph devoted to his role in Kubowski's crimes, was positioned prominently after only the briefest of explorations of Kubowksi's life and involvement.[67]

To some degree the frame that put Amster at the centre of the trial had its own dynamic and goal, and did not need be filled with any content in order to be effective: it simply identified a Jew, and more generally the Jewish legal profession, with crime. Even the most casual of the *Volksblatt*'s readers would walk away with the impression that Amster was in some sense at the centre of this case, and that such involvement of Jews was customary. One can also discern, however, a more sophisticated narrative embedded within the report that wished to establish a very specific kind of criminal identity with 'the Jew Amster' and through him with Jews in general. Throughout the *Volksblatt*'s coverage Amster's professional position of power and trust was highlighted, only to be contrasted with Amster's personal deviousness in exploiting his position:

> The third of the defendants under investigation for the present offence is the *Hof- and Gerichtsadvokat* Doktor Leopold *Amster*. In his office and with his personal intervention the contracts with the job seekers were drawn up and concluded. It was he who described the positions in question to the applicants as splendid, *who threw his authority as a lawyer into the scale to make the individuals trusting* and led them to hand over the so-called deposits. In doing so he was supported most effectively by his solicitor Josef *Borczyk-Glatzer* ...[68]

Josef Borcyk-Glatzer, one should add, was also Jewish, and, by extension, part of the criminal-Jewish enterprise Amster was running.

This narrative of Amster using his authority to lure innocent, trusting victims to their ruin was played up repeatedly. It was, for instance, reiterated when the *Volksblatt* came to discuss his involvement with one Richard Schmal, a relative of his and a 'thoughtless young man' with a history of corruption.[69] Amster knew of his liaison with an affluent lady by the name of Hedwig Binder, and (according to the *Volksblatt*) personally arranged for Schmal to convince his lover to put up the deposit in order for him to take up one of Kubowski's advertised positions. While these events featured in other papers, the emphasis placed upon the idea that Amster cunningly exploiting Schmal's 'thoughtlessness' is unique here, and an extension of the idea that the very person who should be a symbol of justice (and therefore trusted) is in fact a facilitator of criminal activity.

But it was not solely Amster's behaviour prior to the trial that was being analysed as Jewish-criminal. While the *Volksblatt* was on the whole much less descriptive than the *Kronenzeitung*, it paid considerable attention to Amster's 'performance' in court, which unmasked his arrogance and belief that he was above the law. For instance a sub-section with the headline '*Dr Amster's behaviour*' highlighted the fact that he 'sits down, his feet crossed, and *turns his back upon the court.*'[70] His interaction with the witness Binder was likewise characterised as abrupt, aggressive and arrogant.[71] As in the *Kronenzeitung*, some attempt was being made to prove Amster's villainy by clues internal to the trial itself.

The narrative of Amster as a superior criminal who exploited his social status was given further credence by the prosecutor's final speech, which explicitly highlighted the dissimulation he discerned in Amster's performance in front of the court. The prosecutor charged him with 'lying,' and affecting the guise of a 'person with limited mental capacity' whenever questioned about the irregularities of his behaviour.[72] 'Hence,' he concluded, 'it is my duty to tear the mask off Dr Amster and to show him for what he really is – a fraudster!'[73] These words were, of course, reported in all the papers – after all they fit perfectly with the assumption that the most accomplished criminals could be distinguished by their wearing the most sophisticated masks; but they rang with a special significance within the antisemitic framework provided by the *Volksblatt*. Antisemitic tales of Jewish criminality thus consistently employed tropes common to contemporary newspaper narratives of criminality in general, but made it appear that criminal markers were specifically Jewish traits: in a sense crime *per se* was to be made Jewish.

The coverage of the *Reichspost* closely resembled that of the *Volksblatt* with some interesting additions. Again the case was centred upon Amster (headline: '*Fraud Trial Kubowski (Lawyer Leopold Amster as defendant)*').[74] The coverage started off by referring to the 'gang Kubowski-Amster,'[75] but pretty quickly inverted the names to read 'Amster-Kubowski', effectively promoting the lawyer to the head of the consortium.[76] It also paid special attention to the fact that Boreczyk-Glatzer had a previous conviction, in order to characterise Amster's law practice as criminal: 'Without doubt this legally trained crook … felt more comfortable in the company of criminals than among honourable people.'[77] Nor was Amster the only suspect lawyer present in this trial. As in the Schapira case, we find the *Reichspost* creating an association between Amster's defence counsel and the defendant, by pointing to their shared ethnic identity and cunning: 'The defence counsel of the defendant Amster, the Semite Zweigenthal, throws all kinds of antics and attempts to confuse Kubowski with tricky questions.'[78]

Zweigenthal was, in fact, not Amster's defence counsel, a misidentification the *Reichspost* never corrected, but made up for by also implicating his actual counsel, Dr Steger, in Amster's criminality. When commenting on Steger's legal strategy, the *Reichspost* wished to establish that 'the Jewish defence counsel of the Jewish defendant' both were 'cast in the same mould'.[79] It did so by reading Steger's argument that Amster had too little to gain from his suggested role in the fraud for it to make a plausible motive as proof for the general corruptibility of Jews: 'each person has his price, and Dr Steger knows that of a Jewish lawyer!'[80] As before, we encounter evidence for the antisemitic desire to implicate Jews in the subversion of the legal process itself, a charge here articulated by alleging corruption.

A similar strategy was also employed when it came to dealing with the fact that Amster was acquitted of all criminal charges against him 'against all expectations'.[81] The *Volksblatt* reacted to this presumed injustice by brazenly "Jewifying" the entire court, unmasking it as a place not of blind impartiality but of shameless Jewish influence:

> Upon hearing the verdict, the Jews and Jewesses present in court very nearly broke into howls of joy. Amster's defence counsel, Dr Steger, even left the room in tears for a few minutes, and the Jewish auditorium behaved so immodestly [that the judge had to ask them to respect the court].[82]

In this manner the paper could even narrate the very verdict as part of the Jewish crime that had taken place.

The satirical paper *Kikeriki* mirrored the *Reichspost*'s strategy of widening the attack against Amster to a wholesale attack against Jewish lawyers in general. Concurrent with the trial, it published a letter concerning a separate case of a Jewish lawyer's transgression, which detailed the machinations of Jewish law offices.[83] It described such offices as 'robber-chambers [*Räuberkanzlei*]', their staff as a 'band of crooks', that made their money ripping off 'unfortunate people of weak character'.[84] When one such lawyer got suspended, the letter claimed, his machinations were continued by a friend or relative: a 'Dr Levy, if his name is not Kohn.'[85] This letter was followed, in subsequent issues of *Kikeriki*, by a stream of jokes that once again identified Jewish law practices as 'quarters of crime'.[86]

Looking past antisemitic papers to various other papers' reports, one finds variations on the theme of clever criminals exploiting the gullible, but once again notes the total absence of any specifically Jewish angle. The *Illustriertes Extrablatt*, for instance, stressed the intelligence and apparent respectability of the defendants, and like the *Krone* contrasted it to their dastardly deeds.[87] Here Kubowski was the central player, although the paper did pay close attention to Amster, albeit with no reference to his religious or ethnic identity. The *Neue Freie Presse* – after the *Kronenzeitung* perhaps the newspaper most astute at using description for its characterisation of Kubowski as dangerous[88] – was willing to acquit Amster, suggesting his solicitor Borczyck-Glatzer as the true force behind the irregularities in the legal practice: 'The solicitor appears to have been the superior of the two [i.e. between Borczyck-Glatzer and Amster], and at the same time his boss's diabolus...'[89] As ever the criminal hierarchy was established by reference to mental 'superiority' and put into a context of seduction. In the *Neue Freie Presse*, there was no suggestion, however, that the irregularities described were in any way typical of legal practices and certainly no suggestion that this was a Jewish issue.

Business Crimes – Conclusions

Two aspects in the antisemitic construction of Jewish crime have been highlighted so far: first, its interest in constructing deliberate and rational criminals; second, its strategy to construct Jewish criminality by reference to the entire social sphere of the trial (as opposed to a total focus on the defendant). Defence lawyers, witnesses, the public: they all could be narrated as somehow partaking in the spectacle of the trial *qua* Jews, and as furthering the goals of criminality. As a further example of this point one might cite the *Volksblatt*'s coverage of the fraud trial concerning the sudden bankruptcy of the Lemberg *Sparkasse*. It was not sufficient for the paper to prove the criminality of the bank director (who along with all the other accused was *not* Jewish): the whole milieu needed to be implicated as Jewish and criminal: a place of lawlessness, prostitution and usury.[90] It was noted as significant, for instance, that Karpinski, one of the defendants, used to frequent a Jewish public house.[91] In answer to the question of why the police had not intervened earlier, the reader learned that 'the Lemberg *police corps* consists primarily of Jews' and that only the 'coincidence' that one of the policemen was Christian led to any arrests at all.[92] There was also much focus on the witness (later co-defendant) Maria Stefanie Fuhrmann, a 'baptised Jewess'.[93] Her 'outer appearance' was characterised as deceptively 'uninteresting', before being contrasted with the 'rather carefully rehearsed' performance she gave in court.[94] As the trial continued the *Volksblatt* transformed her from a peripheral figure into the (Jewish) key to the affair: a studied liar.[95] When all the defendants were acquitted at the end of an exceptionally lengthy trial (many of the papers had long given up reporting on it, presumably turned off by its exquisite tediousness), the *Volksblatt* was livid: a front-page editorial entitled 'Half-Asia' indicted not only the jury but the whole of Jewish Galicia as lacking 'what in other places is called a public conscience' and connected the depraved moral standards of that Jewish province to the *Neue Freie Presse*'s journalism.[96] Once again the trial was widened into an investigation of society as a whole, and the Jewish role within this society was identified as one that corrupted justice and its access to truth.[97]

This widening of the understanding of the criminal sphere to encompass witnesses, jurors, lawyers, the public and others was a feature that the antisemitic papers shared with other papers, and with criminalistic approaches to crime. Their exploitation of this vision of crime in pointing to Jews as destructive members of society, however, did not spill over into the mainstream discourse. Indeed, one of the crucial results thus far is the highly specialist nature of antisemitic discourse: casual antisemitic remarks in trial reports in newspapers that did not explicitly identify themselves as antisemitic – even the most populist ones like the *Krone*, as well as the socialist *Arbeiter-Zeitung* – were almost entirely non-existent. While it is tempting to point to the Jewish staff and editorial leadership of many of these papers as an explanatory factor, one should remember that such a designation is dangerously close to the antisemites' own dismissal of these papers as '*Judenzeitungen*': it presumes *a priori* that a journalist's Judaism would fully determine his language. Nor would such an argument work for the *Kronenzeitung*, whose political affiliations were if anything conservative and where only a handful of Jews contributed.[98] One should instead conclude that antisemitic discourse was identified as too partisan to be casually employed and that only those papers that wanted to unambiguously affiliate themselves with antisemitic political goals used it. This, in turn, might indicate that antisemitism did not quite acquire the ubiquity and 'invisibility' in this period that is often implied, but remained politically charged even in the manifestation of throwaway remarks or jokes.

Finally, one notes that the antisemitic papers, for all their occasional identification of the 'sons of Israel', a 'tribe' , the 'Kohns and Levys' etc. had no essentialist descriptive language to go with these labels, save the language of the cartoon, where the addition of giant noses and lips, crooked legs and black felt hats made Jews readily recognisable. Jewish criminality, like all other criminality, had to be read primarily through the evidence. Indeed, the descriptions of cunning that marked dangerous criminality in all contemporary newspapers, was appropriated by the antisemitic press as a specifically Jewish trait. Even small-time Jewish criminals, like an 1899 female pickpocket, was characterised by her wily attempt to escape justice by simulating insanity, not by reference to racial features and compulsions.[99] The question whether race *made* Jews commit crime was not explored; the charge was rather that Jews *wanted* to commit crime, and excelled at doing so.

These are preliminary conclusions, based on the analyses of a limited number of commercial crimes. The next section considers a second popular genre in which Jews were associated with crime: vice. It investigates whether the narrative of Jewish criminality changed according to criminal genre.

Sexual Crimes – Leontine von Hervay, Jewish Witch and Bigamist

The trial of Leontine von Hervay (also known as Tamara Bellachini) in late October and early November 1904 inaugurated a series of court scandals that explored aspects of contemporary sexual morality and involved Jews as defendants. As such, they provide this study with a convenient testing ground as to whether there existed a specific narrative of Jews involved in sexual crime, and whether this narrative was distinct from that observed in relation to economic crimes. If the names Hervay, Beer and Riehl ring with some familiarity, this is so because they belong to the pantheon of trials that urged Karl Kraus to publish his virulent attacks against bourgeois hypocrisy with regard to sexual mores, thus precipitating some of *Die Fackel*'s finest writing.

The Hervey case centred around the accusation of bigamy and false registration data. The story began with the marriage of the Mürzzuschlag *Bezirkshauptmann* (a local government official) to the recently arrived Leontine Meurin, who claimed to be the daughter of a Russian duke, and wealthy. Mürzzuschlag was a small community in north-eastern Styria, half-way between Vienna and Graz, and it was not long before the small-town public turned against the outsider. A local paper published a thinly veiled accusation that Leontine's extraordinary stories regarding her birth and wealth were nothing but lies, and hinted that she may not yet have been divorced from a previous husband, i.e. *de facto* a bigamist. A quarrel ensued between husband and wife. Leontine von Hervay ran off to Vienna, making an (alleged) suicide attempt before she was arrested, on the twenty-first of June, on a charge of fraud and bigamy. Her husband, disgraced, elected to end his life with a pistol shot to the heart some three days later. Leontine was put into investigative custody for four months. The charge of fraud was dropped, but the charge of false registration (she faked her age to appear seventeen years younger than she actually was) was added. She was tried in late October.

The trial focused on Leontine's sexually 'immoral' past – her marriage to the Mürzzuschlag *Bezirkshauptmann* was her fifth, and various other extramarital relationships were alleged and 'proven' by reference to her foible for extravagant lingerie. At the heart of the coverage was her identity as the daughter, not of a Russian duke, but of the Jewish street conjurer Bellanchini, and her 'demonic influence' (in the words of her deceased fifth husband's brother who was called in as a character witness) on men. From a legal point of view the accusation of bigamy ran into the problem that Leontine claimed that the marriage to Hervay had been an empty ceremony without legal ratification, enacted to allow the couple to share house and bed without causing a scandal

while waiting for her divorce papers to come through. The priest who had offi-
ciated at the ceremony by contrast claimed that it had been legally binding, but
grudgingly had to admit to severe irregularities. The four-day trial ended with
Hervay/Bellanchini being found guilty of both bigamy and false registration
and sentenced to four months of prison. A separate civil suit would decide
whether she was actually still legally married to her previous husband, a question the criminal court did not pursue to its full conclusion.[100]

It was, in other words, a trivial, local case involving a misdemeanour that
turned into a media sensation through the suicide of a provincial official and
the sheer raciness of the defendant's sexual history. The trial would seem to
lend itself to either a moralistic framing of Leontine von Hervay as a sexually
depraved predator, or else quite simply to a comic tone, with many of its
details being irresistibly and involuntarily funny, such as a hotel porter's wit-
ness-statement that described an officer repeatedly leaving the defendant's hotel
room 'in his underwear,' or Hervay's pathos-ridden injunction that her soul
was as pure as 'this glass of water in front of [her]'.[101]

In the hands of the journalists of the *Deutsches Volkblatt* it was, however,
quite a different narrative that emerged, curiously separate from the accusation
of bigamy or even sexual promiscuity. Rather it aimed to build up Hervay as
a veritable master-criminal, a rational and skilled swindler who was both representative of Jewish dissimulation at large, and in league with Jewish journalistic power that upheld and furthered this kind of criminality.

The coverage started innocently enough on the twenty-ninth of October,
with a headline of '*The trial of Mrs von Hervay*' and no hint of a 'Jewish
angle'.[102] Already the same evening – in reaction to the revelation of Hervay's
supposedly Jewish parentage – the case was totally re-framed under the heading of '*Driven to his Death by a Jewess*.'[103] Hervay's Judaism was exposed and
immediately linked to the 'Jew-press [that] has once again revealed itself in its
full shamelessness and mendacity' because it 'purposefully concealed the true
origins of Mr Hervay's spouse.'[104] The defendant, meanwhile, was systematically built up as a fake, an actress playing at inauthentic emotions, in the manner to which we have already grown accustomed. Her entrance, for instance,
was marked by a 'theatrical bow to the public', and her voice was described as
'affected, whimpering.'[105] On the next day of the trial, most of Hervay's
answers to the court were qualified, by parenthetical asides, as 'affected,'
'cheeky,' 'with pathos', or '*nervous*'.[106] These qualifications served to build up
the image of an actress whose mask occasionally slipped or else betrayed itself
by small incongruities. At one point she is reported to 'start crying loudly.'
Two lines later she is described as 'laughing'.[107] At another instant the reader
learned that 'At these words the *defendant sighs* heavily, waves her hands
around and conducts herself [as though] deeply desperate [*gebärdet sich ganz
verzweifelt*]'.[108] When confronted with an unpleasant witness she 'pretended to
cry her eyes out [*markierte heftige Weinkrämpfe*],'[109] and when the verdict was
read out she 'begins to cry heavily and falls theatrically into the armchair.'[110]

Hervay was thus credited with not a single authentic emotion. Like Nuchem Schapira, she was constructed as an incarnate lie, and it was the close observation of the sheer flurry of enacted emotions that gave her away. Hervay's answers when questioned were often pert and even funny, but the *Volksblatt* maintained a serious tone throughout, narrating her not as a clown, but as a dangerous manipulator. Attention was drawn to her repeated opportunistic conversions, first to Protestantism then to Catholicism, allegedly 'from deep conviction',[111] as well as to her 'unscrupulous greed,'[112] and her exploitation of her unwitting husband.[113] Her sexual mores, or lack thereof, remained curiously in the background. Even when a witness alleged that he suddenly saw through to the Jewess hiding behind the guise of a lady – a moment the *Volksblatt* reported on under the sub-headline of '*The Jewess Emerges*' – it was not her sexual appetites that gave her away but simply the discrepancy between her usual lady-like speech and some sudden mean-spirited crudeness she let slip in his presence ('These are not the words of a *lady*').[114] She was marked as morally depraved, certainly, but her criminality proper was more important to the *Volksblatt* than her status as a fallen woman.

This dual strategy of turning Hervay into a seasoned dissimulator while at the same time accusing the (Jewish) papers of being in league with her came into its own in a page-one lead article on the first of November, in which the defendant was characterised as a 'Jewish monster,' 'Jewish adventuress,' 'cunning person,' 'con-artist of a woman' and 'devilish Jew-woman,' who drove her husband to his suicide, with the support of the 'whole Jewish press [that] has virtually turned the woman ... into a Jewish national saint.'[115] At its climax the editorial brazenly compared the Hervay trial – both in its significance and in what it revealed about the ills of the age – to the Dreyfus trial in which 'the NFP [*Neue Freie Presse*] and of course all other Jewish papers went through thick and thin for the Jewish traitor *Dreyfus*.'[116] The parallel between a case concerning the betrayal of national secrets to a foreign power and Mrs Hervay's alleged bigamy and indiscretion regarding her age – quite distinct entities one might have thought – existed simply in the crime of misinformation on the side of the papers, in spreading untruth in support of a Jewish criminal. The article went on to name explicitly the *Neue Freie Presse*, *Die Zeit*, the *Arbeiter-Zeitung* and the *Neuer Wiener Journal* as representatives of a 'Jewish 'public opinion' willing to excuse and hide everything committed by a member of the Jewish tribe ...'[117] Effectively the function of the press as providers of the truth was here contrasted to the 'Jewish' press's media manipulation that aimed at creating criminal spaces.[118]

The editorial article should also be read in conjunction with the introduction to the final day of trial, that summed up the full gravity of the crime committed:

The significance [of the trial] is not simply that a con-woman, whose past is so caught up in her own web of lies, that one had to invest tremendous amounts of work, money and thought to carve out the naked truth, and of whom the only thing we know with certainty, is that she is a cunning confidence trickster, was sentenced to four months in prison. Rather its significance lies in the victory of truth and justice over the boundless dissimulations, lies and hidden schemes of the Jew-press ... Here too the parallel between Rennes and Leoben [the respective locations of the Dreyfus and Hervay trials] continues.

Even if it hadn't been confirmed by law today that this woman ... is a Jewess, the support of this dear press, that so happily declares its solidarity with criminals of its race, would have proven it as much as the revelations about her life sustained only by fraud and trickery and her impudent behaviour.[119]

When, two days after the trial and alarmed at the defendant's release on bail, the *Volksblatt* reported that a journalist belonging to a 'Jewish paper' had secured a private hour of the 'Jewish innocent's' time, in order to orchestrate a publicity campaign in her favour, it invoked precisely the same spectre.[120] The trial was now conceived as an information battle between the different papers, where truth was pitted against misinformation. But the *Volksblatt* was unperturbed. It promised that 'Israel will hardly win a victory over the philistines.'[121]

Lest the *Volksblatt*'s identification of the press with Hervay – and thus the effective criminalisation of 'Jewish' journalism – be regarded as unique, one need only take a look at *Kikeriki*'s much more succinct but no less biting coverage. The satirical paper had no need for 'live' coverage or descriptive subtleties – Hervay and the press simply became the subject of one of its title page poems:

Who nothing but lies has woven
With truly a Jew's mind for crookery
All agree in Leoben
that she is a con-artist, certainly

Elsewhere people doubt and gripe
In circles namely where
Smart Yids sit and cunningly guide
The public's opinion, go here, go there[122]

Once again we find the same construction of Hervay as a professional and proficient criminal, linked to the accusation that Jewish opinion-makers fostered her dissimulation.

That is not to say that all antisemitic publications dealt with the issue the same way. The *Vaterland* gave the trial minimal coverage, noting in passing that Hervay was the daughter of a 'Russian Jew' and even seemed to applaud that she 'tried to defend herself energetically.'[123] The *Reichspost*, too, limited its coverage to the basics (noting Mrs. Hervay's Judaism, but doing little with it),[124] apart from a lead article on the third of November. Here, however, neither the Jewish dimension, nor the morality of the female defendant received much consideration.[125] Instead, the editorial got worked up about the Catholic priest who (allegedly) conducted a shambolic marriage upon the threat of conversion to Protestantism by Mr Hervay. The paper, in other words, was more concerned about the Protestant threat and susceptibility of priests to blackmail, than any Jewish angle that could be pursued.

Turning to papers of different political persuasions, one finds no antisemitic commentary whatsoever. Hervay's religious affiliation was noted at best in passing, unless it was linked to an attack against the antisemitic invective. In fact, the wholehearted condemnation of Hervay is far rarer than could be assumed when reading Kraus's three articles on the case in *Die Fackel*,[126] that mark the trial as a 'witch hunt', a scandal generated by hypocritical newspapers 'sniffing' around ('*journalistische Schnüffelei*'),[127] built upon small-town envy and narrow-mindedness. The *Arbeiter-Zeitung*, for instance, condemned the trial in words that anticipated Kraus. It explicitly turned against an antisemitic reading of Hervay 'who is the daughter of a Jew, which apparently is the worst part of all,'[128] and openly rejected the verdict as being 'not an investigation about bigamy but about the brand new crime of having a *past*,'[129] which aimed at soothing the 'insulted morality of the petit bourgeoisie [*Spießbürgermoral*].'[130] The sensationalist *Krone*, too, was at pains to reconstruct the milieu that generated the sensation, focusing on the local paper that published the initial satirical piece that got the stone rolling.[131] The *Extrablatt* was more moralistic in tone, condemning Hervay's life style, but even here there was an understanding of the trial as a demonstration of the social politics of Mürzzuschlag, and a cautious condemnation of the verdict.[132] Even the *Neue Freie Presse* – Kraus's self-declared arch-enemy – was restrained in its moralism and made sure to juxtapose Hervay's 'past' with the unflattering description of a sensation-hungry public that stood in large crowds outside the court room and heckled Hervay whenever she spoke.[133]

If Kraus's stance as the only defender of open-mindedness appears somewhat self-styled, he did provided a very astute commentary on the antisemitic coverage (although Kraus, in his anti-liberal attacks against the *Neue Freie Presse*, would also on occasion dip his finger into that particular linguistic pot), mocking for instance the *Volksblatt*'s attempts to turn 'Mrs von Hervay [into] a missionary of the Alliance Israélite sent to that quiet valley in the Alps to vanquish its uptight inmates through "the teaching of Talmudists and Jewish ethicists."'[134] He quoted a ridiculous passage from the *Volksblatt* that claimed that Mrs Hervay was 'clever enough to arrange her actions so that the investigation did not provide the factual basis for the accusation of fraud,' and slyly noted that she was equally clever enough to avoid accusation for 'high treason.'[135] Hervay's actions, in Kraus's treatment, were neither 'criminal nor does one need to claim that they were pathological in order to exculpate her'[136] – one notes the equation of pathology with innocence and criminality with reason. Rather, her actions were 'at best unpleasant.'[137] Kraus was thus a voice of reason, but he is not so much defying the mainstream of public opinion as specifically attacking the antisemitic coverage of the trial.

Our preliminary findings, then, are that in this case of bigamy the question of sexual depravity was subsidiary to the question of truth manipulation for the antisemitic framing of the crime as Jewish. Let us now turn to the Beer scandal and assess whether the same holds true in a case centring on the accusation of homosexual paedophilia.[138]

Sexual Crimes – Theodor Beer, Pederast

On the ninth of February 1904, the lawyers Artur Freund and Heinrich Steger (the same Heinrich Steger we have encountered as Leopold Amster's lawyer) reported Dr Theodor Beer, Professor of Medicine at the University of Vienna, for the crimes of 'violation' (i.e. committing a sexual act with a minor) and 'attempted seduction to the crime of unnatural sexual intercourse.'[139] In the summer of 1902, on three separate occasions, Beer had allegedly shown pornographic photographs to Freund's thirteen-year-old son Oskar and proceeded to touch his penis and demanded that the boy touch Beer's penis in turn. He was also reported to have attempted a similar assault against the fifteen-year-old Gustav Steger, an assault which was, however, rebuffed. The two boys, their physicians and parents were questioned, and a preliminary hearing of Beer scheduled. Beer did not show up for this hearing, but rather decided to leave the country – apparently on the advice of his lawyer Dr Zweigenthal (whom we have already heard mentioned in the Kubowski trial) – going first to his house in Tour de Peilz (Switzerland) then on to Paris, San Francisco, London and Athens. He did not return until the summer of 1905, in order to face trial.[140]

The trial, needless to say, caused a massive sensation, both because of the supposed respectability of its central figure, and because of its sexual subject-matter. The proceedings (25 to 26 October 1905) took place 'behind closed doors' but journalists were allowed access by law and through them many of the details of the case became public knowledge, although the facts of the sexual assault were rendered in varying degrees of explicitness.[141] Significantly, none of the papers offered a clear summary of the actual homosexual activities that had allegedly taken place between Beer and the younger of the two boys – a point of some significance, given that the touching of another man's genitals had an ambiguous status in Austrian law, often being regarded as insufficient for a conviction for homosexuality.[142] The papers also seem to have unanimously misrepresented some of the facts of the case, for instance the identification of a 'physical particularity' of Beer's body (apparently Beer had shaven his pubic hair, but contrary to the reports – if Kraus's account can be trusted – Oskar could not identify this detail).[143]

The case stood and fell with the witness statements of the two now adolescent boys, even though the prosecution endeavoured to paint as immoral a picture of the Beer household as possible in order to further implicate the defendant. Beer was alleged to have been promiscuous, attempting to corrupt his female sexual partners. One witness, gynaecologist Herzfeld, told the court that Beer had attempted to incite one of his late patients to paedophilia, lesbian love and sodomy.[144] His wife's short hair was the subject of a separate series of questions aimed at implicating Beer's sexual preferences, and Beer's wealth was implicated in causing him to suffer from 'megalomania', believing himself to be a 'Nietzschean *Übermensch*' who was beyond society's moral laws.[145]

Beer's defence was two-fold. He admitted that he had photographed the two boys in the nude, both for artistic and scientific reasons (he claimed he was writing a book entitled *The History of the Human Beauty Ideal*) and with their parents' full knowledge. Beer also insisted that the two youthful witnesses had fallen prey to false memories, in turn a function of puberty ('where the mind of young people is filled to the brim with sexual thoughts')[146] and possible pathology (the younger of the two boys had been caught masturbating).[147] The Grossian themes of truth and memory were thus put at the very centre of the trial. Ironically, it was the prosecutor who quoted Gross *in defence* of his crown witnesses' reliability, because the criminalist, in his discussion on reliable and unreliable witnesses, had marked out male adolescents as particularly good observers:

> In Hans Gross's *Handbook for Investigative Judges*, a respected authority on crime, we read that adult boys [sic!] are the best observers of all. Their gaze is clear, sees more openly and with greater focus and is less subjected to outside influences.[148]

The defence counsel reacted to this invocation of a *Sachverständiger* by in turn quoting two rival experts who claimed exactly the opposite: the 'exceptional scholar [Hypolite] Bernheim' and one Dr Siegfried Türk. Türk's book described 'how often children have already been shown to have made up sexual crimes that have been perpetrated against them', while Bernheim reported an experiment in which he induced a boy to believe that his wallet had been stolen via the powers of suggestion.[149] Kraus – one of Beer's most ardent defenders – played the same game by quoting both the psychologist William Stern, whose interest in the subject of suggestion we have already noted in Chapter 2, and (ever the literary) a long passage from Gottfried Keller's *Der grüne Heinrich* that described what contemporary scholars would have called a classic case of auto-suggestion.[150] Keller here recounted how as a child he had evaded his mother's anger at his use of swear words by claiming that he had picked them up from a school-friend; soon he himself came to believe his story and was amazed at the amount of specific detail he could 'recall' about the occasion when these words had been uttered. Beer himself was also directly questioned by the president to assess – as a medical expert of child psychology – whether the two boys would have been capable of 'constructing such an unbelievable narrative of the state of affairs [*Tatbestand*] from their imaginations.'[151] Beer predictably answered in the affirmative, philosophically musing that 'From my own observations I know that I myself am unable to tell dream from truth,' and pointing out that Oskar 'made a pathological impression on me [i.e. on Beer].'[152]

In this entire exchange about the value of the boys' witness statements, nobody ever suggested that they were simply lying. For contemporaries, it seems to have been much easier to believe, or in any case to accept in a court of law, that memory was malleable and flawed. In the words of the defence counsel, holding his final plea: 'It is not the case that the two young people wanted subjectively to speak the untruth, but that that which they said was objectively false.'[153] Thus the narrative of suggestion that we encountered in the psychiatric and criminological literature resurfaces in the contemporary newspapers. Characteristically, this medical discourse focused on witnesses rather than the defendant: he was never conceptualised through the terminology of pathology or any other form of determinism.

The question of truth was also raised on a second level, confronting the public directly with the ambivalent status of trials as truth-narratives. Beer claimed that Zweigenthal – then his lawyer – had advised him to flee the country when the charges had originally been made, rather than face a trial he might very well lose. He quoted Zweigenthal as saying:

> It's tough luck that you aren't guilty, because it is easier under these circumstances to get a guilty person acquitted than an innocent person. If you were guilty, one would simply give the whole thing a psychiatric turn and prove that you're not normal.[154]

Zweigenthal himself, called in as a witness, explained that in his opinion cases involving sexual crimes were particularly hard to defend because less substantial evidence was needed to arrive at a conviction.[155] He also explained that he saw no reason not to advise a man to flee justice, if he had sufficient funds, and 'can live equally well in San Francisco.'[156] A legal expert thus publicly discussed justice in terms of strategy, and shed doubt not only on the judicial process but also on the judgement of a key type of expert witness in many criminal trials, namely the psychiatrist. The prosecutor also questioned Beer about a book he had written, *Weltanschauung eines modernen Kulturmenschen* (*Worldview of a Cultured Modern Man*) which contrasted the 'bold thoughtlessness of the judicial trial based on circumstantial evidence' with the work of the 'true natural scientist, who is used to mistrust his eyes, [and to] repeat experiments a hundred fold ...'[157] For the public the fragility of the truth claim implicit in the form of trial reports was thus powerfully driven home as it became an explicit topic of discussion in the Beer scandal.

After two days of trial, and many minor sensations, such as the appearance of the famed architect Adolf Loos, who testified to the artistic merits of Beer's photography,[158] and the revelation that the defendant had married off his ex-lover with the help of his trusted lawyer Zweigenthal,[159] Theodor Beer was found guilty of a homosexual act (Article 129 1b) but somewhat paradoxically acquitted for 'violation' (Article 128). He was sentenced to three months in prison, stripped of his doctoral title and dismissed from his university position.[160] He was freed on the gargantuan bail of 200,000 crowns.[161] His wife committed suicide in March 1906, after all attempts at a revision of the verdict had failed. Beer's career never recovered and he withdrew to Switzerland.[162]

While all the above could be gleaned from most of the papers covering the case, the actual framing of the case varied tremendously. The coverage in the *Deutsches Volksblatt*, for instance, is a classic study of how a trial could be constructed through headlines and sub-headlines, the designation of various individuals as Jewish, selective, often suggestive omissions, highlighted sections and so on: a construction that was then made explicit in an editorial paragraph or article drawing all the 'Jewish themes' together with apparent coherence. Right from the start the trial was billed as '*A Jewish Scandal,*' and Beer was immediately identified as a 'Jewish university professor.'[163] A column later we learn, via a sub-headline, that Beer was '*Not Jewish, but – Protestant*', a qualification that was not explained but whose meaning is clear: we are told that Beer was, of course, Jewish, and that nobody should be fooled by the flimsy mask of opportunistic conversion. A day later he was identified as a 'clean shaven Jew-descendant,'[164] a phrase that not only emphasised his 'Jewish (racial) nature' but also drew attention to the fact that it would take more than the shaving off of his Jewish beard not to be recognised as such.

But it was not primarily Beer the pervert, whose abominations were hinted at rather than named, often through the use of modest but tantalising ellipses, that provided the case with its Jewish dimension. In fact the *Deutsches Volksblatt* was concerned with constructing the entire *affair* as deeply Jewish, building it up as a Jewish power struggle involving marriage politics (Beer had once been supposed to marry Steger's daughter but had declined) and threats of suits for perversion countered by threats of suits for blackmail. Thus Heinrich Steger was immediately identified as Jewish and a relative of the 'recently oft-mentioned Dr Amster,'[165] and the report on the trial started with a recounting of the various relationships between accusers and defendant. The story here was one of Jews using the law for personal reasons, as a way of settling scores rather than to appease lofty, disinterested justice.[166] Zweigenthal, the crooked lawyer, was, of course, integrated into this narrative. Sub-headlines identified him both in terms of his role as legal counsel full of unethical advice ('*The Jew, Dr Zweigenthal as – adviser and financier*') and as a relative of the odious Beer and hence implicated in his perversion ('*Dr Zweigenthal, the defendant's cousin*').[167] His words about the 'psychiatric turn' and his judgement that affluent persons did better to flee the country were repeatedly printed, and systematically highlighted. In this manner these sly truth-destroying methods could be marked specifically as symptoms of what the paper explicitly described as 'Jewish lawyer-ethics'.[168] Zweigenthal's speech added up to 'truly a spruce confession from a lawyer, from which one can infer what to make of the 'Examination of the Mental State' of some criminal who is to be saved in this manner.'[169] It was thus used to shed doubt on the entire psychological profession which was distrusted as a (Jewish?) force that would hide true criminals and remove them from the grasp of justice.[170] In fact Beer's status as a professional scientist, and his argument that his interest in photographing pubescent nudes was a scientific and artistic endeavour were stressed by the *Volksblatt*, hinting that there was something particularly odious about a type of criminality that masked itself as science (cf. the coverage of the *Reichspost* discussed below).

All of these themes were brought together in a number of editorials on the trial. The introduction to an article entitled '*The Jewish Intelligentsia, (Searchlights on the Beer Trial)*' once again stressed the Jewish milieu of the crime and tried to collapse defendant, accuser and ex-lawyer into one undifferentiated heap.[171] A day previously, the *Volksblatt*'s coverage had already highlighted the 'Jewish amorality and perversion' pervading the case and called it a 'bright searchlight on the activities of baptised and unbaptised Jews, and Jew-descendants.'[172] A rare attempt was made to give some sort of hereditary-pathological racial spin to Beer's sexual perversion: 'The moral defects are hereditary for these Asian invaders, and cannot be extinguished in this race, despite all education.'[173] Crucially, however, the kind of moral insanity that was here alluded to did not impair the rational faculties of the actors: Beer's moral defect was coupled with 'high intelligence' and indeed it was this intelligence that 'marks the criminal's line [*kennzeichnet die Linie des Verbrechers*].'[174] Beer's sexual crimes were also conflated with Jewish commercial immorality: 'How many victims would have fallen prey to the lusty Jew? He had money, after all, and that Jewish business ethic that is devoid of scruples, that says to itself: if it works out, it's allowed.'[175] Somehow his sexual perversion here became a function of a general lack of ethics typically located in business transactions. In this manner Beer's love for boys pointed beyond his personal lack of morality to that of all Jews.

Finally, in a lead article entitled '*Judas's self-exposure*,' the Beer trial was tied to various political events, all of which revealed the 'true nature of Jewdom'.[176] Naturally Jewish journalists were implicated in all this, both by being active participants in various scams, but also, somehow, by their sheer sensationalism, the 'newspaper-Jewry's compulsive snooping.'[177] In the end then the *Volksblatt* could narrate this particular Jewish crime in every possible way: the Jew as an abuser of the justice system (via the Jewishness of the accusers), a destroyer of truth (via Zweigenthal the lawyer), as exploitative capitalist business man, the pathological yet rational pervert, and – by reference to the newspapers – as a scandalmonger.

If the *Volksblatt*'s coverage already threw up a myriad of antisemitic themes, it was the *Reichspost* that gave them their most coherent articulation. Once again we find the identification of Beer as a Jew under the flimsy mask of Protestantism ('the Protestant-baptised Jew Doctor Theodor Beer');[178] once again there was the conflation of accuser, accused and victim via their shared Judaism ('*Steger* [is] a tribesman of Beer', 'Oscar, the son of the Jewish lawyer Arthur Freund').[179] While the actual coverage was much shorter than the *Volksblatt*'s, the core of its antisemitic frame was worked out in a single page-one editorial on the twenty-eighth of October, entitled simply '*The Aliens*'.[180] 'One man has been imprisoned, but a whole race was convicted,'[181] the article opened and from there developed a vision of a trial that bore witness 'not only against the pederast Beer, but also ... against the whole Jewish race.'[182] 'The criminal Beer,' we are told, supplied

> photographic Beervidence of a ring of criminals worse than some rough band of robbers [*hat ... photographische Beer-Platten geliefert*] ... These criminals come from that place, where the 'culture' of our times is commercially produced. These photographs show the naked [*unretouschierte*] personalities of those people who use the slogans intelligence, science, progress as a shield, which they quickly raise when an enraged fist lashes out against their immorality and then scream that the uncouth, uneducated, hostile people wish to destroy the temple of the most holy culture.[183]

In other words, science and culture – those very entities with which Beer endeavoured to explain his interest in the nude pubescent form – were here turned into a cloak worn by the Jewry as a whole that disguised their criminal activities.[184] The article went on to identify the cause of this 'fraud' that had replaced true culture with its Jewish-run simulacrum as the 'financial power of Jewry' who 'put gold-coins upon open eyes.'[185] In order to cement this argument the article then shifted into an anthropological mode, enumerating the 'insight into the family life of rich Jewry' that had been gained in the course of the trial. The editorial ended with yet another repetition of Zweigenthal's dismissive statement about justice and his general lack of ethics, and yet another invocation of the trial's social implications:

> In this trial one has once again seen the incredible danger of Judaism for all states, all people. Christianity cannot be spoilt by it, but it is at work, through tireless infectious activity, at filling the people's intellects with its poisonous matter. Literature, art, law, schooling, all are increasingly permeated by the Jewish spirit, the Jewish will.[186]

One notes the image of infection, of penetrable 'intellects' that were filled up by the influences of the outside world. This conventional antisemitic trope with its pseudo-medical ring was here produced as the outcome of the *Reichspost* careful, dispassionate observation of the trial's vicissitudes. The trial report's logic thus allowed antisemites to 'prove,' in a public theatre of truth, the dangers emanating from 'Jewry' due to their perversion of culture and science.

Kikeriki's coverage of the Beer trial conformed closely to that of *Reichspost* and *Volksblatt*: on the back cover of the *Kikeriki* edition of the fifth of November 1905, its readers found a full-page cartoon dedicated to Beer (see Figure 5.1). Here the university professor stood in a cell, surrounded by three women identified as *Nemesis*, *Themis* and *Justitia*. Beer's cartoon image blended realism – as a portrait the image is a reasonable likeness, judging by various other sketches of Beer (see Figures 5.2 and 5.3) – with the antisemitic iconography of Jews, visible here in Beer's spindly, bandy legs, and over-sized head. One should note

Figure 5.1 'The women's favourite.'
Source. *Kikeriki*, 5 October 1905, back cover.
Captions: Top – 'The women's favourite.'
Bottom (not visible) – 'Virtuous virgins receive Dr Beer in gaol.'
Labels: *Nemesis* (left woman), *Themis* (middle woman), *Justitia* (right woman);
Gallows-Yard (above door). The writing on the food tin combines the Jewish–German
term for 'No' ('*Nix*') with characters that denote kosher (meat).

Figure 5.2 Theodor Beer before the judge.
Source. Title page: *Illustriertes Wiener Extrablatt*, 27 October 1905.

however that both these features were also employed by *Kikeriki* when rendering cartoon images of non-Jewish figures (politicians, Czechs, Englishmen) and hence must be read as ambiguous markers of identity. A much more obvious Jewish aspect located within the image were some Hebrew letters inscribed on a tin of food consumed by Beer: although most of *Kikeriki*'s readers would not be able to read this inscription, the Jewish–German '*Nix*' and the (flawed) Hebrew letters added up to something like 'not kosher'.[187]

The cartoon, in other words, eschewed an unambiguous identification of Beer as Jewish. Rather it depicted him above all as someone who was being fed by Jews. The content of the tin remained an equivocal mixture of food and poison: in one reading, Beer could be understood as being kept alive in jail by his Jewish friends, even after his grave moral fall. In another interpretation, Jews could be seen as having poisoned his food in order to precipitate his immorality. The image drew together the idea of a Jewish conspiracy in which Beer partook, and the invective against Jews permeating and poisoning the body social.

Figure 5.3 Theodor Beer, close-up.
Source. *Illustrierte Kronen-Zeitung*, 26 October 1905, p. 5.

The rest of the press dealt with the trial without ever identifying Beer as Jewish or of Jewish descent. No sustained attempt to connect defendant, accusers and witnesses took place. The theme of truth distortion was present in the non-antisemitic press, but not put into the conspiratorial context encountered above. Zweigenthal in particular was quoted at length, although in some papers, most notably the *Neue Freie Presse*, his words came across as measured, educated and rational, the advice of a pragmatist rather than that of a crook.[188] On the whole, the liberal papers hedged their bets at whether or not they should construct Beer as a straightforward villain, and made sure his defence was given adequate column space. The *Arbeiter-Zeitung*, by contrast, created its own intricate, conspiratorial narrative for the trial that painted Beer as a decadent capitalist, seduced by his money and power to a 'Nietzschean' contempt for ethics, and enjoying preferential treatment by the court.[189] The *Krone* stayed carefully apolitical and focused on defendant and setting: it characterised Beer as cold-blooded and *blasé*,[190] and rendered the court room itself as an infernal place of 'unbearable heat and bad air'.[191] The Beer case thus once again drives home the clear dichotomy between explicitly antisemitic publications and their attempt to 'Judaise' crime, and all other publications here observed, including the socialist and populist press. It also confirms a pattern in which Jewish criminals were set into a larger context of the dangers of truth distortion, and located the Jewishness of a crime not exclusively in the defendant but in the wider networks surrounding it. Let us now turn to a further example, the case of Madame Riehl, who dominated the headlines in early November 1906 with her alleged mistreatment of the young women who worked as prostitutes in her establishment.

Sexual Crimes – Regine Riehl, Brothel Madam

The Riehl case is in many ways paradigmatic of the Viennese coverage of crime in the media of the early 1900s. It demonstrates the way crime-as-news-item could deliberately be created by aggressive, investigative journalism, how a moralising discourse could co-exist with cheerful and thinly disguised voyeurism regarding Vienna's 'underworld' of prostitution and illicit pleasure; and it also gives us further insight into how the antisemitic press could construct the 'Jewishness' of a crime practically at will.[192]

The Riehl sensation was the direct result of a newspaper scoop. A journalist and member of the editorial staff of the *Wiener Illustriertes Extrablatt*, Emil Bader, had secretly observed the legally licensed brothel run by one Regine Riehl, and on the twenty-fourth of June 1906 launched a series of articles accusing both Riehl of ill-treating and incarcerating her staff of prostitutes, and the police force of wilfully tolerating these activities.[193] Bader raised the spectre of '*Mädchenhandel*,' and compared Riehl's enterprise in the *Grünthorgasse* to the brothels of Rio de Janeiro, which in the contemporary literature of white slavery took pride of place as epitomes of depravity and veritable prisons of abducted European maidens.[194] Before the week was out, the *Arbeiter-Zeitung* joined Bader's cause, fuelling the public outcry.[195] A week later, the authorities felt obliged to act and had Riehl arrested.

In its very conception then, the Riehl trial originated in the papers, not simply because they singled out her establishment above all others to be denounced as particularly depraved – a symbol of Viennese vice – but also because their reporting provided the agenda of what was to be investigated. In the court records we find the newspaper reports being treated as central pieces of evidence, along with a ten-page witness report by Emil Bader.[196] The media reported on what it had to a good degree provided itself. This is not to say that the charges levelled had no basis in fact: in the course of the investigation it became clear that the women in question felt their movements had been restricted by Riehl and her employee Antonie Pollak, and that there existed profound irregularities in Riehl's relationship to the supervisory police. Virtually all evidence, however, was non-material, consisting of lengthy and contradictory witness reports.[197] The court files contain no description of the brothel itself, and even the medical data about the prostitutes' state of health is minimal. In the absence of material clues and a crime scene that could be analysed by expert detectives, therefore, the court room in a very real sense became the only locus of evaluation for Riehl's crimes. The trial took place from 2 to 7 November 1906.

Legally, the trial was a complex affair involving a variety of charges against multiple defendants. Riehl stood accused of the restriction of personal freedom, incitement to false testimony (during an initial investigation she had convinced her employees to cover up certain irregularities), violation of the prostitution law and the embezzlement of her employees' profits. Antonie Pollak was charged with complicity in some of these crimes. Alongside these two main defendants, Friedrich König, father of one of the prostitutes, was also charged with complicity in the restriction of personal freedom – he had forced his daughter to work for Riehl. Finally, seven of Riehl's employees were charged with giving false testimony.[198] Concurrently with these criminal charges, the court pursued the civil suit of the prostitutes against their former employer for compensation. This conflation of civil and criminal suits was common in the Austrian legal tradition, and meant that alongside the state prosecutor, a second, private prosecutor - the so-called *Privatbeteiligter* - would be present in court and entitled to question the witnesses and defendants.[199]

All papers here considered covered the trial in considerable detail and unanimously vilified Riehl, Pollak and König, often employing description as a primary means of identifying them as criminal. The *Deutsche Volksblatt*, for instance, introduced the triumvirate according to their hierarchy of evil:

> The defendant Riehl, a small, somewhat heavy person with common, not un-pretty features, has appeared in black clothing, which causes the impression of intentional simplicity. Pollak represents the common type of the allegedly poor old woman, her features are disagreeable, her gaze penetrating. The defendant König is a repulsive man with vulgar features.[200]

One notes, as ever, that the charges of dissimulation went hand in hand with description – Riehl's clothing was *intentionally* simple, Pollak was *allegedly* poor. König, by contrast was described simply as repulsive, and hence was marked as ultimately less of a danger. The same logic holds for the *Krone*, which contrasted Pollak's allegedly innocent appearance and apparent weakness with her actual meanness and vigour which could only be revealed by close observation:

> A 68-year-old little grandmother. The lace cloth on her head, the simple dark clothing, the bent posture lend her a patriarchal something. Her face is full of wrinkles, the somewhat reddened cheeks are fallen in, her deep-seated eyes stare dully at the court. But when she starts to speak, then her features grow more distinct, the voice becomes pointed and hard. One senses that she does not lack the energy to play the slave warder, in spite of her apparent fragility.[201]

The *Kronenzeitung* thus anticipated the prosecutor's statement that described Pollak as 'the superlative of deviousness'[202] – she was being built up as guilty because she was other than what she pretended to be.

The papers were also astonishingly uniform in decrying the moral outrage the trial uncovered, entering into a virtual competition to communicate their shock at the morass uncovered in the capital city's back alleys. Kraus's ironic commentary, structured around the indictment of the other journalists' hypocrisy, was the only real exception.[203] The papers also chose very similar tropes when it came to constructing the prostitutes themselves, principally ambiguous figures in this case, because they played the triple roles of accused, accusers, and damaged parties as well as being part of a profession that would have been regarded as shameful by most contemporaries. Their defence counsel, Wolfgang Pollaczek, seems well aware of this ambiguity, and his strategy reflected the ambivalent feeling these women must have raised in contemporary jurors and news consumers. In his final plea, Pollaczek tried to establish 'the girls' as part of a distinct 'caste of prostitutes' who all shared in the 'common psychology of the prostitute'.[204] In explaining their 'fall', its suddenness and ease, he made uncommitted reference to Lombroso ('one feels one must almost sign up to Lombroso's theory that the prostitute is a psychopathic individual'),[205] but when it came to actually explaining their psychological deviance, Pollaczek's explanatory framework was carefully situated in the actual experience of being a prostitute and thus conformed to the contemporary notion that a person's inner self could be re-configured by outside forces:

> Once the fall has taken place, a peculiar psychological process is set in motion, that totally transforms the prostitutes' souls and causes a reversed mental and ethical development. The sloth, the isolation from the outside world and from any intellectual nourishment causes the gradual dulling of the mind and mental lethargy. The moral depravation ... dulls the emotions ... the lack of protection against exploitation ... petrifies all energy, the odd behaviour of the police confuses their idea about law. The isolation from relatives finally, even causes an intimate attachment to the exploitative procuress, for no human being can live without others.[206]

The prostitutes he defended were thus constructed as weak-willed victims of the realities of their lives. The point of this construction was revealed momentarily. 'This,' the defence counsel finished, 'was the ground on to which such an energetic and intellectually superior person as Regine Riehl sowed the seed for inciting a criminal action.'[207] Once again we note the familiar dynamic of the construction of the master criminal as rational, exploitative, able to mould the mental worlds of her quasi-pathological victims. At the same time there was no need in this explanatory framework to downplay the moral depravity of these victims, i.e. no need to go against received assumptions about the personalities of prostitutes (see Figure 5.4).[208]

Once again the antisemitic press lent its own distinct framework to its trial reports, albeit one that emerged only gradually. The *Deutsche Volksblatt*'s first

The picture once again demonstrates the epistemological logic of the paper's gaze. In spite of the caption, the individual drawings do not actually reveal types but the faces of distinct individuals. At the same time the defendants are legible as prostitutes through a close observation of their stance (hips thrust out, shapely bottom towards the reader), their hats, and the three inches of underwear that peeks out of one woman's skirts (bottom right). An explanatory paragraph inside the paper makes sure that the reader recognises them for what they are in case his or her gaze should prove to be insufficiently experienced.*

Figure 5.4 'Types from the procurer trial against Mrs. Regine Riehl.'
Source. Title page: *Illustrierte Kronenzeitung*, 5 November 1906.

* *Krone*, 5 November 1906, p. 10.

day of coverage did not provide a single hint that this case might have a 'Jewish dimension'. Riehl et al were simply built up as criminals, and the report joined the general outrage about the 'metropolitan morass' in evidence.[209] By the next day, however, the first of the defendants was announced to be Jewish: the report on Antonie Pollak's questioning ran under the sub-headline of '*The redheaded Jewess*':

> She also pleads not guilty, cannot remember a thing, claims continuous illness, and often gives convoluted answers – in the Jewish dialect these are called a 'twist' – so that the president comments: It is impossible to get anything out of you.[210]

Pollak's Jewishness was thus anchored in her evasive way of speaking that escaped questioning. This 'trick' was marked as a particular feature of Jewish speech, as proven by the fact that the Jews even had a specific term for it. Thus Pollak's skill at lying was itself exposed as Jewish and she was implicitly contrasted with Christian defendants who did not have a pre-prepared language of and for dissimulation. Even in such a casual example then, we find the usual logic of marking 'Jewish criminals' as particularly cunning.

The next morning, Riehl, too, was revealed to be a 'Jewish procuress' in a front-page editorial dedicated to revealing '*The brothel's secrets*'.[211] The trial and the picture of vice 'served up every morning on the breakfast table' were here compared to the pornographic products of 'Judapest,' and the predictable tale of the Jewish international network of white slavery was unfolded: 'That Madame Riehl is a Jewess is by no means a coincidence.'[212] Once again the 'Jew-Press' was implicated as the main agent of the circulation of vice through its advertisement sections, which were alleged to be used by procurers.[213] The theme of Jews as merchants of vice was reiterated at the end of the trial, highlighting the idea that vice had destructive effects for society:

> Whom do we see as the acting persons, whom as defendants and flawed key players in this trial? Jews. Regine Riehl is a Jewess; a Jewess is also the accomplice of the shameless procuress. And Jews are almost always the entrepreneurs of vice. They call it and foster it, they poison and spoil the youth. Take notice, Vienna![214]

The image of a 'spoilt youth' thus turned a crime against a number of prostitutes into an attack against the future of society.[215]

Significantly, however, the *Volksblatt* was not content with framing the trial solely by reference to the narrative of white slavery and vice. When, on the sixth of November, the trial turned to the irregularities of the police's behaviour vis-à-vis Riehl, focusing in particular on the activities of agent Piess,[216] the *Volksblatt* stumbled upon an even more promising way of framing the involvement of the Jewry in the scandal:

> The behaviour of the police ... is however now explicable ... It is characteristic that this state of affairs exists specifically in our police corps ... More than half of it is, as is commonly known, Jewified [*verjudet*]. The civil servants and the agent-corps in

particular, who came off so badly in the present trial, contain a disproportional percentage of Jews. It is well known, that corruption prospers much more everywhere where Jews partake, than in places where no Jews are present. Why should the police be an exception? The Jewification of our police is the best way of measuring the corruption and misbehaviour that has taken stronger and stronger hold there ... This state of affairs can only be changed if there is a *de-Jewification* of the police. A reform, no matter how thorough, will achieve nothing ... Individuals like the Jew Piß [*sic*] must disappear from the ranks of our police, even if they are competent – in our police force every Jew is, of course, *a prized expert*. They are festering wounds on the body of the police, that cannot be healed until they are removed.[217]

Once again, Jews could not only be shown as the perpetrators of crime, but also as facilitating crime in a broader sense, by perverting the country's institutions, specifically institutions concerned with truth establishment. From the Jewish lawyer to the Jewish police agent it was only a small step.

The coverage in the *Reichspost* closely conformed to that of the *Volksblatt*. Here there was no mention of any Jewish dimension of the case until a page-one editorial on the eighth of November, entitled '*The Seat of the Infection*.'[218] The '*widespread* infection' in question was that of 'Jewish immorality,' and once again its worst manifestation was located in the abuses of those who wore a badge to uphold the laws, not to help others break them: '... the suspicious policemen and agents are Jews or – a small number – such Christians who through the continuous contact with the Semitic element have to bear the terrible results of the infection.'[219] One notes the medical jargon of contagion, that brings to its logical conclusion a mode of thinking about Jewish crime already present in Thiele's mid-nineteenth century work on Jewish crooks.[220] For the conservative *Reichspost* it was also pertinent to mark this Jewish immorality as 'a mass indictment of our modern society,' once again depicting modernity as a specifically Jewish phenomenon. Like the *Volksblatt*, the *Reichspost* also pointed its antisemitic finger at the press ('The chapter of infection would not be complete, if one didn't spare a thought for its worst agent of circulation: the Jewish press'), and finished off by asserting that this dangerous force remained unpunished: while Riehl had been sentenced to prison and the 'Jewish and pseudo-Christian police-corrupters' had 'received disciplinary punishment', the 'people-seducing [*volksverführende*] Jew-press' was allowed to go on with its dirty labours.[221] One notes that the (suggestive) activities of the press were here directly criminalised and compared to other forms of criminal behaviour. This attack against the 'Jew-press' was reinforced the next day.[222]

Kikeriki, somewhat surprisingly, declined to pay the trial and its Jewish participants much attention, apart from a mild attack against sensational journalism and its identification with Jews,[223] and a half-hearted joke about how Riehl should have pleaded insane in order to get off, that reinforced its narrative about the science of psychology as an agent that obscured justice.[224] The theme of Jewish crime remained an option for antisemitic publications, but it was only the most dedicated papers that took it up with total consistency.

The trial ended in the conviction of all defendants for a majority of the charges levelled at them. Regine Riehl got three and a half years in prison, Antonie Pollak a year. Friedrich König was sent down for eight months.[225] Riehl, for one, felt she had been grossly mistreated, being punished for nothing but simply carrying out her profession. Her lawyer, Gustav Morgenstern, campaigned for a 'resumption of the trial' and his cause was championed by the *Österreichische Kriminalzeitung*, an illustrated paper that uneasily combined an interest in popularising criminological and criminalistics thought and the peddling of trial scandals. Here Morgenstern's appeal – printed in full – provided an excuse for revisiting the trial, almost a year after the actual fact. For over four months every single issue carried news about Riehl, and every single cover picture between mid-July and early September 1907 was dedicated to the topic of sexual mores, giving some sort of indication of how central the Riehl trial was to the discussion of morality at this time. Interestingly, Morgenstern's appeal attempted to invert the victimiser/victim dynamic painted by the trial by recasting the prostitutes working in Riehl's establishment – Riehl's supposed victims – as cunning liars who had engineered the whole affair, helped along, of course, by Bader and his 'clue-sniffing band of journalists,' who were accused of bribing one of the prostitutes to give false evidence against Riehl.[226] Indeed the newspapers with the help of the *'Liga zur Bekämpfung des Mädchenhandels'* (League for the Battle against White Slavery) now stood accused of having artificially created a scandal, pushing the public into a state of frenzy: 'It was simply fashion, a collective fever, a universal intoxication.'[227] Morgenstern thus tapped into the theme of the suggestive powers of the newspapers that so interested crime-experts, alleging that the jury was swayed by this fabricated public opinion. One should add that the *Kriminalzeitung* itself published articles on the theme of suggestion and the limits of witnesses' perception and memory.[228] The language of dissimulation and suggestion thus entered the debate on several levels. In this case, however, Morgenstern's plea fell on deaf ears. No re-trial took place.

Sexual Crimes – Conclusions

The Hervay, Beer and Riehl trials all complement the picture of the antisemitic construction of Jewish criminal activity developed in the previous section. While sexual immorality played a part in this, it was secondary to the presentation of the Jewish offender as rational and in league with various forces that facilitated his or her crimes – the defendant's lawyer, the police, bogus psychiatric evidence, and above all the newspapers. This construction underlay all these trials, even if it was not always entirely coherent: the Beer trial, for instance, demonstrates how supposed Jewish solidarity could be juxtaposed with a narrative that showed one Jew suing the other. In this construction the Jews, paradoxically, were both pre-modern, quasi-tribal creatures (one notes the frequent use of the German '*Stamm*'), but also the perfect modern city-dwellers: they were those who throve in the liberal-capitalist world, who were *suggestors* not *suggestees*, strong-willed, rational, in control, able to exploit their victims.[229]

In extremis, this construction of Jewish crime in the antisemitic press had no need for an actual Jew at the centre of the trial – in part because the whole understanding of crime-as-trial was not straightforwardly focused on the defendant but interested in the whole *ensemble*, including the audience and the journalistic commentators. Thus, in the so-called Weinlich trial in early April 1907, we find an antisemitic commentary in spite of the complete absence of Jews among the accused. The trial centred on a group of three women accused of prostituting young girls, and the nine men who were charged with abusing them, including the so-called 'Child-Devourer,' a mysterious, rich, old paedophile with a 'goatee beard.'[230] The report on the trial in the *Deutsches Volksblatt* ran alongside the heated coverage of the approaching *Reichstagswahlen* in May that invariably were interpreted as a showdown between upright antisemites and treacherous Jews with their socialist allies. Romania was also in the news due to a peasant insurrection, which had antisemitic overtones and was directed, according to the *Volksblatt*, against cruel and unfair Jewish landowners.[231] The trial was thus set against a scene of heightened political antisemitism, and can to some degree be plotted against it. One could also make this point about the Beer trial, which had the 1905 Revolution in Russia (and the alleged Jewish influence upon it) as its backdrop. Unfortunately for the *Volksblatt*, however, the Weinlich trial did not provide a Jewish defendant like the 'Jew-descendant Beer' that would have allowed the paper to establish a convenient link between its coverage of the court events and that of the uprisings. If Jews were to be held responsible for the case, their influence had to be located elsewhere: in the corrupting power of Jewish papers.

In order to construct this narrative, the *Volksblatt* needed first to re-affirm the dangers of such corruption. It did so by stressing that the underage victims of the prostitution ring had not only submitted physically to what was demanded of them, but had been irrevocably changed by their experience: 'their emotions, their thought, their whole way of experiencing resembles that of the seasoned hooker.'[232] Once again we encounter a contemporary vision of the self, in which the most sacred parts of personal identity – the very *way of experiencing* – were malleable, i.e. corruptible by outside influence.

It was precisely this vision of a corruptible self that informed the *Volksblatt*'s subsequent recasting of the Weinlich scandal as a Jewish affair. The lead article on the morning of the seventh of April ran under the heading of 'The Jewish Dominance over Austria-Hungary.'[233] It featured a re-print of an article from the *Kreuzzeitung* (a Berlin conservative/antisemitic daily) presenting a statistical analysis of Jewish influence in Austria, which lingered on the dominance of Jewish lawyers and journalists. Crucially, it characterised Jews as plotting revolution, burning to overthrow the moral, social and political order in Austria. The article seamlessly led the reader to the formally unconnected commentary on the Weinlich scandal. As on the days before, the article bemoaned the 'moral depravity' of the young people involved in the trial who had turned gutter-fiction into reality, a common and telling metaphor, given that there existed a strong cultural narrative that such transformations were in fact possible.[234] Having outlined the full horror of the scandal at hand, the article turned to its causes. The culprit was quickly found.

> It cannot be stated often enough that it is the Jewish press and Jewish literature as a whole which have carried the germ of this moral rot into the public. Among the members of the higher strata of society the adultery and brothel drama has spread its poison, the dirty comedy has sneaked into women's boudoirs, and the common people have been spoilt by pulp fiction [*Kolportageroman*] ... Beyond all this, the *feuilletons* and local news sections of the Jewish press take the stance that the moral views under which our parents were raised, are old and *passé*, that there is nothing more ridiculous than prudishness in things sexual.[235]

The article went on to make the usual charge about the procuring taking place in Jewish papers' personal advertisement sections, and prophesied that morality would not return until the 'the pernicious influence of the journalistic and literary Jewry on the public has found an end.'[236]

In this manner the Jewish press was once again criminalised and cast as being directly responsible for creating child-prostitutes and paedophiles. The press could be narrated as such a powerful tool of influence because by 1900 people (all people, but particularly 'weak' people) were popularly regarded as malleable in their opinions, perceptions and very identities. Secondly, the juxtaposition of the article with the piece on 'Jewish Dominance' not only served to illustrate the latter's point about the high level of Jewish influence within the media, but also created a connection between the press's campaign of immorality and their alleged aim of overthrowing the state. The implication was that Jews were trying to overthrow the state by unfairly subverting people's moral foundations: the press's lack of moderation was not a symptom of ignorance about the effects of their liberalism but part of a larger strategy.

Following this logic virtually any crime could be narrated as a Jewish crime by the antisemitic papers, because criminality itself could be narrated simply as an illustration and symptom of Jewish manipulation. The real crime frequently lay beyond the bounds of the courtroom, in the incarnation of seemingly peripheral Jews, who could be journalists, lawyers or capitalists, all of them plotting the grand perversion of the whole of society through a campaign of misinformation and suggestion.

Having asserted this, one should however add that this strategy was limited to an extremely specialised variety of journalistic output, namely three contemporary publications (the *Volksblatt*, the *Reichspost* and *Kikeriki*), which together did not even approach the circulation numbers of the *Krone* alone. Those papers that worked outside the antisemitic idiom similarly constructed criminals as rational, cunning actors, and paid similar attention to the trial as a spectacle involving a large number of participants (including the public), but their readings for the most part deliberately omitted any religio-ethnic dimension. Here trials were depicted in a variety of forms: as the triumph of modern journalism over the darkness of crime, as the unmasking of the evil machinations of capitalism, or simply as sensations.

One might speculate, however, whether the pattern uncovered broke down in the papers' coverage of violent crimes, including the most Jewish of violent crimes, the ritual murder accusation: after all, criminological thought after Lombroso often centred on compulsively violent criminals.[237] Did newspaper language embrace a tale of essentialist deviance that has so far been conspicuously absent in the reports we have analysed? How were Jews inscribed into violent crimes?

Violent Crimes – The Viennese Ripper

By way of answering these questions one might first turn to one of *fin-de-siècle* Vienna's most gruesome murders, reminiscent of the London Ripper's legendary exploits and one of the limited number of crimes – as opposed to trials – to attract sustained reports in their own right. On the night of the twenty-sixth of December 1898, an unknown assailant killed the forty-one year old Viennese prostitute Franziska Hofer in her flat in Haymerlgasse 27, and savagely mutilated her body, removing her liver in the process.[238] The sensation broke early the next morning after Hofer's sister had discovered the body, and dominated the news for the following week, until New Year's Eve, when a second, unrelated murder, also of a prostitute, displaced public interest to some degree.[239]

Looking over the coverage of the crime, one immediately is struck by the space and time devoted not to speculations about the nature of the perpetrator, let alone his psychopathology, but rather to the scene of crime itself and the forensic facts of the murder. The victim also received sustained attention, an interest sustained in part by the ambivalent connotations evoked by Hofer's occupation. A prostitute had been killed and it fell to the papers to fill this event with moral meaning: was this woman deserving of the reader's pity, or did she in some unspeakable way get what she deserved?[240]

The answer to this question was sought first of all in the story of Hofer's life,[241] but when this did not yield any clear results, it was supplemented by a quasi-Grossian 'reading' of her apartment. The *Deutsches Volksblatt*, for instance, described Hofer's living space in the following terms:

> ... the flat inhabited by the murdered woman is a simply furnished room, but one that has been given a certain homely atmosphere by its inhabitant's good taste. The linen is immaculately white, the furniture has been kept clean. Against one of the walls there stands a red couch with a large floral pattern, over which the photographs of the murder victim's various admirers [are displayed].[242]

This description completely ignored that the space described had since turned into the setting for a ghastly murder, i.e. was no longer homely, clean, immaculate. Instead, it stressed Hofer's poverty and her tidiness, as well as the normality and charm of the place – the bright red sofa, the pictures of the 'admirers' ('*Verehrer*', rather than lovers or even clients), and, most significantly, the 'immaculate' cleanliness of her linen, i.e. of the very space where she plied her trade.[243] Through the description of her living space, the careful observation of discrete, seemingly superficial facts – the linen, the pattern, the lack of dust on the furniture – the reader was implicitly informed that this woman was fundamentally decent, a prostitute yes, but a good prostitute, and a poor one. Hofer's room, filtered through the journalist's gaze, established what her biography could only hint at. There was a truth embedded in its physical minutiae that was absent in the paper's reiteration of her occupation, her criminal record and the story of her love life.

Criminalistic observation also entered the newspaper reports on a second, equally familiar level. Here the clues provided by the crime scene were reiterated as information vital to the investigation. The *Illustriertes Extrablatt*, for instance, made much out of a single '*white button*' that must have fallen off from '*a pair of underpants*', noting explicitly that 'frequently small things [*Kleinigkeiten*] have led to the discovery of murders [*sic*].'[244] All papers also paid detailed attention to the forensic reports about the corpse, and reported these at length.[245] Equally close attention was paid to various witness reports of suspicious men who had been seen in the proximity of Hofer's apartment, and descriptions of their clothing and general appearance were passed on to the readership.[246] All in all, Hofer's murder thus unfolded not unlike a Sherlock Holmes story, clue by clue, even if it were never to find closure.

That is not to say that criminological language – language that would pathologise the criminal and mark him out as 'other' – was completely absent from these reports. From the beginning, for instance, the *Deutsches Volksblatt* covered the case under the headline of '*A beastly murder and robbery*,'[247] and would on occasion bemoan the 'perversity of the monster' who had committed this crime.[248] In themselves, however, these terms are hardly enough to speak of a criminological/pathological construction of the murderer; the terms 'beastly' and 'monster' certainly might be employed as much as general terms of moral outrage as necessarily describing some degenerate other. The term 'perversity' was borrowed directly from the forensic report and was never filled with any specific content: it could be read as little more than a somewhat exotic term of abuse. Indeed it is noticeable that the assumption that the murderer might not be a rational actor did not surface with any conviction until after two or three days' coverage, i.e. only after the forensic report suggested 'perversion' because of the murderer's odd practice of removing some of his victim's head-hair.[249] Considering that Hofer was found with mutilated breasts and a cut-out liver, this disinclination to jump to conclusions about the murder's psychopathology is remarkable. The *Neue Freie Presse* initially reported the crime as a murder and robbery ['*Raubmord*'], pointing out that several of Hofer's possessions were missing,[250] while most of the other papers hedged their bets when it came to describing the murderer's motive.[251] The murderer's insanity was not a foregone conclusion. The criminological language in these crime reports amounted to little more than isolated words, which were integrated into what is at heart an investigative/criminalistic framework.

Other cases of violent crime corroborate this reading. During the trial of Wenzl Benesch for sexual murder in July 1909, the psychiatric experts once again introduced technical terms such as 'degenerate sensuality' and 'sadism' (while at the same time maintaining Benesch's sanity). The terms were taken up by the papers, and re-printed with some regularity.[252] Once again, however, these terms remained unexplored, were juxtaposed with moralistic terminology ('an evil individual'),[253] and lodged within the framework of a trial report with its usual emphasis on witness performance and the minutiae of the evidence.[254] Similarly, a 1907 *Volksblatt* headline concerning the '*Beastly Murder of a Forest Warden*', did not lead to a story about a criminal actor-as-beast, but rather focused on the minutiae of the act itself: its 'beastliness' was simply a function of the violence involved.[255] Sustained constructions of murderers as pathological others in the manner one finds in the late 1920s and early 1930s – I am thinking here of the 'Düsseldorf Vampire' – are hard to come by in this particular historical moment.[256] It is important to stress that the language of a Krafft-Ebing or indeed a Lombroso entered the newspaper discourse largely through medical experts whose psychological evaluations were then integrated into the paper narrative of crime, where they vied with other expert narratives of a more criminalistic nature.

Violent Crimes – A Jewish Murderer

Reports on Jewish violent crimes were harder to manufacture than any other form of crime as all contemporary crime statistics confirmed: Jewish involvement in violent crime was exceptionally rare. Often, antisemitic papers had to import them from far away as in the case of a 1909 article on '*Jewish Revenge*' that told the story of a Jewish girl in Ostrowce in Russian Poland, who wished to convert to Christianity, but was prevented by her two brothers. According to the article the brothers chained her naked to the wall (one notes the sexual overtones) and left her to be eaten by the rats.[257]

While the example implied a sadistic pleasure in violence taken by the Jews, it was not typically the aim of antisemitic publications to construct Jews as especially violent or vengeful – there simply wasn't enough material to support such an assertion. It is best explained as part of the general strategy by antisemitic papers to resolutely print every single instance in which Jews and crime could be connected. At times one senses the more modest desire to prove to their readership that Jews were no less violent than their Gentile neighbours.

This desire is particularly clear in an article on the child abuse perpetrated by Jewish parents, in which their behaviour was used to dispel the 'myth' of Jewish family values being superior to those of Christians.[258]

More typical yet are reports in which violent Jews are once again inscribed into a Jewish social web, and where the crime of creating criminal spaces was highlighted over and above violent criminal act of the individual perpetrator. One example is provided by a 1904 *Reichspost* report on the 'Jew Popper' who abandoned his pregnant lover, spent all her money, and generally behaved abysmally.[259] When his mistreated lover attempted to take revenge, predictably enough by dousing his face in vitriol, the period's weapon of romantic revenge *par excellence*, he wrestled the jar out of her hand and poured it over her face instead. The woman, disfigured, was nevertheless charged with attempt to cause grievous harm. The *Reichspost*'s outrage was not directed primarily against Popper, but against the Jewish press who expressed no sympathy for the woman. Why did it not express sympathy, the *Reichspost* wondered? 'Perhaps because Popper is a – Jew?'[260] As ever the alleged power of Jews to shield villains was worse – and more 'Jewish' – than an individual's vicious behaviour.

Turning to one of the period's very rare genuine murder sensations involving a Jewish defendant (albeit a convert), one similarly finds familiar – if surprisingly muted – tropes of constructing Jewish criminality. On the first of February 1895 the corpse of the respectable Viennese lawyer Isidor Hermann Rothziegel was discovered in his office with a crushed skull and slashed wrists. Within days his solicitor Gustav Eichinger was questioned and arrested, first under a charge of fraud (he had embezzled some of Rothziegel's money), then under the charge of murder. By the fifth of February the newspapers were running detailed biographies of Eichinger. One of the curious details of his former life was his conversion to Judaism for reasons of marriage – the Jewish parents of his future wife, Franziska Rabinowicz, had refused to accept his suit otherwise. Gustav Eichinger changed his name to Abraham, married his wife in a Jewish ceremony, then left the army after some tensions with fellow officers, which to a good part were precipitated by this liaison with a Jewish woman. Eichinger moved to Vienna, lived above his means, and eventually murdered Rothziegel, either to cover up his embezzlement, or else simply to clean out his employer's safe.[261]

The *Deutsches Volksblatt* took some time to find a viable angle for covering the crime. Initially its focus centred on victim[262] and crime scene,[263] much as it had in the Hofer killing described above. A Jewish dimension did not enter until Eichinger emerged as the clear main suspect, and when his biographical information – including his conversion – was made public.[264] As this information was relayed, attempts were made to implicate Eichinger's Jewish wife ('Frau Eichinger was, as you know, arrested under the suspicion of knowledge about the crime').[265] The conversion itself was narrated with reference to Eichinger's economic difficulties, with a suggestion that his parents-in-law manipulated him with their wealth and pressured him into abandoning his religion.[266] At this point, however, the *Volksblatt* was not willing to commit fully to this reading of the murder. It chose to juxtapose this narrative with more gossip about the victim, specifically that Rothziegel had 'an *affair with a married woman*', a piece of news that suggested a murder motivated by revenge and jealousy.[267] Thereafter, the story more or less disappeared from the papers only to re-surface with intensive coverage in the third week of April 1895, when the case came to trial.

By and large this coverage followed familiar patterns. Most papers used description in an attempt to characterise Eichinger at various stages of the trial.[268] They also paid sustained attention to the largely female audience in attendance, with the conventional charge that the court room was being turned into a theatre.[269] The prosecution's construction of the events, likewise, offered few surprises: the reader was presented with a cunning, rational criminal who attempted to create the illusion of suicide while brutally killing his boss for personal profit.[270] Eichinger, in the prosecution's reading, was not born bad. Rather he gradually and rationally embraced criminal means, culminating in minutely planned, pre-meditated murder, in order to extract himself from the consequences of his economic mismanagement.

Unsurprisingly then, much of the trial's focus centred on Eichinger's mental disposition. The defendant pleaded guilty, but claimed temporary insanity during the homicide, as well as a more permanent mental weakness brought on by an accident when an acrobatic display went wrong and precipitated a serious head injury.[271] At one point he went so far as to claim that he had only pretended to be sane during the investigative process for fear of being put in the 'loony bin'.[272] The court psychiatrist, by contrast, judged him to be fully 'accountable', and most of the papers, too, narrated him as a rational entity, often using description as a means to see through any attempts at deception. The *Arbeiter-Zeitung*, for instance, paid much attention to the way Eichinger 'grabs his white shirt collar, as if everything were too tight for him,' an observation that was juxtaposed with the speculation that 'at times it looks like Eichinger wants to simulate insanity.'[273] The *Neue Freie Presse* went a somewhat separate way by introducing a rare criminal-psychological note: it juxtaposed its report on the trial with an article by Moritz Benedikt on 'Moral Insanity,' which somewhat half-heartedly embraced the concept, redefining it as 'inborn or acquired "immorality"'.[274] While one was free to read the article as a commentary on the case, this suggestion was never made explicit. The article was also fully compatible with a reading of Eichinger as a rational actor, who acquired his 'immorality' through years of financial deprivation. His performance in court thus remained central to a decoding of his state of mind.[275]

The *Volksblatt* dismissed Eichinger's attempt at pleading insanity as a ploy fuelled by 'extraordinary cynicism', wishing 'to create the illusion' that the murder was a function of temporary 'mental confusion'.[276] Indeed it was this cynicism that helped unmask Eichinger's true character, and his crime consequently became as much a matter of Rothziegel's murder, as of the wilful misrepresentation of his own person. It was his dissimulation that could be fully verified in the court room, even before the jury came to a formal verdict about his guilt in the homicide.

Surprisingly however, the *Volksblatt* made little attempt to connect Eichinger's cynical cunning to his religious conversion, or indeed his wife's Judaism. Rather the conversion itself was constructed as but another indicator of Eichinger's opportunism and lack of character, in this manner further attesting to his sanity.[277] Nor was there an endless identification of Eichinger as Jewish – he was usually referred to as Gustav, rather than Abraham – or any sustained attempt to implicate his wife or his lawyer, Dr Elbogen, a member of the Austrian Isrealite Union whom we have already encountered at the Klein trial, where he was quite clearly identified as Jewish.

This is not to say that Franziska Eichinger's Judaism and Elbogen's lawyer tricks made no appearance at all in the *Volksblatt*'s coverage. On the penultimate day of the trial the question emerged whether Franziska Eichinger should be called as a defence witness, in order to corroborate her husband's story of desperate financial need, and, one suspects, to make a spectacle of the much touted bonds of passionate love that connected husband and wife. Indeed the *Volksblatt* picked up on this motive behind the planned confrontation, and made a point of attacking the deliberateness of this '*effective* [*effektvolle*] scene' that Elbogen tried to stage.[278] The report also dwelled on Franziska Eichinger's reasons for not testifying: she excused herself, stating that she was planning a pilgrimage to Maria-Lauzendorf, 'despite the fact that she is a Jewess' as the *Volksblatt* put it.[279] The Jewess was lying, the paper implied none too subtly, a point to which it returned when it highlighted the testimony of Eichinger's house warden who claimed '*that she [Mrs Eichinger] had known about her husband's crime.*'[280] But neither accusation was at any point solidified into a concentrated indictment of Jewish criminality: for once there was no editorial that would have drawn the disparate strands of the reports together and offered a coherent antisemitic reading of the crime and its trial. Given the proportions of the Eichinger sensation, and the direct involvement of Jews, this reticence comes as a considerable surprise.

The *Reichspost*'s coverage was similarly muted in its construction of the trial's 'Jewish' dimension, although it did feature a direct attack against Jewish journalists and spectators whose sensationalist habits stood in the way of a accurately appraising the trial:

> [The courtroom is] so full with Jewish, irregular [*nicht ständigen*] reporters, that the *work* of accredited members of the press was made more difficult in an unpleasant manner. This is, after all, a Jewish sensation trial, which explains the presence of masses of Jewesses and other curious women ...[281]

The *Reichspost* thus contrasted the honest labour of 'real' journalism with the alleged Jewish practice of constructing sensations. It left ambiguous whether it was Eichinger's Judaism, the papers' sensationalism, or in fact the Jewish audience's curiosity that turned the present event into a ' Jewish sensation trial'. Indeed it would go on commenting on the 'disgusting spectacle' of the 'female auditorium'[282] throughout the trial, although never again with explicit reference to this audience as Jewish. The story of Eichinger's conversion, and his wife's role in the murder, by contrast, remained relatively unexplored.

The *Ostdeutsche Rundschau* was similarly restrained. Like the *Volksblatt* and the *Reichspost*, it referred to Eichinger largely by his Christian name, Gustav, and neutrally described his wife's family as being 'of Mosaic faith.'[283] It did, however, spend considerable time attacking Eichinger's defence counsel, Elbogen, for his overly theatrical final plea, and the 'Jew papers' that praised 'their tribesman' for it:

> One thing is certain, the auditorium ... is under his spell, and all the *more or less pretty women's eyes hang on his lips* ... All of it, *all*, was a pose, coquetry, crafty, fake [*faustdicke*] modesty ... finishing in a moving appeal to 'justice,' 'humanity' and 'love'.[284]

The Jewish lawyer, as a manipulator of public opinion, was thus introduced into the discourse.

Kikeriki's coverage barely touched on the trial, attacking only its sensationalism.[285] It also ran a joke about how Jewish papers generated crime in order to have sensations to write about, i.e. reiterated the general narrative of the symbiosis between Jewish press and crime, without committing to a specific frame for the Eichinger case.[286]

The Eichinger case thus leaves us with a double impression: on the one hand all the tropes of antisemitic reporting on Jewish crimes are in place and alluded to, on the other there is a reluctance to make more of this trial that could easily been have framed as a story of a respectable Christian – a military officer – falling into the clutches of his Jewish wife and being converted, in the process, into the Jewish murderer Abraham. If one compares the lack of coherence of the construction of Eichinger's criminality to that of the Schapira case of the same year, one is astonished not to find a more sustained narrative.

The reason for this relative reticence may be located in the fact that Jewish murderers were so rare and the conventions of trial reporting still rather fresh, that some insecurity existed on how to deal with it. Things were clearer cut with a financial crime like Nuchem Schapira's forgery fraud. Indeed it took the Hilsner ritual murder trials for the newspapers to fully decide how a violent Jewish criminal could best be inscribed into the antisemitic narrative of Jewish crime that we have thus far encountered.

Conclusions

This chapter has argued that the construction of Jewish crimes within trial reports – by far the most popular, sustained and linguistically rich of contemporary modes of writing about crimes – followed distinct strategies, irrespective of the specific crime. These included constructing the Jewish defendants as rational and cunning, and systematically criminalising other Jews surrounding the trial (lawyers, police-men, spectators, journalists, witnesses, psychiatrists) by charging them with truth distortion. Jewish crimes were thus ultimately crimes against the justice system itself, and, by extension, against society.

Many more examples of this dynamic can be gleaned from the antisemitic papers: one finds Jewish lawyers unmasking themselves as unscrupulous criminals,[287] a Jewish book-dealer who sells pornographic *Schundliteratur*,[288] a Jewish defrauder who preys on the Galician peasantry,[289] and an innocent Christian servant girl who is sued by her Jewish mistress for theft and whose downfall is sealed by the false statements of Jewish witnesses.[290] Indeed an 'exemplary' Jewish witness ('*Jüdischer Musterzeug*') also featured in a fraud case involving Christian defendants, once again giving false witness.[291] There is also the trial of a 'baptised Jew' in Graz, prosecuted by Hans Gross, who had taken on a false identity and pretended to be a member of high society.[292]

Despite this wealth of examples, the articulation of these narratives was clearest in major scandals. These scandals clearly played a key role in the construction of Jewish crime by spelling out a way in which Jewish involvement should be read. The scandals were then loosely connected through a near-continuous chain of crimes and trials associated with Jews, in some more or less artificial manner: they did not need to be as explicit in their narrative structure because the model of how to read them had already been established and would be periodically reiterated through major 'Jewish scandals'. In this manner, a fantasy of a specifically Jewish criminality could be constructed.

The artificiality of the link between Jews and crime in so many of the antisemitic reports, and the absence of the need to have actual Jewish perpetrators to create associations between Jews and crime, point to the limited usefulness of a quantitative analysis that would break the data down according to the type of crime: the figures quoted at the beginning of this chapter give an indication of how ubiquitous the theme was, but in themselves they say little about the antisemitic strategy evident in the papers. A crime was not billed as 'Jewish' because a specific kind of offence had been committed by a Jew. A crime was billed Jewish whenever a Jew could be connected to it – or the investigative and judicial process surrounding it – however peripheral his or her function. Antisemitic meaning was given to this connection through a narrative of Jewish dissimulation/truth-distortion, a narrative spelled out in large scandals.

This narrative was functional because it shared many of the epistemological assumptions and narrative tropes of trial coverage in general, and appropriated them for its own uses. In terms of content, after all, the narratives of Jewish crime encountered in our analysis were by no means original. Rather they recycled long-established antisemitic tropes, above all the identification of Jews with modernity, capitalism and materialism that had found a first flowering during the 1848 revolution and that itself drew upon a long Christian tradition of marking Jews as urban usurers.[293] The conspiratorial aspect of the charge against Jewish criminals, too, was hardly new, and connected with nationalist anxieties about enemies within one's own borders who were motivated by trans-national concerns. What was new to the narrative of Jewish criminality was the success with which antisemitic publications could manipulate the genre conventions in a manner that allowed them to seamlessly integrate their prejudices and develop a vision of Jews as arch-criminals.

The concepts of biological race, degeneracy and heredity did not play an important role in the construction of Jewish crimes (or indeed crimes in general): they had not displaced more traditional antisemitic narratives in the context of crime. Only extremely rarely was the claim made that Jews were criminal because it was 'in their blood'. Indeed the deliberateness of criminal actions was consistently, if implicitly, affirmed: the model for Jewish co-operation in criminal acts was not one of mechanical solidarity but of wilful conspiracy. The term 'race' was, of course, frequently employed, but little effort was made to disentangle the biological, religious and historical meanings: it was used as an identifying tag rather than in itself carrying explanatory force.

Just as biological narratives of Jewish crime did not flourish in the period under consideration either popularly or among scholars, similarly no attempt was made to map criminality onto the Viennese Jewish community sociologically. One might expect, for instance, an attempt to construct the second district, Leopoldstadt – formerly a Jewish ghetto (1625–1670) and in 1910 still host to the largest proportion of Jews in the city, although they never constituted more than a third of its population[294] – as a *Verbrecherviertel*, a criminal quarter, rife with vice. Some contemporary reports on Leopoldstadt as the epicentre of Viennese crime did, in fact, exist. These, however, appeared in the *Österreichische Kriminalzeitung*, i.e. a liberal publication disseminating popular versions of criminological narratives of crime. Here an article that was part of a mini-series entitled 'Forays into the worlds of crime and vice' highlighted the proclivity of 'Thieves Dens' – public houses frequented by criminals – to be located in the second district.[295] Another article, under the colourful title of 'The secrets of Leopoldstadt, prostitution in the second district' recounted a reporter's adventures on and off the *Praterstraße*, 'a true hotbed of crime, disease and meanness, of desolation, despair, and dirt …', which included being picked up by a respectable-looking older woman who turned out to be – much to the reporter's moral outrage – a prostitute.[296] Neither of these articles highlighted Jewish involvement in crime, however, and they represent the only contemporary attempt to write a criminal geography of Vienna. The antisemites conspicuously eschewed locating Jewish criminality spatially – for them it was a cancer that respected no boundaries, social or geographical.[297] The point of their narrative of Jewish crime was not that Jews banded together in one place to plan crimes, but that Jewish influence was making it impossible to locate and punish criminals in general.

Finally, we have found that antisemitic constructions of Jewish crime were an extremely partisan enterprise. Non-antisemitic papers studiously avoided tapping into its language, including Vienna's one truly mass paper, the *Kronen-zeitung*. The picture of antisemitism that thus emerges is one in which use of an antisemitic vocabulary clearly identified papers politically and could not be used casually. This, one might argue, puts pressure upon the thesis that anti-semitism had become 'respectable' across Vienna's social spectrum in the years leading up to the Great War.

Chinese Criminality: A Comparison

The construction of Jewish criminality in the antisemitic press becomes even clearer when compared to contemporary narratives about other – and more exotic – 'others'. We have noted in chapter three that the scholarly treatment of Gypsy crime contrasted starkly with that of Jewish crime. In the popular press it was Chinese criminals that attracted particularly outlandish narratives, in part no doubt because Vienna had no Chinese population to speak of. Thus, the murder of Elsie Sigel, a German immigrant's granddaughter, in distant New York City attracted some excited coverage in the Viennese press, and pro-duced a construction of criminality that throws the narrative of Jewish crime into clear relief.

In late June 1909 the corpse of nineteen-year-old Elsie Sigel was discovered in a suitcase in a New York City flat.[298] Not only was its tenant a Chinese man by the name of Leon K Ling, the love letters also found on the murder scene quickly established Ling as the prime suspect. Racial anxieties were further fuelled by Sigel's romantic involvement with Ling, and – as it turned out – with another Chinese man. The story made its way from the American papers into the London ones and from there conquered the continent.[299] It reached the *Krone* on the twenty-fifth and made its title page with the caption of '*The Secrets of Chinatown, The Murder of Elsie Siegl* [*sic*],' and a picture of a Chinese opium-den juxtaposed with a scene from the actual murder: a Chinese man in western dress strangling a woman on an ottoman (see Figure 5.5). In the opium-den part of the illustration, an elegant lady was being served an opium pipe, while another was busy cutting off a Chinese man's pigtail, at a proximity that sug-gested sexual intimacy. The picture thus establishes a narrative that provided some insight into the 'Secrets of Chinatown' promised in the headline: it could be read sequentially as the seduction of a respectable woman through drugs, that led to an illicit relation in which the lover was externally westernised (the removal of the pigtail), but that nevertheless resulted in her murder at his hands.

The coverage inside spelled out this narrative in greater detail. Sigel was characterised as the naïve daughter of rich parents who wished to convert New York's Chinese population to Christianity. Ling had been one of her students, and had pretended to have been converted. In fact he had become her lover, turned Sigel into his 'unwitting tool', then got bored with the 'white girl'. The *Krone* also hazarded a guess at how the murder took place: '... it is most likely

Figure 5.5 'The Secrets of Chinatown.'
Source. Title page: *Illustrierte Kronenzeitung*, 25 June 1909.

that the Chinese man [*der Chinese*], after seducing the girl, wanted to turn her into a *prostitute* in *Chinatown* to get rid of her; that she resisted and he killed her in a rage.'[300]

Lest one attribute too much blame to Elsie who, in this narrative, seemed to have brought about her own doom through her unwholesome fascination with the Chinese, the *Krone* reminded its readers that she might have not been a willing lover: 'Opium also plays a role. It is not uncommon that young girls are *initiated* by young Chinese men into the *secrets of opium intoxication*, and are then *abused* while they are in a *dream-state*.'[301] As a scenario this was a perfect metaphor for the relationship between victim and perpetrator characteristic of the contemporary conceptualisation of crime: the criminal tricked a hapless victim into a state where she could neither defend herself nor tell truth from lies, then had his evil way.

Indeed the paper established the Chinese as a cunning breed of criminals who organised themselves in gangs according to social status (the paper later mysteriously referred to the 'Hip-Sing-Tong', a gang of 'gamblers and brawlers' and their rivals 'Ong-Long-Tong', who were set to go to war over the affair).[302] Ling himself displayed criminal cunning in his ability to evade the authorities: the *Krone* depicted him as a skilled dissimulator, who frequently impersonated women (see Figure 5.6).

> We have already noted the great difficulties in chasing the Chinese man. These difficulties have now grown immeasurably. For we hear that Leon also used to show himself as an excellent impersonator of women. He used to play his role with such conviction, that it seems likely that the murderer has masked himself as a Chinese woman. The police now is no longer just searching for a Chinese man without a pigtail, but will also have to pay attention to all Chinese women, and it is doubtful that they will find him.[303]

But Ling was not the only crook who demonstrated Chinese cunning in the *Krone*'s narrative of the crime. On the second day of coverage the report focused on Tschong Sing, another Chinese-American who claimed to have witnessed the murder. His testimony was damning for Ling, but Tschong Sing was soon unmasked as an opportunist liar, who wished to use the situation for his own criminal ends. Only the rather brutal sleep deprivation methods of the New York police (here much commended) managed to expose this false witness, who was built up as something of a criminal mastermind:

> According to the police, Tschong Sing is the greatest liar and most cunning person, whom they have ever questioned. Despite the terrible agony of staying awake ... the tough Chinese man's will-power was in no way broken.[304]

While this narrative of cunning, rational master-dissimulators, who were continuously identified as Chinese, corresponds closely to the antisemitic narrative of Jews, it in many ways went even further. For instance, there were passages in the *Krone*'s coverage that offer a straightforwardly racist characterisation of all Chinese, in a language we have rarely if ever encountered in the coverage of Jews, but that may remind us of the criminological treatment of Gypsies. Thus, under a sub-headline of '*The yellow men and the white girls*' the reader learned that the Chinese man ['der Chinese'] is '*dirty, cruel, deceitful and disgustingly sensuous*.'[305] As in the case of Gypsy criminality one can only conclude that

The *Illustriertes Extrablatt* stressed the detective aspects of the case, depicting police officers going through Sigel's love letters and discovering her corpse, as well as providing an image of the perpetrator that resembles a police 'mug-shot'. One also notes the stress on the perfection of Leon/Ling's disguise as a woman (top right).

Figure 5.6 Investigation of the Elsie Sigel murder.
Source. Title page: *Illustriertes Wiener Extrablatt*, 1 July 1909.

such language could only be used for the distant 'other', but was unacceptable and unconvincing for better known minorities.[306] The *Krone* went on to implicate the entire Chinese population of New York for hiding the murderer, by constructing Chinatown as a criminal space. Again, this geographic focus has no real equivalent in the antisemitic coverage of crime that could not easily be mapped onto a specific Jewish space.

Turning from the populist *Krone* to the *Deutsches Volksblatt* we find quite different coverage. Rather than building the murder up as a function of Chinese criminality, as it undoubtedly would have, had Elsie found her end at the hands of a Jewish lover/murderer, the *Volksblatt*'s page-one editorial on the crime focused on the other newspapers' tendencies to glamorise what was at heart a gritty affair of a less than attractive woman of loose morals being presented the bill for her immoral choices by an equally distasteful perpetrator, all in the interest of selling more papers with the newest sensation. Sigel was characterised as a woman who had been 'unable to ensnare a comrade in race', the granddaughter, not of a hero, but of an ordinary immigrant who had been elevated beyond his potential only by circumstance, to wit, the American Civil War.[307] She had been teaching in New York's missionary schools, not out of a sense of Christian duty, but because she had hoped for social elevation through associating with priests and members of high society.[308] Indeed, through this characterisation as a calculating opportunist, Elsie – the murder victim, one should not forget – took on one of the key qualities used to designate criminals. Similarly, the Chinese students under her supervision displayed a criminal's cunning when it came to wooing their teachers in their own quest for social acceptance.[309] A week previously, the *Volksblatt*'s coverage similarly stressed that 'a Chinese man only turns Christian if he regards it to his material advantage'; in this respect the Chinese were compared to Jews, who were charged with similar opportunism.[310] Despite these attempts to establish both the murderer's and the victim's pre-mediated opportunism, however, the lead editorial's focus remained squarely on unmasking the hidden mechanics of various papers' conspiracy to narrate the ordinary as special and thus glamorise crime and turn a hussy into a heroine/victim. Reading the *Volksblatt*, one might come to the conclusion that no grievous crime had taken place at all, and that the entire incident was little but a 'trivial everyday comedy'.[311]

None of this is meant to imply that the *Volksblatt*'s coverage was not racist. At one point it referred to members of various non-Caucasian ethnicities as '*Panoptikernigger*', and its entire coverage was informed by the assumed superiority of white people, and the self-evident need to avoid inter-racial sexual relations.[312] What was absent, however, was the desire to establish the Chinese as a dangerous criminal race, and to enshrine Leon K. Ling as a master-criminal. The coverage throughout was terse and avoided dramatisation. The above quoted scene of Tschong Sing's (here spelled: Dschungsin) interrogation, for instance, was reduced to a single bland paragraph.[313] The *Reichspost* similarly spent little time on the case, avoided building up the Chinese criminals as anything special, and was hostile to Sigel whom it described as a 'dilettante missionary,' implying at the very least incompetence.[314] *Kikeriki* showed even less interest in Chinese criminals: only a single, bland reference was devoted to an affair that made the front pages of all popular papers.[315] The point here cannot be that the *Kronenzeitung* was more racist than antisemitic publications. The point is that a paper that studiously avoided making reference to Jewish criminality had no such qualms when it came to more distant 'others', that the narrative tools it employed were not dissimilar to those antisemitic papers employed for Jews, and that the antisemitic papers' racism was of a highly directed nature.[316]

The Sigel scandal was not the only contemporary incident in which Chinese criminality made headlines. A second interesting treatment of the subject comes from the pages of the *Österreichische Kriminalzeitung*. In a series of articles entitled '*The secrets of a criminal district*,' it turned its attention New York's Chinatown, constructing it as a *Verbecherviertel* par excellence.[317] The article was occasioned by the triumphant announcement (false as it turned out) that Chinatown would soon be torn down to the last house and replaced by a park:

> 'Chinatown', New York's centre of pestilence ... has received its death verdict. [...] Clean people and clean streets will replace the dirty, smelly streets and the yellow devils who call themselves 'sons of heaven', who know how to imbibe the white people with new, bigger and more dangerous vices on top of those they already have.[318]

The author celebrated the tearing down of Chinatown as a great act of exposure: 'The secrets of Chinatown that have caused the New York police force such headaches will only be divulged in their true dimensions and ugliness, when the houses have been levelled and the basements display themselves in the sunlight.'[319] Indeed, he continued, there was much to expose. To prove his point, the author reminisced about all the despicable secrets uncovered when natural forces – the San Francisco earthquake – achieved what New York's city council now wished to put into practice through a man-made effort: 'One discovered secret doors and tunnels, endless passageways that led from one house to the next, chasms and deep wells where the Chinese could easily rid himself of any pursuers, or make his victims disappear.'[320] The sociological and physical space of Chinatown was thus marked as criminal in a variety of ways: its Chinese inhabitants (as a race) were greedy, clever businessmen; they had secret passageways no non-Chinese could penetrate; they filled up their white victims with opium and drink, robbed the men, raped the women whom they desired inordinately; they had a secret criminal government that regulated their ghetto's affairs; they had total group solidarity which made them so very dangerous to hapless white people; they were chain-smokers; and so forth.[321] Once again we note that the stereotype of the Chinese as a criminal race has been taken to a point that the antisemitic invective against Jewish criminality did not – and, I would argue, could not – approach. The simple conflation of ethnicity and crime was only possible for exotic, mystical 'others'. Indeed, the article drew heavily on the tantalisingly alien nature of the subject matter – 'as alien as the fairy tales from *One Thousand and One Arabian Nights*' – that represented a secret world into which readers needed to be 'initiated'.[322] As a test case against Jewish criminality, the treatment of Chinese criminality thus both shows up the centrality of the image of the dissimulating mastermind in the contemporary construction of criminals, but also the limits to which Jews could be criminalised by reference to their 'race' alone.[323]

Notes

1. For example *DV*, 8 March 1900, p. 7.
2. *DV*, 20 September 1905, p. 10
3. *DV*, 25 March 1905, pp. 8–9.
4. *DV*, 25 March 1900, pp. 6–7.
5. *DV*, 23 September 1905, pp. 8–9; *DV*, 24 September 1905, p. 8.
6. For details on *Krida* and other types of fraud, see: Friedrich Hartl, *Das Wiener Kriminalgericht, Strafrechtspflege vom Zeitalter der Aufklärung bis zur Österreichischen Revolution* (Vienna 1973), pp. 395–7.
7. *DV*, 2 January 1895, p. 6.
8. *DV*, 13 June 1909, p. 7.
9. *DV*, 28 October 1904, p. 1.
10. *DV*, 13 September 1899, p. 6.
11. *RP*, 22 September 1905, p. 10. The report focuses on a scandal surrounding two Jewish bookkeepers.
12. *DV*, 16 October 1899, evening edition, p. 5.
13. *DV*, 16 October 1899, evening edition, p. 5.
14. *DV*, 16 Oct 1899, evening edition, p. 5.
15. *RP*, 18 October 1899, 5; *RP*, 21 October 1899, p. 5.
16. *DV*, 18 October 1899, p. 7.
17. Court Documents: Box A 11 93–4 Schapira *et al.* 1895; see esp.: Box 1, Documents 2, 3, 179 ff; Box 2, Document 605 ('Anklageschrift').
18. Cf. *DV*, 18 February 1895, pp. 5–6; *NFP*, 19 February 1895, p. 7; *Extrablatt*, 18 February 1895, p. 4; *RP*, 20 February 1895, p. 4.
19. For example *DV*, 18 February 1895, p. 6.
20. See especially: *Extrablatt*, 20 February 1895, p. 8.
21. *NFP*, 22 February 1895, p. 8.
22. After all, a 'fixed stare' brought on by short-sightedness would only have made literal sense if Herz had not been wearing glasses in court.
23. *NFP*, 22. February 1895, p. 8. The report also stressed his 'utter calm' as he watched the proceedings, another descriptive give-away for the truly cold-blooded criminal.
24. See esp.: *RP*, 23 February 1895, p. 5. The *NFP* was somewhat of an exception on this point, because it largely chose to paraphrase the witnesses. The basic dynamic of clever exploiter/gullible exploitee did however remain in place. See the discussion below.
25. SaW, Gerichtsakte, Box A 11 93–4 (Schapira 1895), 2 Vols.; Vol. 1, Doc. 4.
26. *RP*, 20 February 1895, p. 4.
27. Ibid.
28. *NFP*, 19 February 1895, 8; *Extrablatt*, 18 February 1895, 4; *AZ*, 18 February 1895, 3; *DV*, 18 February 1895, pp. 5–6.

29. *NFP*, 20 February 1895, evening edition, p. 3.
30. *NFP*, 21 February 1895, evening edition, p. 2.
31. *NFP*, 21 February 1895, p. 8.
32. *NFP*, 19 February 1895, p. 7.
33. *AZ*, 18 February 1895, p. 3.
34. See Josef Draxler, 'Vergleich der Zeitungen Reichspost und Vaterland', pp. 59–66.
35. *Vaterland*, 18 February 1895, evening edition, p. 4.
36. *DV*, 18. February 1895, evening edition, p. 5.
37. *RP*, 23. February 1895, p. 5.
38. *DV*, 18. February 1895, evening edition, p. 6.
39. Here quoted from: *DV*, 23 February 1895, p. 6. Re-quoted in: *DV*, 20 September 1905, p. 7.
40. *DV*, 18 February 1895, evening edition, p. 6.
41. *DV*, 21. February 1895, p. 6
42. *RP*, 20 February 1895, p. 4.
43. *RP*, 21 February 1895, p. 5.
44. *RP*, 22 February 1895, p. 5.
45. The misprinting of Gastfreund's name is itself revealing: *Gastfreund* denotes a man who is a 'friend to/of guests', *Gutsfreund* a man who is a 'friend of property'. Freud might have had something to say about this slip of the editorial tongue.
46. *RP*, 26 February 1895, p. 5.
47. '*Oh Muse, singe zur Lyra / Das Lied vom Nuchem Schapira / Der viel verschlagen im Land / die 'Sitt' ünsrer Lait hat erkannt / Die mühelosen Gewinn /Allein nur haben im Sinn / Weil ohne Arbeit verdienen / Das höchste auf Erden ihnen/...*' *Kikeriki*, 24 September 1905, p. 1.
48. *Kikeriki*, 24 September 1905, p. 2.
49. *Kikeriki*, 8 October 1905, p. 9.
50. Cf. Paupié, *Handbuch*, p. 108
51. *OR*, 18 February 1894, p. 2.
52. Mark H. Gelber, 'Ethnic Pluralism and Germanization in the works of Karl-Emil Franzos (1848–1904)', in: *The German Quarterly* 56, 3 (1983), pp. 376–85.
53. *AZ*, 23 February 1895, p. 5.
54. Dr Friedmann's defence speech, as quoted in: *AZ*, 23 February 1895, p. 6.
55. *Krone*, 20 September 1905, p. 7.
56. Ibid., p. 5. See also, for similar terminology: *RP*, p. 21. September 1905, p. 3; *Extrablatt*, 20 September 1905, pp. 5–6; *NFP*, 20 September 1905, p. 9; *AZ*, 20 September 1905, p. 6.
57. *Krone*, 20 September 1905, p. 5.
58. Ibid.
59. Ibid., p. 6.
60. 'Falscher Fünfziger – echte Juden.' The German idiom 'Falscher Fünfziger' designates both a fake bill and a treacherous or deceitful person. *RP*, 21 September 1905, p. 3.
61. For the court materials relating to this (first) Kubowski trial, see: SaW, Gerichtsakte, Box A 11, Fasz. 177-8, No. 2780 (7 Vols.) (Kubowski 1905). The spelling of Kubowsky/Kubovski/Kubowski was inconsistent in papers and official papers alike.
62. Here quoted from: *Extrablatt*, 28 September 1905, p. 8.
63. Ibid.
64. Coverage in the *Kronenzeitung* starts in: *Krone*, 25 September 1905, pp. 10–12; in the *Deutsches Volksblatt* in: *DV*, 25 September 1905, evening edition, pp. 5–6.
65. *DV*, 25 September 1905, evening edition, p. 5. In this instance the paper used the more technical term '*mosaisch*' giving the highlighted biographical detail a veneer of bureaucratic objectivity.
66. Ibid.

67. Ibid., p. 6.
68. *DV*, 25 September 1905, evening edition, p. 5. The italicised emphasis is my own.
69. Ibid., p. 6.
70. *DV*, 27 September 1905, p. 11.
71. *DV*, 28 September 1905, p. 10.
72. *DV*, 30 September 1905, p. 10.
73. Ibid.
74. The coverage starts with: *RP*, 27 September 1905, p. 10.
75. *RP*, 28 September 1905, p. 10.
76. *RP*, 29 September 1905, p. 10.
77. *RP*, 27 September 1905, p. 10. Cf. also: *RP*, 30 September 1905, p. 10.
78. *RP*, 28 September 1905, p. 10.
79. *RP*, 3 October 1905, p. 10.
80. Ibid.
81. *DV*, 1 October 1905, p. 9.
82. Ibid.
83. *Kikeriki*, 28 September 1905, p. 3.
84. Ibid.
85. Ibid.
86. *Kikeriki*, 12 October 1905, p. 1. See also: *Kikeriki*, 8 October 1905, pp. 2, 9.
87. *Extrablatt*, 26 September 1905, p. 8.
88. See in particular: *NFP*, 25 September 1905, evening edition, p. 10.
89. *NFP*, 26 September 1905, 9. See also: *NFP*, 29 September 1905, p. 10.
90. *DV*, 28 October 1899, p. 8.
91. Ibid.
92. Ibid.
93. *DV*, 2 October 1899, evening edition, p. 3.
94. *DV*, 31 October 1899, p. 5.
95. *DV*, 10 November 1899, p. 8.
96. *DV*, 11 November 1899, p. 1.
97. One should note in passing that one defendant in the Lemberg trial claimed that he might have subconsciously acted against his will, due to his morphine consumption. It was this kind of scenario that received close criminological attention at this time. See: reports of 1 November 1899 (various papers).
98. Cf. Dichand, *Kronenzeitung*, pp. 13, 179.
99. *DV*, 13 April 1899, pp. 5–6.
100. This account is based on the parallel reading of the various newspaper accounts for June and for October and November 1904.
101. See: *Krone*, 30 October 1904, p. 7.
102. *DV*, 29 October, 1904, p. 10.
103. *DV*, 29 October, 1904, evening edition, p. 1.
104. *DV*, 29 October, 1904, evening edition, p. 2.
105. Ibid.
106. *DV*, 30 October 1904, pp. 9–10.
107. *DV*, 30 October 1904, p. 9.
108. Ibid.
109. Ibid., p. 10.
110. *DV*, 1 November 1904, p. 8.
111. *DV*, 30 October 1904, p. 9.
112. *DV*, 1 November 1904, p. 7.
113. Ibid., p. 8.
114. *DV*, 30 October 1904, p. 10.

115. *DV*, 30 October 1904, p. 1.
116. Ibid., p. 2.
117. Ibid.
118. On the antisemitic narrative of the Jewish power over the press, cf. Robertson, *Jewish Question*, p. 181.
119. *DV*, 1 November 1904, p. 7.
120. *DV*, 3 November 1904, p. 9.
121. Ibid.
122. '*Die nur Lug und Trug gewoben/Mit echt jüd'schem Gaunersinn/Einig ist man sich in Leoben:/Sie ist eine Schwindlerin/Anderswo gibt es Bedenken/In den Kreisen nämlich wo/ Schlaue Menschen listig lenken/Aller Meinunbg hü! und ho!*' *Kikeriki*, 6 November 1904, p. 1.
123. *Vaterland*, 1 November 1904, p. 7. Tamara Bellachini's father was Italian, not Russian.
124. *RP*, 1 November 1904, p. 6.
125. *RP*, 3 November 1904, pp. 1–2.
126. 'Der Fall Hervay', 'Der Hexenprozess von Leoben', 'Die Memoiren der Frau v. Hervay', originally published in *Die Fackel* in July, November and October 1904, respectively, then collected as part of the 1908 book *Sittlichkeit und Kriminalität* (page references refer to the Frankfurt 1987 edition ed. C. Wagenknecht). On Karl Kraus and *Sittlichkeit und Kriminalität*, see: Theodor W. Adorno, 'Sittlichkeit und Kriminalität, Zum elften Band der Werke von Karl Kraus', in: Theodor W. Adorno, *Noten zur Literatur* (Frankfurt 1977), pp. 366–87; Edward Timms, *Karl Kraus, Apocalyptic Satirist, Culture and Catastrophe in Habsburg Vienna* (New Haven 1986), pp. 61–165; Reinhard Merkel, 'Wo gegen Natur sie auf Normen pochten … Bemerkungen zum Verhältnis zwischen Strafrecht und Satire im Werk von Karl Kraus,' in: Schönert (ed.), *Erzählte Kriminalität*, pp. 607–31.
127. Kraus, 'Der Fall Hervay', p. 103.
128. *AZ*, 1 November 1904, p. 2.
129. Ibid.
130. *AZ*, 2 November 1904, p. 6.
131. *Krone*, 29 October 1904, p. 7.
132. *Extrablatt*, 1 November 1904, p. 2.
133. *NFP*, 31 October 1904, evening edition, p. 9.
134. Kraus, 'Der Fall Hervay', p. 98.
135. Kraus, 'Der Hexenprozess von Leoben', p. 118.
136. Kraus, 'Die Memoiren der Frau v. Hervay', p. 123.
137. Ibid.
138. The following case study has appeared, in abbreviated form, in my article 'Jewish Crimes and Misdemeanours'.
139. Cf. 'Bericht der k.k. Staatsanwaltschaft, 23. April 1901', ÖS, Justizakten, VI – 1 – Schweiz Beer, No 8058/5. For a discussion of the historico-legal context of the crime of 'unnatural sexual intercourse' [*Unzucht wider die Natur*], including a brief summary of the 1847 trial against university professor August Wilhelm Riedl concerning the accusation of the homosexual abuse of a fourteen-year-old boy, see: Hartl, *Wiener Kriminalgericht*, pp. 355–6.
140. ÖS, Justizakten, VI – 1 – Schweiz Beer, No. 8058/5; 8258; 26477.
141. On the admission of journalists to the 'secret trial [*Geheimverhandlung*]' see: ÖS, Justizakten, VI – 1 – Schweiz Beer, No. 24141/5.
142. Article 129 1b of the contemporary Austrian law code. Cf. Karl Kraus's discussion of the legal position in: Kraus, 'Der Selbstmord der Themis', pp. 204–7. The *Arbeiter-Zeitung*'s coverage, characteristically, was the most explicit in its discussion of the charge. Cf. *AZ*, 26 October 1905, p. 6.
143. Ibid., pp. 198–9. *AZ*, 27 October 1905, p. 7.

144. Cf. *AZ*, 26 October 1905, p. 8. The patient in question died prior to the trial.
145. Cf. *AZ*, 27 October 1905, 8; *Krone*, 27 October 1905, p. 11.
146. *NFP*, 25 October 1905, evening edition, p. 5.
147. Cf. *AZ*, 26 October 1905, p. 8; Kraus, 'Der Selbstmord der Themis', pp. 204–5; *Extrablatt*, 26 October 1905, p. 10.
148. *NFP*, 27 October 1905, p. 11.
149. Ibid.
150. Karl Kraus, 'Die Kinderfreunde', *Die Fackel*, November 1905, reprinted in *Sittlichkeit und Kriminalität*, pp. 177–80.
151. *NFP*, 25 October 1905, evening edition, p. 5.
152. Ibid. See also: *Extrablatt*, 25 October 1905, p. 10.
153. *Krone*, 27 October 1905, p. 12.
154. Here quoted from: Ibid., p. 11. Cf. *DV*, 27 October 1905, p. 10.
155. *NFP*, 27 October 1905, 11; *Krone*, 27 October 1905, p. 11; and so on.
156. *DV*, 28 October 1905, p. 8.
157. *DV*, 26 October 1905, p. 8.
158. Cf. *AZ*, 27 October 1905, p. 7; *Extrablatt*, 27 October 1905, p. 11.
159. *RP*, 28 October 1905, p. 1.
160. *NFP*, 27 October 1905, pp. 10–11; *AZ*, 27 October 1905, p. 8.
161. For the court files on the Beer trial, see: Landesgericht für Strafsachen 1905 4586 (Wiener Stadt- und Landesarchiv).
162. See: Sibylee Mulot-Deri, *Sir Galahad, Portrait einer Verschollenen* (Frankfurt am Main 1987), pp. 140 ff.; Tichy and Zwettler-Otte, *Freud*, pp. 258–9.
163. *DV*, 25 October 1905, evening edition, p. 2
164. *DV*, 26 October 1905, evening edition, p. 2.
165. *DV*, 25 October 1905, evening edition, p. 2. For previous coverage of the scandal, see also: *DV*, 24 March 1905.
166. *DV*, 25 October 1905, evening edition, p. 2.
167. *DV*, 26 October 1905, p. 9.
168. *DV*, 28 October 1905, p. 8. See also Kraus's commentary on this point: he maintains that there is nothing 'Jewish' about Zweigenthal's words, but that these are simply honest comments on a perverse justice system. Kraus, 'Die Kinderfreunde', p. 173.
169. *DV*, 28 October 1905, p. 8.
170. One is reminded of Freud's fear that psychoanalysis should be identified as a Jewish science. Cf. Gay, *Freud*, pp. 201–2.
171. *DV*, 28 October 1905, p. 8.
172. *DV*, 27 October 1905, p. 10.
173. Ibid.
174. *DV*, 28 October 1905, p. 8.
175. Ibid.
176. *DV*, 29 October 1905, p. 1.
177. *DV*, 29 October 1905, p. 2.
178. *RP*, 26 October 1905, p. 6.
179. Ibid.
180. *RP*, 28 October 1905, p. 1.
181. Ibid.
182. Ibid.
183. Ibid. The German original puns on the double meaning of 'Platten', denoting both photographic plates, and gangs of criminals that were usually named after their ring-leader (hence 'Beer-Platte'). My translation attempts to capture some of the flavour of the pun.
184. The antisemitic identifation of science as a Jewish trick of some sort is also attested by an antisemitic joke recounted in Arthur Schnitzler's *Der Weg ins Freie*:

'"Ah," said Leo, "that's the person who gave that excellent definition of science in a recent debate about the *Verein* for Public Education."
"Did you not read it?" he asked the others.
They said they could not remember,
"Science," quoted Leo, "Science is that which one Jew copies down from another."
All laughed.' (Schnitzler, *Weg*, pp. 101–2).

185. *RP*, 28 October 1905, p. 1.
186. Ibid., p. 2.
187. Ibid. Like the *Reichspost*, *Kikeriki* here puns on Beer's name, changing '*Perspektive*' into '*Beerspektive*'.
188. *NFP*, 26 October 1905, evening edition, 5; *NFP*, 27 October 1905, pp. 10–11.
189. *AZ*, 27 October 1905, p. 7.
190. *Krone*, 27 October 1905, p. 9.
191. *Krone*, 26 October 1905, p. 5.
192. For a brief introduction to the Riehl case, see: Karin J. Jušek, 'Sexual morality and the meaning of prostitution in Fin-de-Siècle Vienna', in: Jan Bremmer (ed.), *From Sappho to de Sade, Moments in the History of Sexuality* (London 1991 [1989]), p. 136. While Jušek's comments are interesting, her knowledge of the case relies solely on Kraus's rather partisan coverage.
193. *Extrablatt*, 24 June 1906, p. 5. There is some irony to the charge of 'incarceration' since the advantages of '*Kasernierung*' – effectively the imprisonment of prostitutes in brothels as a sanitary measure that would help check the spread of syphilis – had been earnestly debated in the 1880s. Cf. Schrank, *Die Prostitution*, Vol. 2, pp. 3–40.
194. Ibid. On the discourse surrounding *Mädchenhandel*, see my analysis in chapter three.
195. *AZ*, 1 July 1906, p. 7.
196. SaW, Gerichtsakte, Box A 11, Fasz. 200–1, No. 6372 (6 Vols.) (Riehl 1907), Doc. 46 ff.; Doc. 66–75.
197. Ibid. The interview with Riehl alone comes to forty densely filled sides (Doc. 98-120).
198. One should remember here that prostitution itself was legal and regulated by the police. For a brief summary of the legal situation, see: Inge Pronay-Strasser, 'Von Ornithologen und Grashupferinnen, Bemerkungen zur Sexualität um 1900', in: Ehalt, Heiß and Stehl (eds), *Glücklich*, pp. 128–30. See also: Franz X. Eder, 'Sexual Cultures in Germany and Austria 1700-2000', in: Franz X. Eder, Lesley Hall and Gert Helema (eds), *Sexual Cultures in Europe, Themes in Sexuality* (Manchester 1999), pp. 156ff; H. Montane, *Die Prostitution in Wien* (Vienna 1925). On the social milieu from which the prostitutes originated, see: Regina Schulte, *Sperrbezirke, Tugendhaftigkeit und Prostitution in der bürgerlichen Welt* (Frankfurt am Main 1979).
199. SaW, Gerichtsakte, Box A 11, Fasz. 200-1, No. 6372 (6 Vols.) (Riehl 1907), Box 200-1, Z. 6372, Docs. 351 ff. (Vol. 5). Cf. transcript, 'Der Prozess Riehl und Konsorten in Wien', in: *Archiv* 27 (1907), pp. 1–111.
200. *DV*, 2 November 1906, evening edition, p. 3.
201. *Krone*, 3 November 1906, p. 2.
202. Cf. transcript: 'Der Prozess Riehl und Konsorten in Wien', in: *Archiv* 27 (1907), p. 76.
203. Karl Kraus, 'Der Fall Riehl', in: *Die Fackel*, November 1906; 'Wegen Bedenklichkeit', in: *Die Fackel*, November 1906; 'Die Ära nach dem Prozess Riehl', *Die Fackel*, January 1907. All reprinted in: Kraus, *Sittlichkeit und Kriminalität*, pp. 228–51, 252–5, 262–71.
204. Cf. transcript 'Der Prozess Riehl und Konsorten in Wien', pp. 80–1.
205. Ibid. The reference to Lombroso should not come as a surprise. While his thesis on male criminality was heavily criticised, Lombroso's construction of female criminality and prostitution remained influential for decades after its publication in 1893. Cf. Lombroso and Ferrero, *Criminal Woman*, p. 4.

206. Transcript 'Der Prozess Riehl und Konsorten in Wien', in: *Archiv* 27 (1907), pp. 80–1.
207. Ibid., p. 82.
208. There was, however, some variance regarding the construction of the prostitutes' guilt in the various papers. The *Arbeiter-Zeitung*, notably, framed them as innocent victims, 'poor people's daughters'. *AZ*, 3 November 1906, p. 6.
209. *DV*, 2 November 1906, evening edition, p. 3.
210. Ibid.
211. *DV*, 4 November 1906, p. 1. The court documents identify Pollack as '*mosaisch*' and Riehl as Protestant. Protestants were commonly identified as (converted) Jews by the antisemitic press. Whether a conversion from Judaism took place in this case could not be resolved. Cf. SaW, Gerichtsakte, Box A 11, Fasz. 200-1, No. 6372 (6 Vols.) (Riehl 1907), Doc. 98 ff.
212. *DV*, 4 November 1906, p. 1.
213. Ibid.
214. *DV*, 8 November 1906, p. 2.
215. On the association of Jews and white slavery, see: Bristow, *Prostitution*; Kaplan, *Jewish Feminism*, pp. 103–45. See my discussion in chapter three.
216. Josef Piess's name was spelled in a variety of ways (Pieß, Piß, Piss, Piks) by various newspapers; the spelling even lacked consistency in the court records, though his Leumundszeugnis makes him out as "Josef Piess". SaW, Gerichtsakte, Box A 11, Fasz. 200-1, No. 6372 (6 Vols.) (Riehl 1907), no document number (Vol. 4). Since *Leumundzeugnisse* did not include religious affiliation (!), it was impossible to reconstruct whether Piess was indeed Jewish as the *Volksblatt* claimed.
217. *DV*, 7 November 1906, p. 9.
218. *RP*, 8 November 1906, p. 1.
219. Ibid.
220. A.F. Thiele, *Die jüdischen Gauner*. See my discussion in chapter three.
221. *RP*, 8 November 1906, p. 1.
222. *RP*, 9 November 1906, p. 9.
223. *Kikeriki*, 8 November 1906, p. 1 (poem).
224. *Kikeriki*, 18 November 1906, p. 2 ('Offenes Schreiben').
225. Ibid., 110. Riehl's, Pollak's and König's prison terms were made more severe through periodic 'fast days'. Cf. SaW, Gerichtsakte, Box A 11, Fasz. 200-1, No. 6372 (6 Vol.) (Riehl 1907), no document number (Vol. 5).
226. Here quoted from Morgenstern's actual appeal: SaW, Gerichtsakte, Box A 11, Fasz. 200-1, No. 6372 (6 Vols.) (Riehl 1907): 'Antrag um Wiederaufnahme', no document number (Vol. 6). See also: *ÖK*, 18 July 1907, 2; *ÖK*, 25 July 1907, pp. 3–5.
227. Ibid.
228. For example 'Die Suggestion des Verbrechens', *ÖK*, 2 September 1907 4; 'Der Wert der Zeugenaussagen', *ÖK*, 4 July 1907, p. 6.
229. On a literary example of the Jew as 'suggestor' see Daniel Pick's discussion of George de Maurier's Trilby in: Daniel Pick, 'Powers of Suggestion: Svengali and the Fin-de-Siècle', in: Bryan Cheyette and Laura Marcus (eds), *Modernity, Culture and 'The Jew'* (Oxford 1998), pp. 105–25; Daniel Pick, *Svengali's Web, The Alien Enchanter in Modern Culture* (New Haven 2000), pp. 4, 127 ff.
230. *DV*, 6 April 1907, pp. 7–8.
231. Regular coverage, starting *DV*, 21 March 1907, p. 4; on Jewish dimension, see especially *DV*, 31 March 1907, p. 2.
232. *DV*, 6 April 1907, p. 7.
233. *DV*, 7 April 1907, pp. 1–2.
234. *DV*, 7 April 1907, p. 4.
235. Ibid.

236. Ibid.
237. The Klein case, of course, already provides a partial answer to this question, with its accusation of brutal murder and its construction of the perpetrators as rational dissimulators. Cf. chapter four.
238. For a brief, if not entirely accurate, summary of the Hofer murder, see Edelbacher and Seyrl, *Wiener Kriminalchronik*, p. 90.
239. This second murder was that of Anna Spilka. Simon Sosztarich was arrested and convicted for this crime, but the investigation quickly established that he could not also have been responsible for the Hofer killing. Cf. SaW, Gerichtsakte, Box 11, Fasc. 108 (Sosztarich 1899).
240. On the politics of the media-representation of prostitutes who were victims of crime, see: Evans, *Tales*, pp. 166–70, 207–12.
241. See, for instance *DV*, 27 December 1898, evening edition, p. 4. On the importance of biography for mid-nineteenth century 'criminalists', see: Becker, *Verderbnis*, p. 43.
242. *DV*, 27 December 1898, evening edition, p. 4. For a similar description, see. *NFP*, 27 December 1898, evening edition, p. 4.
243. In a separate section her room is once again described as 'very cosy, despite its sparse furnishings.' Ibid.
244. *Extrablatt*, 27 December 1898, p. 4.
245. For example *DV*, 28 December 1898, p. 4; *DV*, 1 January 1898, p. 5; *RP*, 28 December 1898, p. 4; *AZ*, 28 December 1898, p. 6; *NFP*, 28 December 1898, pp. 7–8; *Extrablatt*, 31 December 1898, p. 4.
246. For example *AZ*, 29 December 1898, p. 6; *RP*, 30 December 1898, p. 5; *DV*, 30 December 1898, evening edition, p. 2.
247. For example *DV*, 27 December 1898, evening edition, p. 4.
248. *DV*, 31 December 1898, p. 8. On similar terminology, see also: *Extrablatt*, 31 December 1898, p. 4.
249. Cf. *DV*, 29 December 1898, p. 5; *DV*, 31 December 1898, p. 8.
250. *NFP*, 27 December 1898, p. 4.
251. For example *AZ*, 28 December 1898, p. 6; *Extrablatt*, 28 December 1898, p. 6.
252. See for instance: *DV*, 12 July 1909, pp. 4–5; *DV*, 15 July 1909, p. 8; *Extrablatt*, 15 July 1909, p. 10; *Krone*, 15 July 1909, p. 5.
253. *DV*, 12 July 1909, p. 5.
254. See in particular the emphasis on the testimony of Benesch's wife. Cf. *Extrablatt*, 15 July 1909, p. 9; *Krone*, 15 July 1909, p. 5.
255. *DV*, 17 June 1907, pp. 2–3.
256. On the coverage of the 'Düsseldorf Vampire' case, see: Evans, *Rituals*, pp. 591–610; Claßen, *Darstellung*, pp. 291–320. Maria Tartar argues that even in the "Düsseldorf Vampire" case the papers' coverage was more concerned with the murder victims and with pathologising the public than providing the murderer with a sustained psychological profile. See: Maria Tartar, *Lustmord, Sexual Murder in Weimar Germany* (Princeton 1995), pp. 43–57.
257. *DV*, 29 June 1909, p. 7.
258. *RP*, 23 September 1905, p. 10.
259. *RP*, 10 August 1904, p. 10.
260. Ibid.
261. SaW, Gerichtsakte, Box unnumbered, Fasz. 92, No. 1185 (Eichinger 1895).
262. *DV*, 4 February 1895, evening edition, pp. 1–2.
263. *DV*, 2 February 1895, p. 5.
264. *DV*, 5 February 1895, p. 4.
265. Ibid.
266. Ibid.

267. Ibid., p. 5.
268. *NFP*, 22 April 1895, evening edition, p. 4; *NFP*, 24 April 1895, p. 9; *DV*, 22 April 1895, evening edition, p. 4; *DV*, 23 April 1895, evening edition, p. 3; *AZ*, 22 April 1895, p. 2.
269. *NFP*, 22 April 1895, evening edition, p. 4; *AZ*, 22 April 1895, p. 2; *AZ*, 24 April 1895, p. 5; *RP*, 25 April 1895, p. 4; *DV*, 22 April 1895, evening edition, p. 4; *DV*, 23 April 1895, p. 3; *DV*, 23 April 1895, evening edition, p. 4; *Kikeriki*, 28 April 1895, p. 1.
270. SaW, Gerichtsakte, Box unnumbered, Fasz. 92, No. 1185 (Eichinger 1895), Doc. No. 205, 227.
271. SaW, Gerichtsakte, Box unnumbered, Fasz. 92, No. 1185 (Eichinger 1895), Doc. No. 227. See also: *DV*, 23 April 1895, p. 4
272. See, for instance: *DV*, 23 April 1895, p. 4.
273. *AZ*, 22 April 1895, p. 2.
274. *NFP*, 25 April 1895, pp. 1–2.
275. A second attempt to frame Eichinger's crime as a symptom of a pathology was made by Paul Lindau's *Ausflüge ins Kriminalistische* (Munich 1909), pp. 26–9, in which he articulated a theory of a sudden, spontaneous manifestation of a murderous idea ['*Mordwahn*'], which owed much to Etienne-Jean Georget's rather dated concept of 'homicidal monomania'. See: Jan Goldstein, *Console and Classify: The French Psychiatric Profession in the Nineteenth Century* (Cambridge 1987), pp. 170–2.
276. *DV*, 23 April 1895, p. 3.
277. *DV*, 23 April 1895, p. 4.
278. *DV*, 23 April 1895, p. 4.
279. *DV*, 23 April 1895, evening edition, p. 3.
280. *DV*, 23 April 1895, evening edition, p. 3.
281. *RP*, 23 April 1895, p. 6.
282. *RP*, 25 April 1895, p. 4.
283. *OR*, 22 April 1895, p. 3.
284. *OR*, 24 April 1895, p. 8.
285. *Kikeriki*, 25 April 1895, p. 2; *Kikeriki*, 28 April 1895, p. 1.
286. *Kikeriki*, 28 April 1895, p. 3.
287. *DV*, 4 September 1910, pp. 9–10.
288. *DV*, 23 September 1910, p. 13.
289. *DV*, 12 March 1895, p. 5.
290. *DV*, 1 March 1895, p. 6.
291. *DV*, 13 March 1900, p. 6.
292. *DV*, 11 March 1895, p. 7; *DV*, 12 March 1895, p. 10; *DV*, 13 March 1895, p. 7.
293. Rürüp, 'European Revolution'; Jacob Katz, *From Prejudice to Destruction, Anti-Semitism 1700–1933* (Cambridge, Mass. 1982), pp. 227ff.
294. Ivar Oxaal, 'The Jews of Young Hitler's Vienna: Historical and Sociological Aspects', in: Oxaal, Pollak and Botz (eds), *Jews*, pp. 25–31.
295. *ÖK*, 11 April 1907, p. 5.
296. Ibid.
297. Interestingly there does exist an extended, if fictional, account of depicting Prague's *Judenstadt* as a *Verbrecherviertel*: Gustav Meyrink's 1915 novel *Der Golem*. Indeed the novel even features a Jewish criminal who is depicted with physical and physiological markers compatible with a Lombrosian understanding of criminals (this was underlined by Meyrink's illustrator, Hugo Steiner-Prag, who rendered the book's chief villain with an enormous nose, misshapen face, bulging eyes and manic, crooked grin). Tellingly, the novel was rejected by antisemites and Meyrink himself derided as a 'Jewish' writer. Cf. A. Zimmermann, *Gustav Meyrink und seine Freunde* (Hamburg 1917), pp. 14 and *passim*.
298. The spelling of the murder victim's name varies between Sigel, Siegl and Siegel.

299. Cf. *Daily Telegraph*, 21 June 1909; *NFP*, 23 June 1909, p. 11.
300. *Krone*, 25 June 1909, p. 4. The German 'der Chinese' has subtle racist overtones and could also be translated as 'the Chinaman'.
301. Ibid.
302. *Krone*, 26 June 1909, p. 6.
303. *Krone*, 25 June 1909, p. 3.
304. *Krone*, 26 June 1909, p. 5.
305. *Krone*, 25 June 1909, p. 3.
306. Cf. chapter three.
307. *DV*, 1 July 1909, p. 1.
308. Ibid.
309. Ibid.
310. *DV*, 23 September 1909, p. 6.
311. *DV*, 1 July 1909, p. 1.
312. *DV*, 23 September 1909, p. 6.
313. *DV*, 25 June, p. 10.
314. *RP*, 23 June, p. 7.
315. *Kikeriki*, 4 July 1909, p. 9.
316. On the Sigel murder and its paper coverage, see also: Karl Kraus, 'Die Chinesische Mauer', in: *Der Fackel*, July 1909, reprinted in: Karl Kraus, *Die Chinesische Mauer* (Munich 1964 [1914]), pp. 279–92. Kraus's commentary bears echoes of the *Volksblatt*'s coverage.
317. *ÖK*, July 25 1907, p. 5 and *ÖK*, August 5 1907, p. 5.
318. *ÖK*, July 25 1907, p. 5.
319. Ibid.
320. Ibid.
321. Chinese sexual appetites and perversions feature in several contemporary accounts. See for instance, Schrank, *Mädchenhandel*, p. 64.
322. *ÖK*, July 25 1907, p. 5.
323. For a further example of the construction of the Chinese as a criminal race, and Chinatown as a *Verbrecherviertel*, see: *RP*, 24 September 1905, pp. 1–2.

Chapter 6

THE HILSNER RITUAL MURDER TRIALS

I want to make some remarks about Hitler's opinion of the Jews. ... He said that for a Jew to take advantage, to a certain extent, of a non-Jew, was not punishable according to the Talmud. On the other hand he often dismissed the charge of ritual murder with the remark that it was absolute nonsense, a groundless slander.

Reinhold Hanisch, 'I was Hitler's buddy'[1]

Historiography

At long last, then, let us return to the ritual murder accusation of Polná, and the two trials it precipitated. At first glance the very concept of ritual murder – or 'blood libel' as it is sometimes called – strikes one as irredeemably medieval: a malicious fantasy dreamed up by the spiteful, the fanatical and the plain ignorant. It seems an incongruous atavism in an age that increasingly liked to dress its anxieties and hatreds in scientific clothes. The astonishing frequency of ritual murder accusations in the final decade of the nineteenth century and the opening years of the twentieth has consequently drawn the interest of many a scholar, although precise quantification is complicated by the fact that only a fraction of such accusation crystallised into trials, the most famous of which are the 'affairs' of Tisza-Eszlár (1882 to 1883), Xanten (1891), Konitz (1900 to 1901), the Russian Beilis scandal (1911 to 1913), and, of course, the two Polná trials we are about to discuss. One survey counts eighteen accusations of murder, attempted murder, or 'blood theft', all for ritual purposes, between 1891 and 1899 in the Czech lands alone; another counts fifty reported cases across Europe between 1870 and 1935.[2]

When it comes to analysing these 'modern' ritual murder accusations two basic scholarly strategies can be observed. The first is to place them into the long history of blood libel accusations going back all the way to Thomas of Monmouth's inflammatory description of the 'martyrdom' of a Norwich lad in 1050, and then attempt a trans-historical explanation for the emergence and enduring popularity of this superstition. Very often such explanations make reference to psychological mechanisms such as 'repetition compulsion' and 'projection': the fantasy of Jews slaughtering Christian children or maidens for the sake of their blood is here seen to be tied up with problematic aspects of Catholicism such as the theologically necessary deicide that is committed in the crucifixion of Christ, and the symbolic cannibalism taking place in the consumption of the transubstantiated host.³ Helmut Walser Smith's recent study of the ritual murder accusation of Konitz, *The Butcher's Tale*, takes a somewhat different tack: it combines a micro-historical analysis of local rivalries and antagonisms with an anthropological model that apprehends both the accusations of ritual murder and the riots that frequently surrounded them as rituals of community definition in word and deed that followed a precise 'script' and had to be learned over centuries of re-enactment.⁴ In other words, the Konitz Christian community used the internalised 'rules' and language of the accusation to reinforce the boundaries dividing Christian and Jewish communities in their township. The implication – strengthened by Smith's embedding of the Konitz events in the entire pre-history of ritual murder – seems to be that community building via exclusion lies at the heart of the entire phenomenon, even if local politics shape the specific series of events in any given instance.⁵

Eschewing such global psychological or anthropological models, the second scholarly strategy chooses instead to place each modern occurrence of a ritual murder accusation squarely into the context of the specific socio-economic and political pressures that existed both on a regional and on a local level, and to explain the accusations as a function of economic rivalries and nationalist antagonism brought to a head by modernity's transformational forces. Thus Hillel Kieval, in what is probably the most influential explanatory framework for the Hilsner affair, understands the re-emergence of 'blood libel' accusations in the 1890s both as an articulation of social unrest and as a form of Czech nationalist protest, i.e. as deeply politicised events that can only be understood against a background of Czech grievances at the *fin-de-siècle*.⁶ Towards the end of the nineteenth century Czech nationalist groups had begun to embrace anti-semitism in order to mobilise wider strata of the population, whose traditional suspicion of Jews merged with their anti-Germanism, for their cause.⁷ Jews in the Czech lands had long been identified as culturally German, a long-term effect of the 1782 imperial *Toleranzpatent* that instructed Jews both to educate their children and conduct their internal affairs in German.⁸ The tensions between the German and Czech-speaking populations came to a violent head in the wake of Badeni's language ordinances, issued in November 1897. These proposed that Czech could be used in the internal communications of Czech courts and within Czech bureaucracy, thus threatening German-speaking civil servants who were asked to prove proficiency in Czech if they wanted to hold on to their jobs. If the initial wave of violence originated in the ethnically German population of the Czech lands, there soon followed a Czech nationalist backlash that often conflated anti-German and antisemitic attitudes. This was particularly the case after the repeal of the language ordinances in October 1899, i.e. hard on the heels of the first of the Hilsner trials of mid-September of that year. The riots in the Moravian townships of Batelov (eleventh of October), Holešov (twenty-second of October), and Wšetin (twenty-sixth of October) thus combined antisemitic sentiments nurtured by the ritual murder affair (Jews were consistently the primary targets) with nationalist antagonisms.[9] Polná itself, located on the Bohemian–Moravian border, was also witness to violence against the small Jewish population of just over three hundred souls (as compared to a Czech Catholic population of around five thousand), despite the fact that these Jews spoke a mixture of Czech and German and were reasonably well integrated into local life.[10] The importance of Czech nationalist politics for the Hilsner trial is further underlined by the involvement of Tomaš Masaryk and Karel Baxa – the first speaking for an Enlightened Czech nationalist tradition that for all its (and Masaryk's personal) ambivalence about Jews saw the ritual murder superstition as a stain upon the honour of the Czech people, the second an antisemitic nationalist populist and soon-to-be mayor of Prague.[11] Quite literally, then, the struggle over Hilsner's guilt or innocence had political implications for the entire Habsburg Empire that was struggling so desperately to contain the various nationalist and separatist movements throughout its realms.

Despite the undeniable importance of seeing the events of Polná in this context of a political struggle within Czech society, this chapter wishes to advocate a different vision of the Hilsner trials by highlighting a very different sort of context, namely that of the construction of criminality in the contemporary press.[12] It will test to what extent the seemingly so outlandish charge of ritual murder conformed to the narrative of Jewish criminality uncovered thus far. And while it has no interest in denying that the nationalist-inflected antagonism against Jews must bear much of the blame for the development of the scandal, emphasis is placed on the extent to which both local action against Hilsner and his fellow Jews as well as local understanding of the events that unfolded were dependent on deliberate orchestration at the hands of organised, urban antisemites and their newspaper publications. The chapter thus argues that the Hilsner ritual murder trial has to be understood with reference to such distinctly modern journalistic strategies as the investigative 'scoop' and such modern criminological categories as 'suggestion', rather than being reduced to the simple re-emergence of a century-old superstition. Whatever 'script' ritual murder accusations followed, therefore, it had not – as Helmut Walser Smith maintains – been acquired and retained in the collective memory over centuries of ritual repetition, but was absorbed in the very contemporary language of the modern trial report and as such was contingent on the existence of modern mass media and the high rates of literacy typical for the modern era.

The Accusation Against Leopold Hilsner – Origin and Contexts

The first thing one needs to understand about the Hilsner ritual murder accusation is that, from its very conception, it was a media creation. Its origins lay not in the Bohemian town of Polná, but in two antisemitic publishing houses located in Vienna and Prague respectively. While it is true that the rumour that a ritual murder had taken place arose locally, it was through the work of two journalists that it was given shape and circulation. Within days of the discovery of Anežka Hrůzová's allegedly bloodless corpse in the woods around Polná, the antisemitic editor of the České Zájmi, Jaromír Hušek, published an article accusing the Jew Leopold Hilsner of murder for ritual purposes.[13] The issue was confiscated, unsurprisingly, and – in a curious move to ally himself with the German antisemitic movement, despite their obvious political differences – Hušek responded by addressing a letter to the antisemitic parliamentarian Schneider in Vienna, asking him to challenge the confiscation.[14] Hušek also left for Polná to pursue his investigations on site. Meanwhile Schneider passed on the story to the *Deutsches Volksblatt*. The paper smelled a scandal, printed its first, ill-informed article about the crime,[15] and soon dispatched its own investigator to Polná in order to poke around, the editor Hans Arnold Schwer.[16] Schwer, along with Hušek and, for a short period, Ludwig Weng, a journalist in the employ of the Munich-based *Der Reichsdeutsche*, began asking questions and writing a series of inflammatory articles.[17] Schwer's investigation and need for 'evidence' was soon further motivated by the threat of a libel suit by the Jewish butcher Moric Kurzweil of the Bohemian town of Golčov–Jeníkov/Goltsch-Jenikau, whom Schwer had implicated in the crime along with other Jews.[18] Schwer later claimed to have interviewed as many as 180 people as part of his investigation, and was no doubt helped along by his friendly relations with the town's major Rudolf Sadil.[19] His methods included getting Hilsner's mentally retarded brother drunk, in order to uncover incriminating evidence.[20] Schwer passed his information on to the local investigators of the crime, Augustin Sedlák and Josef Klenovec. As a result the prosecution's evidence, gathered by the investigative judges Reichenbach and Baudyš, in co-operation with Sedlák and Klenovec, came to reflect the biases of Schwer's investigative work. The point here need not be that the evidence was entirely fictional or fabricated. What is obvious, however, is the extent to which the parameters of the trial were the direct function of the *Volksblatt*'s investigative journalism, and did not simply arise from rural antisemitic convictions or Czech nationalist politics.[21] It was the strange alliance between German antisemites with anti-Czech and pan-Germanic attitudes with an anti-German Czech antisemitic agitator that made sure that the Polná murder became the biggest news story of the year throughout the Empire and beyond.

Another important context for the Hilsner affair was the Dreyfus scandal.[22] The trial of Alfred Dreyfus, a French army officer charged with passing on state secrets to the German arch-enemy, finished only days before the first of the two Polná sensations took hold of the papers, and it was not unusual to find reports on both scandals in a single issue of a given paper.[23] Dreyfus's alleged betrayal thus became a natural point of reference for the Hilsner trial, especially amongst the antisemites who focused on Dreyfus's Judaism, and the support he found amongst the Zolas of his nation. Indeed the state prosecutor in the first Hilsner trial explicitly referred to it as 'Austria's Dreyfus trial,' a label that stuck.[24] Similarly, earlier ritual murder trials, in particular those of Konitz and Tisza-Eszlár, were frequently used as a point of reference, both by those in the antisemitic camp, and by their enemies.[25] These trials were often regarded by liberal commentators as demonstrations of the public's ignorance and irrational antisemitism, while antisemites saw them as testing the independence of judicial investigations from the influence of Jewish money and journalistic clout. We will encounter both of these perspectives as we analyse the paper coverage of the Hilsner trials.

The Two Trials

Before turning to this coverage, however, it will be helpful to outline the events of the trials themselves.[26] The first Hilsner trial took place in the regional court in the Bohemian city of Kutná Hora (German designation: Kuttenberg), from 12 to 17 September 1899. Hilsner was charged with both murdering and assisting in the murder of the nineteen year old seamstress Anežka Hrůzová (Agnes Hruza in German). Hilsner's defence counsel Zdenko Auředníček was confronted with two separate prosecutors: Antonín Schneider-Svoboda representing the state, and Karel Baxa, a Czech antisemite and nationalist politician, later to become mayor of Prague. Baxa was a so-called '*Privatbeteiligter*,' a kind of private prosecutor representing the Hrůza family's civil suit. It was he who pursued the accusation of ritual murder most vigorously. One should note, however, that Hilsner was not prosecuted for ritual murder – no such statute existed in Austro-Hungarian law – and that, throughout the first trial, no direct reference was made to the 'ritual' motive until the final pleas. Nevertheless the evidence, as presented by the prosecution, was heavily geared towards this supposed motive. One of its key components was a forensic report, made out by the local Polná medical team, that described Hrůzová's body as having been virtually free of blood, and her throat slashed in what Baxa later described as the 'characteristic cut' of ritual slaughter.[27] Nor was the missing blood to be found at the crime site, where only a tiny puddle had been discovered. Thus, the medical evidence pointed to the blood having been collected and removed.

The prosecution could also present a number of witnesses who reported seeing Hilsner in suspicious circumstances near the crime site, in the company of two Jewish strangers. These witnesses (Čink, Skareda, Huber and others) reported having overheard snatches of suspicious conversations, and having seen a suspicious parcel being handed around among the Jews – presumed to have been the blunt-ended knife used by Jewish butchers for ritual slaughter. The descriptions of Hilsner's companions were astonishingly detailed, and reflected rural antisemitic stereotypes: the alleged conspirators were 'bent' and 'hobbling' respectively, ugly, unshaven, dressed in Jewish smocks, and forever sucking on cigarettes.[28] The single most important witness, perhaps, was one Petr Pešák (German spelling: Peter Peschak), who claimed to have observed Hilsner and companions near the crime site at approximately the time of the murder. This alleged identification took place at a distance of seven hundred yards.[29]

Hilsner's defence counsel argued that the evidence presented by the prosecution was circumstantial and contradictory. Auředníček maintained that Hilsner had never exhibited any violent behaviour; that no individual could accurately identify a human being at such a distance; and, in his final plea, that the supposed motive for the killing – ritual murder – was a fairy tale, disproved by the historical record. The prosecution's entire premise was therefore proclaimed null and void. Auředníček also complained that František Wehr, a convicted murderer incarcerated in a Prague prison, who might have been in the Polná area around the time of the Hrůzová murder, and whose description fitted one of the witness statements, was never investigated.

The trial was accompanied by local antisemitic agitation. Postcards depicting the corpse with its throat slit wide open, brochures about ritual murder and antisemitic leaflets were distributed among the population and seem even to have been sent to jurors' houses.[30] Hilsner busts could be purchased in local market stalls, in order to be vilified.[31] At the same time, Tomáš Garrigue Masaryk, Professor of Philosophy at the Czech University in Prague, and later the first president of the Czechoslovak Republic, took a stand against the ritual murder accusation, publishing a series of widely read articles trying to disprove the charge, and offering alternative ways of interpreting the evidence: for instance, that Anežka Hrůzová had been killed somewhere else and was later carried to the site where she was found.[32] Masaryk also maintained that the doctors who had produced the forensic report had been victims of the suggestive power of the ritual murder rumour and had misdiagnosed the case.[33] We will see that the charge of suggestion was made on all kinds of levels by both the paper coverage and other scholarly treatments of the case.

After five days of trial Hilsner was acquitted of the charge of murder, but found guilty of assisting in the murder of Anežka Hrůzová. His lawyer appealed and the Viennese supreme court, reviewing the case, requested a second forensic report. This was supplied by the (Czech) Prague medical faculty, and was phrased largely as a critique of the initial investigation. The new report maintained that sufficient amounts of blood had been present at the scene of the crime, and suggested sexual 'sadism or fetishism' as the true motive of the crime, although it did acknowledge that a mentally 'normal' rapist could also be postulated if one assumed that he had been interrupted in his crime, or become scared half-way through.[34] The argument for sexual perversion was seen to be supported by the odd distribution of garments and rags found surrounding the corpse – a total of forty-four individual items had been found – that made no rational sense. It should, however, be mentioned that Hrůzová's hymen was intact, and that no wounds consistent with a sexual assault were attested. The evidence for a sexual motive was thus tenuous at best.

The second forensic report supplied sufficient grounds for a re-trial, this time at the district court in Písek. In the run-up to this second trial the prosecution – once again prompted by the antisemitic press – busied itself gathering new evidence (circumstantial in nature and heavily dependent on questionable witnesses) that Hilsner was also involved in the murder of one Marie Klímová (German spelling: Marie Klima).[35] Klímová had gone missing in the woods around Polná on the seventeenth of July 1898(!) and her supposed corpse (the body was too decayed to make identification certain) was found on the twenty-seventh of October of the same year. The second Hilsner trial, running for an astonishing seventeen days, from the twenty-sixth of October to the fourteenth of November, thus examined the evidence for two separate murders. This time, the Písek state prosecutor, Malijovský, explicitly discarded the ritual murder motive, while Baxa, still the *Privatbeteiligter*, continued to pursue it, if somewhat more cautiously, preferring to speak of a 'Jewish sect' and 'religious fanaticism' rather than implicating all Jews.[36] Baxa also shifted to attacking those hostile to the ritual murder charge more explicitly, accusing them of conspiratorial motives:

> A conspiracy was forged against law and justice! I have to state this publicly, because that which happened after the Kuttenberg trial does not correspond to the path of justice. One has to speak here about corruption, not of the authorities, but rather of the corruption by the public press, which, like a vampire wished to turn injustice into justice.[37]

If he was more cautious about implicating all Jews in the ritual murder charge, Baxa did not hesitate to charge them with a conspiracy that aimed at saving Hilsner: 'Here, dear jurors, you see a defendant, who is supported not only by his defence counsellors, but - as we have heard from the mouth of the certainly typical [Jewish] witness Anton Bretisch – the entirety of Jewry.'[38] The Klíma family was also represented by their own *Privatbeteiligter* Dr. Pevny, who in contrast to Baxa stuck to the traditional role of his office and consequently played no major part.

The evidence, shaped by Schwer's investigative focus and the Kutná Hora trial, continued to focus on Hilsner's Jewish accomplices, and thus remained heavily tied to the ritual murder charge. Auředníček and his co-defence counsel Vodička had to defend Hilsner against both the implicit ritual murder charge and the accusation of sexual deviance implied by the second medical report. In the end the jury re-affirmed the initial verdict: Hilsner was acquitted of both murder charges, but found guilty of assisting in the murders. He was sentenced to death. The sentence was commuted by imperial pardon, and Hilsner was eventually freed after the Great War. Leopold Hilsner died in 1928, by all accounts physically exhausted and mentally confused.[39]

This summary may give the reader some indication of the internal complexity of the case, a complexity that was further augmented by Hilsner's false confession after the first trial which led to a separate charge of false accusation. In prison, scared by a fellow inmate who told him the noise he was hearing from their cell window was the erection of the gallows, he had accused two former acquaintances, Wassermann and Erbmann, of having committed the murder, both of whom had watertight alibis (one had been far away from Polná, the other in hospital). The trials were also surrounded by a multitude of rumours, scandals and false reports. Here one might cite the mystery of a perfume vial, allegedly filled with Hrůzová's blood, the clumsy attempt by Hilsner's senile aunt to provide him with an alibi by means of a transparent lie, and the libel suit raised against some newspapers, which had suggested that Hrůzová had been killed not by Hilsner but by his mother and sister – a theory that was in fact widely discussed and has some plausibility for anyone familiar with the facts of the case. Perhaps more than any other trial here analysed, the Hilsner trials thus provided newspapers with such a rich texture of facts, rumour and courtroom drama, that the possibilities of construction through selection, emphasis and editorial commentary were endless.

At the same time, the mechanics of reporting the trials were far more difficult than was usually the case. Kutná Hora had no publicly accessible telephone or telegraph station,[40] and even in the better equipped Písek, some journalists complained about the sheer difficulty of getting the news 'home'.[41] Despite these technical challenges, however, the journalistic attention paid to the trials was enormous. In both trials the number of reporters and illustrators outnumbered the small audience: only twenty tickets were given out in Kutná Hora, forty in Písek, although it is clear that substantially more spectators managed to sneak into the court room at times.[42] More than half of the 'public' in attendance, then, belonged to a professional class whose job was to allow the public at large access to the sensation – an access mediated through carefully constructed narrative frameworks. Let us now turn to how this army of journalists put the trials into words.

Newspaper Coverage of the First Hilsner Trial

Let me begin with the antisemitic coverage. One should remember here that this coverage was shaped above all by the fact that, unlike all the other cases discussed thus far, the Hilsner trials already had an antisemitic narrative embedded in the accusation of ritual murder, and above all, in the spin given the proceedings by Karel Baxa whose crude antisemitic invective was meant to appeal to his own Czech constituency.[43] The material with which the antisemitic papers – instrumental in producing the evidence in the first place – set to work was thus of a wholly different order than in those cases where the anti-semitic dimension had to be teased out and imposed upon a trial.

The most obvious antisemitic frame provided by the *Deutsches Volksblatt* in its coverage of the first Hilsner trial rested in the systematic emphasis placed upon all evidence pointing towards ritual murder. This narrative was con-structed via a string of sub-headlines (for example '*No blood puddle, no stains*';[44] '*Extra help for bleeding dry*'[45]) that left no doubt that Hilsner was the murderer, and that the prosecution's/Baxa's version of the events was accurate. These sug-gestive sub-headings were helped along by a lavish amount of bold print and the periodic use of exclamation marks next to paragraphs, at times in a font four or five times as big as the rest of the coverage, such as when an expert wit-ness stated that the murderer did not want to kill his victim when he bludg-eoned her, but only render her unconscious.[46] The strategy was further re-enforced by the systematic omission or abbreviation of statements made by defence witnesses or the defence counsel – they were present in this coverage, but came across as weak, devoid of facts. Thus, in the reports of the final pleas, Baxa's statement was related in some detail, with the juiciest bits declaiming the '*Christian virgin's martyrdom*' and the murderers' '*ritual motive*' set in bold,[47] while Auředníček plea was largely paraphrased and only received two short paragraphs.[48]

Significantly, the proof for ritual murder was sought primarily through the evidence provided by the trial, rather than by means of a historical argument, or through references to the Talmud's supposed injunctions to kill Christians.[49] Even if this reticence might to some degree reflect fears of censorship, one should note that the antisemitic language in circulation posited that the truth about ritual murder could be conclusively established through the truth mech-anisms of the trial. This insistence that the facts by themselves should tell the story of the ritual murder in turn led the *Volksblatt* to emphasise that it took the utmost care with facts. In order to express its concern with detail, the paper would, for instance, print the occasional word in the original Czech, to vouch-safe the absolute accuracy of a particularly important statement: 'Beneath the corpse one found an inconsequential puddle of blood (*nepatrna louz krve*) about the size of a flat hand (*dlau* [*sic*]).'[50] A similar intention can be attested for the *Volksblatt*'s occasional venture into a criminalistic mode, for instance when it included a map depicting the Březina woods and nearby Polná, marking the crime site to acquaint its readers with the region's geography and thus provid-ing them with a quasi-detective gaze.[51]

The emphasis placed upon the accuracy of the *Volksblatt*'s coverage tied in directly to the second strand of the newspaper's antisemitic frame for the trial. In a string of articles and editorial commentaries on the investigative process and the trial the *Volksblatt* sought to prove the complicity of the Jewish press in the crime under investigation, and its attempts to cover up the truth, by highlighting the 'Jew-press's' 'falsifications' and 'omissions,' particularly where other paper editors had been reluctant to dwell on evidence supporting the rit-ual murder motive.[52] By pinpointing the inaccuracies in the other newspapers' reporting, the *Deutsches Volksblatt* wanted to enter into a battle of facts – for facts, in the truth-regime of the court room, established truth. The mistakes in the so-called Jewish papers were thus seen not simply as shoddy journalism, but as a deliberate strategy of sabotaging justice: 'Viennese Jewry wishes to bring confusion into the Polna murder affair by all means. Since it does not work with bribery and false witnesses, they now try it by throwing around accusations.'[53]

A comment about a meeting of the *Jüdischer Volksverein* condemning the ritual murder accusation similarly vowed that 'here at the Polna murder there will be no obscuration, no bribery ... and also no indifferent rural population, that with the help of false witnesses turns *a Jewish murderer into a Christian one*.'[54] Yet another article, entitled '*Murder in Polna (Hülsner's Accomplices – the Jew-Press)*'[55] attacked the Jewish 'misrepresentation' of Hilsner's confession which the *Volksblatt* in turn 'verified'.[56] It also rejoiced that the Jews had failed in their attempt to declare Hilsner insane, thus marking psychiatric reports as a Jewish strategy to get criminals off the hook, and stressing how central Hilsner's (and his alleged accomplices') rationality was to the antisemitic nar-rative of events.[57] In fact, the accusation that the Jews tried to cover up the truth of the murder by declaring the murderer insane and a 'necrophiliac' was raised already during the investigation of the crime.[58] The murder the *Volks-blatt* narrated to its readers was not the action of a man-beast, but that of sane, rational conspirators. The antisemitic narrative of a rational murderer thus directly contradicted Lombroso's understanding of ritual murders as an atavis-tic act perpetrated by primitive people.[59]

The same narrative of a Jewish attempt to de-rail justice and protect Hilsner also emerged in other contexts. On the fifteenth of September, for instance, the coverage of the trial revealed that the investigator Wenzel Daniek, who, like so many others, had poked around Polná and asked questions, and who allegedly was a proud member of the Christian Social Party – was in reality '*in the Jew-gold*.'[60] This '*seemingly harmless man [...] had for years been an agent of Samuel Goldberger's international detective agency, Praterstraße No. 37*, which advertises its services in all Jew-papers.'[61] The message conveyed by such side-line scandals was clear. The Jews were doing everything to protect one of their own, a crim-inal, in the same way they had done in the Dreyfus trial. This accusation was further reinforced by stressing that Auřední̌ček, too, was a hired hand: his steep salary of 15,000 crowns, we are told with some emphasis, was covered by the Vienna-based '*Oesterreichisch-israelitische Union*.'[62]

As in so many trial reports, 'significant description' served once again to dif-ferentiate heroes and villains in this drama about truth, and did so without making reference to any facts beyond those visible in the trial itself. The Kutná Hora court-room, for instance, was described as 'light and friendly... Above the president's table there hangs a little picture, showing the emperor in his youth. That is the room's only ornament.'[63] It was, in other words, a no-non-sense space of justice, patriotic, sympathetic and Spartan. The 'president' (whose lenient treatment towards Baxa throughout the trial helped the antisemitic cause immeasurably) likewise found the *Volksblatt*'s approval for his competent, even military appearance:

> The judge, a high, imposing figure with closely cropped white hair and a white goatee beard, makes the impression of an energetic personality, as may be necessary for this trial, that could bring incidents of *incalculable* significance.[64]

The respective descriptions of Auředníček and Baxa established a contrast between shifty hack and the dependable man of principle:

> Hülsner's defence counsel, *Dr Aurednicek*, a relatively young man, shows every sign of excitement. He makes hasty movements, turns to all sides, looks around the room, and frequently drums with his hand on the desk.
> The much better impression is made by the prosecutor of the civil suit, *Dr Baxa*, whose calm, confident posture allows one to conclude that this man will pursue his goal from immutable conviction.[65]

Similarly, Hrůzová's mother was described in terms that aimed to bring out her suffering and Christian devotion ('The head is covered by a black silk cloth, a prayer book is in her hands')[66] while the 'crown witness' Pešák was built up as the very height of confidence and trustworthiness:

> Peschak is a man of middling height, whose military education can be seen. He speaks in a highly articulated manner and so loudly that the president has to ask him whether that is his way. He answers that he used to be a soldier and that he has become used to answering quickly. The man gives witness, sharply and confidently... Hülsner loses his stoic calm for a moment.[67]

Hilsner himself received relatively little descriptive attention, apart from the passing comment that described his reactions to witness statements in a manner suggesting a guilty conscience.[68] This reticence may be explained by the fact that Hilsner, by all accounts, was not the most imposing of men, and did not lend himself to descriptive rendering as a criminal mastermind. Nor did the *Volksblatt* feel the need to establish his Jewishness via physiognomic description, in contrast to some of the Czech antisemitic publications that, in illustrations that look nothing like any of the photographs we have of the accused, provided him with stereotypical 'Jewish' features.[69] For the *Volksblatt* – a paper edited by a man steeped in von Schönerer's racist discourse – Hilsner's Judaism was an objective fact that did not need to be corroborated by a big nose or weak legs.

In fact, the only occasion on which description in a much cruder antisemitic idiom was invoked, was when the paper found itself tied to witness statements that described in such lurid detail Hilsner's two phantom accomplices, the 'bent' and the 'hobbling' Jew. This happened when two Jews,

Wassermann and Erbmann, were arrested, following Hilsner's (false) confession in jail. Borrowing its description from a Prague daily, Wassermann was described in a manner reminiscent of the larger-than-life cartoon images of Jews peddled in *Kikeriki*. He was said to possess 'bulging eyes, jutting lips, totally abnormally ugly facial features, the right foot lame,' and was identified as a '*ritual butcher [Schächter]*' by profession.[70] The trouble with this kind of description was both that it was utterly interchangeable, and factually inaccurate. Thus a few days earlier, Erbmann, was described in almost identical terms: '*Erbmann is ... of middling height, has a round face, an upturned nose, bad teeth, a red beard, is bald, is lame in the right foot, leans on a stick when he walks.*'[71] Wassermann, in this earlier report, did not yet hobble, nor was he a butcher but rather a '*trained baker*' which, as a profession, had rather fewer murderous connotations.[72]

Erbmann and Wassermann, of course, turned out not to be viable suspects after all, because both could provide an alibi. As this fact emerged, the *Deutsches Volksblatt*, glibly changed to a cautious, criminalistic tone: 'We have reasonable suspicions that Hülsner *has not named the true accomplices.*'[73] In the evening edition the theme was taken up again and the descriptions were now explicitly compared to witness descriptions and found wanting, despite the fact that they were clearly based on these in the first place.[74] The *Volksblatt* thus plotted its own detective gaze against the lying criminal Hilsner who gave false witness. This did not stop the *Volksblatt* from later re-iterating the Prague paper's description of Wassermann, on the off chance that his alibi would not hold after all.[75] On a small scale, then, this example illustrates the tensions between the crude, referential descriptive strategies of localising Jewish criminality employed by the witnesses, and the far more open-ended sign-systems typically employed in newspaper description.

Moving on to the other antisemitic publications, one finds a similar dual strategy of focusing upon the evidence for ritual murder provided by the prosecution, and implicating Jewish journalists in supporting the criminal through a campaign of dissimulation. The *Reichspost*, for instance, carefully struck a pose of impartiality, in which its own open mind towards the ritual murder question was contrasted to the 'blind fury' of the 'Jew-press' that dismissed the motive outright.[76] By the same logic, the *Reichspost* maintained, one could also declare sexual murder a fairy tale, without weighing the evidence. The Jewish press, the *Reichspost* charged, tried to spread a 'veil of forgetting and silence' over the affair.[77] The paper also repeated the old accusation that the Jewish dominance over the press was a conscious strategy, masterminded by Moses Montefiore.[78] Like the *Volksblatt*, the *Reichspost* pretended that a ritual murder was proven beyond doubt simply by the weight of impartial evidence presented in court, while simultaneously minimising the coverage of defence witnesses or Auředníček's often perceptive attacks upon prosecution witnesses, omitting key answers to his cross-examination of witnesses and thus deliberately misrepresenting its results.[79] The *Vaterland* went so far as to not even summarise, let alone quote, Auředníček's final plea.[80] The overall effect of such selective reporting was both that the reader felt he was in possession of all the facts, and that this chain of facts simply did not give Hilsner, or his sympathisers, a leg to stand on.

Kikeriki's satirical coverage of the first Hilsner trial was extensive, and more than any other paper it routinely linked the Dreyfus and the Hilsner trials. Its main theme throughout was that of the distortion of the truth. Visual and linguistic reference was made to the ritual murder accusations via drawings of Jewish slaughter knives, and puns on 'bleeding Justice dry,'[81] but the main thrust was to uncover the conspiratorial attempt by Jews to suppress the truth. The back cover of the issue of the twenty-first of September, for example, showed armed guards jealously guarding 'The truth about Polna'.[82] A similar joke implied that uncomfortable truths were being suppressed as early as the investigative process. Under the title of '*After the familiar (Polna) pattern*' the reader was treated to a fictional snippet of a witness interrogation:

> Investigative judge: 'You want to claim with certainty that the defendant Itzig Schnorreles [a fictional name, presumably 'typically Jewish' like Kohn or Levy] ran across the square on that day at the specified hour?'
> Witness: 'I can give an oath on that. If by *nothing* else, I recognised him by his long, brown caftan, the long *pajes*, the ...'
> Investigative judge: 'That does not belong here – you are not to be concerned with the caftan and the *pajes*.' (To the secretary): 'Write – 'On the specified hour I saw a man hurry across the square whom I believed to recognise as Itzig Schnorreles.' There – sign it.'[83]

Here the investigative judge downplayed a witness's certainty to mere 'belief' – 'a wish to claim' – and stripped his description of all details that would have authenticated it and pointed to a Jewish perpetrator.

Another joke focused on the alleged dominance of Jews in the journalistic realm, but this time more optimistically assumed that in the Hilsner trial the truth for once would come out, despite Jewish attempts to sabotage it. Taking up the oft-repeated phrase that 'the people's voice' had identified Hilsner as a probable culprit, *Kikeriki* printed the following 'Monologue' by some unnamed Jew, identified by his heavy *Mauschel*: 'Why [do] they say, 'the people's voice' has spoke there in Polna, when our people make the public opinion?'[84]

Jokes such as these were further complemented by a cartoon cover that showed a number of Viennese 'Jewish' papers – incarnated as fat Jewesses with grotesque lips and noses, dressed in skirts made out of newspapers – begging 'Rothschild' [a common cipher for Jewish money] to provide them with funds for both Dreyfus's and Hilsner's 'cause' (see Figures 6.1 and 6.2).[85] In other words the narrative we noted in the *Volksblatt* and *Reichspost* of implicating Jewish journalism as antithetical to the truth-finding mission of the Kutná Hora court is played up both visually and verbally.

Top caption (not shown): 'Earned Dishonestly [*Unredlich verdient*].'
Bottom caption: 'Rothschild. "Very well, dear children, you'll all get your portion."'

Figure 6.1 'Earned Dishonestly'.
Source. *Kikeriki*, 24 September 1899, p. 1.

Top caption: 'Comparison'
Labels: 'Jewish Money Bag for Cover-Ups': 'The Polna Scandal'
Bottom caption: 'Big'/'Bigger'/'The Biggest'

Figure 6.2 'Comparison.'
Source. *Kikeriki*, 19 November 1899, p. 3.

Turning to the liberal and other papers we find a direct inversion of the anti-semitic picture. Virtually all liberal papers highlighted the antisemitic agitation that took place in Polná and Kutná Hora, and often drew attention to the *Volksblatt*'s role in constructing Hilsner's guilt, and Schwer's questionable strategies for obtaining incriminating evidence.[86] The agitation, moreover, was held to have had a suggestive effect on the population, the witnesses, and perhaps even the jurors. This is particularly clear in the *Neue Freie Presse*'s coverage that, in an outraged editorial discussing the verdict, reminded its readers not

> to raise a stone against the peasants and small businessmen, who, under the influence not only of the terrifying deed but also under the suggestion of many months of planned agitation, finally witnessed to what was asked of them ... After all this suggestion more and more took hold of the court itself ...'[87]

In the same article the paper decried that it was 'shameful' that 'all jurors, a court, a whole city and its surrounding area come to a verdict virtually [as though] hypnotised ...'[88] In other words, according to the *Neue Freie Presse*, it was the antisemites who destroyed any chance of arriving at the truth about the murders through a wilful campaign of dissimulation that overwhelmed all those called upon to judge Hilsner. This attack against the antisemites' suggestive hold on the public and jurors was at times supplemented by the charge of actual corruption. Thus the *Neue Freie Presse* exposed one of the jurors as a 'businessman who has a part in the publication of postcards about the murder', i.e. an antisemitic profiteer, who was far from impartial.[89] For many of the liberal papers the combination of corrupt justice and suggestion via agitation was responsible for Hilsner's conviction.

The *Österreichische Wochenschrift* pushed the conspiratorial angle of this accusation even further. This self-consciously Jewish publication was edited by Rabbi Joseph Bloch who had made his name by provoking an 1883 libel suit filed by the antisemite August Rohling over Rohling's expert witness statement, made in the context of the Tisza-Eszlar trial, that Jews did indeed practice ritual murder.[90] Now, faced with another blood libel affair some twenty years later, the *Wochenschrift* maintained that some of the witnesses heard in Kutná Hora were simply false, planted by the *Volksblatt*:

> *The antisemitic press-boys' audacious, brutal lying goes beyond all boundaries. It virtually terrorises justice ... and the editors of the Deutsches Volksblatt have false witnesses at their disposal whenever needed ... The population of that area has been roused close to insanity by several months' worth of agitation.*[91]

The argument that the antisemites were destroying justice in the Hilsner trial was augmented by the more or less subtle allegation in many papers that the judge was far from impartial. Particular emphasis was given for instance to the fact that he at one point made what the *Extrablatt* described (in a sub-headline) as '*A physiognomic remark*':

> '*President: 'Was the man a Jew?' – Witness: 'How can I know that?' – President: 'Of course you can know that. One sees that, more or less.' (Stormy laughter among the jurors and the antisemitic journalists)'*[92]

The description of the audience's reaction told the *Extrablatt*'s readers not only that the antisemitic journalists delighted in the president's remark, but that the jurors, too, partook in the merriment, and thus stood as a clear indictment of the corruption of justice taking place in this court of law.

Another strategy evident in most non-antisemitic papers – and once again a direct mirror image of the antisemites' strategy – was to give Auředníček and the defence witnesses space and time to express themselves. This is particularly evident in the above-mentioned expert/layman controversy.[93] When it came to printing the worst of the antisemitic invective aired in court by Baxa, the liberal papers had to make a difficult decision: either give him sufficient newsprint in order to expose the rampant antisemitic agitation of the occasion, or else shut him up altogether. The *Extrablatt*, for one, did not print Baxa's final plea, explaining to their readers that they would not like to be insulted by it,[94] while the *Neues Wiener Tagblatt* and other liberal dailies printed all pleas at length, highlighting the most offensive statements.[95]

When it came to Hilsner, the liberal dailies also found themselves in an ambiguous situation. Auředníček, one should remember, walked a tightrope between stressing his client's stupidity, and not pathologising him sufficiently to make him a prime suspect for his own version of the probable motive – sadism. It was a subtle strategy and most papers did not quite know how to follow this lead, printing Auředníček's characterisation without comment, and devoting little description to Hilsner himself. The *Österreichische Wochenschrift*, unconcerned whether Hilsner was guilty or not, but desperate to disprove the ritual murder charge, chose to ignore Auředníček's construction and push Hilsner into a pathological mode: 'Leopold Hilsner is a mentally deficient [*schwachsinnig*], work-shy human being, known to be violent and without morals, who was a strain on his mother who herself depended on charity.'[96] A later article noted that 'Certainly the idea for such a murder could arise in the head of a not fully sane person via its description,'[97] i.e. that a ritual murder could be committed by some pathological person acting out antisemitic propaganda. It is clear that Hilsner, 'a morally depraved and mentally inferior subject,'[98] was to some degree built up as such a criminal imitator. The point here is clear: just as the antisemites wanted a rational criminal actor, coolly acting out a kind of violent crime that was collective and conspiratorial in nature, the *Wochenshrift* wished to prove that Hilsner was a pathological freak, whose actions could in no way be connected to Judaism.[99]

But the *Wochenschrift* also had a different scenario up its journalistic sleeve. If the culprit had not been some pathological other, such a rational, '*intelligent murderer*' must have faked the ritual murder with the specific intention to '*place suspicion upon any Jew who might have been in the woods at the critical time.*'[100] This 'cunning' ploy pointed towards a 'probably antisemitic' murderer.[101] Once again we find the direct inversion of the antisemitic construction of the case, in which the fantasy of an antisemitic conspiracy is articulated.

The *Neue Freie Presse* provided perhaps the oddest construction of Hilsner. While, following Auředníček, it stressed Hilsner's 'minimal mental powers,'[102] it was also curiously concerned with establishing whether or not Hilsner was a 'noticeable Jewish type'.[103] Its conclusion was that Hilsner was 'barely noticeably' Jewish,[104] but it must come as a surprise that the question was raised at all. The NFP also mentioned that Hilsner 'speaks about Jews, the Jewish walk, the holidays of the Jews in an alien tone, as though he did not belong to them at all.'[105] The comment is odd, both because it could equally well apply to the *Neue Freie Presse*'s own liberal-assimilationist ideology, but also precisely because this was one of the very few occasions in which the *Neue Freie Presse* acknowledged terms like 'Jews' and 'Jewish walk' as conceptual categories. Indeed the passage is unique in all the material I have analysed, and points to the upheaval and confusion the Hilsner trial must have caused. All other liberal papers studiously avoided working with the word 'Jew' as a conceptual category denoting anything other than Hilsner's religion. The *Wochenschrift*, self-consciously Jewish and as such more comfortable with the language of race as a tool to establish Jewish distinctiveness against assimilationist tendencies, went a separate way here: it stressed Jewish racial identity in an article about the 'anthropology of Jews,'[106] maintained that Jews, as a people, were not prone to violence,[107] and backed up this assertion with some crime statistics.[108]

One will have noted that with Auředníček's invocation of sadism as a possible motive – he makes direct reference to Krafft-Ebing here – some criminological angle entered the trial, and that the *Wochenschrift*'s speculation about Hilsner's pathology also fitted into this category. The antisemites, naturally, stayed clear of this reading of the case, intent on apprehending a rational criminal. Most of the liberal dailies also paid little attention to this reading of the crime, and certainly did not launch into criminal-psychological elucidation of the type of criminal capable of sexual murder. The only context in which the term 'atavism' was ever used, was to stigmatise the ritual murder 'superstition' itself as primordial and sick.[109] The criminalistic reading, with an emphasis on experts, witnesses, blood stains and court-room dynamics, remained the master-narrative of the trial throughout.

Turning from the liberal and Jewish media to the socialist *Arbeiter-Zeitung*, one finds a similar strategy of coping with the trial. The antisemitic coverage, above all that of the *Deutsches Volksblatt*, and its role in collecting evidence against Hilsner was attacked and exposed,[110] while Auředníček's arguments were given a prominent place.[111] A leading article published in response to the verdict, entitled '*An Un-cultural trial*',[112] flatly denied that there had been sufficient evidence to convict Hilsner, an argument the paper had already made for the Dreyfus trial some nine days previously.[113] It also highlighted the 'atmosphere' in which the verdict had been made, blaming antisemitic agitation for the population's 'crazy, superstitious, blood fairy-tale [*Blutmärchenaberglaube*]'.[114] Like the *Wochenschrift* it went on to pathologise Hilsner (or any other possible culprit), in this manner reducing the crime to the act of an individual:

Top caption: 'From the upcoming yearly report about the blessed activities of the "Austrian-Israelite Union."'
Middle caption: 'Monday, 10 AM, the "Austrian-Israelite Union" approaches the Justice Minister about the Polna affair.'
Bottom caption: 'Monday, 10.30 AM Hilsner is freed. Hruza's mother and brother are arrested and incarcerated.'
Labels: 'Prison' (sign above building); 'Hilsner free' (sign held by man)
The cartoon endeavoured to demonstrate the power held by the Jews over the Austrian justice system.

Figure 6.3 'From the upcoming yearly report ...'
Source. *Kikeriki*, 22 October 1899, p. 1.

And what if Hilsner murdered the young girl in that animal bloodlust, if all of a sudden that beast in man broke free inside him that Emile Zola described in his famous book – what would be proven by that? Only the depraved imagination of the professional antisemite can charge a religion with the crime of a single human being; a religion, moreover, that gave humanity the law: 'Thou shalt not kill.'[115]

Again we note that a criminological note entered the discourse only in order to counter the antisemitic argument that depicted the murder as the deed of rational conspirators.

The *Kronenzeitung*, of course, did not yet exist in 1899. Its conservative forerunner, the *Reichswehr* (edited by the *Krone*'s later publisher Gustav Davis) attempted to provide nothing more than a bland and neutral coverage of the case.[116] The ritual murder accusation was here identified as a partisan position upheld by the Young Czech party, and as such dismissed.[117] Overlooking the entire spectrum of fin-de-siècle coverage of the case, one notes that the term *Blutmärchen* ('blood fairy-tale') was as much or more in circulation as the phrase 'ritual murder'. Only dedicatedly antisemitic publications openly supported the ritual murder narrative, and accused Jews at large of being supportive of Hilsner: the sources paint a picture of a public sphere in which such a position was understood to have very specific political origins (Figure 6.3).

Newspaper Coverage of the Second Hilsner Trial

The reports on the second Hilsner trial followed the parameters laid down by the first, but further developed the narratives of truth distortion, suggestion, and conspiratorial attempts to influence justice. *Kikeriki*, for instance, devoted several full page cartoons to this theme (see Figures 6.4 and 6.5). It also introduced the idea that it was not just Jewish journalists who were shielding Hilsner, but that Jewish scientists – the members of the Prague medical faculty responsible for the second forensic report – used false and spurious knowledge to pervert justice and get a Jewish criminal off the hook. To this end it printed a satirical article entitled: '*Very scientific false-expert report [Schlechtachten] by Professor Maseltoff*'.[118] In this 'false-expert report' the lack of blood in the corpses was explained by the fact that 'both murdered girls suffered from *anaemia*'; it then went on to turn the facts of the case upside down, transforming victims into perpetrators:

> I am convinced that Leopold *Hülsner* is totally innocent and that both murdered girls were obviously bribed by the antisemites and caused the deadly wounds themselves. I have numerous expert opinions by Europe's greatest medical capacities that confirm that among sexually perverse individuals such suicides are common ... Thus, on the basis of all psychiatric and medical authorities, I can boldly claim that in this case no lust/sexual murder took place.[119]

The same trope of a false, deceptive and deceiving 'Jewish science' was upheld in yet another article in which a 'scientific expert opinion' 'proved' Hilsner's

Labels: 'Jew-Press' (on paper); 'Jewish Money-Bag' (on the overcoat); 'Justice' (pillar). Bottom caption (not shown): 'Kikeriki: "Am I wrong – or are there some that tower over justice?"'

Figure 6.4 'In Pisek.'
Source. *Kikeriki*, 4 November 1900, p. 4.

innocence with similar absurdity.[120] This argument was taken up by Baxa himself, who described the second forensic report as 'a piece of fantasy,'[121] implying that it was not a product of science but rather part of the stream of Jewish misinformation.

The *Ostdeutsche Rundschau* meanwhile, raised the stakes concerning the power of Jewish journalists as the shapers of public opinion. Rhetorically, it asked its readers why people were unwilling to accept the existence of a Jewish religious fanatic, but would not bat an eyelid if someone were to recount a murder featuring a Muslim or Christian fanatic. It provided the following

Das verschleierte Bild zu Pisek.

Top caption: 'The veiled picture in Pisek'
Bottom caption (not shown): 'Justice Minister: "Let's play it safe! I've got to blindfold her, or else she might end up seeing the accomplices."'
The cartoon depicts Baxa in the act of revealing the truth, with the president and the justice minister trying to stop him. This 'truth' is Jewish, as demarked by the bandy legs, and the 'original Talmud' that serves as a pedestal. Once again we encounter a narrative of the antisemitic attempt to unveil a truth others wished to keep hidden.

Figure 6.5 'The veiled picture in Pisek.'
Source. *Kikeriki*, 22 November 1900, p. 4.

answer: 'This shows how fully we all are under the spell of Jewry. That also goes for those, who think of themselves as good antisemites, or at least think that they are fully independent of the Jews.'[122] In other words, the power of the Jewish press went beyond organising and co-ordinating the views of Jews and their friends. In the *Rundschau*'s version it insidiously imposed itself upon the entire public, even those who thought of themselves as independent of it.

The veracity of the ritual murder accusation itself, debunked by the verdict of the medical faculty, drifted somewhat into the background during the second Hilsner trial, although a publication like the *Deutsches Volksblatt* did its utmost to maintain it as the most plausible motive for the murder,[123] and to emphasise evidence against sexual murder: 'all body parts that have to be considered in the case of a sexual murder are *not injured*'.[124] One should also note that a 'sexualisation' of the ritual murder charge was not part of the *Volksblatt*'s narrative – it ran counter not only the insistence on the ritual aspects of the deed, but also against the assumption of a rational, volitional criminal.[125] The *Reichspost* chose to sit on the fence, stressing both the evidence for a ritual murder, and considering other possible motives.[126] It wilfully misrepresented the state prosecutor's speech as being similarly undecided about the motive.[127] Only when the jurors' verdict confirmed Hilsner as an accomplice in murder, did it revert wholeheartedly to celebrating proof of a murder for 'religious' reasons.[128]

Both the *Volksblatt* and *Reichspost* also presented their own versions of the accusation of truth distortion. The *Volksblatt*, for instance, referred to a 'Hülsner-syndicate' when discussing the charge (made by Baxa) that defence witness Bulova [German spelling: Bulowa] had allegedly attempted to blackmail a prosecution witness to withdraw certain incriminating statements.[129] Similarly, the paper was more than ever inclined to ascribe a cunning rationality to Hilsner himself, whose clumsy denial of even the most obvious facts here became a 'web of lies with which he has surrounded himself'.[130] The *Reichspost*, meanwhile, systematically identified all Jewish witnesses as Jewish, even in cases when their statements did not contribute to Hilsner's defence, as in the case of two Jews who were unable confirm his alibi.[131] All Jews, this strategy implied, were potentially part of this larger criminal conspiracy, a conspiracy that included the attempt to 'pin suspicion of the murder of Agnes Hruza on her mother and brother,' and thus turn victims into perpetrators.[132] It once again tapped into the standard trope of associating the attendant journalists with Hilsner by reference to their shared 'descent'.[133] The *Reichspost* also made much of an anonymous letter that claimed Baxa and Pešák had met in a secret meeting in order to 'fix' Pešák's witness statement. The paper denounced this letter as a 'Jewish trick' which, far from implicating Baxa, shed light on the Jewish strategy of disseminating false facts.[134] It then went straight into another diatribe that accused the witness Bulova of influencing public opinion.[135] Finally, when it came to commenting on the verdict and Hilsner's second conviction, the *Reichspost* was at pains to defend the jurors against the accusation that they 'had allowed themselves to be ruled by ... suggestion.'[136]

The liberal press paid similarly detailed attention to issues of truth distortion, suggestion and conspiracy. This is unsurprising, given that the final days of the trial itself were dedicated to a veritable battle of truths, with Baxa and Auředníček accusing one another of agitation and the destruction of justice.[137] The *Neue Freie Presse*, for instance, took up the question of Jewish witnesses, and described them as terrorised old people, afraid of saying anything 'that could be judged as taking the defendant's side.'[138] It also printed a lead article on the Konitz perjury trial (a follow-up to the Konitz ritual murder trial), in which a number of witnesses had clearly given false witness. Significantly, the *NFP* here went a long way towards exculpating the accused by locating the true cause of their false witness statements in 'the suggestive power of a widespread opinion.'[139] Similarly an editorial article reporting on the verdict of the Hilsner trial a few days later, stressed that the jurors had 'stood under the compulsive idea [*Zwangsvorstellung*] of ritual murder,' and that their opinions and verdict did not reflect the 'facts' of the case, but rather represented an 'opinion suggested [*suggeriert*] through countless influences ...'[140]

What was absent in the reports on the second trial is the *Neue Freie Presse*'s emphasis on Hilsner's Judaism found during the first trial. The defendant was described in some detail, a description that played up his complacency, simplicity and excitability, pointing not necessarily to Hilsner's innocence, but debunking the idea that this was a master criminal.[141] This treatment was complemented by a positive description of the state prosecutor Malijovský, who was established early on as a good, trustworthy man.[142] The paper's construction of the trial did not aim at depicting Hilsner as a victim, but was directed simply against the antisemitic narrative surrounding the trial. In this construction Malijovský and Baxa were adversaries, rather than accomplices.

The *Extrablatt* was somewhat less explicit in the attention paid to the idea of suggestion and agitation. Indeed it downplayed both trials by not giving them quite the coverage – and certainly not the visual coverage – it would lavish on less politicised trials, and sometimes tried to de-politicise it by stressing the humorous aspects of a day's events. Nevertheless even here the editors felt compelled to pay attention to the accusations of truth distortion raised in the court by Baxa, Auředníček and others. For instance, the *Extrablatt* devoted time and space to Auředníček's exploration of Jewish witnesses, as well as to the entire discussion of whether or not public opinion had been wilfully influenced.[143]

The *Arbeiter-Zeitung* once again came out strongly against the antisemitic version of events, stressing the theory of sexual murder developed by the Prague medical faculty, and paying attention to other suspects.[144] In an article running under the heading of '*Sensations and Sensation-Creation*,' it also criticised the sensationalism of the affair, and the star-status of witnesses who fed the public with ever more detailed accounts of what they had seen or heard.[145] The implication was clearly that justice was in danger of succumbing to the spectacle surrounding it, an anxiety that we have noted many times before.

The *Arbeiter-Zeitung* also provides us with yet another fine example of how nuanced description could serve as a tool either to discredit a person, or else to establish their credentials. We have already discussed the *Volksblatt*'s description of 'crown-witness' Pešák in the first trial, that built him up as trustworthy by stressing his military manner, and the sheer confidence with which he made his pronouncements. The *Arbeiter-Zeitung* reported on Pešák's appearance in the second trial at some length, and here too his loud voice and military background were stressed, if to a quite different effect:

> He speaks in a loud voice that carries through the room and in a tone that is meant to create, even for the smallest of details, the impression of fullest conviction for this detail. The witness wears his military medals. No man in all of Polna, he says, moved his stick back and forth when walking in the same manner as Leopold *Hilsner*.[146]

Here the very details that turned him into an impressive, believable witness elsewhere were subtly ridiculed. Pešák was marked as an actor whose 'tone is meant to create' a certain effect in his audience; his military medals were part of his act; his claim about Hilsner's style of moving his stick is preposterous. The ironic nature of the passage is already announced in the sub-headline that introduced the above description: '*The crown witness with the eagle eyes.*'[147] The passage went on to show up certain inconsistencies in Pešák's statement, and then showed him engaging in theatricals, performing 'in a nasal, imitating tone of voice how he is being teased by Jews [about his claim to have perfect eyesight], to the merriment of a part of the audience.'[148] What elsewhere might be narrated as a funny antisemitic aside here became part of an indictment that showed Pešák as biased, frivolous, theatrical, untrustworthy. We are reminded that, depending on which newspaper narrated it, a witness statement could be framed as a triumph or catastrophe, even if the words uttered were not changed. One should also remember that certain words were also simply read differently by different audiences.

But apart from attacking the antisemitic version of the crime and trial, the *Arbeiter-Zeitung* also tried to frame it within its own ideological parameters. In a remarkable quasi-sociological article entitled '*Pisek Trial Images: The Defendant and his friends*,' Hilsner and some of the witnesses who had been acquainted with Hilsner were marked as members of the *Lumpenproletariat* ('beggar-proletariat'), society's 'fifth estate'.[149] More specifically they were identified as a special subsection of these work-shy poor: 'the Jewish *Lumpenproletariat*'.[150] The *Arbeiter-Zeitung* here launched into a socio-historical narrative of the Jewish ghetto, which was held to have fostered bonds of solidarity among Jews. While this might once have saved poor Jews from starvation, these very bonds now served as a means of suppressing workers. Rich capitalist Jews were eager to maintain the guise of solidarity, and provide the poorest of Jews with scraps

> to keep sedate the rebellious spirit. The discarded trousers given to the Jewish Schnorrer is a weapon in the class war among the Jewry ... They are all – the witnesses of the ritual murder as much as the accused – plants that grow best in the same soil, namely the morass of capitalism.[151]

This is about as close as the *Arbeiter-Zeitung* ever came to endorsing antisemitism. One notes that the deviousness that was here exposed was not that of the Jews in general, but of the capitalist, property-owning Jews whose charity was nothing but a strategy to avoid revolution. At the same time this invective gave the paper an opportunity to reinforce a key dividing line between proletariat and vagrants, by highlighting the lazy, good-for-nothing nature of the *Lumpenproletariat*, a theme to which it returned in its commentary on the verdict. Here, too, an antisemitic note entered through a stress on the 'characteristics of the ghetto' acquired by Jews such as Hilsner, but again this was not taken further.[152]

It would be wrong, however, to overly-emphasise these rare antisemitic asides, unique in the *Arbeiter-Zeitung*'s coverage of crime. The focus of its coverage lay elsewhere. Like the *Neue Freie Presse*, it ran an article on the perjury trial of Konitz, wondering openly whether the witnesses were lying or whether they themselves believed all the nonsense that they had put forward.[153] The article tended towards the latter explanation and stressed the role of Wilhelm Bruhn, the editor of the antisemitic Berlin daily, *Die Staatsbürgerzeitung*, in implanting these memories in the witnesses: like Schwer, Bruhn had investigated the crime himself.

Reporting on the Písek verdict a few days later, the *Arbeiter-Zeitung* highlighted the flimsiness of the evidence, the discrepancy between the medical report and the verdict that acquitted Hilsner of murder but condemned him for assistance in murder, and above all, the indifference of the jurors who had come to this verdict.

> When they were about to withdraw to discuss the verdict, they were busy writing *postcards*, and when they came back, their first thoughts were once again those postcards. Despite the fact that they were given the entire, voluminous evidence, they only needed five quarter-hours for their discussion.[154]

Its report ended in impressionistic description of the crowd outside, including such images as the triumphant shouts of 'an old mother [*altes Mütterchen*]' who celebrated Hilsner's demise.[155] In short it was a narrative in which Hilsner had not been judged fairly: jurors and public had long decided on his guilt.

Bloch's *Wochenschrift*, finally, dedicated much of its coverage to reiterating its argument that public opinion had been manipulated through 'fanatical agitation,'[156] with the aim of 'impregnate[ing] the atmosphere in Pisek with the bloody superstition of ritual murder'.[157] Even more than in its commentary on the first trial, the *Wochenschrift* highlighted the 'suggestive effect of this agitation,'[158] for example by juxtaposing the coverage on Pešák's witness statements with an article on '*"Retro-active" Suggestion and Hallucinations of Witnesses*', a reprint of a scholarly article by one Professor Eulenburg, very much in the style of similar articles that could be found in Gross's *Archiv* or Aschaffenberg's *Monatsschrift*.[159] The article made a straightforward case for 'collective suggestion' in which people 'are reduced to the play-thing of the invading suggestions, originating in themselves or others.'[160] Sources of this 'suggestion by others' ['*Fremdsuggestion*'] included: 'gossipmongers, or the agitatory "public opinion" [i.e. the newspapers] and its distributors, or the vociferousness of the lawyers and the inquisitorial astuteness of the investigative judge …'[161]

While the article stressed that some people were more suggestible than others (it specifically mentioned 'primitive people ... [and] women and children'), it principally allowed for the possibility that anyone could be subject to suggestion given the right circumstances. When it came to giving examples of such suggestion, the author pointed to the murder trials of Xanten and Konitz, both of which had been tried under the auspices of ritual murder accusations. Konitz, specifically, was marked as having provided a 'fertile soil for breeding such "retroactive hallucinations"'.[162] Suggestion was thus identified as a common and dangerous threat to the truth-finding process of the trial. The theory's applicability to the Hilsner case was obvious, and indeed we will find numerous examples of precisely this kind of treatment of the Hilsner trial when we turn to discussing criminological treatments of the trial in the next section. The *Wochenschrift* in any case reiterated this point a few weeks later under the heading of '*Ritual Murder Witnesses*', referring the interested reader to Forel and Bernheim's books on the suggestion phenomenon.[163]

Despite this emphasis on suggestion, the *Wochenschrift* nevertheless implied elsewhere that conscious dissimulation might also have played a part in dictating the outcome of the case.[164] It also charged the antisemites with being disingenuous even in their antisemitism: not all agitation came from conviction, some was simply a way of making profit – by selling agitatory postcards for example.[165] Once again one notes how the construction of the case by this self-consciously Jewish publication mirrors precisely the antisemitic narrative of conspiratorial, disingenuous Jews.

The coverage of the Hilsner trial thus confirms our analysis of reports on other types of 'Jewish' crime: rather than highlighting Hilsner's potential pathological deviance the vast bulk of the public discourse was focused on capturing the details of both investigation and court-room events, and charging the ideological enemy with the distortion of truth and influencing the course of justice. At times, the latter narrative made explicit reference to the criminological discourse about suggestion. The final section of this chapter will consider how the scholarly literature of crime itself dealt with the Hilsner trials.

Criminologists and the Hilsner Trial

The Hilsner trial provoked some of the most coherent formulations of the theory of suggestion, perhaps unsurprisingly so, given that even popular analyses frequently had recourse to the argument that the witnesses were not consciously lying, but rather had been misled by their own perceptions and memories. The most detailed of these was provided by Arthur Nussbaum's 1906 book entitled *Der Polnaer Ritualmordprozess, Eine kriminalpsychologische Untersuchung auf aktenmässiger Grundlage* [*The Polna Ritual Murder Trial, A Criminal-Psychological Examination Based on the Documentary Record*], a study commissioned by Zdenko Auředníček in 1904. His book came with a preface by the illustrious Franz von Liszt, Nussbaum's mentor at the University of Berlin.[166] Liszt praised the 'unique importance' of both the book and the trial itself for 'the cultural history of the nineteenth century's final moments', and announced that the book served both as an analysis of the trial as such and as a key contribution to the 'psychology of witnessing'.[167] Indeed the structure of the book reflected this double aim: it presented the reader with an exploration of the evidence in the two Hilsner trials through the prism of a psychological theory developed in the first half of the book.

The theory's key axiom was that the witnesses were not lying, but had mis-perceived, and misremembered the truth, resulting in 'natural, normal false tes-timon[ies] without intention or knowledge'.[168] Nussbaum was here quoting a phrase used by Auředníček – one notes again how much the discourse of sug-gestion had already become part of the trials. Like other writers on suggestion discussed in chapter two, Nussbaum developed his vision of a penetrable sub-ject whose mastery over his or her self was imperfect at best, and stressed that, unlike hypnotism, suggestion was not dependent on any specific procedure or even the intention to be suggestive:

> The suggestion, i.e. the creation of above mentioned [mental] disturbances on behalf of third parties does not require, as shown by empirical studies, the introduction of a hypnotised (dream-like) state or of a conscious effort of suggestion by the other side [i.e. the side that causes suggestion].[169]

Nussbaum went on to explain that emotional agitation facilitates suggestion, and that 'the more lively this agitation, the more the defensive mechanism against the re-interpretation of consciousness's content is disabled.'[170] In this context, Nussbaum allotted special status to ritual murder trials, in which 'pas-sions are whipped up' to such a degree that mass-suggestion became a common phenomenon.[171] Indeed, ritual murder cases were shown to have such power over people's perceptions, that they could be regarded 'as a distinct criminal-psychological category.'[172]

No-one, Nussbaum explained, was principally immune against suggestion. It was part of the existential condition of humanity, rooted in biology: 'The danger of the falsification of memory and misguidance of judgement is rooted [...] in the psychological conditions of the faculties of memory and reason as such.'[173] Once again we get a clear sense of how 'criminal-psychology' was in many ways more comfortable pathologising the public as a whole, rather than some criminal 'other', and how, as a consequence, the dividing line between normality and degeneracy was eroded.

Significantly, however, Nussbaum went on to rescue some individuals from the implications of this rather bleak anthropology, which, taken *ad absurdum*, could easily have led to total epistemological nihilism. The reader soon learned that not all men were equal in the face of suggestion. On the one hand there were those who were particularly suggestible:

Apart from the lack of intellectual and moral development – the witnesses belong almost typically to the lower strata of society, are rural and small-town people – one should here name: hysteria, puberty, greed and personal vanity.[174]

Nussbaum went on to discuss the example of witness Pešák, claiming that his greed (the town of Polná had offered a reward for information about the murder) had contributed, without his knowledge, to the development of false memories, such as his famed identification of Hilsner at a distance of over seven hundred yards.[175]

In contrast to suggestible individuals such as Pešák, others were better suited to holding off the onslaught of false memory and perception:

> What we have said about the difficulty of correct interpretation [of sensory data] does, of course, principally hold true for experts and judges to an even higher degree than witnesses, but here often – if not always – there exist certain counterweights against this tendency of misinterpretation, i.e. the degree to which education, specialised knowledge, sense of duty and the ability for self-criticism are developed.[176]

Duty – the cornerstone of de-ontological, Protestant ethics in a Kantian mould – as well as education (another key liberal virtue) thus helped to sustain the liberal self and keep it free from the pollutive effects of suggestion. If Nussbaum was building up a dichotomy here between an educated urban elite and rural backwardness, he also established further hierarchies within the elite: 'On average, the judges are under greater threat [of suggestion] than the expert witnesses who are given guidance by the more specific kinds of questions asked and by their specialised knowledge ...'[177]

The ideal observer, then, was the scientist who dispassionately records events and compared them to a body of objective knowledge he has gathered under laboratory conditions. All of this fits perfectly, of course, with Gross's own project of data collection exemplified by his books and the *Archiv*. Indeed, Nussbaum's own volume was full of examples of such expert knowledge: the text was complemented by a number of reports made by expert witnesses on various aspects of the trial, including a re-evaluation of the cause of Hrůzová's death, and an experiment determining the possibility of recognising individuals at a distance of 676 metres.[178] These reports remind us once again just what kind of observation was regarded 'good observation'. Thus, the expert discussing the cause of Hrůzová's death cut the throats of two female corpses and that of a lion, hanging the latter upside down in order to gauge the amount of blood lost post-mortem.[179] The other expert was similarly resourceful: he had domestic servants walk up and down on his father's country estate, asking 'a coachman, a shepherd, a lady and five gardeners' to describe what they could or could not see. In other words, good observation was based on empirical study under 'laboratory' conditions, made by a qualified expert. It was then recorded and provided a discrete piece of objective truth. Nussbaum, of course, also regarded himself as an expert able to arrive at objective truth, fortified by his training in criminal psychology and law.

When it came to locating the source of the suggestion experienced by the Polná witnesses, Nussbaum pointed his finger both at the investigative process itself ('the question-answer game of the interrogation creates a mental disposition within the witness that virtually triggers the previously latent hallucinatory phenomena'),[180] and above all at the proliferation of antisemitic publications. He highlighted in particular the power of images – police sketches, newspaper drawings, trick photography – to imprint themselves upon people's memories:

> What one sees in these pictures is truly gruesome, and the memory cannot free itself from this disgusting vision. If one considers that the great majority of country people regard anything in print as to some degree true ... one can gain some insight into how strong the suggestion-effect of these papers must have been, imprisoning both perception and mind.[181]

Nussbaum was here referring to illustrated Czech antisemitic papers, and to the illustrated brochures that were sold around Polná. We have already seen that the same argument was raised against Viennese antisemitic publications. Interestingly, in Nussbaum's reading, the 'blood-libel agitators' themselves not only stood outside the suggestive effects of their own propaganda, but were marked as opportunistic, 'business-astute' rational actors who simply 'discovered a particularly clever way of imbuing the thinking of the people with antisemitic concepts'.[182]

Another interesting aspect of Nussbaum's treatment of the Hilsner trial was its willingness to draw on both criminological and criminalistic knowledges, and combine them in a manner that once again demonstrates that these should not be seen as incompatible modes of inquiry. Not only did Nussbaum use criminal-psychology – a discipline initially devoted to criminal abnormality – to explore witness behaviour, he also was not averse to combining his criminalistic inquiry into physical evidence with the criminological inquiry into Hilsner's character, his sexual and family history, physical traits and other details. The same ten-pages section considering the motives for the crime provided both information about Hilsner's sexual history and childhood maladies, and recalled the (lack of) forensic evidence for a sexual assault against Hrůzová.[183] Here, once again, the 'real' of the forensic evidence was a way of testing psychological assertions. The criminalistic inquiry remained privileged, not because it was more important, but because only the flawless recovery of evidence provided a basis for criminological speculation. In the present case the recovery was far from flawless; Nussbaum indicated, for instance, that the victim's anus was not examined.[184]

Nussbaum's book thus provides a perfect bridge between the concepts and concerns of criminology/criminalistics, as outlined in chapter two, and the ways in which crime and criminality were narrated in the popular medium of the press. For once the connection was explicitly established and the common epistemological preoccupations directly addressed. One notes how much of

Nussbaum's book was anticipated in the newspaper coverage of the crime, but also how much this coverage itself referred back to criminological accounts of suggestion. Indeed antisemitic parliamentarians would soon attack Nussbaum's study itself as a dangerous suggestive force.[185]

Nor was Nussbaum's book the only criminological account that tried to provide a theoretical framework for the trials. Erich Sello's *Die Irrtümer der Strafjustiz und ihre Ursachen*, a book dedicated to 'Hans Gross, the creator and master of today's criminalistic science,' also devoted a chapter to the affair.[186] Sello had read Nussbaum's earlier account and clearly agreed with its analysis, highlighting the antisemitic agitation's suggestive effect on the masses. Indeed, at that point Sello had already written a pamphlet on the psychology of sensation trials, marking newspapers as the key agents of 'contagion' through which suggestion was transmitted.[187] Sensations and their suggestive effects were here portrayed as 'a disease of the people [*Volkskrankheit*],' and a 'symptom of the general neurasthenic disposition of our time' – one notes yet again how the discourse on suggestion tended to pathologise the masses.[188] The pamphlet ended with the impassioned plea that the press practice a 'conscientious self-limitation' in order to become a 'teacher and leader [*Führerin*] – not a seductress [*Verführerin*] of the people'.[189] Ironically, our analysis of newspaper trial reports suggests that the papers styled themselves precisely in the pedagogic role Sello invoked: they guided their readers' gaze towards significant details and thus schooled their detective skills.

Apart from the criminological commentators who analysed the trial in terms of witness psychology, the Hilsner trial also invited commentary by Hans Gross himself, albeit of a surprising nature. In a review published in his *Archiv*, Gross dismissed Nussbaum's book without even making a reference to his theory of suggestion, a theory that in other places Gross did much to support.[190] Instead, he attacked Nussbaum for factual inconsistencies, the subjective use of language, alleged generalisations about criminal behaviour, and, above all, for his uninvited commentary on what was an Austrian trial, held in the Czech language, involving 'Czech justice officials, Czech expert witnesses, Czech witnesses.'[191] Gross argued that the Prussian Nussbaum was not entitled to his own opinion.

While this dismissal is surprising and may be attributed to hurt patriotism, there is also evidence that Gross, despite his interest in suggestion, had no desire to debunk this or any ritual murder trial as a judicial farce.[192] Gross, for one, did not see any necessary reason to doubt that Hilsner was the culprit. Indeed in several articles and book reviews Gross time and again maintained that one could not *a priori* maintain that all ritual murder accusations were nonsensical, because 'blood-superstition' existed among many peoples throughout the world.[193] The possibility that a Jewish sect, or an individual Jew committed a murder in order to obtain blood therefore had to be acknowledged, even if it was absurd to believe that the Jewish religion as a whole partook in this ritual. One of the reasons why Gross stressed this argument – apart from his personal antisemitism evident in occasional asides[194] – was his theory that superstition was a much overlooked motive that could explain a number of otherwise mysterious crimes.[195]

Consequently, Gross's own treatment of the Hilsner trial considered it in terms of his 'psychopathic superstition' hypothesis. In his discussion, he grouped it together with three other cases: the Konitz murder of a male teenager, Ernst Winter, which we have already encountered, the 1894 murder of Anna Isser in Würtenbert, and the 1878 murder of one Therese S. in the Graz area. These four murders were all connected in Gross's analysis, by the fact that, in all of them, the murderer had distributed shreds of the victim's clothing, or else cut-off body parts, in a most peculiar manner.

The most interesting aspect of Hrůzová's murder for Gross was thus not the alleged bloodlessness of the corpse but the odd distribution of her clothes around the murder site. Gross argued that this peculiarity could be best explained by the perpetrator's superstitious belief that this act of distribution would somehow protect him from detection, or else entitle him to murder with impunity. This superstition he classified as 'psychotic' – a term that denoted abnormality of any kind[196] – because it had become 'disproportionate' for the perpetrators, whom he held to be 'psychologically inferior, work-shy, [and] socially valueless ...'[197]

Gross backed up his assertions by pointing to the confession of Johann Hofer, Therese S.'s murderer. Hofer, after twenty years in prison, requested to be pardoned, arguing that he had committed his crimes in a 'ruined mental state' brought on by a beating he had received at the hands of a butcher's apprentice to whose cruel treatment of a calf Hofer had objected.[198] As part of this confession Hofer described his superstitious belief that by removing part of the victim's petticoat and keeping it, he would be safe from harm.

Gross dismissed Hofer's confession as obviously fabricated in many of its details, but maintained that the account of his superstitious motive for tearing her dress was truthful and offered the key not only to his crime, but to all four murders under discussion. None of the four crimes could be explained by any rational motive, and defied explanation unless one assumed that superstition played a part. Gross later added other cases to this count, all of which he argued were structurally similar (including one featuring a criminal with cannibalistic tendencies), and hence should also be explained by recourse to his theory of 'psychopathic superstition.'[199]

Even taken on its own terms, Gross's theory had many inconsistencies: he grouped together very disparate crimes, gave no conclusive demonstration of what precise sort of superstition led to the criminals' odd behaviour, and seemed to make no real differentiation between the motive for the act itself and the motive for the distribution of garments/body parts. More significantly, one is led to wonder why Gross would have come to a treatment of the Hilsner trial that in many ways seems rather out of character with his usual criminal-istic preoccupations. After all, in his attempt to explain the perceived irrationality of the murders, we find Gross making direct assertions about the psychopathology of criminals, classifying them as mentally abnormal and inferior.[200] One should note, however, that Gross did not locate the perpetrator's pathology in a wider narrative of psychological or physical deviance: they were pathological only in so far as they are abnormally superstitious. Nor was it Gross's claim that this theory would explain all murders committed for an apparently irrational purpose, or in an apparently irrational way. Rather, by discussing four cases, and adding more on in the later article, Gross merely wished to establish a morphology of a certain type of violent crime: his project remained additive and descriptive. Indeed, the theory also intended to refute a reading of the crimes under discussion that described the murderers as sexually perverse: Gross dismissed the sexual motive as secondary and unconvincing.[201] In other words, 'psychopathic superstition' could also be read as an attempt to warn against the classification of all 'dim-wits' who commit violent actions as sexual deviants.[202]

Nevertheless it is striking that Gross never acknowledged the issues of suggestion and truth distortion that were so central to many of the debates surrounding the trial. In fact, rather than corroborating Nussbaum's vision of suggestible masses, Gross in this instance postulated hyper-suggestible, superstitious perpetrators, thus taking all political relevance out of the case, and reducing it to the matter of a freak murder. One can only conclude that Gross took this position either to avoid being drawn into the battle over the trial, or in order to side with those who had identified Hilsner as the murderer without taking on the antisemitic mantle.

Gross's idea that superstition could provide a convincing argument for 'irrational' murders in general, and alleged ritual murders specifically, gained support from a 1909 article by Hellwig, published in the *Zeitschrift für die gesamte Strafrechtswissenschaft*,[203] but was criticised heavily by Nussbaum himself, clearly peeved at the cold reception his book had found in Gross's *Archiv*.[204] In his final word on the affair, Nussbaum, by then a professor at Columbia, did not mince words and accused Gross of having been biased 'perhaps subconsciously, by prejudice and outside agitation', and of devising a theory that was 'wholly unfounded and misleading.'[205] Although he did not elaborate on this, the drift of the accusation was clear: like the witnesses, Gross had fallen victim to antisemitic suggestion, or else had antisemitic leanings to begin with. For Nussbaum suggestion thus remained the master key that could not only explain the mis-trials, but also the willingness of laymen and experts alike to accept the false verdicts.

Conclusion

The ritual murder trials of Leopold Hilsner can thus be integrated into narratives of Jewish crime more generally and into the contemporary criminological debates surrounding suggestibility, witness reliability and the difficulties of establishing 'good knowledge' through the complex procedures of investigation and trial. This is not to deny that the political context of Czech nationalism (and the economic rivalries and social grievances it expressed) provided an important local context, as did community needs for self-definition in an age of constant change. Nationally and internationally, however, the Hilsner affair was encountered above all as news, and hence was absorbed into popular culture according to the logic of such news. The understanding of the 'meaning' of the affair was thus shaped by contemporary assumptions about what a Jewish criminal should look like, the conventions of trial reporting, and the narratives of truth distortion that were so central to these.

One should add that the interaction between investigative journalism, tropes of trial reporting, and fashionable psychological concepts can also be observed in the Konitz ritual murder affair. Here, too, a professional anti-semitic journalist did much to shape the evidence; here, too, mutual accusations of truth distortion and references to suggestion littered the public discourse about the trial. The historical truth of ritual murder accusations was by comparison a side issue: as ever the crime that was to be (un)covered took place not just in the past but right there and then, in the court room, the newspaper column and the alleged struggle over justice itself.

Notes

1. Reinhold Hanisch, 'I was Hitler's buddy, Part II', in: *New Republic*, 12 April 1939, pp. 271–2.
2. Georg R. Schroubek, 'Der "Ritualmord" von Polna, Traditioneller und moderner Aberglaube', in: Rainer Erb and Michael Schmidt (eds), *Antisemitismus und jüdische Geschichte* (Berlin 1987), p. 157; Myriam Kubbovy, 'Matzoh, Red Wine and the Eucharist', *Jewish Spectator* 29 (1964), pp. 21–5.
3. Ernest A. Rappaport, 'The Ritual Murder Accusation, The Persistence of Doubt and the Repetition Compulsion', in: Alan Dundes (ed.), *The Blood Libel Legend: A Casebook in Anti-Semitic Folklore* (Madison, Wisc. 1991), pp. 304–35; Alan Dundes, 'The Ritual Murder or Blood Libel Legend, A Study of Anti-Semitic Victimisation Through Projective Inversion', in: ibid., pp. 336–76; Sigrun Anselm, 'Angst und Angstprojektionen in der Phantasie vom jüdischen Ritualmord', in: Rainer Erb (ed.), *Die Legende vom Ritualmord, Zur Geschichte der Blutbeschuldigung gegen Juden* (Berlin 1993), pp. 253–65. Anselm's essay does locate psychological projection within the nineteenth century gothic revival, but shares its ahistorical view of psychology with the other essays here mentioned.
4. Helmut Walser Smith, *The Butcher's Tale, Murder and Anti-Semitism in a German Town* (New York 2002).
5. For a longer discussion of Smith's study, including a critique of his concept of ritual, see my review in *Central Europe* 2, 1 (2004), pp. 66–8.
6. Hillel Kieval, *The Making of Czech Jewry, National Conflict and Jewish Society in Bohemia, 1870–1918* (Oxford 1988), p. 66. See also: Hillel J. Kieval, 'Jews, Czechs and Germans in Bohemia before 1914', in: Robert S. Wistrich (ed.), *Austrians and Jews in*

the Twentieth Century, From Franz Joseph to Waldheim (New York 1992), pp. 19–37; Hillel J. Kieval, 'Death and the Nation: Ritual Murder as Political Discourse in the Czech Lands', in: *Jewish History* 10, 1 (1996), pp. 75–91; Hillel J. Kieval and Francoise Main, 'Antisémitisme ou Savoir Social? Sur la Genèse des Procès Modernes Pour Meurtre Rituel', in: *Annales. Histoire, Science Sociales* 49, 5 (1994), pp. 1091–105.

7. Kieval, *Making*, pp. 70–1. Cf. Jiří Kovtun, *Tajuplná Vražda, Případ Leopoldna Hilsnera* (Prague 1994), pp. 46–53, 275–86. On antisemitic attitudes in Czech popular literature, and their connection to Czech nationalism, see: Robert B. Pynsent, 'Obchod a smyslnost. České spisovatelky a židé okolo přelomn stoleti', in: *Sbornik Prací Filosofické Faculty Brněské University* 43 (1996), pp. 23–39. Pynsent stresses that there is no necessary link between nationalism and antisemitism, and that not all Czech antisemitism was rooted in anti-Germanism.

8. This is not to claim that German-speaking Czech Jews were simply absorbed in the gentile German-speaking population of Prague and elsewhere; there existed a sharp division in the private sphere of both populations. Cf. Gary B. Cohen, *The Politics of Ethnic Survival: Germans in Prague 1861–1914* (Princeton 1981), pp. 322–3.

9. Cf. Albert Lichtblau, 'Die Debatten über die Ritualmordbeschuldigungen im österreichischen Abgeordnetenhaus am Ende des 19. Jahrhunderts', in: Erb (ed.), *Legende*, pp. 271–3. Lichtblau also shows how, in the Viennese parliamentary debate surrounding the Hilsner trial, pan-Germanist antisemites were keen to prove that the Czech riots had a purely antisemitic as opposed to nationalist motivation. Ibid., p. 275.

10. Schroubek, 'Ritualmord', 151–2; František Červinka, 'The Hilsner Affair', in: Dundes (ed.), *Blood Libel Legend*, reprinted from the Leo Baeck Institute Year Book XIII, 1968, p. 143.

11. On Masaryk's involvement in the Hilsner trial, and his ambivalence regarding the 'Jewish Question', see: Steven Beller, 'The Hilsner Affair: Nationalism, Anti-Semitism and the Individual in the Habsburg Monarchy at the Turn of the Century', in: Robert B. Pynsent (ed.), *T. G. Masaryk (1850–1937), Vol. 2, Thinker and Critic* (London 1989), pp. 52–76; Michael J. Riff, 'The Ambiguity of Masaryk's Attitudes on the 'Jewish Question', in: ibid., pp. 77–87; Hillel Kieval, 'Masaryk and Czech Jewry, The Ambiguities of Friendship', in: Stanley B. Winters (ed.), *T.G. Masaryk (1850–1937), Vol. 2 Thinker and Politician* (London 1990), pp. 302–21.

12. For an attempt to place modern ritual murder trials into the context of other sorts of trials dealing with Jews (and thus into the context of modern antisemitism), see: Albert S. Lindemann, *The Jew Accused, Three Antisemitic Affairs (Dreyfus, Beilis, Frank) 1894–1915* (Cambridge 1991).

13. Cf. Kovtun, *Tajuplna vražda*, pp. 62–4.

14. Lichtblau, 'Die Debatten', pp. 270–92.

15. *DV*, 12 April 1899, p. 9. Several misspellings of names occur in this report; Hrůzová's name in particular was repeatedly misspelled. At this point the *Volksblatt* clearly had very limited information about the crime.

16. Nussbaum, *Der Polnaer Ritualmordprozess*, pp. 9–14.

17. See especially: *DV*, 18 May 1899, evening edition, 2 and the following days.

18. Cf. *ÖW*, 22 September 1899, p. 694.

19. Nussbaum, *Der Polnaer Ritualmordprozess*, pp. 35–7. Schwer published some of this evidence in: Hans Arnold Schwer, *Die Wahrheit über die Morde in Polna* (Vienna 1900).

20. *Přelíčení s Hilsnerem před porotou v Kutné Hoře pro vraždu v Polné: Doslovný otisk stenogrfických protokolů* (Prague 1899), pp. 131–3.

21. Cf. Schroubek, 'Der Ritualmord von Polná', pp. 161–2; Kovtun, *Tajuplna vražda*, pp. 62–71, 122–4.

22. On the Dreyfus trial, see: Lindemann, *The Jew Accused*, pp. 94–128; Jean-Denis Bredin, *The Affair: The Case of Alfred Dreyfus* (New York 1986). On the reception of the

Dreyfus case in the Austrian press, see: Sigmund Scheichl 'Österreichische Reaktionen auf die Dreifus-Affäre', in: *Relations franco-autrichiennes 1870–1970, Austriaca Special Colloque* (1986), pp. 241–59.

23. This is most obvious in *Kikeriki*, 21 and 24 September 1899; see also: *Extrablatt*, 12 September 1899, *Wiener Tagblatt*, 17 September 1899, and so on. References to the Dreyfus case in the coverage of the Hilsner trials were common in all newspapers here discussed.

24. Cf. Nussbaum, *Der Polnaer Ritualmordprozess*, p. 4. The *Deutsches Volksblatt* used this label as early as the twenty-eight of April: *DV*, 28 April 1899, p. 10.

25. On the Tisza-Eslár (also spelled: Tiszaeszlár) 'ritual murder' and its trial, see: Paul Nathan, *Der Process von Tisza-Eszlar: Ein Antisemitisches Culturbild* (Berlin 1892); Andrew Handler, *Blood Libel at Tiszaezlar* (New York 1980). On the Konitz trial, see: Anon., *Der Konitzer Mord, Ein Beitrag zur Klärung* (Breslau 1900); Max Lebermann von Sonnenberg, *Der Blutmord in Konitz mit Streifenlichtern auf die strafrechtliche Stellung der Juden im Deutschen Reiche* (Berlin 1901); Smith, *The Butcher's Tale*; Christoph Nonn, *Eine Stadt sucht einen Mörder; Gerücht, Gewalt und Antisemitism im Kaiserreich* (Göttingen 2002). Nonn stresses sensationalism and self-promotion over endemic antisemitism in his explanation of the ritual murder accusation (pp. 188–94). He also points to contemporary socio-economic pressures, however (p. 196). The newspaper coverage of the 1892 Xanten Ritual Murder trial is briefly summarised in: Daniela Kasischke-Wurm, *Antisemitismus im Spiegel der Hamburger Presse während des Kaiserreichs (1884–1914)* (Hamburg 1997), pp. 175–82.

26. This account is based on: *Přelíčení s Hilsnerem*; Maximilian Paul-Schiff, *Der Prozeß Hilsner, Aktenauszug* (Vienna 1908); Zdenko Auředníček, *Materiale zum Prozess gegen Leopold Hilsner, Vorgelegt der kk General-Prokuratur* (Vienna 1910); J.A. Bulowa, *Zum Polnaer Ritualmordprozess im Stadium vor dem Zweiten Urteile. Ein Brief an die Herren Professoren der gerichtlichen Medizin und an alle ehrlichen Menschen überhaupt* (Berlin 1900); J.A. Bulowa, *Der Polnaer Ritualmordprozess* (Berlin 1900); Gustav Toužil, *Polna 29.3.1899. Ermordung der Agnes Hruza und der sensationelle Prozess Hilsner vor dem Kuttenberger Schwurgerichte* (Kuttenberg 1899), Schwer, *Die Wahrheit*; and a critical, parallel reading of the various newspaper accounts.

27. See his final plea in the Písek, reprinted in: Paul-Schiff, *Der Prozeß Hilsner*, pp. 123–7.

28. On the discourse of cigarette smoking as a marker for eastern Jews, see: Gilman, *Jew's Body*, p. 58. While Gilman's argument provides an explanation for the witness statements, it does not, as we shall see, explain the descriptive strategies employed for Jews in the press.

29. *Přelíčení s Hilsnerem*, pp. 179 ff., 238 ff.

30. Cf. Bohumil Černý, *Vražda v Polné* (Prague 1968), plates 33–45, 105–12, 176–84.

31. Nussbaum, *Der Polnaer Ritualmordprozess*, p. 18.

32. Tomáš G. Masaryk, *Die Notwendigkeit der Revision des Polnaer Prozesses* (Vienna 1899); Tomáš G. Masaryk, *Die Bedeutung des Polnaer Verbrechens für den Ritualmordaberglauben* (Berlin 1900). See also: Kovtun, *Tajuplna vražda*, pp. 236–42. Masaryk's involvement in the Hilsner affair is also analysed in Ernst Rychnovsky (ed.), *Masaryk und das Judentum* (Prague 1931). The reliance of many present day commentators on the Hilsner trial on what is at best a biased and shaky source is remarkable.

33. Masaryk, *Notwendigkeit*, p. 14.

34. *Gutachten der böhmischen medizinischen Fakultät in der Strafsache Leopold Hilsner, 25.5.1900* (Prague 1900), reprinted in: Nussbaum, *Der Polnaer Ritualmordprozess*, pp. 220–41. For Nussbaum's discussion of the motive, see: Ibid., p. 239.

35. Attempts to blame the same Jewish murderer for both corpses were made literally within days of the discovery of Hrůzová's corpse. Cf. *DV*, 15 April 1899, p. 7. See also: *DV*, 18 May 1899, evening edition, p. 3.

36. See his final plea in the Písek trial, reprinted in: Paul-Schiff, *Der Prozeß Hilsner*, pp. 123–7 and in various papers on the thirteenth of November 1900.
37. Here quoted from: *Extrablatt*, 13 November 1900, p. 9. The versions in various papers differ slightly and differ again from the version in: Paul-Schiff, *Der Prozeß Hilsner*, p. 123, though the key components of the speech are constant.
38. Ibid.
39. Cf. Egon Erwin Kisch, 'Zum Tode Leopold Hilsners', in: *Berliner Morgenpost*, 16 January 1928.
40. Cf. *DV*, 16 September 1899, 8. The *Volksblatt* here complained that the Jewish newspapers were allowed access to a Jewish factory owner's telephone, i.e. had an unfair advantage in disseminating their (false) version of events.
41. *RP*, 17 October 1900, p. 6.
42. Cf. the numbers cited by: *AZ*, 13 September 1899, p. 6; *Extrablatt*, 12 September 1899, p. 9; *NFP*, 26 October 1900, p. 6; *NFP*, 28 October 1900, p. 6; *AZ*, 26 October 1900, p. 6; *RP*, 26 October 1900, p. 6.
43. On the importance of the Hilsner trial for Czech nationalism, see: Kieval, *Making of Czech Jewry*, pp. 73–83.
44. *DV*, 16 September 1899, p. 6.
45. *DV*, 16 September 1899, p. 7.
46. *DV*, 15 September 1899, evening edition, p. 3; *DV*, 16 September 1899, p. 5.
47. *DV*, 16 September 1899, evening edition, p. 3.
48. *DV*, 17 September 1899, p. 5.
49. For the exception to this rule, see: *DV*, 3 October 1899, evening edition, p. 2. For the most part, however, the *Volksblatt* was even willing to accept the murder as the act of a fringe group of fanatics with no link to 'mainstream' Judaism. Cf. *DV*, 18 April 1899, p. 3.
50. *DV*, 12 September 1899, evening edition, p. 2. The Czech for palm, '*dlaň*', is misspelled, rather deflating the *Volksblatt*'s claim to accuracy.
51. *DV*, 13 September 1899, p. 6.
52. For example: *DV*, 15 April 1899, p. 7; *DV*, 18 April 1899, p. 3; *DV*, 18 April 1899, evening edition, p. 3; *DV*, 18 May 1899, evening edition, p. 2; *DV*, 16 September 1899, evening edition, pp. 2–3; *DV*, 13 September 1899, p. 9; *DV*, 11 October 1899, evening edition, p. 2; *DV*, 26 September 1899, p. 4; *DV*, 16 September 1899, p. 8.
53. *DV*, 11 October 1899, evening edition, p. 2.
54. Ibid.
55. *DV*, 25 September 1899, evening edition, 4. Hilsner's name was frequently rendered 'Hülsner' by the *Volksblatt* and other German language publications.
56. Ibid.
57. Ibid.
58. *DV*, 18 April 1899, evening edition, p. 2 and *DV*, 19 April 1899, p. 2.
59. Cf. Lombroso, *Verbrecher*, p. 56.
60. *DV*, 15 September 1899, p. 8. In the *Volksblatt*, the italicised sections were set in broad double font.
61. Ibid.
62. *DV*, 12 September 1899, evening edition, p. 1.
63. *DV*, 12 September 1899, evening edition, p. 1.
64. Ibid.
65. Ibid.
66. Ibid.
67. *DV*, 14 September 1899, evening edition, p. 2.
68. *DV*, 16 September 1899, p. 7.
69. See, for instance, *Pražky Illustrovaný Kurýr*, 28 October 1900, title page; *Hlasu Národa*, příloha, 13 September 1900, 24 September 1900.

70. *DV*, 3 October 1899, p. 4. The highlighted sections are similarly highlighted in the original.
71. *DV*, 25 September 1899, evening edition, p. 5.
72. Ibid.
73. *DV*, 27 September 1899, p. 8.
74. *DV*, 27 September 1899, evening edition, p. 2.
75. *DV*, 3 October 1899, p. 4. See discussion above.
76. *RP*, 13 September 1899, p. 1.
77. Ibid.
78. Ibid.
79. *RP*, 19 September 1899, p. 1; *RP*, 17 September 1899, p. 4.
80. *Vaterland*, 16 September 1899, p. 6.
81. *Kikeriki*, 1 October 1899, p. 3.
82. *Kikeriki*, 21 September 1899, p. 4.
83. *Kikeriki*, 21 September 1899, p. 2.
84. *Kikeriki*, 24 September 1899, p. 3. The use of *Mauschel* in the cartoon is difficult to render in English.
85. *Kikeriki*, 24 September 1899, p. 1.
86. For example: *NFP*, 12 September 1899, p. 8; *NFP*, 15 September 1899, p. 8; *Extrablatt*, 15 September 1899, p. 9; *NWT*, 17 September 1899, p. 2; *WT*, 17 September 1899, p. 9.
87. *NFP*, 17 September 1899, p. 1.
88. *NFP*, 17 September 1899, p. 2.
89. *NFP*, 12 September 1899, p. 8.
90. On Bloch, and the Rohling affair, see: Wistrich, *Jews of Vienna*, 270–309.
91. *ÖW*, 15 September 1899, p. 678.
92. *Extrablatt*, 16 September 1899, p. 9.
93. See for instance: *Extrablatt*, 16 September 1899, p. 9
94. *Extrablatt*, 17 September 1899, p. 23.
95. *NWT*, 17 September, pp. 8–10.
96. *ÖW*, 15 September 1899, p. 677.
97. *ÖW*, 29 September 1899, p. 715.
98. *ÖW*, 2 September 1899, p. 690.
99. One or two of the liberal papers hint at a similar reading. See, for instance, *NWT*, 17 September, p. 1. See also the discussion of the *Arbeiter-Zeitung*'s coverage below.
100. *ÖW*, 22 September 1899, p. 690.
101. Ibid.
102. *NFP*, 13 September 1899, p. 6.
103. Ibid. See also his initial description in which he is marked as 'not much of a Jewish type, that only emerges when he speaks'. *NFP*, 12 September 1899, evening edition, p. 2.
104. *NFP*, 13 September 1899, p. 6.
105. Ibid.
106. *ÖW*, 6 October 1899, pp. 736–8. The article explored Jewish racial identity via its discussion of William Ripley's lectures on the 'racial geography of Europe'. See also: *ÖW*, 6 October 1899, p. 730 for a statement of Jewish racial pride.
107. *ÖW*, 22 September 1899, p. 690.
108. *ÖW*, 13 October 1899, p. 756.
109. For example: *NWT*, 17 September 1899, p. 1.
110. For example: *AZ*, 14 September 1899, p. 6.
111. For example: *AZ*, 15 September 1899, pp. 6–7; *AZ*, 17 September 1899, p. 6.
112. *AZ*, 17 September 1899, p. 1. The German '*Unkulturprozess*' denies the frequently raised antisemitic claim that this was a trial of cultural historical importance.
113. *AZ*, 8 September 1899, p. 3.

114. Ibid.
115. *AZ*, 17 September 1899, p. 1. The novel in question is Zola's *La Bête Humaine*, which seems to have been widely read in contemporary Vienna (cf. Lindau, *Ausflüge*, pp. 104–6). Its creation of a murderer unable to help himself when aroused by a woman's flesh, drew on an amalgam of Lombroso, Morel, Georget and Pinel.
116. Cf. Paupié, *Handbuch*, p. 138.
117. *RW*, 12 September 1899, p. 3.
118. *Kikeriki*, 1 November 1900, p. 3.
119. *Kikeriki*, 1 November 1900, p. 3.
120. *Kikeriki*, 8 November 1900, p. 2.
121. Paul-Schiff, *Der Prozeß Hilsner*, p. 124.
122. *OR*, 15 November 1900, p. 6.
123. *DV*, 25 October 1900, evening edition, pp. 1–2.
124. *DV*, 25 October 1900, evening edition, p. 2.
125. Contra Bristow, *Prejudice*, pp. 4, 46, 82.
126. *RP*, 26 October 1900, p. 11.
127. *RP*, 12 November 1900, p. 5.
128. *RP*, 17 November 1900, p. 1.
129. *DV*, 28 October 1900, p. 5.
130. *DV*, 15 November 1900, p. 1.
131. *RP*, 1 November 1900, p. 6.
132. *RP*, 30 October 1900, p. 9.
133. *RP*, 26 October 1900, p. 6.
134. *RP*, 10 November 1900, p. 6.
135. Ibid.
136. *RP*, 17 November 1900, p. 1. The paper here echoed a similar statement made by Baxa in his final plea ('reply to the defence'). Cf. Paul-Schiff, *Der Prozeß Hilsner*, p. 143.
137. Ibid., pp. 123–7; 130–40; 143 ff.
138. *NFP*, 1 November 1900, p. 8.
139. *NFP*, 11 November 1900, p. 1.
140. *NFP*, 15 November 1900, p. 1.
141. *NFP*, 25 October 1900, evening edition, p. 1; *NFP*, 26 October, p. 6.
142. *NFP*, 25 October 1900, p. 7.
143. *Extrablatt*, 14 November 1900, pp. 9–10.
144. For example *AZ*, 31 October 1900, p. 8; *AZ*, 3 November 1900, p. 8.
145. *AZ*, 14 November 1900, p. 6.
146. *AZ*, 30 October 1900, p. 6.
147. Ibid.
148. Ibid.
149. *AZ*, 10 November 1900, p. 7.
150. Ibid.
151. Ibid.
152. *AZ*, 15 November 1900, p. 9.
153. *AZ*, 11 November 1900, p. 9.
154. *AZ*, 15 November 1900, p. 9.
155. Ibid.
156. *ÖW*, 2 November 1900, p. 777.
157. Ibid., p. 778.
158. Ibid.
159. *ÖW*, 9 November 1900, pp. 801–2.
160. Ibid., p. 802.
161. Ibid.

162. Ibid.
163. ÖW, 30 November 1900, p. 858. Bernheim, Die Suggestion; Forel, Der Hypnotismus. The Wochenschrift's reference was to the third edition of Forel's text.
164. ÖW, 2 November 1900, p. 778.
165. Ibid.
166. Nussbaum, Der Polnaer Ritualmordprozess, pp. v–vii. Originally Liszt had been commissioned to write a book about the Hilsner trial 'from the standpoint of "criminological psychology"' but he passed the job on to his student Nussbaum. See: Arthur Nussbaum, 'The "Ritual-Murder" Trial of Polna', in: Historica Judaica 9 (1947–8), p. 61. See also: NFP, 13 March 1906, evening edition, p. 4. Franz von Liszt's interest in suggestion and the psychology of witnessing is also evident from the work of another of his students, Louis William Stern. See, for example: L.W. Stern, 'Zur Psychologie der Aussage', in: Zeitschrift für die gesamte Strafrechtswissenschaft 23 (1906), pp. 65–6.
167. Arthur Nussbaum, Der Polnaer Ritualmordprozess, pp. v–vii.
168. Ibid., p. 4.
169. Ibid., p. 6.
170. Ibid., p. 7.
171. Ibid.
172. Ibid.
173. Ibid., p. 6.
174. Ibid., p. 33.
175. Ibid.
176. Ibid., p. 6.
177. Ibid.
178. Westenhoeffer, 'Ueber die Ursache des Todes der Agnes Hruza', in: ibid., pp. 241–57; Paul Silex, 'Aerztliches Gutachten über das Erkennen von Personen in einer Distanz von 676 m mit Bezug auf den Fall Peter Pesak', in: ibid., pp. 257–9.
179. Westenhoeffer, 'Ueber die Ursache des Todes der Agnes Hruza', in: ibid., pp. 247, 248.
180. Nussbaum, Der Polnaer Ritualmordprozess, p. 33.
181. Ibid., pp. 16–17.
182. Ibid., p. 16.
183. Ibid., pp. 146–56.
184. Ibid, p. 150.
185. NFP, 13 March 1906, evening edition, p. 4.
186. Erich Sello, Die Irrtümer der Strafjustiz, Erster Band: Todesstrafe und lebenslängliches Zuchthaus in richterlichen Fehlsprüchen neuerer Zeit (Berlin 1911), pp. 239 ff. For the dedication to Gross, see p. iii.
187. Erich Sello, Zur Psychologie der cause célèbre, Ein Vortrag (Berlin 1910), p. 11 and passim. See also: Erich Sello, Die Hauprozesse und ihre Lehren (Berlin 1908), pp. 131 ff.
188. Sello, Zur Psychologie, p. 43. For a present day psycho-historical analysis of blood libel cases that employs similar metaphors, see: Tamás Kende, 'The Language of Blood Libels in Central and East European History', in: Lázló Kontler (ed.), Pride and Prejudice, National Stereotypes in 19th and 20th century Europe East and West, CEU History Department Working Paper Series (Budapest 1995), pp. 91–104.
189. Ibid., p. 44.
190. Hans Gross, book review of Nussbaum, Der Polnaer Ritualmordprozess, in: Archiv 26 (1907), pp. 366–8.
191. Ibid., p. 368.
192. Hurt vanity might also have played a part: Nussbaum's book explicitly dismissed Gross's own theory of 'psychotic superstition' (see below), even though he made extensive use of his Handbuch and various of the Archiv's articles. Cf. Arthur Nussbaum, Der Polnaer Ritualmordprozess, pp. 205 ff.

193. Hans Gross, 'Buchbesprechung: Anonymous, *Der Konitzer Mord, Ein Beitrag zur Klärung* (Breslau 1900)', in: *Archiv* 4 (1900), pp. 363–5. Hans Gross, 'Buchbesprechung: D. Chwolson, *Die Blutanklage und sonstige mittelalterliche Beschuldigungen der Juden, Eine historische Untersuchung nach den Quellen* (Frankfurt am Main 1901 [1880])', in: *Archiv* 9 (1902), pp. 240–1; Hans Gross, 'Buchbesprechung: Carl Mommert, *Menschenopfer bei den alten Hebräern* (Leipzig 1905)', in: *Archiv* 24 (1906), p. 176; Hans Gross, 'Buchbesprechung: Carl Mommert, *Der Ritualmord bei den Talmudjuden* (Leipzig 1905)', in: *Archiv* 24 (1906), p. 176; Hans Gross, 'Buchbesprechung: Maximilian Paul-Schiff, *Der Prozeß Hilsner, Aktenauszug* (Vienna 1908)', in: *Archiv* 29 (1908), p. 314; Hans Gross, 'Buchbesprechung: Albert Hellwig, *Ritualmord aund Aberglaube* (Minden i.W. o.J.)', in: *Archiv* 59 (1914), p. 377. See also Gross's articles on 'psychopathic superstition' discussed below.
194. See for instance: Hans Gross, *Handbuch*, p. 556.
195. Hans Gross, 'Psychopathischer Aberglaube', *Archiv* 9 (1902), pp. 253–82; Hans Gross, 'Zur Frage vom psychopathischen Aberglauben', *Archiv* 12 (1903), pp. 335–40. See also: Hans Gross, 'Buchbesprechung: Maximilian Paul-Schiff, *Der Prozeß Hilsner, Aktenauszug* (Vienna 1908)', in: *Archiv* 29 (1908), p. 314; Robert Gaupp, 'Zur Lehre vom psychopathischen Aberglauben', in: *Archiv* 28 (1907), pp. 20–48; Hans Gross, *Handbuch*, pp. 354 ff. Hans Gross's interest in superstition draws on Avé-Lallement's own classification of many criminals as superstitious. Cf. Avé-Lallement, *Das Deutsche Gaunertum* Vol. 2, pp. 20 ff.
196. Cf. Wetzell, *Inventing*, p. 145.
197. Hans Gross, 'Psychopathischer Aberglaube', in: *Archiv* 9 (1902), pp. 279–80.
198. Ibid., p. 276.
199. Hans Gross, 'Zur Frage vom psychopathischen Aberglauben', *Archiv* 12 (1903), pp. 335–40.
200. His description of the murderers echoes that of 'work-shy' vagabonds and petty criminals elsewhere. Cf. Gross, 'Degeneration und Deportation', p. 70. It contrasts starkly to the deliberate and rational criminality he assumes elsewhere.
201. In itself this dismissal of a sexual motive is puzzling given the nature of some of these cases. In one, the 1864 Tirsch murder, the murderer famously ate the sexual organs he had removed from his victim's body. Cf. Arthur Nussbaum, 'The "Ritual-Murder" Trial of Polna', in: *Historica Judaica* 9 (1947–8), p. 66.
202. Hans Gross, 'Zur Frage vom psychopathischen Aberglauben', p. 340.
203. Albert Hellwig, 'Blutmord und Aberglaube, Fakten und Hypothesen', in: *Zeitschrift für die gesamte Strafrechtswissenschaft* 30 (1909/1910), pp. 149–74. Hellwig differed from Gross on some points. For instance, for him superstitious criminals need not be 'pathological'.
204. Arthur Nussbaum, 'Ueber Morde aus Aberglauben', in: *Zeitschrift für die gesamte Strafrechtswissenschaft* 30 (1909/1910), pp. 813–52; Nussbaum, 'The "Ritual-Murder" Trial', pp. 57–74. See also Hellwig's 'Blutmord und Ritualaberglauben' in: *Der Grenzbote* 77 (1913), pp. 149 ff. in which Hellwig partially reverses his position, and to some degree comes to endorse Nussbaum's suggestion thesis.
205. Nussbaum, 'The "Ritual-Murder" Trial', p. 64.

Chapter 7

CONCLUSIONS

Do you believe that there is a Christian on earth, and were he the most noble, the most just and faithful man, one single Christian, who in some moment of anger, of ill-humour, of wrath even against his best friend, against his lover, his wife, if these were Jews or of Jewish descent, did not hold their Judaism against them, at least to themselves? ... There is none, I assure you.

Arthur Schnitzer, The Road to the Open.[1]

When did I overcome in myself the antisemitism of the common people? Well, really, in my own feeling perhaps never, only in my reason ...

Tomáš G. Masaryk, quoted in Karel Čapek, President Masaryk Tells His Story.[2]

[N]either at school, nor at the University, nor in the world of literature, have I ever experienced the slightest suppression or indignity as a Jew.

Stefan Zweig, The World of Yesterday.[3]

This book has presented a number of interlocking arguments concerning the themes of crime and antisemitism in Vienna during the two decades leading up to the First World War. The first of these arguments concerned the shape of both popular and scientific thought about crime in that period. The most basic point made here – although hardly a mainstay of the critical literature – was that popular thinking about criminals was not overshadowed by biological models. Indeed the most popular of genres in which narratives of the criminal were articulated – the trial report – followed a logic in which criminal rationality rather than biological (or sociological) determinism defined the perpetrator. This narrative was free of any moral ambiguities: criminals were not victims of inner compulsions beyond their control. It also allowed the reader to enter into a battle of wits in which his or her observatory sophistication was pitted against the criminal's dissimulative skill. The narrative logic of the trial report thus placed the consumer of crime sensations into a privileged place –

that of the expert observer – that was explicitly marked off against the ignorant masses that comprised the *Publikum*, i.e. the wider public.

About the assertion that trial reports were indeed the most popular form of consuming knowledge about crime, there can, I believe, be little doubt. Of course popular fictional accounts about crime were also in circulation, most typically detective yarns inspired by Conan Doyle, whose Sherlock Holmes series was widely read and imitated in Austria. Many such stories were English or American imports and were translated *en masse*.[4] All such fiction featured a broadly criminalistic take on crime, i.e. it regarded crime above all as a problem of investigative technique and was thus compatible with the image of criminality conjured up by the papers.[5] Popular non-fiction about crime, for example the so-called *Pitaval* tradition, was often a direct extension of journalistic output.[6] Here crimes, and particularly trials, were written up and collected in a format that mimicked many of the trial report's conventions; in fact they were often penned by the same journalists who had initially covered the cases. Occasional examples of more reductionist readings of criminality did exist in contemporary popular non-fiction, most notably Paul Lindau's *Ausflüge ins Kriminalistische* (1909). Even here determinist constructions of criminality sat side-by-side with 'forensic' treatments of crime that treated the court room as a dramatic space, in which the *Publikum* interacted with defendants who 'give more or less the impression of actors who have carefully studied and memorised their roles.'[7] Finally, there were a number of contemporary quasi-anthropological texts that sought to penetrate the world of crime in the manner of the investigative journalist: Max Winter's *Im dunkelsten Wien* ['In Darkest Vienna'] (1904) and Emil Kläger's *Durch die Wiener Quartiere des Elends und Verbrechens* ['Journey Through Quarters of Despair and Crime'] (1909).[8] These texts, penned by professional journalists, focused on urban poverty and presented a more or less explicitly socialist narrative of crime in which economic deprivation was the most important root cause of crime.[9] Kläger's book originated in a very popular slide show of the Viennese underworld at the *Urania* theatre in Vienna.[10] His construction of criminals situated them biographically and did provide physiognomic readings, but these did not add up to any semiotics of criminal types.[11] When it came to describing crime in action – a pickpocket's exploits – his report focused on the observatory powers of the trained detective he was shadowing.[12] Both his and Winter's account gave a new twist to the trial journalist's promise to provide his readers with access beyond the surface of criminality by following the criminal out of the court room and into his or her squalid night shelter.[13] At the same time they implicitly questioned whether most of these criminals were no more than hungry, unfortunate wretches rather than the devious masterminds who filled the trial columns. In terms of sheer circulation, none of these texts compare with the daily dose of trial reports that represented the bread and butter of Vienna's most popular papers, and formed a central feature in even the most sophisticated dailies, comparable perhaps to the status of sport in present-day news culture.

I have further argued that the popular knowledge of crime disseminated by these newspapers was not as much at odds with scientific views of crime as might be supposed from reading much of the historiography of criminology. The degree to which deterministic models of criminality – and through them, narratives of criminals as 'others' – dominated the discourse has often been exaggerated, although it did, of course, represent an important and, with a view to the Nazi abuse of criminological research, fateful innovation of nineteenth-century social-scientific thought. I have argued that rival knowledges of crime came into existence at the end of the nineteenth century, which, much like the newspapers, focused on investigation over classification, and did not assume any anthropological, social or psychological difference between criminal actors and the rest of the population. If any line of demarcation was conjured up by criminalistics, it was that between good and bad observers, the suggestible and the intellectually superior, the scientist and the public at large. As such it reproduced the same division that was implied by the trial reports' narrative logic. The Austrian criminalist Hans Gross was at the forefront of this rival knowledge of criminality, and made explicit its critique of the methods and assumptions of deterministic criminologies, even if Gross at times tapped into such determinism himself.

Criminalistic science and newspaper trial reports (and, for that matter, contemporary detective fiction) thus produced harmonising narratives of criminality.[14] Criminology proper – i.e. medical, deterministic visions of the criminal – by contrast did not move the public imagination much at this point, very much in contrast to present-day culture where both views of the criminal find ample popular representation in film and television, from mass-murderer shockers such as the films *The Silence of the Lambs* (Jonathan Demme, 1991) and *Se7en* (David Fincher, 1995) to the current popularity of the television series *Crime Scene Investigations* (Anthony Zuiker, from 2000) and its various spin-offs. One might add that the first crime novels focusing on psychopathologies and psycho-biographies stemmed from the early 1930s and did not take off as a sub-genre until the 1940s.[15]

One should be careful, however, not to explain away the lack of popular enthusiasm for deterministic narratives of crime by simply assuming a popular ignorance about this model of criminality. It is striking, after all, that newspapers did not feel they had to go into long paroxysms of explanation when medical authorities raised questions of 'compulsion' or 'sadism' during a trial. In fact there is some evidence – inconclusive because the rules of the genre were still fluid and because the Austrian newspaper landscape was comparably barren – that deterministic narratives of criminality had been rehearsed on occasion in the late 1870s and early 1880s. Thus the *Extrablatt* constructed one Katharina Steiner, a sometime prostitute who was tried and convicted of murder, as being endowed with a 'criminal nature', and as a member of a 'criminal family' that had fostered this nature for generations.[16] Indeed the paper stuck to this construction even after Steiner's acquittal in response to the real murderer coming forward, insisting on her criminality against the evidence of her innocence. I know of no comparable construction from the 1890 to 1914 period: here such essentialism was studiously eschewed.

Once one accepts that the scholarly engagement with criminality was more diverse than is often realized, and more linked to contemporary popular narratives thereof, it might come as less of a surprise that Jewish criminality was also not narrated in terms of a racial criminality (in the biological sense of the term). Neither physical nor psychological criminal stigmata were mapped onto Jewish bodies and minds. Given the enduring popularity of the theory of degeneracy at the *fin-de-siècle* and beyond, it would have been possible for anti-semitic scientists to mark Jews as a degenerate race and hence driven to deviance, but instead it was precisely the Jews' vitality in the modern age that was contrasted with the difficulties many others in the population were experiencing in adjusting to modernity's demands. This logic made Jews into convenient symbols of all those modern institutions and phenomena despised by many antisemites, including capitalism, materialism, secularisation, and scientific progress. Even their alleged propensity towards nervous disorders did not necessarily sketch them as victims of modernity; after all the discourse of neurasthenia was an ambivalent one that could just as well point to adjustment rather than maladjustment to an admittedly 'nervous' age.[17]

Jewish criminality, then, was narrated as a rational, volitional and competent criminality, and had been narrated in much the same manner throughout the nineteenth century. Modern criminologists reiterated this narrative with minor adjustments. Only fringe antisemitic voices marked this criminality as a race-feature in a strict biological sense. The analysis of Viennese trial reports shows that the same narrative of modern criminality was also upheld by antisemites in this popular medium. Significantly this was true even for the paper that was most steeped in a racial invective against Jews of a distinctly Schönerian cast, the *Deutsches Volksblatt*: rationality and cunning were the dominant themes, physiological characterisations of the defendants as Jewish were conspicuous in their absence and the roots of their criminality (for example in racial predisposition) left largely unexplored. One might say, then, that Lueger's antisemitism with its heavily anti capitalist and anti-modern overtones, dominated also within the genre of the trial report. The merging of racial narratives of Jews with criminal biological narratives predicted by various cultural historians was not in evidence in this period. At the same time it is clear that crime reporting was a central *locus* in which sustained antisemitic narratives were disseminated. This routine usage of crime as a vehicle to expose Jews as dangerous to society only emerged in the early to mid-1890s; the Steiner case mentioned above, for instance, would have attracted close antisemitic scrutiny fifteen or twenty years later – Steiner was Jewish – but at the time neither of the two main antisemitic papers had been founded as of yet, and *Kikeriki* had not yet embraced an antisemitic focus.[18] While the case did draw antisemitic commentary, there simply did not exist a central venue that would have allowed antisemites to disseminate this commentary effectively, and to emplot it in a larger narrative of Jewish crime.[19]

The logic of the antisemitic narrative of Jewish crime was virtually independent of the type of crime that had been committed. While the construction of Jews as rational, modern criminals might come as little surprise in the context of business crimes, it held equally true for sexual and violent crimes (though few enough of either were actually committed by Jews). Indeed, this antisemitic logic extended even to the Hilsner ritual murder trial; the construction of Hilsner as anything but a rational actor was more typically a strategy of philosemitic publications rather than one antisemites embraced. This blanket treatment of Jewish crime went hand in hand with the antisemitic strategy of not focusing on the defendant, but on any Jew involved in the trial who could be charged with the deliberate obstruction of justice. This move away from the defendant to a vision of crime in which each trial was always also a trial of the efficacy of the entire justice system was facilitated by two genre conventions of the trial report in both antisemitic papers and elsewhere: first, the practice of turning the courtroom itself into an investigative scene in which all participants had to be examined and evaluated, and second, the assumption that dissimulation was the most significant marker of criminality. These conventions allowed antisemitic publications to glibly move from the contemplation of the defendant's guilt to, say, the (Jewish) medical faculty's examination of evidence, the (Jewish) lawyer's 'unfair' strategies, or the (Jewish) newspapers' attempt to entrance a 'suggestible' public with their lies. In this manner the narrative of a Jewish conspiracy that aimed at dismantling the justice system's access to objective truth could be endlessly reiterated – one notes that the supposedly very modern Jew was here endowed with the ability to maintain his distinctly pre-modern tribal solidarity and thus beat gentiles both at the game of adjusting to the times and at preserving his communal identity. This conspiratorial charge, in turn, found an echo in the anxiety evident in contemporary criminological literature that the age of the masses also signalled an age where epistemological certainty was hard to come by, because it was consistently being sabotaged by the ordinary citizen. The antisemitic papers not only reproduced this anxiety, but also disassociated the reader from the general public who were being fooled by the Jews' strategies. Just as in other papers, the antisemitic trial reader's gaze was that of an observational elite.

The difference between antisemitic newspapers and those of other political persuasions thus did not lie in their strategies of narrating criminality. Both identified rationality and deception as key criminal markers, both conducted an 'investigation' of the trial (and, through it, of society) rather than trying to categorise the perpetrator according to set typologies. Rather, the difference lay in the simple fact that while the antisemitic publications went out of their way to create some sort of connection between Jews and crime, the other papers scrupulously avoided dwelling on a given defendant's (or lawyer's, witness's or victim's) Judaism and, in fact, very rarely made reference to Jews at all. This will come as no great surprise in the case of the liberal publications that, after all, upheld assimilationist politics. In the case of the *Kronenzeitung*, however, with its explicit populism and mass circulation, as well as that of the *Arbeiter-Zeitung*, whose use of antisemitic tropes has been much debated, this result may lead to a tentative re-assessment of the thesis that antisemitism had become acceptable and respectable throughout Viennese society in the decade leading up to the Great War. What the treatment of crime – i.e. a *sujet* that certainly in the *Kronenzeitung* was primarily apolitical entertainment for the 'common man' – indicates, I think, is how much antisemitic narratives remained politicised even after Lueger's electoral victory in the late 1890s.

The point here cannot be that Vienna was not an antisemitic society in the years under consideration: the political success of the Christian Social Party, although not reducible to its antisemitism, clearly speaks for the attraction of that ideology for a substantial part of the electorate, and the sheer amount of antisemitic output that circulated in Vienna points with equal clarity to the vigour that Jew-hatred, in its many guises, enjoyed, even if contemporary anti-semitic publications amounted to only a small part of the total print output of the day. Nor can there be much doubt that antisemitic stereotypes had been successfully enough disseminated as to be recognisable to all but the most protected of society's members. It is less clear, however, whether antisemitism had truly achieved widespread respectability up and down the social ladder, if one takes this characterisation to mean its absorption into culture to a degree that antisemitic language – jokes and jibes, throw-away assumptions about the difference between gentile and Jew – had become so ubiquitous as to have turned 'invisible' for its users. Rather, I would suggest that most Viennese knew that antisemitic comments were a language used by a certain political camp, and that using it meant identifying oneself with that camp. As such, antisemitic comments did not creep into news coverage by accident, and were deemed too political by the truly populist press. In the case of the *Arbeiter-Zeitung* this means that its occasional use of an antisemitic idiom in its political commentary was a careful and conscious strategy rather than a blind absorption of popular invective; there was no such thing as being 'innocently' antisemitic. It is here that antisemitism contrasted with other forms of xenophobia which carried little political import: the *Krone* could be racist about the Chinese, but did not wish to alienate readers by embracing a discourse that remained clearly linked to party-politics. Of course the language of newspapers and the language of the street are hardly identical; but one must also assume that the limits of what could be decently said in newspapers could hardly be entirely independent from what could be decently said amongst strangers. In private circles, of course, one was free to transgress – but one knew, too, that one was transgressing. One might go so far as to say that antisemitism remained somewhat of a 'forbidden' language used only by those who prided themselves on their defiance of good social manners (which is not to say that there were not many of those, both in the public and the private arena).

This conclusion must by necessity remain tentative and represent an approximation formulated to challenge another approximation that conjures up a far more casually antisemitic society. The quotations that open this chapter give some indication about how complex a phenomenon antisemitism really was in this Austria in the age of Franz Joseph. On the one hand we have Arthur Schnitzler's indictment, formulated in the context of a novel dealing with Zionism, antisemitism and Viennese Jew-gentile relations, that even the most philosemitic contemporary was familiar with antisemitic language, and would find him- or herself tapping into this language when angered.[20] The quotation, however, also points to a recognition on the part of this person that such language was somehow wrong and shameful, and should perhaps not be uttered aloud, but rather only thought to oneself. As such the statement might equally be interpreted as a fair description of many 'white' Englishmen's or Americans' relationship to racial slurs. Tomáš Masaryk's confession, made to the Czech novelst and playwright Karel Čapek, that a rural antisemitism, which he absorbed in his childhood years may have remained ingrained in him despite his rational rejection thereof, does much to support this characterisation of the nature of antisemitism as something that can be at one and the same time ubiquitous and shameful.[21] Stefan Zweig's denial that antisemitism managed to cast any shadow over his life – made in the context of a nostalgic declaration of love to an age gone past and as such not entirely trustworthy – might suggest that it was at least possible to treat antisemitism as something that happened elsewhere and involved specific people rather than everyone.[22] Far be it from this book to reduce this complexity to some new formula about the nature of Viennese antisemitism before the First World War. All that can be stated with certainty is that, of all the people enjoying their daily dose of crime in the papers, only those who identified themselves as antisemites by their choice of newspaper would come across any narrative of Jewish crime. For everyone else – i.e. the vast majority of the population – this narrative did not exist.

I do not believe that this is a comforting conclusion, and I hope it will not be misconstrued as an attempt to 'whitewash' Vienna in 1900 in any way. If my book does suggest a rethinking of the easy penetration of the masses by casual antisemitic thought, this has to put into the context of the horrendous crimes Austrians committed a generation further on. Antisemitism flourished after the war, helped along by the tremendous agitation that met the influx of Galician war refugees into Vienna and Lower Austria, with all the social pressures that the displacement of tens of thousands of hungry, destitute people implies.[23] Certainly in the universities antisemitism achieved a new flowering amongst the student population.[24] By the early 1930s the electoral success of the Nazi party was to a good part due to voters with middle-class, even intellectual, backgrounds: civil servants, architects and business men.[25] The *Anschluss* movement and the Great Depression further fostered antisemitic sentiments. It remains astonishing, nevertheless, that, when Hitler's hatred of Jews turned into an exterminatory policy, Austrians – some eight percent of the Reich's population – should (according to one count) furnish almost fourteen percent of SS-members, forty per cent of the staff in death camps, and three-quarters of camp commandants.[26] It is equally astonishing how many 'ordinary' Austrians quietly or enthusiastically witnessed, collaborated in and actively benefited from the theft of Jewish property. One must either assume that the Nazi propaganda machinery had finally made convinced antisemites out of many sections of society, or – no less disturbingly – that the tens and hundreds of thousands of Austrians who, directly or indirectly, played their part in the Holocaust were willing to use antisemitic phrases to rationalise away their crimes out of pure opportunism – i.e. that much of the population were never radicalised but humiliated, beat, robbed, expelled and finally killed Jews anyway (or tolerated this humiliation, beating, robbery, expulsion and murder).[27] Vienna 1900 remains at the beginning of this journey into the abyss because of the simple fact that it gave rise to successful articulations of modern antisemitism that served both as models and as germ cells for later incarnations. All that can be at dispute is how widely antisemitic ideas were accepted; through a scholarly exploration of this dispute we can but hope to better understand the nature, content and modes of dissemination of an ideology that so deeply and painfully marked the modern world.

The narrative of Jewish criminals, finally, both continued in the Nazi period and underwent significant modifications. While notions of Jews as malign financial and criminal geniuses, as manipulators of public opinion and so on, remained a mainstay of antisemitic discourse, they were joined by a much more racially reductive vision of Jewish crime that cancelled out any need to pursue the strategies of narrating crimes found in the Viennese papers. The Hilsner case, for instance, was re-narrated in a special edition of the National Socialist *Stürmer* on the occasion of the invasion of the Czechoslovak Republic in 1938.[28] Here the trial was embedded in the framework of race science: much of the paper was dedicated to a racial classification of Slavs and Jews (complete with photographic evidence). In the discussion of the Hilsner case itself, all possible ambiguities had been removed: Hilsner's co-conspirators were named, the question of motive solved (murder with the aim of gaining blood), a timetable for the ritual slaughter was provided. 'Significant description' was unnecessary when all the facts of the case were clear and neatly conformed to the ideology of race. While German criminologists continued to question whether or not criminals should be regarded as different from the general population well into the 1930s,[29] the Nazis systematically privileged those researchers whose narrative of crime was compatible with their racial vision of the world.[30] It was in this climate that, in 1936, Johann von Leers presented a paper on 'The criminality of Jewry' at a conference on the theme of 'Jews in legal studies', arguing that Jews historically formed a 'criminal counter-race' i.e. were constitutionally criminal.[31] At the same time this narrative of a criminal race coexisted with one much closer to the pre-War conceptualisation of

Jewish crime this book has analysed. Thus, at the very same conference, another contributor, one Max Mikorey, presented a paper entitled 'Jewry in Criminal Psychology'.[32] Mikorey's thesis was that the Jews, starting with Lombroso, had come up with the false science of criminal psychology in order to sabotage their host states' justice systems whose moral authority in punishing criminals was undercut by the notion that criminality was a mental or physiological disorder. He also implicated psychoanalysis and Jewish statisticians of crime in this Jewish attempt to destroy society through bad science. Here the antisemitic fantasy of Jewish manipulators aiming at the destruction of law and order through their fostering of crime was reiterated, and the Jews' modernity (underlined by their prominence in the social sciences) rather than their race-nature was indicted. In the absence of any semblance of a public sphere, it was no longer possible to voice a challenge to either of the two narratives; the tale of the Jewish criminal ruled supreme until the short-lived Thousand Years Reich came to an end.

Notes

1. Schnitzler, *Der Weg ins Freie*, p. 234.
2. Karel Čapek, *President Masaryk Tells His Story* (London 1934), p. 29.
3. Stefan Zweig, *The World of Yesterday, An Autobiography* (New York 1943), p. 25.
4. A good example for imported detective fiction of the most populist sort are the Nick Carter stories, originally published in New York (from 1886 onwards): Various authors, *Nick Carter, Amerika's grösster Detektiv* (Vienna n. d.). German-language Sherlock Holmes stories that claimed to be translations but were in fact clever works of imitation and pastiche were also in mass circulation, most famously *Detective Sherlock Holmes und seine weltberühmten Abenteuer* in more than two hundred instalments (Berlin 1907–1911).
5. Cf. Wiener, *Reconstructing*, p. 224. Note that even crude stories would at times contain explicit discussions of detective technique. See for instance Willy Grünes's *Der Detektive* [sic], a serialised novel in the *Deutsches Volksblatt* (late June 1909). One should also note that detective novels would, before long, start to make explicit reference to Hans Gross: fictional detectives would consult his *Handbuch* for advice, while fictional criminals would do the same in order to dream up some particularly devious ploy. (Cf. Green, *Mountain*, p. 21). One should also note that the one near-contemporary literary masterpiece that was, in parts, organised around the theme of crime, Musil's *Der Mann ohne Eigenschaften*, explored crime by focusing on the criminal's trial and the trial's reception by the public, and was in fact based on newspaper trial reports of an actual crime. Robert Musil, *Der Mann ohne Eigenschaften* Vol. 1 (Berlin 1930), Book 1, Chapter 18 and *passim*. Cf. Karl Corino, 'Ein Mörder macht Literaturgeschichte, Florian Großrubatscher, ein Modell für Musils Moosbrugger', in: Josef Strutz (ed.), *Musil Studien* 11 (Munich 1983), pp. 130–47. See also: Walter Fanta, *Die Entstehungsgeschichte des 'Mannes ohne Eigenschaften' von Robert Musil* (Vienna 2000), pp. 143 ff. Musil's novel was first published in 1930, but was in large parts written much closer to the period here considered.
6. For example Hugo Friedländer, *Interessante Kriminalprozesse von Kulturhistorischer Bedeutung, Darstellung merkwürdiger Strafrechtsfälle aus Gegenwart und Jüngstvergangenheit nach eigenem Erlebnissen* 10 Vols. (Berlin 1910–1914); Edmund Otto

Ehrenfreund (ed.), *Der Wiener Pitaval, Eine Sammlung der interessantesten Wiener Kriminalfälle des letzten Jahrhunderts von Ubald Tartaruga* 4 Vols. (Vienna 1913); Gustav Roscher, R. Frank and H. Schmidt (eds), *Der Pitaval der Gegenwart, Almanach interessanter Straffälle* 8 Vols. (Leipzig 1904–1914). On Gross's approval of such collections, see: Hans Gross, 'Buchbesprechung: Der Pitaval der Gegenwart (Leipzig 1907)', in: *Archiv* 28 (1907), p. 395. On the Pitaval tradition, see also: Hügel, *Untersuchungsrichter*, pp. 83–6.

7. Lindau, *Ausflüge*, pp. 18 ff.; 53 ff.; 75 ff; 106.

8. Max Winter, *Im dunkelsten Wien* (Vienna 1904); Emil Kläger, *Durch die Wiener Quartiere des Elends und Verbrechens, Ein Wanderbuch aus dem Jenseits* (Vienna 1908). See also: Ernst Lohsing, 'Buchbesprechung: Emil Kläger, *Durch die Wiener Quartiere des Elends und Verbrechens, Ein Wanderbuch aus dem Jenseits* (Vienna 1908)', in: *Archiv* 32 (1909), pp. 349–50; Hamann, *Hitlers Wien*, p. 216. In flavor these projects are comparable to Hans Ostwald's contemporary exploration of Berlin, especially: Hans Ostwald, *Dunkle Winkel in Berlin, Großstadt Dokumente Band 1* (Berlin 1904).

9. Max Winter was in charge of the *Arbeiter-Zeitung*'s *Gerichtsaal* column. Cf. Kunz, 'Die Geschichte der *Arbeiter-Zeitung*', p. 79. On contemporary socialist explanations of crime more generally, see: Grassmann, *Weg der Kriminologie*, pp. 115–44.

10. The photographs were supplied by his colleague Hermann Drawe. Hamann is mistaken when she attributes the photographs to Kläger himself (*Hitler's Wien*, p. 216).

11. Kläger, *Wiener Quartiere*, pp. 115–32.

12. Ibid., pp. 83–92.

13. One could add that Winter's and Kläger's project found a literary echo in Schnitzler's *Der Weg ins Freie* in which a socialist activist proposed to investigate Vienna's impoverished underbelly by similarly investigative means. Schnitzler, *Der Weg ins Freie*, p. 245.

14. The relationship between scientific and popular knowledge should not necessarily be viewed according to a 'trickling down' model. Recent sociological work on narratives of the 'eastern European/Russian Mafia' for instance, suggests that scientific narratives are as likely to mimic journalistic ones as to anticipate them. Cf.: Arno Pilgram, 'Wirklichkeitskonstruktionen'.

15. Cf. Stephen Knight, *Crime Fiction 1800–2000, Detection, Death, Diversity* (New York 2004), pp. 146–52.

16. *Extrablatt*, 14 February 1882, evening edition, p. 1.

17. This reinterpretation of neurasthenia became particularly fashionable after 1900. Cf. Radkau, *Zeitalter*, pp. 264 ff. Radkau also argues that the supposed propensity of Jews for neurasthenia was not used to stigmatize them as 'different' (p. 334).

18. *Kikeriki*'s only comment on the case highlighted Steiner's status as a prostitute, not as a Jew. *Kikeriki*, 23 February 1882, p. 4 (cartoon).

19. On antisemitic reactions to the Steiner case, see: *ÖW*, 22 September 1899, p. 695, in which the false accusation of Steiner is discussed in the context of the Hilsner trial.

20. See the discussion of Schnitzler and his views on antisemitism in: Schorske, *Fin-de-Siècle Vienna*, pp. 10–15; Rolf-Peter Janz and Klaus Laermann, *Arthur Schnitzler: Zur Diagnose des Wiener Bürgertums im Fin-de-Siècle* (Stuttgart 1977), pp. 155–74; Wistrich, *Jews of Vienna*, p. 607; Norbert Abels, *Sicherheit ist nirgends, Judentum und Aufklärung bei Arthur Schnitzler* (Königstein 1982). On the relation of Viennese Jewish novelists and playwrights and antisemitism more generally, see: Ruth Kluger, 'The theme of antisemitism in the work of Austrian Jews', in: Sander Gilman and Steven T. Katz (eds), *Anti-Semitism in Times of Crisis* (New York 1991), pp. 173–87.

21. Beller, 'Masaryk', pp. 56–7.

22. On Zweig's steadfast faith in enlightenment humanism which shaped his nostalgic view of the pre-war period, see: Leo Botstein, 'Stefan Zweig and the Illusion of the Jewish European', in: Marion Sonnenfeld (ed.), *Stefan Zweig* (Albany 1983), pp. 90–2.

23. Pauley, *Prejudice*, pp. 67–9, 81–3.
24. Ibid., pp. 89–101.
25. Gerhard Botz, 'The Changing Patterns of Social Support for Austrian National Socialism', in: S.U. Larsen, Bernt Havel and Jan P. Myklebust (eds), *Who were the Fascists?, Social Roots of European Fascism* (Bergen 1980), pp. 202–23. See also: Adam Wandruszka, 'Österreichs politische Struktur: Die Entwicklung der Parteien und politischen Bewegungen', in: Heinrich Benedikt (ed.), *Geschichte der Republik Österreich* (Vienna 1954), p. 405.
26. Pauley, *Prejudice*, p. 297.
27. Simon Wiesenthal famously estimated that Austrians could be held responsible for killing three million Jews. For a discussion of the importance of ideology vis-à-vis economic opportunism (and the interaction of the two factors) for an understanding of Austrian antisemitism under the Nazi regime, see: Gerhard Botz, 'Ausgrenzung, Beraubung und Vernichtung, Das Ende des Wiener Judentums unter der nationalsozialistischen Herrschaft (1938–1945)', in: Botz *et al.*, *Zerstörte Kultur*, pp. 315–39.
28. *Der Stürmer*, Sondernummer November 1938.
29. For the existence of non-deterministic narratives of criminality during the late 1920s, see for instance Franz Exner's sociological analysis of wartime criminality in Austria. Exner clearly assumed rational criminals who were merely reacting to socio-economic hardship. (Franz Exner, *Krieg und Kriminalität in Österreich* (Vienna 1927)). Exner – like Gross – also maintained that one could not study the criminal without studying the police, prosecutors and judges involved. He called for a sociology of criminological knowledge alongside any criminological inquiry (Franz Exner, 'Kriminalsoziologie', in: Alexander Elster and Heinrich Lingemann (eds.), *Handwörterbuch der Kriminologie* (Berlin 1933–36), vol. 2, 10–11). As for the 1930s: as late as 1936 to 1937, Hellmuth Mayer maintained that it was not degenerates but often quite talented, socially underprivileged individuals who were prone to crime. (Hellmuth Mayer, *Das Strafrecht des deutschen Volkes* (Stuttgart 1936); Hellmuth Mayer, 'Kriminalpolitik als Geisteswissenschaft,' in: *Zeitschrift für die gesamte Strafrechtswissenschaft* 57 (1937), pp. 1–27.)
30. Wetzell, *Inventing*, p. 182.
31. Johann von Leers, 'Die Kriminalität des Judentums,' in: *Das Judentum in der Rechtswissenschaft, Band 3: Judentum und Verbrechen* (Berlin 1936), pp. 5–60. Cf.: Wetzell, *Inventing*, pp. 187–9.
32. Max Mikorey, 'Das Judentum in der Kriminalpsychologie,' *Das Judentum in der Rechtswissenschaft, Band 3: Judentum und Verbrechen* (Berlin 1936), pp. 61–7. Cf.: Wetzell, *Inventing*, pp. 187–9.

BIBLIOGRAPHY

Unpublished Primary Sources

PaHS, Kriminaldokumentation K14, H 14A, B14.
PaHS, Akte 'Polizeiwesen 1900–1906'.
SaW, Gerichtsakte, Box unnumbered, Fasz. 92, No. 1185 (Eichinger 1895).
SaW, Gerichtsakte, Box A 11, Fasz. 93–4 (2 Vols.) (Schapira 1895).
SaW, Gerichtsakte, Box A 11, Fasz. 108 (Sosztarich 1899).
SaW, Gerichtsakte, Box A 11, Fasz. 126, No. 8392 (Kohn 1899).
SaW, Gerichtsakte, Box A 11, Fasz. 177–8, No. 2780 (7 Vols.) (Kubowski 1905).
SaW, Gerichtsakte, Box A 11, Fasz. 177, No. 2780 Vol. 2 (Reiter 1905).
SaW, Gerichtsakte, Box A 11, Fasz. 176, No. 1162 (Nemecek 1905).
SaW, Gerichtsakte, Box A 11, Fasz. 200–1, No. 6372 (6 Vols.) (Riehl 1907).
SaW, Gerichtsakte, Box A 11, Fasz. 257, No. 5782 (Klingenberger 1909).
ÖS, Justizakten, VI – l – Schweiz – Beer.
ÖS, Justizakten, VI H 4652 (Hilsner) (mostly lost).
ÖS, Justizakten, I R I 5 (Hilsner).
ÖS, Justizakten, VI – l – Frankreich – K 11 (Klein) (mostly lost).
ÖS, Druckschriften IV Allg 1898–1909 (3038–50) Pressedelikte.

Published Primary Sources

a) Periodicals, Newspapers, Journals, Parliamentary Documents

Allgemeine Zeitschrift für Psychiatrie und psychiatrisch-gerichtliche Medizin
Arbeiter-Zeitung
Archiv für Criminalanthropologie und Criminalistik
Der Stürmer
Deutsches Volksblatt
Die Fackel
Die Welt
Die Zeit
Illustrierte Kronenzeitung
Illustriertes Wiener Extrablatt
Monatsschrift für Kriminalpsychologie und Strafrechtsreform

Neue Freie Presse
Neues Wiener Tagblatt
Österreichische Kriminalzeitung
Österreichische Wochenschrift
Ostdeutsche Rundschau
Polizei-Anzeiger
Reichspost
Reichswehr
Stenografisches Protokoll über die Sitzungen des Hauses der Abgeordneten des österreichischen Reichsrats in den Jahren 1892 und 1893, 9. Session, Vol. 7 (Vienna 1893), 11 November 1892.
Wiener Bilder, Illustriertes Familienblatt
Wiener Illustrierte Kriminalzeitung
Wiener Tagblatt
Zeitschrift für Demographie und Statistik der Juden
Zeitschrift für die gesamte Strafrechtswissenschaft
Zentral-Polizei-Blatt

b) Monographs, Pamphlets and Novels

Altschul, Theodor, *Hypnotismus und Suggestion im Leben und in der Erziehung* (Vienna 1900).

Anonymous, *Der Konitzer Mord, Ein Beitrag zur Klärung* (Breslau 1900).

Aschaffenburg, Gustav, *Das Verbrechen und seine Bekämpfung: Kriminalpsychologie für Mediziner, Juristen und Soziologen, ein Beitrag zur Reform der Strafgesetzgebung* (Heidelberg 1903).

_____ and Dr H. Partenheimer (eds), *Bericht über den VII. Internationalen Kongreß für Kriminalanthropologie* (Heidelberg 1912).

Auředníček, Zdenko, *Materiale zum Prozess gegen Leopold Hilsner, Vorgelegt der k.k. General-Prokuratur* (Vienna 1910).

Austerlitz, Fritz, *Pressefreiheit und Presserecht, Eine Studie über den Preßgesetzentwurf* (Vienna 1902).

Austerlitz, R., *Suggestion, Roman aus der Berliner Gesellschaft*, Hölzer's Roman-bibliothek Vol. 42 (Vienna n.d.).

Avé-Lallement, Friedrich Christian Benedikt, *Das Deutsche Gaunertum in seiner social-politischen, literarischen und linguistischen Ausbildung zu seinem heutigen Bestande*, 4 Vols. (Leipzig 1858–1862).

_____ *Physiologie der deutschen Polizei* (Leipzig 1882).

Baer, Abraham-Adolph, *Der Verbrecher in anthropologischer Beziehung* (Leipzig 1893).

Bechterew, W. von, *Suggestion und ihre sociale Bedeutung*, translated by R. Weinberg (Leipzig 1899).

Benedikt, Moriz, *Anatomische Studien von Verbrechergehirnen für Anthropologen, Mediziner, Juristen und Psychologen* (Vienna 1879).

Berg, Alexander, *Judenbordelle, Enthüllungen aus dunklen Häusern* (Berlin 1892).

_____ *Judenhyänen vor dem Strafgericht zu Lemberg, ein bestätigender Nachtrag zu seiner Schrift 'Judenbordelle'* (Berlin 1893).

Bernheim, Hyppolite, *Die Suggestion und ihre Heilwirkung*, translated by Sigmund Freud, ed. M. Kahane (second edition) (Leipzig 1896).

Bertillon, Alphonse, *Identification anthropométrique, instructions signalétiques* (Paris 1893 [1885]).

_____ *Das anthropometrische Signalement*, translated by V. Sury, (Bern 1895).

Börner, Wilhelm, *Die Schundliteratur und ihre Bekämpfung* (Vienna 1908).

Bresler, Johannes, *Die Simulation von Geistesstörungen und Epilepsie* (Halle 1904).

Brunner, Karl, *Unser Volk in Gefahr, Ein Kampfruf gegen die Schundliteratur* (Dusseldorf 1909).

Bulowa, J.A., *Zum Polnaer Ritualmordprozess im Stadium vor dem Zweiten Urteile. Ein Brief an die Herren Professoren der gerichtlichen Medizin und an alle ehrlichen Menschen überhaupt* (Berlin 1900).

_____ *Der Polnaer Ritualmordprozess* (Berlin 1900).

Burckhard, Max, *Der Entwurf eines neuen Pressegesetzes* (Vienna 1902).

Collins, Wilkie, *The Moonstone* (London 1998 [1868]).

Das Comite zur Abwehr antisemitischer Angriffe in Berlin (eds), *Die Kriminalität der Juden in Deutschland* (Berlin 1896).

Diez, H., *Das Zeitungswesen* (Leipzig 1919).

Dostoevsky, Fyodor, *Demons*, translated by Richard Pevear and Larissa Volokhonsky, (London 1994 [1871]).

Drähms, August, *The Criminal, His Person and Environment* (New York 1900).

Ehrenfreund, Edmund Otto (ed.), *Der Wiener Pitaval, Eine Sammlung der interessantesten Wiener Kriminalfälle des letzten Jahrhunderts von Ubald Tartaruga*, 4 Vols. (Vienna 1913).

Elster, Alexander and Heinrich Lingemannn (eds), *Handwörterbuch der Kriminologie* (Berlin 1933–1936).

Exner, Franz, *Krieg und Kriminalität in Österreich* (Vienna 1927).

Forel, August, *Der Hypnotismus: seine psycho-physiologische, medicinische, strafrechtliche Bedeutung und seine Handhabung* (Stuttgart 1891).

_____ *Der Hypnotismus und die suggestive Psychotherapie. Vierte umgearbeitete Auflage* (Stuttgart 1902 [1889]).

Fosdick, Raymond, *European Police Systems* (Montclair 1969 [1914]).

Frey, Thomas, (a.k.a. Fritsch, Theodor) *Antisemiten-Katechismus, Eine Zusammenstellung des wichtigsten Materials zum Verständnis der Judenfrage* (sixth edition, Leipzig 1888).

Friedländer, Hugo, *Interessante Kriminalprozesse von Kulturhistorischer Bedeutung, Darstellung merkwürdiger Strafrechtsfälle aus Gegenwart und Jüngstvergangenheit nach eigenem Erlebnissen* 10 Vols. (Berlin 1910–1914).

Fröhlich, Rudolph Alois, *Die gefährlichen Klassen Wiens, Darstellung ihres Entstehens, ihrer Verbindungen, ihrer Taktik, ihrer Sitten und Gewohnheiten und ihrer Sprache. Mit belehrenden Winken über Gaunerkniffe und einem Wörterbuch der Gaunersprache* (Vienna 1851).

Fuld, Ludwig, *Das jüdische Verbrecherthum, Eine Studie über den Zusammenhang zwischen Religion und Kriminalität* (Leipzig 1885).

Galton, Francis, *Inquiries into Human Faculty and its Development* (New York 1883, reprinted Bristol, England 1998).

_____ 'Photographic Composites', in: *The Photographic News* 29 (17–24 April 1885), pp. 234–45.

_____ *Fingerprints* (London 1892).

Garr, Max, *Die Inseratsteuer* (Vienna 1909).

Gentz, W., 'Berufsverbrecher', in: E. Bunke (ed.), *Deutsches Gefängniswesen, Ein Handbuch* (Berlin 1928), pp. 334–52.

Gross, Alfred, 'Kriminalpsychologische Tatbestabdsforschung', in: *Juristisch-Psychiatrische Grenzfragen* 5, 7 (1907), pp. 1–56.

Gross, Hans, *Criminalpsychologie* (Graz 1898).

_____ *Handbuch für Untersuchungsrichter als System der Kriminalistik (Dritte Vermehrte Auflage)* (Graz 1899).

_____ *Encyclopädie der Kriminalistik* (Leipzig 1901).

_____ *Gesammelte Kriminalistische Aufsätze* Vol. 1 (Leipzig 1902).

_____ *Gesammelte Kriminalistische Aufsätze* Vol. 2 (Leipzig 1908).

Guglia, Eugen, *Wien, Ein Führer durch Stadt und Umgebung, mit 6 Karten, 11 Plänen und 15 Grundrissen* (Vienna 1908).

Hanisch, Reinhold, 'I was Hitler's buddy, Part II', in: *New Republic* (12 April 1939), pp. 271–2.

Heldt, *Die Schundliteratur* (Leipzig 1908).

Hellwig, Albert, *Ritualmord aund Aberglaube* (Minden i.W. n.d.).

_____ 'Blutmord und Ritualaberglauben' in: *Der Grenzbote 77* (1913), pp. 149–57.

Herz, Hugo, *Verbrechen und Verbrechertum in Österreich, Kritische Untersuchungen über Zusammenhänge von Wirtschaft und Verbrechen* (Tübingen 1908).

Hitler, Adolf, *Mein Kampf* (Munich 1943 [1925]).

Jacobs, Joseph, 'The Jewish Type, and Galton's Composite Photographs,' in: *The Photographic News* 29 (April 24, 1885), pp. 234–45.

Jaeger, Johannes (ed.), *Hinter Kerkermauern, Autobiographien und Selbstbekenntnisse, Aufsätze und Gedichte von Verbrechern, Ein Beitrag zur Kriminalpsychologie, Mit einem Vor- und Nachwort von Univ.-Prof Dr Hans Gross* (Berlin 1906).

Jagemann, Ludwig von, *Handbuch der gerichtlichen Untersuchungskunde* (Heidelberg 1838).

Jewish Encyclopaedia (New York 1901–1906).

Jung, Carl Gustav, 'Die psychologische Diagnose des Tatbestandes', in: *Juristisch-psychiatrische Grenzfragen, Zwanglose Abhandlungen*, ed. A. Finger, A. Hoche and J. Bresler, Bd. 4, Heft 3 (Halle 1906), pp. 1–47.

'Junius' (pseudonym), *Das Judenthum und die Tagespresse: Ein Mahnwort in ernster Stunde* (Leipzig 1879).

Kant, Immanuel, *Critique of Practical Reason and Other Works on the Theory of Ethics*, translated by T. K. Abbott (London 1879 [1788]).

Kisch, Egon Erwin, 'Zum Tode Leopold Hilsners', in: *Berliner Morgenpost*, 16 Jan 1928.

Kläger, Emil, *Durch die Wiener Quartiere des Elends und Verbrechens, Ein Wanderbuch aus dem Jenseits* (Vienna 1908).

Kočmata, Karl F., *Jugend und Schundliteratur, Eine energisches Wort gegen systematische Volksvergiftung* (Vienna n.d. (1908?)).

Krafft-Ebing, Richard von, *Grundzüge der Kriminalpsychologie* (Erlangen 1872).

_____ *Psychopathia Sexualis, Mit besonderer Berücksichtigung der conträren Sexualempfindungen, Klinisch-forensische Studie, 8. verbesserte und theilweise vermehrte Auflage* (Stuttgart 1893 [1886]).

Kraus, Karl, *Sittlichkeit und Kriminalität* (Frankfurt am Main 1987 [1908]).

_____ *Die Chinesische Mauer* (Munich 1964 [1914]).

Kreuzer, M., 'Ueber anthropologische, physiologische und pathologische Eigenheiten der Juden', in: *Die Welt* 27–9 (5, 12 and 19 July, 1901).

Kubin, Alfred, *Die andere Seite* (Reinbek bei Hamburg 1995 [1909]).

Lange, Johannes, *Verbrechen als Schicksal: Studien an kriminellen Zwillingen* (Leipzig 1929).

Le Bon, Gustave, *Psychologie des foules* (Paris 1896).

Leers, Johann von, 'Die Kriminalität des Judentums', in: *Das Judentum in der Rechtswissenschaft, Band 3: Judentum und Verbrechen* (Berlin 1936), pp. 5–60.

Leppin, Paul, 'Das Gespenst der Judenstadt', in: Oskar Wiener (ed.), *Deutsche Dichter in Prag* (Vienna 1919), pp. 197–202.

Lichtenberg, Georg Christoph, *Schriften und Briefe* Vol. III, (ed.) Wolfgang Promies (Frankfurt am Main 1994).

Lichtenstein, Albert, *Der Kriminalroman (Grenzfragen der Literatur und Medizin Heft 7)* (Munich 1908).

Lindau, Paul, *Ausflüge ins Kriminalistische* (Munich 1909).

Liszt, Franz von, 'Das Problem der Kriminalität der Juden', in: *Festschrift für die juristische Fakultät in Giessen zum Universitäts-Jubiläum*, hrsg. Reinhard Frank (Giessen 1907).

Lombroso, Cesare, *L'uomo delinquente studiato in rapporto alla antropologia, alla medecina legale, ed alle discipline carcerarie* (Milan 1876).

_____ *L'antisemitismo e le science moderne* (Turin 1894).

_____ *Der Antisemitismus und die Juden im Lichte der modernen Wissenschaft*, translated by H. Kurella (Leipzig 1894).

_____ *Der Verbrecher (Homo Delinquens) in anthropologischer, ärztlicher und juristischer Beziehung* 3 Vols., translated by M. O. Fraenkel (Hamburg 1890–1896).

_____ *L'uomo delinquente* Vol. I–III, ed. F. Bocca (Turin 1896–1897).

_____ *Die Ursachen und Bekämpfung des Verbrechens*, translated by H. Kurella and E. Jentsch (Berlin 1902).

_____ *Crime, Its Causes and Remedies*, translated by Henry P. Horton (London 1911 [1896–1897]).

Lombroso, Cesare and Guglielmo Ferrero, *Criminal Woman, the Prostitute and the Normal Woman*, translated by and with a new introduction by Nicole Hahn Rafter and Mary Gibson (Durham, NC 2004).

Masaryk, Tomáš G., *Die Notwendigkeit der Revision des Polnaer Prozesses* (Vienna 1899).

_____ *Die Bedeutung des Polnaer Verbrechens für den Ritualmordaberglauben* (Berlin 1900).

Mayer, Hellmuth, *Das Strafrecht des deutschen Volkes* (Stuttgart 1936).

Mexin, S., *Der Mädchenhandel* (Basel 1904).

Meyrink, Gustav, *Der Golem* (Berlin 1998 [1915]).

_____ *Der weiße Dominikaner* (Munich 1978 [1921]).

Mikorey, Max, 'Das Judentum in der Kriminalpsychologie', in: *Das Judentum in der Rechtswissenschaft, Band 3: Judentum und Verbrechen* (Berlin 1936), pp. 61–7.

Möbius, Paul Julius August, *Ueber Entartung* (Wiesbaden 1900).

_____ *Geschlecht und Entartung* (Halle 1903).

Montane, H., *Die Prostitution in Wien* (Vienna 1925).

Musil, Robert, *Der Mann ohne Eigenschaften* Vol. 1 (Berlin 1930).

Näcke, Paul, *Verbrechen und Wahnsinn beim Weibe mit Ausblicken auf die Kriminalanthropologie überhaupt, Klinisch-Statistische, Anthropologisch-Biologische und Craniologische Untersuchungen* (Vienna 1894).

_____ (ed.), *Die Gehirnoberfläche von Paralytischen, Ein Atlas von 49 Abbildungen nach Zeichnungen* (Leipzig 1909).

Nathan, Paul, *Der Process von Tisza-Eszlar: Ein Antisemitisches Culturbild* (Berlin 1892).

Niceforo, A. and Heinrich Lindenau, *Die Krimialpolizei und ihre Hilfswissenschaften* (Groß-Lichterfelde-Ost 1910).

Nordau, Max, *Entartung* (Berlin 1886).

_____ *Die conventionellen Lügen der Kulturmenschheit* (Leipzig 1889 [1883]).

Nussbaum, Arthur, *Der Polnaer Ritualmordprozess* (Berlin 1906).

_____ 'The "Ritual-Murder" Trial of Polna', in: *Historica Judaica* 9 (1947–1948), pp. 57–74.

Ostwald, Hans, *Dunkle Winkel in Berlin, Großstadt Dokumente Band 1* (Berlin 1904).

Paul-Schiff, Maximiliam, *Der Prozess Hilsner* (Vienna 1908).

Petting, Otto, *Wiens antisemitische Presse* (Vienna 1896).

Ploetz, Alfred, *Die Tüchtigkeit unserer Rasse und der Schutz der Schwachen* (Berlin 1895).

Pollak, Heinrich, *Dreißig Jahre aus dem Leben eines Journalisten* (Vienna 1894).

Přelíčení s Hilsnerem před porotou v Kutné Hoře pro vraždu v Polné: Doslovný otisk stenogrfických protokolů (Prague 1899).

Roscher, Gustav, *Großstadtpolizei, Ein praktisches Handbuch der deutschen Polizei* (Hamburg 1912).

Roscher, Gustav, R. Frank and H. Schmidt (eds), *Der Pitaval der Gegenwart, Almanach interessanter Straffälle* 8 Vols. (Leipzig 1904–1914).

Ruppin, A. 'Der Rassenstolz der Juden', *Zeitschrift für Demographie und Statistik der Juden* 6 (1910), pp. 88–92.

Schäffle, Albert Eberhard Friedrich, *Bau und Leben des sozialen Körpers* (Tübingen 1881).

Schimmer, Karl Eduard, *Wien in Wort und Bild, Illustrierter Führer durch Wien, seine Sehenswürdigkeiten und Umgebungen, mit 25 Illustrationen und einem collorierten Plan* (Vienna 1900).

Schnitzler, Arthur, *Der Weg ins Freie* (Frankfurt am Main 1990 [1908]).

_____ *My Youth in Vienna*, translated by Catherine Hutter (New York 1979).

Schrank, Josef, *Die Prostitution in Wien in historischer, administrativer und hygienischer Beziehung*, 2 Vols. (Vienna 1886).

_____ 'Prostitution in Madrid', in: *Deutsche Vierteljahrsschrift für öffentliche Gesundheitspflege* 31, 3 (1889).

_____ *Die Regelung der Prostitution in Kairo* (Vienna 1890).

_____ *Die amtlichen Vorschriften, betreffend die Prostitution in Wien in ihrer administrativen, sanitären und strafgerechtlichen Anwendungen* (Vienna 1899).

_____ *Der Mädchenhandel und seine Bekämpfung* (Vienna 1904).

Schrenck-Notzing, Albert von, *Über Suggestion und Erinnerungsfälschung im Berchthold Prozeß* (Leipzig 1897).

_____ *Kriminalpsychologische und Psychopathologische Studien, Gesammelte Aufsätze aus den Gebieten der Psychopathia Sexualis, der gerichtlichen Psychiatrie und der Suggestionslehre* (Leipzig 1902).

Schulze, Ernst, *Die Schundliteratur, Ihr Wesen, Ihre Folgen, Ihre Bekämpfung* (Halle 1911).

Schwenken, K., *Notizen über die berüchtigsten jüdischen Gauner und Spitzbuben welche sich gegenwärtig in Deutschland und an dessen Grenzen herumtreiben nebst genauer Beschreibung ihrer Person, nach Criminalakten und sonstigen zuverlässigen Quellen bearbeitet und in alphabetischer Ordnung zusammengestellt* (Marburg 1820).

Schwer, Hans Arnold, *Die Wahrheit über die Morde in Polna* (Vienna 1900).

Seidl, Joseph, *Der Jude des 19. Jahrhunderts, oder warum sind wir Antisemiten?* (Munich 1900).

Sello, Erich, *Die Hauprozesse und ihre Lehren* (Berlin 1908).

_____ *Zur Psychologie der cause célèbre* (Berlin 1910).

_____ *Die Irrtümer der Strafjustiz, Erster Band: Todesstrafe und lebenslängliches Zuchthaus in richterlichen Fehlsprüchen neuerer Zeit* (Berlin 1911).

Stern, William L., *Zur Psychologie der Aussage, Experimentelle Untersuchungen über Erinnerungstreue* (Berlin 1903).

_____ *Beiträge zur Psychologie der Zeugenaussage, Mit besonderer Berücksichtigung von Problemen der Rechtspflege, Pädagogik, Psychiatrie und Geschichtsforschung* (Berlin 1904).

_____ *Die Aussage als geistige Leistung und als Verhörsprodukt, Experimentelle Schüleruntersuchungen* (Leipzig 1904).

_____ *Psychologische Tatbestandsdiagnostik, Beiträge zur Psychologie der Aussage* 2 Vols. (Leipzig 1903–6).

Stoll, Otto, *Suggestion und Hypnotismus in der Völkerpsychologie* (Leipzig 1904).

Thiele, A. F., *Die jüdischen Gauner in Deutschland, ihre Taktik, ihre Eigenthümlichkeiten und ihre Sprache nebst ausführlichen Nachrichten des in Deutschland und an dessen Grenzen sich aufhaltenden berüchtigten jüdischen Gauner, Nach Kriminalakten und sonstigen zuverlässigen Quellen bearbeitet und zunächst praktischen Criminal- und Polizeibeamten gewidmet, 1. Band, 2. Auflage* (Berlin 1842 [1842]).

Tönnies, Ferdinand, *Kritik der öffentlichen Meinung* (Berlin 1922).

Toužil, Gustav, *Polna 29. 3. 1899. Ermordung der Agnes Hruza und der sensationelle Prozess Hilsner vor dem Kuttenberger Schwurgerichte* (Kuttenberg 1899).

Various authors, *Nick Carter, Amerika's grösster Detektiv* (Vienna, n.d.).

Verax, Severus, *Die öffentliche Meinung von Wien. Wiener Pressegeschichten* (Zurich 1899).

Wassermann, Rudolf, *Beruf, Konfession und Verbrechen. Eine Studie über die Kriminalität der Juden in Vergangenheit und Gegenwart* (Munich 1907).

Weber, Max, *Gesammelte Aufsätze zur Soziologie und Sozialpolitik* (Tübingen 1924).

Weininger, Otto, *Geschlecht und Charakter* (Vienna 1904 [1903]).

_____ *Über die letzten Dinge* (Vienna 1904).

Wertheimer, Max, *Experimentelle Untersuchungen zur Tatbestandsdiagnostik* (Leipzig 1905).

Windt, Kamillo and Siegmund Kodiček, *Daktyloskopie, Verwertung von Fingerabdrücken zu Identifizierungszwecken, Lehrbuch zum Selbstunterricht für Richter, Polizeiorgane, Strafanstaltsbeamte, Gendarmen etc.* (Vienna 1904).

Winter, Max, *Im dunkelsten Wien* (Vienna 1904).

Wulffen, Erich, *Psychologie des Verbrechers, Ein Handbuch für Juristen, Ärzte, Pädagogen und Gebildete aller Stände* Vol. 1 (Lichterfelde-Ost 1908).

_____ *Gauner und Verbrechertypen* (Lichterfelde-Ost 1910).

Zimmermann, A., *Gustav Meyrink und seine Freunde* (Hamburg 1917).

Zimmermann, Karl Wilhelm, *Der Dieb in Berlin oder Darstellung ihres Entstehens, ihrer Organisation, ihrer Verbindungen, ihrer Taktik, ihrer Gewohnheit und ihrer Sprache. Zur Belehrung für Polizeibeamte und zur Warnung für das Publikum. Nach praktischer Erfahrung* (Berlin 1847).

Zweig, Stefan, *The World of Yesterday, An Autobiography* (New York 1943).

Secondary Sources

Abels, Norbert, *Sicherheit ist nirgends, Judentum und Aufklärung bei Arthur Schnitzler* (Königstein 1982).

Adorno, Theodor W., 'Sittlichkeit und Kriminalität, Zum elften Band der Werke von Karl Kraus', in: Theodor W. Adorno, *Noten zur Literatur* (Frankfurt am Main 1977), pp. 366–87.

Althoff, Martina *et al.* (eds), *Integration und Ausschließung, Kriminalität und Kriminalpolitik in Zeiten gesellschaftlicher Transformation* (Baden-Baden 2001).

Anderson, Benedict, *Imagined Communities, Reflections on the Origins and Spread of Nationalism* (London 1983).

Anselm, Sigrun, 'Angst und Angstprojektionen in der Phantasie vom jüdischen Ritualmord', in: Rainer Erb (ed.), Die Legende vom Ritualmord, Zur Geschichte der Blutbeschuldigung gegen Juden (Berlin 1993), 253–65.

Arendt, Hannah, On Revolution (London 1973).

Arkel, Dirk van, Antisemitism in Austria (Leiden 1966).

Asquith, Ivan, 'The Structure, ownership and control of the Press 1780–1855, in: George Boyce, James Curran and Pauline Wingate (eds), Newspaper History, from the Seventeenth Century to the Present Day (London 1978), pp. 98–118.

Auer, Olga, 'Beginn der Parteipresse in Österreich mit besonderer Berücksichtigung der Parteientwicklung' (Ph.D. Diss. Univ. Wien 1951).

Auerbach, Nina, Private Theatricals, The Lives of the Victorians (Cambridge, Mass. 1990).

Baldwin, P.M., 'Liberalism, Nationalism and Degeneration: The Case of Max Nordau', Central European History 13 (1980), pp. 99–120.

Bauer, Irene, 'Diebinnen und Betrügerinnen in Wien um die Jahrhundertwende. Zur Sozialgeschichte der Frauenkriminalität', in: Jahrbuch des Vereins für Geschichte der Stadt Wien Vols. 44–5 (1988-9), pp. 187–227.

Becker, Peter, 'Randgruppen im Blickfeld der Polizei. Ein Versuch über die Perspektivität des "praktischen Blicks"', in: Archiv für Sozialgeschichte 32 (1992), pp. 283–304.

_____ 'Vom "Haltlosen" zur "Bestie". Das Polizeiliche Bild des "Verbrechers" im 19. Jahrhundert', in: Alf Lüdtke (ed.), 'Sicherheit' und 'Wohlfahrt'. Polizei, Gesellschaft und Herrschaft im 19. und 20. Jahrhundert (Frankfurt am Main 1992), pp. 97–113.

_____ 'Wie sieht ein Verbrecher aus?', Damals 26 (1994), p. 45.

_____ 'Kriminelle Identitäten im 19. Jahrhundert', Historische Anthropologie 1 (1994), pp. 142–57.

_____ 'Changing Images: The Criminal as seen by the German Police in the Nineteenth Century', History of European Ideas 19, 1–3 (1995), pp. 78–85.

_____ 'Die Rezeption der Physiologie in Kriminalistik und Kriminologie: Variationen über Norm und Ausgrenzung', in: Philipp Sarasin and Jakob Tanner (eds), Physiologie und industrielle Gesellschaft. Studien zur Verwissenschaftlichung des Körpers im 19. und 20. Jahrhundert (Frankfurt am Main 1998), pp. 453–90.

_____ Verderbnis und Entartung, Eine Geschichte der Kriminologie des 19. Jahrhunderts als Diskurs und Praxis (Göttingen 2002).

_____ 'The Criminologists' Gaze at the Underworld, Toward an Archaeology of Criminological Writing', in: Peter Becker and Richard Wetzell (eds), Criminals and Their Scientists: The History of Criminology in International Perspective (Cambridge 2006), pp. 105–36.

Becker, Peter and Richard Wetzell (eds), Criminals and Their Scientists: The History of Criminology in International Perspective (Cambridge 2006).

Beirne, Piers, 'Adolphe Quetelet and the Origins of positivist criminology', American Journal of Sociology 92, 5 (March 1987), pp. 1140–69.

_____ 'Inventing Criminology: The "Science of Man" in Cesare Beccaria's Dei Delitti e Della Pene,' in: Piers Beirne (ed.), The Origins and Growth of Criminology, Essays on Intellectual History 1760-1945 (Aldershot 1994), pp. 777–820.

Beller, Steven, 'Class, Culture and the Jews of Vienna, 1900', in: Ivar Oxaal, Michael Pollak and Gerhard Botz (eds), Jews, Antisemitism and Culture in Vienna (London 1987), pp. 39–51.

_____ Vienna and the Jews 1867-1938, A Cultural History (Cambridge 1989).

_____ 'The Hilsner Affair: Nationalism, Anti-Semitism and the Individual in the Habsburg Monarchy at the Turn of the Century', in: Robert B. Pynsent (ed.), T.G. Masaryk (1850-1937), Vol. 2, Thinker and Critic (London 1989), pp. 52–76.

Benhabib, Seyla, 'Models of the Public Space: Hannah Arendt, the Liberal Tradition, and Jürgen Habermas', in: Craig Calhoun (ed.), *Habermas and the Public Sphere* (Cambridge, Mass. 1992), pp. 73–98.

Benjamin, Walter, *Charles Baudelaire: A Lyric Poet in the Era of High Capitalism* (London 1983).

Berkowitz Michael, 'Unmasking Counterhistory: An Introductory Exploration of Criminality and the Jewish Question', in: Peter Becker and Richard Wetzell (eds), *Criminals and Their Scientists: The History of Criminology in International Perspective* (Cambridge 2006), pp. 61–84.

Bienert, Michael, *Die eingebildete Metropole, Berlin im Feuilleton der Weimarer Republik* (Stuttgart 1992).

Blasius, Dirk, *Kriminalität und Alltag, zur Konfliktgeschichte des Alltagslebens im 19. Jahrhundert* (Göttingen 1978).

_____ 'Einfache Seelenstörung', *Eine Geschichte der deutschen Psychiatrie 1800–1945* (Frankfurt am Main 1994).

Bollinger, Ernst, *1840–1930: Die Goldenen Jahre der Massenpresse* (Freiburg, Switzerland 1996).

Bolton, Richard (ed.), *The Contest of Meaning: Critical Histories of Photography* (Cambridge, Mass. 1989).

Bonß, Wolfgang, *Die Einübung des Tatsachenblicks* (Frankfurt am Main 1982).

Booth, Michael R., 'Nineteenth-Century Theatre', in: John Russell Brown (ed.), *The Oxford Illustrated History of Theatre* (Oxford 1995), 299–340.

Borch-Jacobson, Mikkel, *Remembering Anna O., A Century of Mystification*, translated by Kirby Olson (New York 1996).

Botstein, Leo, 'Stefan Zweig and the Illusion of the Jewish European', in: Marion Sonnenfeld (ed.), *Stefan Zweig* (Albany 1983).

Botz, Gerhard, 'The Changing Patterns of Social Support for Austrian National Socialism', in: S. U. Larsen, Bernt Havel and Jan P. Myklebust (eds), *Who were the Fascists?, Social Roots of European Fascism*, (Bergen 1980).

_____ 'Ausgrenzung, Beraubung und Vernichtung, Das Ende des Wiener Judentums unter der nationalsozialistischen Herrschaft (1938–1945)', in: Gerhard Botz, Ivar Oxaal, Michael Pollak and Nina Scholz (eds), *Eine zerstörte Kultur, Jüdisches Leben und Antisemitismus in Wien seit dem 19. Jahrhundert* (Vienna 2002), 315–39.

Botz, Gerhard, Ivar Oxaal, Michael Pollak and Nina Scholz (eds), *Eine zerstörte Kultur, Jüdisches Leben und Antisemitismus in Wien seit dem 19. Jahrhundert* (Vienna 2002).

Boyce, George, James Curran and Pauline Wingate (eds), *Newspaper History, From the Seventeenth Century to the Present Day* (London 1978).

Boyer, John W., 'Karl Lueger and the Viennese Jews', in: *Leo Baeck Institute Year Book* Vol. 26 (1981), 125–41.

_____ *Political Radicalism in Late Imperial Vienna. Origins of the Christian Social Movement 1848–1897* (Chicago 1981).

_____ *Culture and Political Crisis in Vienna: Christian Socialism in Power, 1897–1918* (Chicago 1995).

Brand, Dana, 'From the Flâneur to the Detective: Interpreting the City in Poe', in: Tony Bennett (ed.), *Popular Fiction: Technology, Ideology, Production, Reading* (London 1990).

Brantlinger, Patrick, *Bread and Circuses, Theories of Mass Culture as Social Decay* (Ithaca 1983).

Bremmer, Jan (ed.), *From Sappho to de Sade, Moments in the History of Sexuality* (London 1991 [1989]).

Breuer, Mordechain and Michael Graetz, *German–Jewish History in Modern Times Vol. 1: Tradition and Enlightenment 1600–1780*, (ed.) Michael A Mayer and Michael Brenner, translated by William Templer (New York 1996).

Brooke, Iris, *Western European Costume, 17th to Mid-19th Centuries, and Its Relation to the Theatre* (London 1940).

Brooks, Peter, *The Melodramatic Imagination, Balzac, Henry James, Melodrama and the Mode of Excess* (New Haven 1995).

Bristow, Edward J., *Prostitution and Prejudice, The Jewish Fight against White Slavery 1870–1939* (Oxford 1982).

Bürger, Peter, *Das Verschwinden des Subjekts, Eine Geschichte der Subjektivität von Montaigne bis Barthes* (Frankfurt am Main 1998).

Buranelli, Vincent, *The Wizard from Vienna* (London 1976).

Bynum, W. F. and Roy Porter (eds), *Companion Encyclopaedia of the History of Medicine*, 2 Vols. (London 1993).

Calhoun, Craig, (ed.), *Habermas and the Public Sphere* (Cambridge, Mass. 1992).

Cameron, Deborah and ElizabethFrazer, *Lust to Kill: A Feminist Investigation of Sexual Murder* (New York 1987).

Čapek, Karel, *President Masaryk Tells His Story* (London 1934).

Carlson, Marvin, *The German Stage in the Nineteenth Century* (Metuchen, NJ 1972).

Černý, Bohumil, *Vražda v Polné* (Prague 1968).

Červinka, František, 'The Hilsner Affair', in: Alan Dundes (ed.), *The Blood Libel Legend: A Casebook in Anti-Semitic Folklore* (Madison, Wisc. 1991), pp. 142–57.

Chalaby, Jean K., *The Invention of Journalism* (London 1998).

Cheyette, Bryan and Laura Marcus (eds), *Modernity, Culture and 'the Jew'* (Oxford 1998).

Claßen, Isabella, *Darstellung von Kriminalität in der deutschen Literatur, Presse und Wissenschaft 1900 bis 1930* (Frankfurt am Main 1988).

Clair, Jean, Cathrin Pichler and Wolfgang Pircher (eds), *Wunderblock, Eine Geschichte der modernen Seele, Ausstellungskatalog* (Vienna 1989).

Cocks, H.G., 'Trials of character: the use of character evidence in Victorian sodomy trials', in: R.A. Melikan (ed.), *Domestic and International Trials, 1700–2000, The Trial in History Vol. II* (Manchester 2003), pp. 36–53.

Cohen, Gary B., *The Politics of Ethnic Survival: Germans in Prague 1861–1914* (Princeton 1981).

Cohn, Norman, *Warrant for Genocide, The Myth of the Jewish World Conspiracy and the Protocols of the Elders of Zion*, Brown Judaic Studies 23 (Chica, Calif. 1981 [1969]).

Cole, Simon A., *Suspect Identities, A History of Fingerprinting and Criminal Identification* (Cambridge, Mass. 2001).

Connelly, Mark Thomas, *The Response to Prostitution in the Progressive Era* (Chapel Hill 1990).

Corino, Karl, 'Ein Mörder macht Literaturgeschichte, Florian Großrubatscher, ein Modell für Musils Moosbrugger', in: Josef Strutz (ed.), *Musil Studien 11* (Munich 1983), pp. 130–47.

Crary, Jonathan, *Techniques of the Observer: On Vision and Modernity in the Nineteenth Century* (Cambridge, Mass. 1990).

Curran, James, 'Mass Media and Democracy', in: James Curran and Michael Gurevitch (eds), *Mass Media and Society* (New York 1991), pp. 82–117.

Curran, James and Michael Gurevitch (eds), *Mass Media and Society* (New York 1991).

Curtis, L. Perry, *Jack the Ripper and the London Press* (New Haven 2002).

Danker, Uwe, *Räuberbanden im Alten Reich um 1700, Ein Beitrag zur Geschichte von Herrschaft und Kriminalität in der Frühen Neuzeit* (Frankfurt am Main 1988).

Daston, Lorraine, 'Baconian Facts, Academic Civility, and the Prehistory of Objectivity', in: *Annals of Scholarship* 8, 3–4 (1991), pp. 333–65.

Daston, Lorraine and Peter Galison, 'The Image of Objectivity', *Representations* 40, Special Issue: Seeing Science (Autumn 1992), pp. 81–128.

Daston, Lorraine and Katherine Park, *Wonders and the Order of Nature* (New York 1998).

Dichand, Hans, *Illustrierte Kronenzeitung, Die Geschichte eines Erfolges* (Vienna 1977).

Dienst, Heide and Edith Saurer (eds), *Das Weib existiert nicht für sich* (Vienna 1990).

Dölling, Dieter, 'Kriminologie im Dritten Reich', in: Ralf Dreier und Wolfgang Sellert (eds), *Recht und Justiz im 'Dritten Reich'* (Frankfurt am Main 1989).

Draxler, Joseph, 'Vergleich der Zeitungen Reichspost und Vaterland in Bezug auf die Probleme der Zeit von 1894–1911' (Ph.D. Diss. Univ. Wien 1948).

Dreier, Ralf und Wolfgang Sellert (eds), *Recht und Justiz im 'Dritten Reich'* (Frankfurt am Main 1989).

Dürkop, Marlis, 'Zur Funktion der Kriminologie im Nationalsozialismus', in: Udo Reifner und Bernd Sonnen (eds), *Strafjustiz und Polizei im Dritten Reich* (Frankfurt am Main 1984), pp. 97–120.

Dundes, Alan (ed.), *The Blood Libel Legend: A Casebook in Anti-Semitic Folklore* (Madison, Wisconsin 1991).

_____ 'The Ritual Murder or Blood Libel Legend, A Study of Anti-Semitic Victimisation Through Projective Inversion', in: Alan Dundes (ed.), *The Blood Libel Legend: A Casebook in Anti-Semitic Folklore* (Madison, Wisc. 1991), pp. 336–76.

Edelbacher, Max and Harald Seyrl, *Wiener Kriminalchronik, Zweihundert Jahre Kriminalistik und Kriminalität in Wien* (Vienna 1993).

Eder, Franz X., 'Sexual Cultures in Germany and Austria 1700–2000', in: Franz X. Eder, Lesley Hall and Gert Helema (eds), *Sexual Cultures in Europe, Themes in Sexuality* (Manchester 1999), pp. 138–72.

_____, Lesley Hall and Gert Helema (eds), *Sexual Cultures in Europe, Themes in Sexuality* (Manchester 1999).

Efron, John M., *Defenders of the Race, Jewish Doctors and Race Science in Fin-de-Siècle Europe* (New Haven 1994).

Egmond, Florike, *Underworlds, Organised Crime in the Netherlands 1650–1800* (Cambridge 1993).

Ehalt, Hubert Ch., Gernot Heiß and Hannes Stekl (eds), *Glücklich ist wer vergißt..?, Das andere Wien um 1900* (Cologne 1986).

Eisenstein, Elisabeth L., 'Some Conjectures about the Impact of Printing on Western Society and Thought: A Preliminary Report', *Journal of Modern History* 40, 1 (1968), pp. 1–56.

Ellenberger, Henri F., *The Discovery of the Unconscious, The History and Evolution of Dynamic Psychiatry* (New York 1970).

Engelsing, Rolf, *Massenpublikum und Journalistentum in Nordwestdeutschland* (Berlin 1966).

_____, *Analphabetentum und Lektüre, Zur Sozialgeschichte des Lesens in Deutschland zwischen feudaler und industrieller Gesellschaft* (Stuttgart 1973).

Erb, Rainer (ed.), *Die Legende vom Ritualmord, Zur Geschichte der Blutbeschuldigung gegen Juden* (Berlin 1993).

Erb, Rainer and Michael Schmidt (eds), *Antisemitismus und jüdische Geschichte* (Berlin 1987).

Evans, Richard J. (ed.), *The German Underworld: Deviants and Outcasts in German History* (London 1988).

_____ *Kneipengespräche im Kaiserreich, Die Stimmungsberichte der Hamburger politischen Polizei 1892-1914* (Reinbeck bei Hamburg 1989).

_____ *Rituals of Retribution, Capital Punishment in Germany 1600-1987* (London 1997).

_____ *Tales from the German Underworld, Crime and Punishment in the Nineteenth Century* (New Haven 1998).

_____ 'Social Outsiders in German History: from the sixteenth century to 1933', in: Robert Gellately and Nathan Stoltzfus (eds), *Social Outsiders in Nazi Germany* (Princeton 2001), pp. 20–44.

Falkmayer, Hugo, *Die Presse in der österreichischen Gesetzgebung* (Vienna 1951).

Fanta, Walter, *Die Entstehungsgeschichte des 'Mannes ohne Eigenschaften' von Robert Musil* (Vienna 2000).

Finzsch, Norbert and Robert Jütte (eds), *Institutions of Confinement, Hospitals, Asylums, and Prisons in Western Europe and North America 1500-1950* (Cambridge 1996).

Foucault, Michel, *Discipline and Punish: The Birth of the Prison*, translated by A. Sheridan (New York 1977).

Fraenkel, Josef (ed.), *The Jews in Austria, Essays on Their Life, History and Destruction* (London 1970 [1967]).

Frisby, David, *Fragments of Modernity: Theories of Modernity in the Work of Simmel, Kracauer and Benjamin* (Cambridge 1988).

_____ (ed.), *Simmel in Wien, Texte und Kontexte aus dem Wien der Jahrhundertwende* (Vienna 2000).

Fritzsche, Peter, *Reading Berlin 1900* (Cambridge, Mass. 1996).

_____ '"Eyes Peeled!" Anonymity, Anxiety, and Surveillance in the Metropolis', unpublished paper presented at the IFK Vienna, 14 December 2001.

Frommel, Monika, 'Internationale Reformbewegung zwischen 1880 und 1920', in: Jörg Schönert (ed.), *Erzählte Kriminalität, Zur Typologie von narrativen Darstellungen in Strafrechtsflege, Publizistik und Literatur zwischen 1770 und 1920* (Tübingen 1991), pp. 467–95.

Frühwald, Wolfgang (ed.), *Zur Sozialgeschichte der deutschen Literatur von der Aufklärung bis zur Jahrhundertwende* Vol. 1 (Tübingen 1985).

Gadebusch Bondio, Mariacarla, *Die Rezeption der kriminalanthropologischen Theorien von Cesare Lombroso in Deutschland von 1880-1914* (Husum 1995).

Garland, David, 'Criminological Knowledge and Its Relation to Power, Foucault's Genealogy and Criminology Today', *The British Journal of Criminology* 32, 4 (Autumn 1992), pp. 403–22.

_____ 'Of Crimes and Criminals, The Development of Criminology in Britain', in: Mike Maguire, Rod Morgan, Robert Reiner (eds), *The Oxford Handbook of Criminology* (Oxford 1994), pp. 17–68.

Gay, Peter, *Freud, A Life for Our Time* (London 1989).

_____ *Kult der Gewalt: Aggression im bürgerlichen Zeitalter*, translated by Ulrich Enderwitz (Munich 1996).

_____ *Schnitzler's Century, The Making of Middle Class Culture 1815-1914* (New York 2002).

Geehr, Richard S., *Karl Lueger, Mayor of Fin-de-Siècle Vienna* (Detroit 1989).

Gelber, Mark H., 'Ethnic Pluralism and Germanization in the works of Karl-Emil Franzos (1848-1904)', *The German Quaterly* 56, 3 (1983), 376–85.

Gellately, Robert and Nathan Stoltzfus (eds), *Social Outsiders in Nazi Germany* (Princeton 2001).

Gibson, Mary S., *Born to Crime, Cesare Lombroso and the Origins of Biological Criminality* (Westport, Conn. 2002).

_____ 'The "Female Offender" and the Italian School of Criminal Anthropology', in: *European Studies* 12 (1982), pp. 155–65.

Gilman, Sander L., *Jewish Self-Hatred: Anti-Semitism and the Hidden Language of the Jews* (Baltimore 1986).

_____ *The Jew's Body* (New York 1991).

Gilman, Sander L. and Steven T. Katz (eds), *Anti-Semitism in Times of Crisis* (New York 1991).

_____ *The Case of Sigmund Freud, Medicine and Identity at the Fin de Siècle* (Baltimore 1993).

_____ 'Psychotherapy', in: W.F. Bynum and Roy Porter (eds), *Companion Encyclopaedia of the History of Medicine* Vol. 2 (London 1993), pp. 1029–49.

Gilman, Sander L. and J. Edward Chamberlin (eds), *Degeneration: The Dark Side of Progress* (New York 1985).

Ginzburg, Carlo, 'Morelli, Freud and Sherlock Holmes: Clues and Scientific Method," translated by Anna Davin, *History Workshop* 9 (1980), pp. 5–36.

Golding, Ann, *Sex, Religion and the Making of Modern Madness, The Eberbach Asylum and German Society 1815–1849* (Oxford 1999).

Goldstein, Jan, *Console and Classify, The French Psychiatric Profession in the Nineteenth Century* (Chicago 1987).

Gombrich, E.H., *Jüdische Identität und jüdisches Schicksal, Eine Diskussionsbemerkung* (Vienna 1997).

Goodman, Nelson, *Languages of Art* (Indianapolis 1976).

Gould, Alan, *A History of Hypnotism* (Cambridge 1992).

Gould, Stephen J., *The Mismeasure of Man, Revised and Expanded Edition* (London 1996).

Grassberger, Roland, 'Österreich und die Entwicklung der Kriminologie zur selbstständigen Wissenschaft', *Wissenschaft und Weltbild* 18, 4 (1965), pp. 277–89.

Gray, Richard, 'Sign und Sein, The Physiognomikstreit and the Dispute over the Semiotic Constitution of Bourgeois Individuality', *Deutsche Vierteljahrsschrift für Literaturwissenschaft und Geisteswissenschaft* 66 (1992), pp. 300–32.

_____ *About Face, German Physiognomic Thought from Lavater to Auschwitz* (Detroit 2004).

Green, Martin, *Mountain of Faith, The Counterculture Begins, Ascona 1900–1920* (London 1986).

Grunberger, Richard, 'Jews in Austrian Journalism', in: Josef Fraenkel (ed.), *The Jews in Austria, Essays on Their Life, History and Destruction* (London 1970 [1967]).

Habermas, Jürgen, *Strukturwandel der Öffentlichkeit, Untersuchungen zu einer Kategorie der bürgerlichen Gesellschaft* (Frankfurt am Main 1996 [1961]).

Hacking, Ian, *The Taming of Chance* (Cambridge 1990).

Hahn Rafter, Nicole, *Creating Born Criminals* (Urbana 1997).

_____ 'Seeing and Believing: Images of Heredity in Biological Theories of Crime', *Brooklyn Law Review* 67 (2001), pp. 1–30.

_____ 'Space, Gender, and Representation in Lombroso's "La donna delinquente"', unpublished conference paper, IFK Vienna 14 December 2001.

Hamann, Brigitte, *Hitler's Wien, Lehrjahre eines Diktators* (Munich 1998).

Handler, Andrew, *Blood Libel and Tiszaeszlar* (New York 1980).

Haney, Walter, 'Die Illustrierte Kronenzeitung, ein Beitrag zur Geschichte der Wiener Presse' (Ph.D. Diss. Univ. Wien 1950).

Hardt, Hanns, *Social Theories of the Press, Early German and American Perspectives* (London 1979).

Harris, Ruth, *Murder and Madness, Medicine, Law and Society in the Fin-de-Siècle* (Oxford 1989).

Harrowitz, Nancy A., *Antisemitism, Misogyny and the Logic of Cultural Difference, Caesare Lombroso and Matilde Serao* (London 1994).

Hartl, Friedrich, *Das Wiener Kriminalgericht, Strafrechtspflege vom Zeitalter der Aufklärung bis zur Österreichischen Revolution* (Vienna 1973).

Hauer, Anna, 'Sexualität und Sexualmoral in Östereich um 1900, Theoretische und Literarische Texte von Frauen', in: Wiener Historikerinnen (ed.), *Die ungeschriebene Geschichte, Historische Frauenforschung, Dokumentation 5. Historikerinnentreffen* (Vienna 1985).

Hehemann, Rainer, *Die 'Bekämpfung des Zigeunerwesens' im Wilhelminischen Deutschland und in der Weimarer Republik, 1871–1933* (Frankfurt am Main 1987).

Hein, Robert, 'Studentischer Antisemitismus in Österreich' in: *Beiträge zur österreichischen Studentengeschichte 10* (Vienna 1984).

Hellwing, Isaak A., *Der Konfessionelle Antisemitismus im neunzehten Jahrhundert in Österreich* (Vienna 1972).

Henning, Jörg, 'Gerichtsbestattung in deutschen Tageszeitungen 1850–1890', in: Jörg Schönert (ed.), *Erzählte Kriminalität, Zur Typologie und Funktion von narrativen Darstellungen in Strafrechtspflege, Publizistik und Literatur zwischen 1770 und 1920, Vorträge zu einem interdisziplinären Kolloquium, Hamburg 10–12 April 1985* (Tübingen 1991), pp. 349–68.

Hering, Karl-Heinz, *Der Weg der Kriminologie zur selbständigen Wissenschaft* (Mainz 1966).

Hermann, Arthur, *The Idea of Decline in Western History* (New York 1996).

Höbling, Lothar, 'Der österreichisch-ungarische Mädchenhandel in den Akten des Bundespolizeidirektionsarchivs Wien' (M.A. Diss. Univ. Wien 1996).

Hödl, Klaus, *Als Bettler in der Leopoldstadt, Galizische Juden auf dem Weg nach Wien* (Vienna 1994).

_____ *Die Pathologisierung des jüdischen Körpers* (Vienna 1997).

Hoffmann, Ludger, 'Vom Ereignis zum Fall, Sprachliche Muster zur Darstellung und Überprüfung von Sachverhalten vor Gericht', in: Jörg Schönert (ed.), *Erzählte Kriminalität, Zur Typologie und Funktion von narrativen Darstellungen in Strafrechtspflege, Publizistik und Literatur zwischen 1770 und 1920, Vorträge zu einem interdisziplinären Kolloquium, Hamburg 10–12 April 1985* (Tübingen 1991), pp. 87–114.

Hohmann, Joachim S., *Geschichte der Zigeunerverfolgung in Deutschland* (Frankfurt am Main 1981).

Holiczki, Walter, 'Die Entwicklung der Gerichtsberichterstattung in der Wiener Tagespresse von 1848 bis zur Jahrhundertwende' (Ph.D. Diss., Univ. Wien 1972).

Horn, David G., *The Criminal Body, Lombroso and the Anatomy of Deviance* (London 2003).

_____ 'Blood Will Tell: The Vascular System and Criminal Dangerousness', in: Christopher Forth and Ivan Crozier (eds), *Body Parts: Critical Explorations in Corporeality* (Lanham, Md. 2005).

Hügel, Hans-Otto, *Untersuchungsrichter – Diebesfänger – Detektive. Theorie und Geschichte der deutschen Detektiverzählungen im 19. Jahrhundert* (Stuttgart 1978).

Hundert, E.J., 'The European Enlightenment and the History of the Self', in: Roy Porter (ed.), *Rewriting the Self, Histories from the Renaissance to the Present* (London 1997), pp. 72–83.

Hunt, Lynn, *Politics, Culture and Class in the French Revolution* (London 1992).

Hurwitz, Emanuel, *Otto Gross, Paradies Sucher zwischen Jung und Freud, Leben und Werk* (Zurich 1979).

Imm, Konstantin and Joachim Linder, 'Verdächtige und Täter. Zuschreibung von Kriminalität in Texten der "schönen Literatur" am Beispiel des Feuilletons der "Berliner Gerichtszeitung", der Romanreihe "Eisenbahnunterhaltungen" und Wilhelm Raabes "Horaker" und "Stopfkuchen"', in: Wolfgang Frühwald (ed.), *Zur Sozialgeschichte der deutschen Literatur von der Aufklärung bis zur Jahrhundertwende* Vol 1 (Tübingen 1985), pp. 21–96.

Janik, Allan, 'Viennese Culture and the Jewish Self-Hatred Hypothesis: A Critique', in: Ivar Oxaal, Michael Pollak and Gerhard Botz (eds), *Jews, Antisemitism and Culture in Vienna* (London 1987), pp. 75–87.

Janik, Allan and Stephen Toulmin, *Wittgenstein's Vienna* (New York 1973).

Janz, Rolf-Peter and Klaus Laermann, *Arthur Schnitzler: Zur Diagnose des Wiener Bürgertums im Fin-de-siècle* (Stuttgart 1977).

Jay, Martin, *Downcast Eyes, The Denigration of Vision in Twentieth-Century French Thought* (Berkeley 1993).

Jervis, John, *Exploring the Modern* (Oxford 1998).

John, Michael, 'Obdachlosigkeit – Massenerscheinung und Unruheherd in Wien der Spätgründerzeit', in: Hubert Ch. Ehalt, Gernot Heiß and Hannes Stekl (eds), *Glücklich ist wer vergißt..?, Das andere Wien um 1900* (Cologne and Graz 1986), pp. 174–94.

John, Michael and Albert Lichtblau, *Schmelztiegel Wien* (Vienna 1990).

Johnson, Eric A., 'The Roots of Crime in Imperial Germany', *Central European History* 15 (1982), pp. 351–76.

_____ *Urbanisation and Crime, Germany 1871–1914* (Cambridge 1995).

Johnson, Paul, *The Birth of the Modern* (London 1991).

Johnston, William M., *The Austrian Mind, An Intellectual and Social History 1848–1938* (Berkeley,Cal., 1972).

Jušek, Karin J., 'Sexual morality and the meaning of prostitution in Fin-de-Siècle Vienna', in: Jan Bremmer (ed.), *From Sappho to de Sade, Moments in the History of Sexuality* (London 1991 [1989]), pp. 123–42.

_____ 'Ein Wiener Bordellroman: Else Jerusalems Heiliger Skarabäus', in: Heide Dienst and Edith Saurer (eds), *Das Weib existiert nicht für sich* (Vienna 1990), pp. 139–47.

Kaplan, Marion A., *The Jewish Feminist Movement in Germany, The Campaigns of the Jüdischer Frauenbund, 1904–1938* (London 1979).

Karl, Friedrich R. and Leo Hamalian (eds), *The Existential Imagination, From de Sade to Sartre* (London 1973).

Kasischke-Wurm, Daniela, *Antisemitismus im Spiegel der Hamburger Presse während des Kaiserreichs (1884–1914)* (Hamburg 1997).

Katz, Jacob, *From Prejudice to Destruction: Anti Semitism 1700–1933* (Cambridge, Mass 1980).

Kaupen-Haas, Heidrun and Christian Saller (eds), *Wissenschaftlicher Rassismus, Analysen einer Kontinuität in den Human- und Naturwissenschaften* (Frankfurt am Main 1999).

Kende, Tamás, 'The Language of Blood Libels in Central and East European History', in: Lázló Kontler (ed.), *Pride and Prejudice, National Stereotypes in 19th and 20th century Europe East and West*, CEU History Department Working Paper Series (Budapest 1995), pp. 91–104.

Kershaw, Ian, *Hitler, 1889–1936: Hubris* (London 1998).

Kielwein, Gerhard (ed.), *Entwicklungslinien der Kriminologie* (Cologne 1985).

Kieval, Hillel J., *The Making of Czech Jewry, National Conflict and Jewish Society in Bohemia, 1870–1918* (Oxford 1988).

_____ 'Masaryk and Czech Jewry: The Ambiguities of Friendship', in: Stanley B. Winters (ed.), *T.G. Masaryk (1850–1937) Vol. 1: Thinker and Politician* (London 1990), pp. 302–21.

_____ 'Jews, Czechs and Germans in Bohemia before 1914', in: Robert S. Wistrich (ed.), *Austrians and Jews in the Twentieth Century, From Franz Joseph to Waldheim* (New York 1992), pp. 19–37.

_____ 'Death and the Nation: Ritual Murder as Political Discourse in the Czech Lands', *Jewish History* 10, 1 (1996), pp. 75–91.

Kieval, Hillel J. and Francoise Main, 'Antisémitisme ou Savoir Social? Sur la Genèse des Procès Modernes Pour Meurtre Rituel', *Annales. Histoire, Science Sociales* 49, No. 5 (1994), pp. 1091–105.

Kluger, Ruth, 'The Theme of Anti-Semitism in the Work of Austrian Jews', in: Sander L. Gilman and Steven T. Katz (eds), *Anti-Semitism in Times of Crisis* (New York 1991), pp. 173–87.

Knight, Stephen, *Crime Fiction 1800–2000, Detection, Death, Diversity* (New York 2004).

Kontler, Lázló (ed.), *Pride and Prejudice, National Stereotypes in 19th and 20th Century Europe East and West*, CEU History Department Working Paper Series (Budapest 1995).

Koszyk, Kurt, *Deutsche Presse im 19. Jahrhundert* (Berlin 1966).

Kovtun, Jiří, *Tajuplná Vražda, Případ Leopoldna Hilsnera* (Prague 1994).

Kreutzahler, Birgit, *Das Bild des Verbrechers in Romanen der Weimarer Republik, Eine Untersuchung vor dem Hintergrund anderer gesellschaftlicher Verbrecherbilder und gesellschaftlicher Grundzüge der Weimarer Republik* (Frankfurt am Main 1987).

Kubbovy, Myriam, 'Matzoh, Red Wine and the Eucharist', *Jewish Spectator* 29 (1964), pp. 21–5.

Kunz, Ruprecht, 'Die Geschichte der Arbeiterzeitung von ihrer Gründung zur Jahrhundertwende' (Ph.D. Diss. Univ. Wien 1949).

Kuschej, Hermann and Arno Pilgram, 'Fremdenfeindlichkeit im Diskurs um "Organisierte Kriminalität",' in: Karin Liebhart *et al.* (eds), *Fremdbilder-Feindbilder-Zerrbilder* (Klagenfurt 2002).

Lamott, Franziska, 'Professor Dr Hans Gross gegen seinen Sohn', in: Jean Clair, Cathrin Pichler und Wolfgang Pircher (eds), *Wunderblock, Eine Geschichte der modernen Seele, Ausstellungskatalog* (Vienna 1989), pp. 611–19.

_____ 'Weibliche Emanzipation als Symptom und Delikt. Die Frauenfrage im kriminologischen Diskurs der Jahrhundertwende', *Zeitschrift für Sexualforschung* 5 (1992), pp. 25–40.

_____ 'Liebe, Tod und Strafrecht, Strategien der Angstabwehr in der Kriminologie der Jahrhundertwende', in: *Sozialwissenschaftliche Informationen* 21 Heft 2 (1992), pp. 82–94.

Laver, James, *Drama, Its Costume and Décor* (London 1951).

Lebermann von Sonnenberg, Max, *Der Blutmord in Konitz mit Streifenlichtern auf die strafrechtliche Stellung der Juden im Deutschen Reiche* (Berlin 1901).

Ledl, Alexandra, 'Die Gerichtssaalsberichterstattung in der ersten österreichischen Republik in den Parteiorganen der Christilich-Sozialen und Sozialdemokraten von 1918 bis 1939' (Ph.D. Diss., Univ. Wien 1990).

Leps, Marie-Christine, *Apprehending the Criminal: The Production of Deviance in Nineteenth-Century Discourse* (Durham 1992).

Lerg, Winfried Bernhard and Michael Schmolke, *Massenpresse und Volkszeitung, Zwei Beiträge zur Pressegeschichte des neunzehnten Jahrhunderts* (Assen 1968).

LeRider, Jaques, *Modernity and Crises of Identity, Culture and Society in Fin-de-Siècle Vienna*, translated by Rosemary Morris (Cambridge 1993).

_____ 'Hans Gross, criminologue, et son fils Otto Gross, "délinquant sexuel" et psycho-analyste', in: Britta Rupp-Eisenreich and Justin Stegl (eds), *Kulturwissenschaft im Vielvölkerstaat, Zur Geschichte der Ethnologie und verwandter Gebiete in Österreich ca. 1780–1918 / L'Anthropologie et L'Etat Pluri-Culturel, Le cas de l'Autriche, de 1780 à 1918 environ* (Vienna 1995), pp. 229–40.

Lerner, Paul, *Hysterical Men, War Psychiatry and the Politics of Trauma in Germany, 1890–1930* (Ithaca 2003).

Lesky, Erna, *Die Wiener Medizinische Schule* (Graz 1978 [1965]).

Leuschen-Seppel, Rosemarie, *Sozialdemokratie und Antisemitismus im Kaiserreich, Die Auseinandersetzung der Partei mit den konservativen und völkischen Strömungen des Antisemitismus 1871–1914* (Bonn 1978).

Lichtblau, Albert, 'Die Debatten über die Ritualmordbeschuldigungen im österreichis-chen Abgeordnetenhaus am Ende des 19. Jahrhunderts', in: Rainer Erb (ed.), *Die Legende vom Ritualmord, Zur Geschichte der Blutbeschuldigung gegen Juden* (Berlin 1993), pp. 270–92.

Liebhart, Karin et al. (eds), *Fremdbilder-Feindbilder-Zerrbilder* (Klagenfurt 2002).

Lindemann, Albert S., *The Jew Accused, Three Antisemitic Affairs (Dreyfus, Beilis, Frank) 1894–1915* (Cambridge 1991).

Lorenz, Maren, *Kriminelle Körper – Gestörte Geister, Die Normierung des Individuums in Gerichtsmedizin und Psychiatrie der Aufklärung* (Hamburg 1999).

Lüdtke, Alf (ed.), *'Sicherheit' und 'Wohlfahrt'. Polizei, Gesellschaft und Herrschaft im 19. und 20. Jahrhundert* (Frankfurt am Main 1992).

Lury, Celia, *Prosthetic Culture, Photography, Memory and Identity* (New York 1998).

MacIntyre, Alasdair, *After Virtue, A Study in Moral Theory* (London 1981).

Maguire, Mike, Rod Morgan and Robert Reiner (eds), *The Oxford Handbook of Criminology* (Oxford 1994).

Margarethe, Jakob, 'Das Deutsche Volksblatt und seine politische Geschichte in den Jahren 1889–99' (Ph.D. Diss., Univ. Vienna 1937).

Martschukat, Jürgen, *Inszeniertes Töten, Eine Geschichte der Todesstrafe vom 17. bis zum 19. Jahrhundert* (Cologne 2000).

Marxen, Klaus, 'Zum Verhältnis von Strafrecht und Gerichtserstattung in der zweiten Hälfte des 19. Jahrhunderts', in: Jörg Schönert (ed.), *Erzählte Kriminalität, Zur Typologie und Funktion von narrativen Darstellungen in Strafrechtspflege, Publizistik und Literatur zwischen 1770 und 1920, Vorträge zu einem interdisziplinären Kollo-quium, Hamburg 10–12 April 1985* (Tübingen 1991), pp. 369–74.

Marzin, Florian E., *Okkultismus und Phantastik in den Romanen Gustav Meyrinks* (Essen 1986).

Mayerhofer, Rainer, 'Die Entwicklung der Lokalberichterstattung in der Wiener Tages-presse von 1848 bis 1900' (Ph.D. Diss. Univ. Vienna 1972).

Megill, Alan (ed.), *Rethinking Objectivity* (Durham, N.C. 1994).

Melikan, R.A. (ed.), *Domestic and International Trials, 1700–2000, The Trial in History Vol. II* (Manchester 2003).

Merkel, Reinhard, 'Wo gegen Natur sie auf Normen pochten ..., Bemerkungen zum Ver-hältnis zwischen Strafrecht und Satire im Werk von Karl Kraus', in: Jörg Schönert (ed.), *Erzählte Kriminalität, Zur Typologie und Funktion von narrativen Darstellungen in Strafrechtspflege, Publizistik und Literatur zwischen 1770 und 1920, Vorträge zu einem interdisziplinären Kolloqium, Hamburg 10–12 April 1985* (Tübingen 1991), pp. 607–31.

Mitchell, W.J.T., *Iconology, Image, Text, Ideology* (Chicago 1986).

Molin-Pradel, Mario, 'Friedrich Austerlitz, Chefredakteur der Arbeiter-Zeitung' (Ph.D. Diss., Univ Vienna 1963).

Mosse, Georg L., *Towards the Final Solution: A History of European Racism* (London 1978).

Mosse, Werner E., Arnold Paucker and Reinhard Rürüp (eds), *Revolution and Evolution: 1848 in German-Jewish History* (Tübingen 1981).

Müller-Dietz, Heinz, 'Literatur und Kriminalität', in: *Juristenzeitung* 39 (1984), pp. 699–708.

_____ 'Kriminologie und Literatur. Ein Literatur-Bericht', in: Gerhard Kielwein (ed.), *Entwicklungslinien der Kriminologie* (Cologne 1985), pp. 59–91.

_____ 'Kriminalität und Kriminalitätsverarbeitung in der Fackel, Zur Justiz-, Strafrechts und Pressekritik von Karl Kraus', in: Jörg Schönert (ed.), *Erzählte Kriminalität, Zur Typologie und Funktion von narrativen Darstellungen in Strafrechtspflege, Publizistik und Literatur zwischen 1770 und 1920, Vorträge zu einem interdisziplinären Kolloquium, Hamburg 10–12 April 1985* (Tübingen 1991), pp. 571–605.

Mulot-Deri, Sibylle, *Sir Galahad, Portrait einer Verschollenen* (Frankfurt am Main 1987).

Nonn, Christoph, *Eine Stadt sucht einen Mörder, Gerücht, Gewalt und Antisemitismus im Kaiserreich* (Göttingen 2002).

Nye, Robert A., *Crime, Madness and Politics in Modern France, The Medical Concept of National Decline* (Princeton 1984).

Oxaal, Ivar, Michael Pollak and Gerhard Botz (eds), *Jews, Antisemitism and Culture in Vienna* (London 1987). Translated into German as: *Eine zerstörte Kultur: Jüdisches Leben und Antisemitismus in Wien seit dem 19. Jahrhundert* (Vienna 2002).

Patterson, Michael, *The Revolution in German Theatre 1900–1933* (Boston 1981).

Pauley, Bruce F., *From Prejudice to Persecution, A History of Austrian Anti-Semitism* (Chapel Hill 1992).

Paupié, Kurt, *Handbuch der österreichischen Pressegeschichte Band 1: Wien* (Vienna 1960).

Pearson, K., *The Life of Francis Galton*, 3 Vols. (Cambridge 1914–1930).

Péter, László and Robert B. Pynsent (eds), *Intellectuals and the Future in the Habsburg Monarchy 1890–1914* (London 1988).

Pick, Daniel, *Svengali's Web, The Alien Enchanter in Modern Culture* (New Haven 2000).

_____ 'Powers of Suggestion: Svengali and the Fin-de-Siècle', in: Bryan Cheyette and Laura Marcus (eds), *Modernity, Culture and 'the Jew'* (Oxford 1998), pp. 105–25.

_____ 'Stories of the Eye', in: Roy Porter (ed.), *Rewriting the Self, Histories from the Renaissance to the Present* (London 1997), pp. 186–99.

_____ *Faces of Degeneration, A European Disorder c. 1848–1918* (Cambridge 1989).

Pilgram, Arno 'Zur Auswirkung der Kriminalitätsdarstellung in den Massenmedien. Annahmen und ihre Folgen', *Österreichische Zeitschrift für Soziologie* 4 (1979), pp. 107–19.

_____ *Kriminalität in Österreich, Studien zur Soziologie der Kriminalitätsentwicklung* (Vienna 1980).

_____ 'Wirklichkeitskonstruktionen im Vergleich: Polizei und Unternehmer im Ost-West-geschäft über "Organisierte Kriminalität"', in: Martina Althoff et al. (eds), *Integration und Ausschließung, Kriminalität und Kriminalpolitik in Zeiten gesellschaftlicher Transformation* (Baden-Baden 2001).

Po-Chia Hsia, R. and Hartmann Lehmann (eds), *In and Out of the Ghetto, Jewish-Gentile Relationships in late Medieval and Early Modern Germany* (Cambridge 1995).

Pollack, Michael, 'Cultural Innovation and Social Identity in Fin-de-Siècle Vienna', in: Ivar Oxaal, Michael Pollack and Gerhard Botz (eds), *Jews, Antisemitism and Culture in Vienna* (London 1987).

Poovey, Mary, '"Scenes of an Indelicate Character": The Medical "Treatment" of Victorian Women', *Representations* 14 (1986), pp. 137–68.

Porter, Roy (ed.), *Rewriting the Self, Histories from the Renaissance to the Present* (London 1997).

_____ *The Greatest Benefit to Mankind, A Medical History of Humanity from Antiquity to the Present* (London 1997).

Pulzer, Peter, *The Rise of Political Antisemitism in Germany and Austria* (New York 1964).

Pyckett, Lyn, *Engendering Fictions, The English Novel in the Early Twentieth Century* (London 1995).

Pynsent, Robert B. (ed.), *T.G. Masaryk (1850–1937), Vol. 2, Thinker and Critic* (London 1989).

_____ 'Conclusory Essay: Decadence, Decay and Innovation', in: Robert B. Pynsent (ed.), *Decadence and Innovation, Austro–Hungarian Art at the Turn of the Century* (London 1989), pp. 111–248.

_____ (ed.), *Decadence and Innovation, Austro–Hungarian Art at the Turn of the Century* (London 1989).

_____ 'Obchod a smyslnost. České spisovatelky a židé okolo přelomn stoleti', *Sbornik Prací Filosofické Faculty Brněské University* 43 (1996), pp. 23–39.

Radkau, Joachim, *Das Zeitalter der Nervosität, Deutschland zwischen Bismark und Hitler* (Munich 1998).

Rappaport, Ernest A., 'The Ritual Murder Accusation, The Persistence of Doubt and the Repetition Compulsion', in: Alan Dundes (ed.), *The Blood Libel Legend: A Casebook in Anti-Semitic Folklore* (Madison, Wisc. 1991).

Regener, Susanne, 'Metaphysik des Bösen, Zur Anschauungspraxis von Kriminalmuseen', in: Heidrun Kaupen-Haas and Christian Saller (eds), *Wissenschaftlicher Rassismus, Analysen einer Kontinuität in den Human- und Naturwissenschaften* (Frankfurt am Main 1999), pp. 304–26.

_____ *Fotographische Erfassung, Zur Geschichte medialer Konstruktion des Kriminellen* (Munich 1999).

Rhodes, Henry, *Alphonse Bertillon: Father of Scientific Detection* (London 1956).

Riff, Michael A., 'The Ambiguity of Masaryk's Attitudes on the "Jewish Question"', in: Robert B. Pynsent (ed.), *T.G. Masaryk (1850–1937) Vol. 2, Thinker and Critic* (London 1989).

Ripellino, Angelo Maria, *Magic Prague*, translated by David Newton, (ed.) Michael H. Heim (London 1995 [1973]).

Robertson, Ritchie, *The Jewish Question in German Literature, 1749–1939, Emancipation and Its Discontents* (Oxford 1999).

Rozenblit, Marsha L., *The Jews of Vienna, 1867–1914: Assimilation and Identity* (New York 1983).

Rubin, Miri, *Gentile Tales, The Narrative Assault on Late Medieval Jews* (New Haven 1999).

Rupp-Eisenreich, Britta and Justin Stegl (eds), *Kulturwissenschaft im Vielvölkerstaat, Zur Geschichte der Ethnologie und verwandter Gebiete in Österreich ca. 1780–1918/ L'Anthropologie et L'Etat Pluri-Culturel, Le cas de l'Autriche, de 1780 à 1918 environ* (Vienna 1995).

Rürüp, Reinhard, 'The European Revolution of 1848 and Jewish Emancipation', in: Werner E. Mosse, Arnold Paucker, Reinhard Rürüp (eds), *Revolution and Evolution: 1848 in German-Jewish History* (Tübingen 1981).

Rychnovsky, Ernst (ed.), *Masaryk und das Judentum* (Prague 1931).

Sarasin, Philipp and Jakob Tanner (eds), *Physiologie und industrielle Gesellschaft. Studien zur Verwissenschaftlichung des Körpers im 19. und 20. Jahrhundert* (Frankfurt am Main 1998).

Scheichel, Siegurd Paul, 'Österreichische Reaktionen auf die Dreifus-Affäre', in: *Relations franco-autrichiennes 1870–1970, Austriaca Special Colloque* (1986), pp. 241–59.

_____ 'The Contexts and Nuances of Anti-Jewish language: Were all the "Antisemites" Antisemites?', in: Ivar Oxaal, Michael Pollack and Gerhard Botz (eds), *Jews, Antisemitism and Culture in Vienna* (London 1987), pp. 89–110.

Schenda, Rudolf, *Volk ohne Buch, Studien zur Sozialgeschichte der populären Lesestoffe 1770–1910* (Frankfurt am Main 1970).

Schenk, Michael, *Rassismus gegen Sinti und Roma. Zur Kontinuität der Zigeunerverfolgung innerhalb der deutschen Gesellschaft von der Weimarer Republik bis in die Gegenwart* (Frankfurt am Main 1994).

Schönert, Jörg (ed.), *Erzählte Kriminalität, Zur Typologie und Funktion von narrativen Darstellungen in Strafrechtspflege, Publizistik und Literatur zwischen 1770 und 1920, Vorträge zu einem interdisziplinären Kolloquium, Hamburg 10–12 April 1985* (Tübingen 1991).

Schorske, Carl E., *Fin-de-Siècle Vienna: Politics and Culture* (London 1981).

Schreder, Stephan, *Der Zeitungsleser, Eine soziologische Studie mit besonderer Berücksichtigung der Zeitungsleserschaft Wiens* (Vienna 1934).

Schroubek, Georg R., 'Der "Ritualmord" von Polna, Traditioneller und moderner Aberglaube', in: Rainer Erb and Michael Schmidt (eds), *Antisemitismus und jüdische Geschichte* (Berlin 1987), pp. 149–71.

Schuller, Marianne, '"Entartung," Zur Geschichte eines Begriffs, der Geschichte gemacht hat', in: Heidrun Kaupen-Haas and Christian Saller (ed.), *Wissenschaftlicher Rassismus, Analysen einer Kontinuität in den Human- und Naturwissenschaften* (Frankfurt am Main 1999), pp. 122–36.

Schulte, Regina, *Sperrbezirke, Tugendhaftigkeit und Prostitution in der bürgerlichen Welt* (Frankfurt am Main 1979).

Schulz, Andreas, 'Der Aufstieg der vierten Gewalt, Medien, Politik und Öffentlichkeit im Zeitalter der Massenkommunikation', *Historische Zeitschrift* 270 (2000), pp. 65–97.

Sekula, Allan, 'The Body and the Archive', in: Richard Bolton (ed.), *The Contest of Meaning: Critical Histories of Photography* (Cambridge, Mass. 1989), pp. 343–88.

Seliger, Maren and Karl Ucakar, *Wien, Politische Geschichte 1740–1930, Entwicklung und Bestimmungskräfte Grossstädtischer Politik, Teil 2: 1896–1934* (Vienna 1985).

Sengoopta, Chandak, *Otto Weininger, Sex, Science and Self in Imperial Vienna* (Chicago 2000).

_____ *Imprint of the Raj, How Fingerprinting was Born in Colonial India* (London 2003).

Sennet, Richard, *The Fall of Public Man* (Cambridge 1976).

Shorter, Edward, 'Women and Jews in a Private Nervous Clinic in Late Nineteenth-Century Vienna', *Medical History* 33, 2 (1989), pp. 149–83.

Silbernagel, Nikolaus, 'Kriminalberichterstattung' (Ph.D. Diss. Univ. Wien 1979).

Smith, Anthony, *The Newspaper, An International History* (London 1979).

Smith, Helmut Walser, *The Butcher's Tale, Murder and Anti-Semitism in a German Town* (New York 2002).

Southern, Richard, *The Seven Ages of the Theatre* (London 1962).

Stamprech, Franz, 'Die kleinen Blätter Wiens' (Ph.D. Diss. Univ. Wien 1954).

Staudacher, Anna, 'Die Aktion "Girondo". Zur Geschichte des internationalen Mädchenhandels in Österreich-Ungarn um 1885', in: Heide Dienst and Edith Saurer (eds), *Das Weib existiert nicht für sich* (Vienna 1990), pp. 97–138.

Strasser, Peter, *Verbrechermenschen, Zum kriminalwissenschaftlichen Erzeugen des Bösen* (Frankfurt am Main 1984).

Sulloway, Frank J., *Freud, Biologist of the Mind, Beyond the Psychoanalytic Legend* (New York 1979).

Swales, Martin, 'Liberalism and Hedonism, Arthur Schnitzler's Diagnosis of the Viennese Bourgeoisie', in: László Péter and Robert B. Pynsent (eds), *Intellectuals and the Future in the Habsburg Monarchy 1890–1914* (London 1988), pp. 13–28.

Szajkowski, Zoza, 'The Impact of the Beilis Case on Central and Western Europe', *Proceedings of the American Academy of Jewish Research* 31 (1963), pp. 197–218.

Tagg, John, *The Burden of Representation. Essays on Photographies and Histories* (New York 1988).

Tartar, Maria, *Lustmord, Sexual Murder in Weimar Germany* (Princeton 1995).

Tichy, Marina and Sylvia Zwettler-Otte, *Freud in der Presse, Rezeption Sigmund Freuds Psychoanalyse in Österreich 1895–1938* (Vienna 1999).

Timms, Edward, *Karl Kraus, Apocalyptic Saint, Culture and Catastrophe in Habsburg Vienna* (New Haven 1986).

Toury, Jacob (ed.), *Der Eintritt der Juden ins Deutsche Bürgertum: Eine Dokumentation* (Tel Aviv 1972).

_____ *Die jüdische Presse im Österreichischen Kaiserreich, Ein Beitrag zur Problematik der Akkulturation 1802–1918* (Tübingen 1983).

Traum und Wirklichkeit, Wien 1870–1930, Ausstellungskatalog zur 93. Sonderausstellung des Historischen Museums der Stadt Wien (Vienna 1985).

Trilling, Lionell, *Sincerity and Authenticity* (Oxford 1971).

Ulbricht, Otto, 'Criminality and Punishment of the Jews in the Early Modern Period', in: R. Po-Chia Hsia and Hartmann Lehmann (eds), *In and Out of the Ghetto, Jewish–Gentile Relationships in Late Medieval and Early Modern Germany* (Cambridge 1995), pp. 49–70.

Vyleta, Daniel Mark, 'Jewish Crimes and Misdemeanours: In search of Jewish Criminality (Germany and Austria, 1890–1914)', *European History Quaterly* 35, 2 (2005), pp. 299–325.

_____ Review: 'Helmut Walser Smith, *The Butcher's Tale, Murder and Anti-Semitism in a German Town*', *Central Europe* 2, 1 (2004), pp. 66–8.

_____ 'Was Early Twentieth-Century Criminology a Science of the 'Other'? A Re-evaluation of Austro-German Criminological Debates', *Cultural and Social History*, 3, 4 (2006).

Wachsmann, Nikolaus, *Hitler's Prisons* (New Haven 2003).

Wagner, Nike, *Geist und Geschlecht: Karl Kraus und die Erotik der Wiener Moderne* (Frankfurt am Main 1982).

Wagner, Patrick, *Volksgemeinschaft ohne Verbrecher, Konzeptionen und Praxis der Kriminalpolizei in der Zeit der Weimarer Republik und des Nationalsozialismus* (Hamburg 1996).

Walkowitz, Judith R., *City of Dreadful Delight, Narratives of Sexual Danger in Late-Victorian London* (London 1992).

Wandruszka, Adam, 'Geschichte einer Zeitung. Das Schicksal der "Presse" und "Neuen Freien Presse" von 1848 bis zur zweiten Republik', (Ph.D. Diss., Univ. Vienna 1958).

_____ 'Österreichs politische Struktur: Die Entwicklung der Parteien und politischen Bewegungen', in: Heinrich Benedikt (ed.), *Geschichte der Republik Österreich* (Vienna 1954).

Weindling, Paul, *Health, Race and German Politics Between National Unification and Nazism 1870–1945* (Cambridge 1989).

Weitzmann, Walter R., 'Die Politik der jüdischen Gemeinde Wiens zwischen 1890 und 1914', in: Gerhard Botz, Ivar Oxaal, Michael Pollak and Nina Scholz (eds), *Eine zerstörte Kultur, Jüdisches Leben und Antisemitismus in Wien seit dem 19. Jahrhundert* (Vienna 2002), pp. 211–12.

Wetzell, Richard F., 'The Medicalization of Criminal Law Reform in Imperial Germany', in: Norbert Finzsch and Robert Jütte (eds), *Institutions of Confinement, Hospitals, Asylums, and Prisons in Western Europe and North America 1500–1950* (Cambridge 1996), pp. 275–83.

_____ *Inventing the Criminal, A History of German Criminology, 1880–1945* (Chapel Hill 2000).

Wexler, Paul, 'Languages in Contact: The Case of Rotwelsch and the Two Yiddishes', in: R. Po-Chia Hsia and Hartmann Lehmann (eds), *In and Out of the Ghetto, Jewish–Gentile Relationships in Late Medieval and Early Modern Germany*, pp. 109–24.

White, Hayden, *The Content of the Form, Narrative Discourse and Historical Representation* (Baltimore 1987).

Whiteside, A.G., *The Socialism of Fools, Georg Ritter von Schönerer and Austrian Pan-Germanism* (Berkeley 1975).

Wiener Historikerinnen (ed.), *Die ungeschriebene Geschichte, Historische Frauenforschung, Dokumentation 5. Historikerinnentreffen* (Vienna 1985).

Wiener, Martin J., *Reconstructing the Criminal, Culture, Law and Policy in England 1830–1914* (Cambridge 1990).

Wilson, Elizabeth, 'The Invisible Flâneur', in: Sophie Watson and Katherine Gibson (eds), *Postmodern Cities and Spaces* (Oxford 1995), pp. 59–79.

Winters, Stanley B., (ed.), *T.G. Masaryk (1850–1937) Vol. 1: Thinker and Politician* (London 1990).

Wistrich, Robert S., *Socialism and the Jews: The Dilemmas of Assimilation in Germany and Austria–Hungary* (London 1982).

_____ 'Sozialdemokratie, Antisemitismus und die Wiener Juden', in: Gerhard Botz, Ivar Oxaal, Michael Pollak and Nina Scholz (eds), *Eine zerstörte Kultur, Jüdisches Leben und Antisemitismus in Wien seit dem 19. Jahrhundert* (Vienna 2002), pp. 187–95.

_____ *The Jews of Vienna in the Age of Franz Joseph* (Oxford 1990).

_____ (ed.), *Austrians and Jews in the Twentieth Century, From Franz Joseph to Waldheim* (New York 1992).

Wolff, Larry, *Postcards from the End of the World, An Investigation into the Mind of Fin-de-Siècle Vienna* (London 1989).

Wright, Gillham Nicholas, *A Life of Sir Francis Galton, From African Exploration to the Birth of Eugenics* (Oxford 2001).

Wright, Gordon, *Between the Guillotine and Liberty* (New York and Oxford 1983).

INDEX

Lightning Source UK Ltd.
Milton Keynes UK
UKOW06f0840191116
288021UK00025B/863/P